From Paradise to the Promised Land

From Paradise to the Promised Land

An Introduction to the Pentateuch

T.D. Alexander

PATERNOSTER PRESS

Baker Academic
A Division of Baker Book House Co

08 07 06 05 04 03   7 6 5 4 3 2

Paternoster Press is an imprint of Authentic Media,
P.O. Box 300, Carlisle, Cumbria, CA3 0QS, UK
Website: www.paternoster-publishing.com

Baker Academic is a division of Baker Book House Company
P.O. Box 6287, Grand Rapids, MI 49516-6287
Website: www.bakeracademic.com

British Library Cataloguing in Publication Data
A catalogue record for this book is available from the British Library

ISBN 1-84227-136-9

Library of Congress Cataloging-in-Publication Data

Alexander, T. Desmond
    From paradise to the promised land : an introduction to the Pentateuch / T. Desmond
Alexander.—2nd ed.
       p. cm.
    Includes bibliographical references and index.
    ISBN 0-8010-2597-4 (pbk.)
    1. Bible. O.T. Pentateuch—Criticism, interpretation, etc. I. Title.
BS1225.52 .A44 2002
222'.1061—dc21   2002023062

Cover Design by FourNineZero
Typeset by WestKey Ltd, Falmouth, Cornwall, UK
Printed in The United States of America

To
Margaret,
Bob and Janet

Contents

Preface

The idea of writing an introductory guide to the first five books of the Bible arose following a brief period of teaching Asian theological students in Singapore in 1990. My experience there confirmed what had been evident to me in Ireland: most students of theology and religious studies have at best a very limited understanding of the basic contents of the Pentateuch. While they are vaguely familiar with the better-known stories of Genesis and Exodus, few could claim to have a clear understanding of the Pentateuch as a whole. What was lacking was a good guide to the text, a book that was suited to the needs of such students. To this end, what now appears as Part 2 of this edition was published in 1995 under the title *From Paradise to the Promised Land*.

Because this former volume focused deliberately on the contents of Genesis to Deuteronomy, it provided no detailed discussion of contemporary academic approaches to the Pentateuch. To address this shortcoming, Part 1 has now been added. The present volume, therefore, seeks to (a) guide the reader through the maze of modern approaches to the Pentateuch, and (b) focus on the main themes of the Pentateuch, viewed as a unified literary work, by drawing on the best insights of recent research into Hebrew narrative techniques.

To these a further aim has been added which strictly speaking is not required in an introduction to the Pentateuch. I have sought to outline briefly the many ways in which the Pentateuchal material is taken up and used in the NT. Two considerations have encouraged me to do this. First, many students of theology and religious studies approach the Pentateuch from a Christian perspective and are naturally interested in how this material relates to the beliefs and practices of the NT church. Secondly, and perhaps more importantly from a purely academic perspective, the NT documents reveal how the Pentateuchal texts were understood in a period and culture much closer to that of the Pentateuch than our own. It is interesting, therefore, to compare the NT understanding of the Pentateuch with that of twenty-first-century readers. To what extent is there agreement on the meaning of the text?

Having stated the general aims of this study, some further comments may help clarify the overall approach adopted here. Although this volume seeks to explain the contents of the Pentateuch, it is not a verse-by-verse commentary on the text. An abundance of commentaries already exists, as noted in the bibliography on pages 281–84. Yet, while they are especially helpful in explaining shorter units of material – for example, individual verses or chapters – they tend by their very nature to atomise the text into small units. Consequently, they sometimes fail to highlight themes which are spread across entire books, especially when such themes do not appear to be of particular importance in any single passage. Studying the biblical texts by means of commentaries can be compared to looking at the separate pieces of a jigsaw puzzle. While we may find something of interest in each piece, it is only when all the pieces are put together that we get the complete picture. It is with this larger picture that we wish to engage in this study of the Pentateuch.

Not only may commentaries fail to give a complete picture, but also they may even unintentionally give a distorted picture. By atomising the text and considering each unit independently there is ever present the danger of misinterpreting these shorter passages. This may be illustrated using the jigsaw puzzle again. Examined on its own a single piece may appear to show one thing, yet when placed alongside its matching pieces it may reveal something quiet different. Obviously, knowledge of the wider context is vital for under-standing the individual components of something larger. Unfortunately, scholars have not always appreciated adequately the dangers that exist in inter-preting a biblical book unit by unit without taking into account sufficiently the broader context.

Alongside these shortcomings must be placed a further and much more fundamental problem. For the past two centuries the academic study of the Pentateuch has been dominated by methods which seek primarily to elucidate how the present text came into being; these methods are surveyed in Part 1. Encouraged by the hope of uncovering the pre-history, both literary and oral, of the received text, scholars have expended an inordinate amount of time and energy on developing the methodologies of *source* and *form* criticism. Several consequences of this should be noted. First, these methods have resulted in the text being dissected in a variety of ways. No longer is the Pentateuch generally considered to be a literary unity – which regardless of how it was composed, it now is. Rather, it is commonly viewed as a collection of literary documents and/or oral accounts linked together by editorial (or redactional) additions. Most scholarly research on the Pentateuch has sought to (a) discover the existence of these hypothetical sources, (b) explain the process by which they were combined to form the present text, and (c) relate the existence of these earlier sources to the history and religious development of the Israelites prior to the final composition of the Pentateuch in the exilic or post-exilic period. While scholarly endeavours to address these issues have not been wanting, the past two decades have witnessed a substantial rejection of results which for several immediately preceding generations of scholars seemed assured. At the present time much uncertainty exists regarding how and when the Pentateuch was composed. It could even be asked, given our present knowledge, if it is actually possible to determine with any confidence the process by which it came into being.

A second consequence of biblical scholarship focusing its resources on the pre-history of the text has been a failure to elucidate clearly the meaning of the Pentateuch in its received form. Relatively little has been said about the final form of the Pentateuch. Most studies have focused on the sources underlying the present text. Three factors have possibly contributed to this lack of interest in the Pentateuch as received.

1. In the past source-critical studies have generally portrayed the earliest stages in the composition of the Pentateuch as the most interesting and important. In marked contrast the contribution of the final editor was considered to be insignificant. Consequently, there was little incentive to examine in detail his work. Moreover, when scholars did consider it they generally looked only at the material assigned specifically to him. It was believed to be inappropriate or unnecessary to consider the entire Pentateuch in order to establish an understanding of the final redactor.

2. Many scholars appear to have assumed that a detailed explanation of the pre-history of the Pentateuch reveals all that needs to be known about the text as received. However, as R. Polzin has rightly observed:

   > Traditional biblical scholarship has spent most of its efforts in disassembling the works of a complicated watch before our amazed eyes without apparently realising that similar efforts by and large have not succeeded in putting the parts back together again in a significant or meaningful way.[1]

   We need to recognise that the Pentateuch, as we now have it, is much more than the sum of its component parts.

3. Scholars have tended to consider the study of the Pentateuch in its final form as less demanding and, therefore, of less academic value, than the investigation of its hypothetical sources.[2] Such reasoning is fallacious, how-

---

[1] R. Polzin, '"The Ancestress of Israel in Danger" in Danger', *Semeia* 3 (1975), 82–3.

[2] Interestingly, a similar observation was voiced by Gerhard von Rad in 1938 when he remarked, 'On almost all sides the final form of the Hexateuch has come to be regarded as a starting point barely worthy of discussion, from which the debate should move away as rapidly as possible in order to reach the real problems underlying it.' See, *The Problem of the Hexateuch and Other Essays* (Edinburgh: Oliver & Boyd, 1966), 1.

ever. The value of the final form of the Pentateuch should not be judged on the basis of the ease or otherwise of studying it. Rather, such study should be undertaken because of the inherent importance of the text as a unified literary work.[3] While some still fail to take seriously the study of the Pentateuch in its final form, it is encouraging to see that many more scholars now recognise the importance of doing so.

Even if one grants the importance of source and form criticism, there are various arguments which strongly favour an approach that gives prominence to the final form of the Pentateuch.

First, this is the form in which the text has been received. Whatever the process by which it was composed, it is now a coherent literary work. Even if, as seems very likely, various sources were used in its composition, it must be recognised that the final editor, whoever he (or she?) may have been, appropriated all the source material as his own and used it to compose the present narrative which begins in Genesis and continues through to the end of Deuteronomy. It is, therefore, essential to view the entire Pentateuch as reflecting the outlook of the final editor, not merely those portions which are normally assigned to the last editorial stage.

Secondly, a detailed and comprehensive study of the Pentateuch in its final form must have priority in sequence over the approaches of source and form criticism. It is methodologically unsound to explore the pre-history of the text without having established a clear understanding of how the present text is constructed as a literary work. To do otherwise is to set the cart before the horse. Similarly, on pedagogical grounds, it is surely improper to expect students to appreciate and apply critical methods before they have understood the content and literary structure of the received text. Unfortunately, it is frequently the case that students are introduced to scholarly opinions regarding the process by which the text was composed, without knowing what the text itself is saying.

Thirdly, new literary approaches to the study of Hebrew narrative provide fresh insights into the meaning of many Pentateuchal passages. Frequently, these insights offer new ways of approaching problems which in the past were resolved by resorting to source or form critical solutions. Scholars in general are now more confident about taking seriously the present integrity of the text.

---

[3] By this I mean that the books of Genesis to Deuteronomy are linked together in such a way that while they may be viewed as separate entities, it is clear that they have been made dependent upon one another, with the later books presupposing a knowledge of the earlier ones and the earlier books being incomplete without the addition of the later ones. In this connection it should also be noted that on this basis the Pentateuch itself is incomplete and is linked in a special way to the material in Joshua to 2 Kings.

Fourthly, a clear understanding of the final form of the Pentateuch is important if we are to appreciate how it influenced later writers. The writers (and earliest readers) of the NT were all pre-critical in their understanding of the Pentateuch; they did not think in terms of different literary and/or oral sources underlying the text, each reflecting different theologies. For them the Pentateuch was a single entity; this was how they understood and interpreted it. All of these reasons argue for an approach which treats with respect the received text of the Pentateuch.

From the preceding comments it will be evident that the position adopted in Part 2 of this book differs markedly from that often followed by others. The object of our study is the final form of the Pentateuch as it has been handed down to us in the Hebrew text. Little attention will be given to possible sources or the process of composition; much has been written on this elsewhere, as will be observed in Part 1. Rather, it is our aim to map out the terrain of the Pentateuch as it now stands by drawing attention to its main features. To enable the reader to assimilate the contents of the Pentateuch more easily the material is usually approached book by book. Sometimes attention is focused on major themes running throughout entire books. Elsewhere, shorter blocks of material which deal with specific subjects are examined. The intention has been to allow the text to determine the approach which seems most appropriate. For example, the themes of 'seed', blessing and land run throughout the book of Genesis.[4] On the other hand, the account of the building of the tabernacle dominates most of the final third of the book of Exodus. When blocks of material are examined I have tried to follow the natural divisions of the text.

References to the rest of the OT have been kept to a minimum. To have included all the relevant material would have added considerably to each chapter and shifted the focus of the book from the Pentateuch to the OT as a whole.

While I have sought to include in Part 2 the best insights of contemporary studies, to keep the presentation as straightforward as possible I have deliberately avoided engaging in a detailed critique of the views of other scholars. Three factors have persuaded me to adopt this approach. First, to interact meaningfully with all that has been said would have taken this study far beyond an introductory guide. Secondly, since many writers discuss the Pentateuchal material from the perspectives of source and/or form criticism, it

---

[4] While I have tended to restrict the study of particular themes to individual books, it should be noted that certain themes could not be restricted in this way (e.g. land, descendants, blessing). While such themes tend to be dominant in one book, they may, however, be picked up elsewhere in the Pentateuch as important motifs echoing earlier material. As such, they are important indicators to the overall unity of the Pentateuch in its received form.

has to be recognised that they are addressing very different issues from those being examined here. While this does not automatically exclude the possibility of meaningful interaction, it does make it much more difficult to achieve. Moreover, it would have required for every passage under consideration a detailed discussion of past and contemporary views on the process by which it was composed; something which would have added considerably to the length of this volume. Thirdly, the primary purpose of Part 2 is to focus the reader's attention on the content of the Pentateuch itself, rather than on the diverse opinions of contemporary scholars. For those interested in following up individual topics I have included suggestions for further reading at the end of the book.

A number of chapters have appeared in print elsewhere; these have been modified and updated to varying degrees to conform to the overall pattern of presentation adopted in this volume. Some of the material in chapters 3 and 5 first appeared in the author's book, *Abraham in the Negev: A Source-critical Investigation of the Genesis 20:1–22:19.*[5] The discussion of the Passover in chapter 4 incorporates some material from the author's article, 'The Passover Sacrifice' in R.T. Beckwith and M. Selman (eds.), *Sacrifice in the Bible.*[6] Chapters 6 and 9 first appeared as 'The Composition of the Sinai Narrative in Exodus xix–xxiv',[7] and 'Genealogies, Seed and the Compositional Unity of Genesis',[8] respectively. Chapter 12 was originally published as 'Abraham Reassessed Theologically: The Abraham Narrative and the New Testament Understanding of Justification by Faith', in R.S. Hess, P.E. Satterthwaite and G.J. Wenham (eds.), *He Swore an Oath: Biblical Themes from Genesis 12–50.*[9] Much of the material in chapters 13–16 was first published in 1994 in the *New Bible Commentary (21st Century Edition)* and I am grateful to the publishers, Inter-Varsity Press, for permission to reproduce this in a modified form.

Except where otherwise indicated, biblical quotations are from the NIV, and all biblical references follow the English rather than the Hebrew scheme of numeration. All Hebrew words have been transliterated according to standard practice; however, where for the ordinary reader the transliteration does not reflect the actual pronunciation of a Hebrew word I have added this in parenthesis.

For providing me with helpful observations on sections of this study I am grateful to John Brew, Claude-Bernard Costecalde, Ian Hart, James McKeown, Alan Millard, Albert Ong, David Palmer and Paul Williamson.

---

[5] (Carlisle: Paternoster Press, 1997).

[6] (Carlisle/Grand Rapids: Paternoster/Baker, 1995), 1–24.

[7] *VT* 49 (1999), 2–20.

[8] *TynBul* 44.2 (1993), 255–70.

[9] (Cambridge; Tyndale House, 1993), 7–28. (2nd edn.; Grand Rapids/Carlisle: Baker/Paternoster, 1994).

Needless to say they can in no way be held responsible for the shortcomings that remain. I wish also to express my thanks to the staff of Paternoster Press for their valuable assistance in the final stages of the production of this book. For the loving support which I receive so consistently from my wife, Anne, I am deeply grateful, not forgetting the contribution made to this by our children, Jane and David, who constantly remind me that there is more to life than books. To my mother and Anne's parents, this book is dedicated with love.

SOLI DEO GLORIA

Abbreviations

AB	Anchor Bible
ABD	Anchor Bible Dictionary
ABR	*Australian Biblical Review*
AJBI	*Annual of the Japanese Biblical Institute*
AOAT	*Alter Orient und Altes Testament*
AUSS	*Andrews University Seminary Studies*
BA	*Biblical Archaeologist*
BARev	*Biblical Archaeology Review*
BASOR	*Bulletin of the American Schools of Oriental Research*
Bib	*Biblica*
BibBh	*Bible Bhashyam*
BJRL	*Bulletin of the John Rylands Library*
BR	*Biblical Research*
BRev	*Bible Review*
BS	*Bibliotheca Sacra*
BSC	Bible Student's Commentary
BT	*The Bible Translator*
BTB	*Biblical Theology Bulletin*
BZ	*Biblische Zeitschrift*
BZAW	Beihefte zur Zeitschrift für die alttestamentliche Wissenschaft
CBC	Cambridge Bible Commentaries on the New English Bible
CBQ	*Catholic Biblical Quarterly*
CTJ	*Calvin Theological Journal*
CTM	*Concordia Theological Monthly*
CTQ	*Concordia Theological Quarterly*
CurTM	*Currents in Theology and Mission*
DSB	The Daily Study Bible
EgT	*Eglise et Théologie*
Enc	*Encounter*
ETL	*Ephemerides Theologicae Lovanienses*

EvQ	*The Evangelical Quarterly*
ExpTim	*The Expository Times*
FOTL	Forms of Old Testament Literature
GTJ	*Grace Theological Journal*
HS	*Hebrew Studies*
HTR	*Harvard Theological Review*
HUCA	*Hebrew Union College Annual*
IBS	*Irish Biblical Studies*
ICC	International Critical Commentary
Imm	*Immanuel*
Int	*Interpretation*
ITC	International Theological Commentary
ITS	*Indian Theological Studies*
JAAR	*Journal of the American Academy of Religion*
JANES	*The Journal of the Ancient Near Eastern Society*
JANESCU	*The Journal of the Ancient Near Eastern Society of Columbia University*
JAOS	*Journal of the American Oriental Society*
JBL	*Journal of Biblical Literature*
JETS	*Journal of the Evangelical Theological Society*
JJS	*Journal of Jewish Studies*
JNES	*Journal of Near Eastern Studies*
JNSL	*Journal of Northwest Semitic Languages*
JRT	*Journal of Religious Thought*
JSOT	*Journal for the Study of the Old Testament*
JSOTSS	Journal for the Study of the Old Testament Supplement Series
JSS	*Journal of Semitic Studies*
JTS	*Journal of Theological Studies*
JTSoA	*Journal of Theology for Southern Africa*
LB	*Linguistica Biblica*
LTJ	*Lutheran Theological Journal*
MT	Masoretic Text
NAC	New American Commentary
NCB	New Century Bible
NDBT	*The New Dictionary of Biblical Theology*
NETR	*The Near East School of Theology Theological Review*
NIBCOT	New International Biblical Commentary Old Testament
NICOT	New International Commentary on the Old Testament
NIV	New International Version
NT	New Testament
Or	*Orientalia*

OT	Old Testament
OTL	Old Testament Library
OTM	Old Testament Message
OTS	*Oudtestamentische Studiën*
PIBA	*Proceedings of the Irish Biblical Association*
PSTJ	*The Perkins Journal*
RB	*Revue biblique*
Rel	*Religion*
ResQ	*Restoration Quarterly*
SBLMS	Society of Biblical Literature Monograph Series
SJT	*Scottish Journal of Theology*
StudBT	*Studia Biblica et Theologica*
SVT	Supplement to Vetus Testamentum
SwJT	*Southwest Journal of Theology*
TD	*Theology Digest*
TDOT	Theological Dictionary of the Old Testament
Them	*Themelios*
TI	Text and Interpretation
TJ	*Trinity Journal*
TNB	*The New Blackfriars*
TOTC	Tyndale Old Testament Commentaries
TynBul	*Tyndale Bulletin*
VR	*Vox Reformata*
VT	*Vetus Testamentum*
WBC	Word Biblical Commentaries
WEC	Wycliffe Exegetical Commentary
WTJ	*The Westminster Theological Journal*
ZAW	*Zeitschrift für die alttestamentliche Wissenschaft*

Maps
and
Diagrams

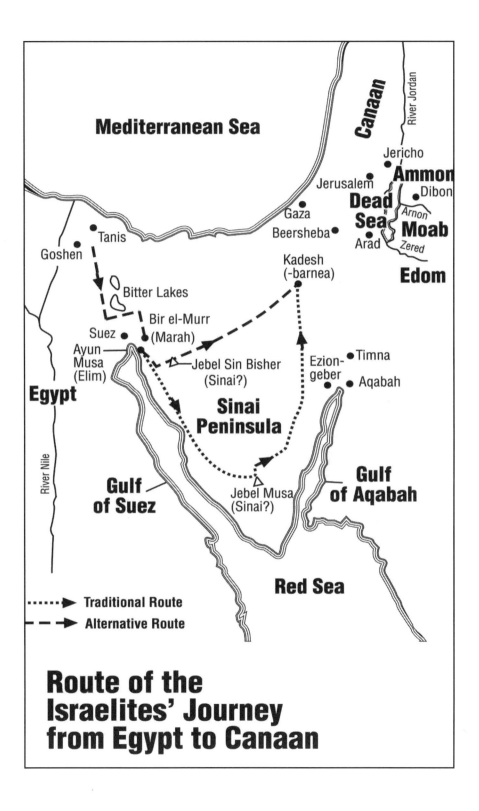

Route of the
Israelites' Journey
from Egypt to Canaan

The Israelite Camp

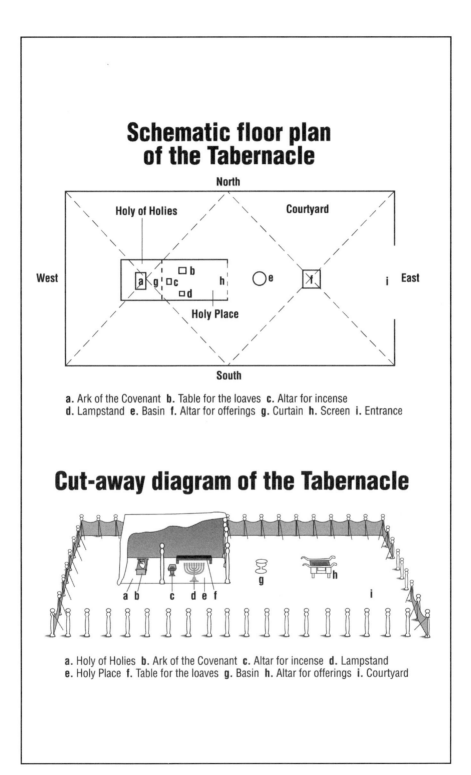

Schematic floor plan of the Tabernacle

North

Holy of Holies

Courtyard

West

a g b c d h e f i **East**

Holy Place

South

a. Ark of the Covenant **b.** Table for the loaves **c.** Altar for incense
d. Lampstand **e.** Basin **f.** Altar for offerings **g.** Curtain **h.** Screen **i.** Entrance

Cut-away diagram of the Tabernacle

a b c d e f g h i

a. Holy of Holies **b.** Ark of the Covenant **c.** Altar for incense **d.** Lampstand
e. Holy Place **f.** Table for the loaves **g.** Basin **h.** Altar for offerings **i.** Courtyard

Part 1
Pentateuchal Criticism

1

Introduction to Pentateuchal Criticism

Since at least the third century AD the term Pentateuch (derived from the Greek *pentateuchos*, 'five-volume work') has been used to denote the first five books of the Bible (i.e. Genesis, Exodus, Leviticus, Numbers and Deuteronomy). Jewish tradition has favoured the designation Torah, usually translated as 'law', although 'instruction' would perhaps be more accurate. Penned originally in Hebrew, the books of the Pentateuch were already important texts by at least the fourth century BC, and over the years they have had a significant influence, both knowingly and unknowingly, upon the religious outlook of Jews, Christians and Moslems. In spite of this, most people today have only a passing familiarity with their contents, and much within them is likely to strike the modern reader as strange and/or incomprehensible.

For an introduction to the *contents* of these five books, the reader should consult Part 2. The opening chapters, in Part 1, provide an introduction to contemporary academic approaches to the Pentateuch and offer a critique of them from an evangelical perspective. After almost a century of relative stability, Pentateuch criticism is currently in a state of turmoil as various theories vie with each other in an attempt to dethrone the Documentary Hypothesis as *the* explanation for the process by which these books were composed. Naturally, it is not possible to do justice to all that has been said, and the present writer is conscious of the limitations of what follows. Nevertheless, it is hoped that this contribution may provide a basis for and a stimulus to further study.

Before focusing on the Documentary Hypothesis, it may be helpful to survey briefly how the Pentateuch has been approached in the modern period. During the past two hundred and fifty years scholarly research on the Pentateuch has developed around four main methods: *source* criticism; *form* criticism; *traditio-historical* criticism and *literary* criticism. Since each method addresses a specific set of issues, it is important to understand how they differ from each other. Moreover, as we shall observe, the rise of each method signalled a new stage in the study of the Pentateuch.

1.1. Source Criticism

Source criticism was the first of these four methods to be employed, and it has established itself as a major tool in Pentateuchal criticism. This method, which to some extent originally came into being by chance, seeks to uncover the *literary* sources which may have been used in the composition of the books of Genesis to Deuteronomy. Although pushed into the background by other methods during most of the twentieth century, it continues to exercise considerable influence particularly in relation to the exegesis of the Pentateuchal books and scholarly reconstructions of the history of ancient Israel. In chapter 2 we shall trace the development of this method from its origins in the middle of the eighteenth century through to the end of the nineteenth century, by which time there evolved the influential *Documentary Hypothesis* of Graf, Vatke and Wellhausen. For the present it is sufficient to note that this hypothesis proposes that four distinctive source-documents were combined over a period of five or six centuries to produce the Pentateuch as we now know it, the end of this process coming in the fifth century BC.

1.2. Form Criticism

Following the almost universal acceptance of the Documentary Hypothesis, biblical scholars turned, not surprisingly perhaps, to consider the *oral* phase that was thought to lie behind the source-documents. Pioneered by Hermann Gunkel in the early decades of the twentieth century, a new methodology arose, subsequently termed form criticism. This approach sought to analyse the Pentateuchal material into different categories on the assumption that each had its own particular life setting (technically known as *Sitz im Leben*). By identifying the form of a particular passage, it was thought possible to recover the historical context in which the material was composed. Fundamental to the development of this method was the belief that Genesis consisted of numerous short episodes which originally circulated both orally and independently of each other. Only at a much later stage were these oral compositions brought together and committed to writing, eventually creating the four source-documents from which the Pentateuch was composed. A fuller description of this method comes in chapter 3.

1.3. Traditio-historical Criticism

Having determined (a) the earliest oral forms of the Pentateuchal material, and (b) the four main source-documents, the next stage in the history of

Pentateuchal criticism was to describe the process by which the former were combined to produce the latter. Since this method was interested in the *history of the traditions* underlying the Pentateuch, it was designated traditio-historical criticism. Two of the main scholars associated with the development of this approach are Gerhard von Rad and Martin Noth. Regarding their contribution, see chapter 3.

The preceding three methods all focus on the process by which the Pentateuch was composed. Form criticism identifies the earliest oral stage, traditio-historical criticism describes the process leading up to the formation of the longer written source-documents, and, finally, source criticism explains how the source-documents were brought together to create the Pentateuch as we now have it. In subsequent chapters we shall outline in more detail the use and results of these methods, at the same time evaluating the success of each in achieving its objectives.

1.4. Literary Criticism

The past twenty years have witnessed the introduction of a new method of viewing the Pentateuch, known as literary criticism. While interest remains strong in uncovering the process by which the Pentateuch was composed, many scholars either have or are gradually recognising the need to comprehend the Pentateuch in its final form. This shift in emphasis entails a switch from a diachronic ('through time') to a synchronic ('at the same time') reading of the text. Instead of locating portions of the text in different historical periods, literary criticism seeks to understand the Pentateuch as a coherent, unified work composed at one specific point in time. Literary criticism recognises that the Pentateuch cannot be understood solely on the basis of the components that have been used in its construction; the whole is much greater than the sum of its parts.

Two further dimensions of literary criticism ought to be noted. First, the designation literary criticism embraces a wide range of differing approaches that may be used to interpret texts (e.g. structuralism, deconstruction, reader-response). It is worth remembering that scholars primarily interested in the study of modern literature have developed many of these approaches. Secondly, some proponents of literary criticism adopt a very ambivalent attitude towards historical issues. They are primarily interested in the text alone, viewing questions concerning the growth of the text and its historical context as irrelevant to their particular approach. While there may be a place for adopting an a-historical reading of some texts, it needs to be asked if this is really appropriate for the study of the Pentateuch.

In theory, the four methods outlined above are complementary, asking different questions of the Pentateuch. In practice, however, literary criticism, by revealing more clearly how the biblical text is constructed, has challenged many of the results obtained by the other methods. For this reason, in recent years literary criticism has had a major impact upon the study of the Pentateuch, and continues to do so. Nevertheless, the results obtained by the other methods still enjoy substantial support. Consequently, as we move into the twenty-first century, the academic study of the Pentateuch is marked by a greater diversity of opinions than possibly at any stage in the modern period. What follows, therefore, makes no claim to be a comprehensive description of all current views. Rather, it is designed to (a) explain how the present state of affairs came into being, (b) evaluate some of the more influential contributions, and (c) offer some tentative suggestions as to how Christians may best approach the Pentateuch as an important theological text.

2

The Rise of the Documentary Hypothesis

Contemporary approaches to the Pentateuch have their roots in the seventeenth and eighteenth centuries. For this reason, in this chapter we shall survey, briefly and somewhat selectively, the development of source criticism, as applied to the Pentateuch, from the period of the Enlightenment to the end of the nineteenth century. This historical overview provides an important introduction to the topics which we shall explore in more detail throughout the rest of Part 1 of this book. It will also help us understand more clearly some of the different directions being pursued in contemporary discussions.

The origin of source criticism as a critical method may be traced back to the middle of the eighteenth century.[1] From somewhat unusual beginnings it became the dominant tool for the study of the Pentateuch. Undoubtedly, this development owed much to the new climate of intellectual freedom associated with the Enlightenment, which permitted the questioning of traditional views. Although the source criticism of the Pentateuch developed largely through a slow process of evolution, with new ideas being introduced and refined, it is possible to distinguish a number of distinctive stages. These are helpful in highlighting various models which may be used to explain the process by which the Pentateuch was composed (see 2.6).

2.1. The Older Documentary Hypothesis

In 1753 a leading French medical professor, Jean Astruc (1684–1766), published in Brussels a work entitled *Conjectures sur les mémoires originaux dont il paraît que Moyse s'est servi pour composer le livre de la Genèse*, in which he argued that Moses had compiled Genesis from older documents. Astruc made three important observations regarding Genesis: (a) certain events are recorded more

---

[1] For a fuller history of Pentateuchal Criticism up to the 1960s, see R.J. Thompson, *Moses and the Law in a Century of Criticism since Graf* (VTS 19; Leiden: Brill, 1970); cf. J.W. Rogerson, *Old Testament Criticism in the Nineteenth Century* (London: SPCK, 1984).

than once (e.g. the creation; the flood); (b) God is designated by the names Elohim and Yahweh;[2] (c) certain events are reported before other events, although chronologically they occur later. These observations suggested to Astruc that Genesis was composed of older records, and so he proceeded to 'decompose' Genesis. In one column, which he termed A, he placed those passages which used the divine name Elohim.[3] Next to this first column he placed a second, B, containing passages employing Yahweh.[4] However, it soon became apparent that two columns would not suffice. A third column, C, was introduced for those passages which (a) were repetitions of events already included in both columns A and B, and (b) did not employ any divine designation. To this column Astruc assigned with certainty only two verses (Gen. 7:20, 23). Other passages that did not contain the name of God still required attention. When Astruc noticed that the remaining passages recorded events foreign to the history of the Hebrew people, he placed them in a fourth column, D.[5] With regard to this final column, Astruc thought it unlikely that it once formed a continuous document. Rather, it consisted of fragments from other minor documents. Finally, Astruc was unable to assign certain verses to any particular column. These verses he felt could be common to two or three of the original documents (Gen. 7:24 to A, B and C; Gen. 9:28, 29 to A and B). Astruc proposed that Moses had originally placed these four columns side by side, but unfortunately a later copyist mistakenly combined them together, and so created the continuous narrative which now constitutes Genesis.

Some fifteen years after the death of Astruc, Johann Gottfried Eichhorn (1752–1827) published his *Einleitung in das Alte Testament.*[6] In the second volume (1781) of this three-volume work Eichhorn investigated the authorship and composition of the biblical books. Concerning Genesis he maintained the orthodox view of Mosaic authorship; indeed, he argued that Moses

---

[2] In most modern English versions of the Bible, Elohim is translated as 'God', and Yahweh as 'LORD'. In older versions, the divine name Yahweh occasionally occurs as Jehovah. For consistency the terms 'Yahweh', 'Yahwist' and 'Yahwistic' are used throughout this historical survey even when writers under discussion use 'Jehovah', 'Jehovist' and 'Jehovistic'.

[3] Genesis 1:1–2:3; 5:1–32; 6:9–22; 7:6–10, 19, 22; 8:1–19; 9:1–10, 12, 16, 17; 11:10–26; 17:3–27; 20:1–17; 21:2–32; 22:1–10; 23:1–20; 25:1–11; 30:1–23; 31:4–27; 31:51–32:2; 32:24–33:16; 35:1–27; 37:1–36; 40:1–48:22; 49:1–28.

[4] Genesis 2:4–26; 6:1–8; 7:1–5, 11–18, 21; 8:20–22; 9:11, 13–15, 18–27; 10:1–11:9; 11:27–13:18; 15:1–17:2; 18:1–19:28; 20:18–21:1; 21:33–34; 22:11–19; 24:1–67; 25:19–26:33; 27:1–28:5; 28:10–29:35; 30:24–31:3; 31:48–50; 32:3–32; 33:17–20; 38:1–30; 39:1–23; 49:1–28.

[5] Genesis 14:1–24; 19:29–38; 22:20–24; 25:12–18; 26:34, 35; 28:6–9; 34:1–31; 35:28–36:43.

[6] (Leipzig: Bey Weidmanns Erben und Reich, 1780–1783).

was particularly well suited to be the author. Moses, however, had employed older written records, and Eichhorn held that it was possible to discern in most of Genesis elements of two distinct documents. These documents could be distinguished (a) by the divine epithet employed, and (b) by repetitions in the text. Apart from certain minor modifications Eichhorn followed the division suggested by Astruc, although he asserted that Astruc did not influence him.[7]

A further significant development in the source analysis of Genesis occurred in a work by Karl David Ilgen (1763–1834) which was published at Halle in 1798, entitled *Die Urkunden des jerusalemischen Tempelarchivs in ihrer Urgestalt als Beytrag zur Berichtigung der Geschichte der Religion und Politik*. Ilgen, the successor of Eichhorn at Jena, suggested that Genesis comprised seventeen individual documents. These were, however, composed by merely three authors, two of whom used the divine name Elohim, whereas the third employed the epithet Yahweh. Ilgen referred to them by the terms *Sepher Eliel Harischon* (First Elohist), *Sepher Eliel Haschscheni* (Second Elohist) and *Sepher Elijah Harischon* (First Yahwist). He concluded that the First Elohist was responsible for ten sections of Genesis, the Second Elohist for five sections and the Yahwist for two sections. Ilgen's contribution was important in that he was the first to forward the idea that more than one author used the divine name Elohim. This idea, however, did not gain recognition among scholars until it was advocated afresh by Hermann Hupfeld in 1853 (see below).

The position adopted by Astruc, Eichhorn and Ilgen for the source analysis of Genesis is sometimes referred to as the *Older Documentary Hypothesis*. This particular approach represents the earliest phase of the source criticism of the Pentateuch. The conclusions reached by these early critics were based mainly upon a consideration of the book of Genesis alone. Apart from the early chapters of Exodus, no attempt was made to extend the theory to include the other books of the Pentateuch. Furthermore, as a methodology source criticism arose more by chance than by design. It was the presence of particular phenomena in Genesis that led Astruc, Eichhorn and Ilgen to propose the existence of earlier literary sources, and these same phenomena continued to form the basis of future scholarly research. Consequently, from its inception source analysis of the Pentateuch has relied heavily upon the presence in Genesis of differing names for God, and apparently duplicate accounts of the same events.

2.2. The Fragmentary Hypothesis

The initial phase of source criticism was followed by a second, which differed in two important respects.

---

[7] Cf. T.K. Cheyne, *Founders of Old Testament Criticism* (London: Methuen, 1893), 23.

1. Attention was no longer focused solely on Genesis. The Pentateuch as a whole became the object of source analysis, and this was to have an important bearing on future studies.
2. It was argued that the sources were of such a fragmentary nature that they could not be viewed as documents. The idea that Genesis was composed from extensive documents was rejected. As a result, the Older Documentary Hypothesis gave way to the *Fragmentary Hypothesis.*

The earliest exponent of the Fragmentary Hypothesis was a Scottish Roman Catholic priest called Alexander Geddes (1737–1802). In 1792, he published in London the first volume of a work entitled *The Holy Bible, or the Books accounted Sacred by Jews and Christians, otherwise called the Books of the Old and New Covenants, with various readings, explanatory notes and critical remarks.* This volume contained a new translation of the Pentateuch and the book of Joshua. Later, in 1800, Geddes published another book on the Pentateuch, *Critical Remarks on the Hebrew corresponding with a new translation of the Bible.* In both of these works Geddes rejected Mosaic authorship of the Pentateuch. Instead, he argued that the Hexateuch ('six-volumes'; i.e. Genesis to Joshua) had been composed by an editor, living in Jerusalem during the reign of Solomon, who had combined together numerous fragments. Geddes suggested that these fragments originated from two separate circles of tradition, one of which used the divine name Elohim, the other Yahweh. Geddes was influenced in favour of a fragmentary explanation of the sources by what he observed concerning the legal codes in the latter part of the Pentateuch. These, especially by their independent and self-sufficient nature, supported the idea that various fragments, rather than extensive documents, had been combined together to form the Pentateuch as we now have it.

In his *Commentar über den Pentateuch* (vols. 1–2 [1802]; vol. 3 [1805]), Johann Severin Vater (1771–1826) developed the position adopted by Geddes. Vater regarded the book of Deuteronomy as the nucleus around which the Pentateuch had been constructed. He separated it from the other books of the Pentateuch, and argued that certain differences between the regulations in Deuteronomy and Leviticus could only be explained by positing multiple authorship. These differences chiefly concerned the relationship between priests and Levites, and their respective incomes. Vater then proceeded to discover some thirty-nine fragments that were used in the compilation of the Pentateuch shortly prior to the exile. He also equated part of Deuteronomy with the law-book found in the time of Josiah (2 Kgs. 22).

Partial support for the Fragmentary Hypothesis came from Wilhelm Martin Lebrecht de Wette (1780–1849), a scholar who was to play a significant role in the development of critical thinking on the Pentateuch.[8] In his doctoral thesis of 1805, *Dissertatio Critico-Exegetica qua Deuteronomium a prioribus Pentateuchi libris diversum alius cujusdam recentioris auctoris opus esse monstratur*, de Wette proposed that Deuteronomy had been composed in the time of king Josiah (c. 621 BC) and was to be equated with the Book of the Law mentioned in 2 Kings 22. De Wette was convinced that the books of Joshua to Kings displayed no knowledge of Deuteronomic legislation prior to the time of Josiah. This was especially so as regards Deuteronomy's emphasis upon a central sanctuary and its laws on kingship (Deut. 17:14–20). This view of Deuteronomy was to become very influential in future discussions.

Later in his *Beiträge zur Einleitung in das Alte Testament* (vol. 1 [1806]; vol. 2 [1807]), de Wette developed further his thinking on the Pentateuch. Having already placed the origin of Deuteronomy in the reign of Josiah, he considered the dating of Leviticus. On the basis of its legislation he concluded that it did not originate in the time of Moses. At the earliest Leviticus could be dated to the reign of Solomon. De Wett also argued that the cultic history recorded in the books of Joshua and Chronicles was unreliable, and so could not be used to reconstruct the development of cultic practices. He maintained that the oldest sections of the Pentateuch came from the time of David, and later editors drew upon these fragments in order to compile the whole Pentateuch. While maintaining a fragmentary approach to the rest of the Pentateuch, de Wette rejected the position of Geddes and Vater as regards Genesis. He suggested that in Genesis, and as far as Exodus 6, one main Elohistic document had been supplemented by sections from a Yahwistic source, or perhaps several such sources. This view of Genesis was to find substantial support among later scholars. Finally, it should be noted that de Wette revised his thinking on the composition of the rest of the Pentateuch, and in the final two editions of his *Lehrbuch der historisch-kritischen Einleitung in die kanonishcen und apokryphischen Bücher des Alten Testament*[9] he rejected the Fragmentary Hypothesis.

2.3. The Supplementary Hypothesis

In 1823 Heinrich Georg August Ewald (1803–1875) proposed that the Hexateuch was composed of an Elohistic work that formed the *Grundschrift*

---

[8] For a fuller discussion of de Wette's contribution, see J.W. Rogerson, *W. M. L. de Wette Founder of Modern Biblical Criticism: An Intellectual Biography* (JSOTSS 120; Sheffield, JSOT Press, 1992).

[9] (Berlin: G. Reimer; 1840[5]; Berlin: G. Reimer, 1845[6]).

(basic document).[10] The compiler of this original Elohistic document had incorporated into it older sections, e.g. the Decalogue and the Book of the Covenant. Subsequently, one employing the divine name Yahweh paralleled this Elohistic document. Eventually this later Yahwistic source, along with certain other material, was incorporated into the original Elohistic document. This theory has become known as the *Supplementary Hypothesis.*

In 1836 Friedrich Bleek published a work on Genesis, entitled *De libri Geneseos origine atque indole historica observationes quaedam contra Bohlenum,* in which he argued that a Yahwistic editor during the period of the early monarchy supplemented an earlier Elohistic document (the *Grundschrift*). Significantly, Bleek viewed this Yahwistic editor as the compiler of Genesis. He also maintained that the Yahwistic supplements were from a parallel document. Later, during the reign of Josiah, a further redaction of the Pentateuch occurred when the compiler of Deuteronomy gave the Hexateuch its present form.

In his *Geschichte des Volkes Israel bis Christ*[11] Ewald modified his earlier position by arguing that within the Pentateuch there were sections which could not be assigned to the Elohistic, Yahwistic or Deuteronomic documents. Ewald proposed that there were two Elohistic sources, one of which he designated the Book of Origins because of its concern to explain the origins of the Sabbath, circumcision and bloodless meat. These two continuous Elohistic sources were combined and later supplemented by the work of the Yahwistic redactor (or editor). By adopting this position, Ewald combined the approaches of the Older Documentary Hypothesis and the Supplementary Hypothesis.

2.4. The New Documentary Hypothesis

The Supplementary Hypothesis, however, did not gain many adherents. This was probably due to the impact made by an alternative theory proposed by Hermann Hupfeld (1796–1866). In his *Die Quellen der Genesis und die Art ihrer Zusammensetzung von neuem untersucht*[12] Hupfeld returned to a purely documentary explanation for the composition of Genesis, rejecting the idea of later supplements. While Hupfeld reverted to the approach first suggested in the Older Documentary Hypothesis, he also incorporated the results of subsequent studies. His theory was based primarily on the book of Genesis. Underlying Genesis, Hupfeld suggested, there were three independent continuous sources; two of these employed the divine name Elohim, whereas

---

[10] H.G.A. Ewald, *Die Komposition der Genesis kritisch untersucht* (Braunschweig: L. Lucius, 1823).

[11] (7 vols. Göttinger: Dieterich, 1843–59 ET of vol. 1, London, 1869).

[12] (Berlin: Wieganat und Grieben, 1853).

the third used Yahweh. An editor who exercised considerable freedom in his use of the sources combined these documents together to form Genesis. Hupfeld called the older of the Elohistic documents the *Urschrift* ('original'). Significantly, two-thirds of the total *Urschrift* came in the initial nineteen chapters of Genesis and resembled closely the Elohist of Astruc and Eichhorn. With Genesis 20 the *jüngerer* or *second Elohist* commenced, and in the subsequent chapters of Genesis it was the more dominant of the two Elohistic documents. Concerning the *Urschrift*, Hupfeld noted that it had a particular interest in priestly matters; later this document became known as the *Priestly* or P.

In 1854 Eduard Riehm obtained widespread support for the earlier view of de Wette that Deuteronomy had been composed independently of the other books of the Pentateuch.[13] When Hupfeld's theory of the composition of Genesis was extended to include the whole of the Pentateuch, Riehm's conclusions were incorporated. This resulted in the view, sometimes designated as the *New Documentary Hypothesis*, that the Pentateuch was composed of four documents which were combined by a redactor. Concerning the dating of the sources it was proposed that they should be placed in the order: Urschrift or First Elohist (P); Jüngerer or Second Elohist (E); Yahwist (J);[14] Deuteronomy (D).[15]

The position advocated by Hupfeld gained support from a number of scholars. Two scholars in particular deserve special mention. A student of Hupfeld, Edward Böhmer, carefully separated the text of Genesis into the three sources, P, E, and J.[16] Böhmer also offered an alternative dating of the sources. He placed the *Urschrift* (P) in the reign of David, the Yahwist (J) in the time of Elisha (ninth century) and the Second Elohist (E) in the reign of Jeroboam (c. 793–753 BC). Finally, a redactor combined these documents during the reign of Josiah (c. 639–609 BC). In 1869 Theodor Nöldeke provided, in his *Untersuchungen zur Kritik des Altes Testament*,[17] what was to become accepted as the definitive outline of the *Urschrift* P. However, in contrast to Böhmer he dated the *Urschrift* to the period shortly after the reign of Solomon.

---

[13] E. Riehm, *Die Gesetzgebung Mosis im Lande Moab* (Gotha: Friedrich Andreas Perthes, 1854).

[14] The siglum 'J' is derived from the German spelling 'Jahve'.

[15] Cf. de Wette, *Lehrbuch der historisch-kritischen Einleitung in die kanonischen und apokryphischen Bücher des Alten Testaments* (8th edn.; revised by E. Schrader; Berlin: G. Reimer, 1869).

[16] E. Böhmer, *Das erste Buch der Thora* (Halle, 1862).

[17] (Kiel: Schwers'sche, 1869).

2.5. The Documentary Hypothesis of Graf, Vatke and Wellhausen

The assertion of the New Documentary Hypothesis that the Pentateuch was composed of four documents found general acceptance. However, a further development was to occur which modified the theory significantly. Although most scholars were prepared to accept the division of the Pentateuch into four documents, doubts were expressed about Hupfeld's dating of these sources. Eventually, a new theory regarding the order of the documents was formulated and propagated chiefly through the labours of three scholars, Karl Heinrich Graf (1815–1869), Wilhelm Vatke (1806–1882) and especially Julius Wellhausen (1844–1918).

In his *Die geschichtlichen Bücher des Alten Testament: zwei historisch-kritische Untersuchungen* (1866) Graf adopted the view of de Wette that Deuteronomy was from the time of Josiah. By comparing the cultic legislation contained in the rest of the Pentateuch with that of Deuteronomy, Graf observed that the JE legislation was earlier than D, whereas the P material was later.[18] Like de Wette, he also rejected the historical witness of the book of Chronicles to the cultic institutions. Graf, however, took matters further by arguing that references to the tabernacle in P were merely fictional. The tabernacle itself had never existed; the detailed descriptions of it were based on the temple of the post-exilic period.

Concerning the composition of the Pentateuch, Graf initially maintained a type of supplementary hypothesis, arguing that the narrative sections that composed the Urschrift of Genesis were early. However, Graf's views were criticised by various scholars with the result that in 1869 he adopted a modified form of the New Documentary Hypothesis; in contrast to Hupfeld, Graf dated the *Urschrift*, or First Elohist (P), after Deuteronomy. Support for Graf's position came from the Dutch scholar Abraham Kuenen (1828–1891). In 1869–70 he published a work entitled *De Godsdienst van Israël*, in which he also argued that Hupfeld's *Urschrift* ought to be dated to the post-exilic period.

Vatke's contribution to the debate over the ordering of the sources arose from his interest in the work of the philosopher Hegel. Influenced by Hegel's views on the development of civilisation, Vatke argued that there were three distinctive stages in the development of Israelite religion which could be

---

[18]   Graf was influenced by his teacher Eduard Reuss. According to J. Blenkinsopp, *The Pentateuch* (London: SCM, 1992), 7, 'Reuss pointed out that the pre-exilic prophets betray no familiarity with the Mosaic legal system, and that the ritual law in particular, closely related as it is to Ezekiel, could not have originated earlier that the exilic period (sixth century BC).'

aligned with the Pentateuchal sources. The earliest phase, as witnessed in JE, was a religion that emphasised nature/fertility. The next stage of religious development, as reflected in D, centred on the spiritual and ethical ideas associated with the eighth-century prophets. Eventually, there evolved out of these a conception of religion that was legalistic in outlook, emphasising the importance of cultic rituals involving priests and sacrifices.

Marrying the views of Graf and Vatke, Wellhausen propagated this revised Documentary Hypothesis with remarkable skill and conviction. His views appeared first in 1876–77 in a series of offprints for the *Jahrbücher für deutsche Theologie*, entitled 'Die Composition des Hexateuchs'. These were later reprinted in the second volume of *Skizzen und Vorarbeiten*.[19] In 1878 there appeared Wellhausen's *Geschichte Israels I*[20] which was published in future editions under the title *Prolegomena zur Geschichte Israels*.[21] Relying on the work of the scholars who preceded him, Wellhausen argued cogently that the Pentateuch was composed of four distinct documents. The earliest of these was the Yahwistic source, J. The next document was the Elohistic source, E. Subsequently, these two sources were combined by an editor whom Wellhausen designated the 'Jehovist' (R^{JE}). For Wellhausen this redactor played such an important role in shaping the Hexateuch that in his *Prolegomena* he focuses attention principally on the Jehovist, rather than on J and E as separate sources. Later, in the time of Josiah, the book of Deuteronomy, D, was composed.[22] This first edition of Deuteronomy was subsequently expanded by the addition of narrative, homiletic and legal material. Since this additional material showed a knowledge of JE but not P, Wellhausen concluded that JE and D were combined before P was added. Then during the fifth century BC the Priestly document P (Hupfeld's *Urschrift*) was composed. This occurred when an independent Priestly narrative, which recorded the covenants associated with Adam, Noah, Abraham and Sinai, was expanded by the addition of extensive Priestly legislation. Finally, P too was combined with the earlier material. By so ordering the sources Wellhausen produced the now famous sequence J, E, D, P. While Wellhausen recognised the existence of four main sources, he also believed that the sources underwent redactional modifications. Consequently, the process by which the Pentateuch was composed was exceptionally complex.

---

[19] (Berlin: G. Reimer, 1885). This was later reprinted with additional material in *Die Composition des Hexateuchs und der Historischen Bücher des Alten Testaments* (Berlin: G. Reimer, 1889).

[20] (Berlin: G. Reimer, 1878).

[21] ET, *Prolegomena to the History of Israel* (Edinburgh: A. & C. Black, 1885).

[22] For a critique of this dating of Deuteronomy, see G.J. Wenham, 'The Date of Deuteronomy: Linchpin of Old Testament Criticism', *Them* 10 (1985), 15–20; and *Them* 11 (1985), 15–8.

Although Wellhausen was somewhat uncommitted concerning the dating of J and E, subsequent scholars tended to favour a date for J in the second half of the ninth century BC, with E being composed about a century later. Nicholson writes, 'according to the Wellhausen "school" the documents were dated as follows:

J: c. 840 BC

E: c. 700

D: c. 623

P: c. 500–450'.[23]

Throughout Europe Wellhausen's views were generally well received. In his native Germany most scholars quickly adopted his approach. In Holland, Kuenen propounded the views of Wellhausen in his *Historisch-Critisch Onderzoek naar het Onstaan en de Verzameling van de Boeken des Ouden Verbonds*.[24] In France, E. Reuss, who many years earlier had influenced Graf, supported the new theory in his *L'Histoire sainte et la loi*,[25] and in Britain William Robertson Smith became an important advocate of the new theory.[26] Indeed, the influence of the new hypothesis was such that by the year 1890 the views of Graf, Vatke and Wellhausen gained almost total acceptance in the world of biblical scholarship.

2.6. Models for Explaining the Composition of the Pentateuch

Before proceeding to consider in more detail various aspects of the Documentary Hypothesis, we should observe briefly how the stages identified above reflect three different models by which the composition of the Pentateuch may be described.

The *documentary* theories may be thought of as viewing the Pentateuch like a rope which is made up of several coloured strands. Woven together, these strands run throughout the Pentateuch, with occasionally one colour being

---

[23] E.W. Nicholson, *The Pentateuch in the Twentieth Century: The Legacy of Julius Wellhausen* (Oxford: Clarendon Press, 1998), 21.

[24] (Vol. 1; 2nd edn.; Leiden: P. Engels en zoon, 1885. ET, *An Historico-critical Inquiry into the Origin and Composition of the Hexateuch;* London: Macmillan, 1886; based on 2d ed. of *Historisch-Critisch*).

[25] (Paris: Libraire Sandoz et Fischbacher, 1879).

[26] Cf. *The Old Testament in the Jewish Church* (Edinburgh: A. & C. Black, 1881); *The Prophets of Israel* (Edinburgh: A. & C. Black, 1882).

more dominant than the others. Since each strand has its own distinctive features, it is possible to distinguish it from the rest. In the case of the Documentary Hypothesis, the process by which the rope was formed initially involved two strands being combined, to these another strand was added, and then later yet another.

In contrast to the rope-model of the Documentary Hypothesis, *fragmentary* theories view the Pentateuch like a chain composed of assorted links. These links are made from different types of material and may vary greatly in their size and shape; some, however, may share common features. The Pentateuch was created when these links were joined together. An important aspect of this approach is that the Pentateuch may be viewed as having been composed of blocks or sections of material which originally had nothing in common. These were subsequently joined end to end in order to create a longer work.

The third model, corresponding to *supplementary* theories, views the Pentateuch as a coloured string which is stretched out in a line. The string is then broken in various places and other pieces of different coloured strings are knotted in, adding to the length of the original string. As a result the finished string has one dominant colour supplemented by others.

All these models seek to explain the existence within the Pentateuch of features that convey either a sense of unity or diversity. As we shall observe later, although there can be little doubt that diverse materials have been brought together to form the Pentateuch, it is also apparent that the narrative is more unified that many scholars allow.

2.7. Distinctive Vocabulary

For source criticism to work, it is necessary to have definitive criteria by which source-documents can be clearly distinguished from each other. Fundamental to uncovering the source-documents is the assumption that each author has his/her own style of writing. Since it is not always possible to define a writer's literary style with precision, vocabulary provides the best index by which to determine authorship. As we have already observed, it was the unusual distribution of the divine names, Yahweh and Elohim, which first prompted scholars to discern the presence of two sources in the book of Genesis. Beginning here, source critics proceeded to develop vocabulary lists for each of the main source-documents.[27] While in theory vocabulary is a very suitable criterion for distinguishing sources, in practice complications exist.

---

[27] Examples of such lists may be found in various works. In particular, see S.R. Driver, *An Introduction to the Literature of the Old Testament* (9th edn.; Edinburgh: T. & T. Clark, 1913), 116–59.

The presence of a particular word or phrase in various passages need not indicate a common source-document; this could be due to the fact that all the relevant passages address the same subject. For example, the expression 'with all your heart and with all your soul' is generally taken to be characteristic of the D source, occurring within the Pentateuch only in Deuteronomy 4:29; 6:5; 10:12; 11:13; 13:3; 26:16; 30:2, 6, 10.[28] All, however, come in exhortatory speeches addressed by Moses to the Israelites as they prepare to enter into the promised land of Canaan. The context clearly determines the presence of this expression. Moreover, the lengthy speeches in Deuteronomy represent one of the few places were Moses addresses at length the people of Israel using his own words; elsewhere he more often mediates God's words to the Israelites. In the light of these observations, it is reasonable to conclude that the expression 'with all your heart and with all your soul' is indicative of a particular individual speaking in a distinctive context. This hardly justifies its use as a criterion for source analysis.

Two words taken by source critics to be synonyms and, consequently, assigned to separate sources, on closer inspection may be found to have slightly different connotations; this in turn may account for the use of one term in preference to the other in certain contexts. For example, the geographical name Horeb is frequently said to be indicative of the E source; the other sources use 'Sinai'.[29] Yet, from a study of how both words are used in the Pentateuch, it is apparent that Horeb refers to a broad region, within which lies a smaller area known as Sinai. On this basis the use of the term Horeb in Exodus 17:6, for example, is determined by geographical considerations rather than the presence of the E source.

A survey of all the supposedly distinctive vocabulary reveals that on occasions words taken to be typical of one source occasionally come in passages assigned to another source. This clearly undermines completely the usefulness of the term for distinguishing source-documents. Even if just one exception is noted, what guarantee can a source critic have that another exception does not exist? For example, the expression 'land of Canaan' is normally taken to be typical of the P source (e.g. Gen. 12:5; 17:8).[30] Yet, its presence in various verses that may be attributed to either J or E (cf. Gen. 35:6; 42:5, 7, 13, 29, 32; 44:8) clearly undermines its usefulness as a P criterion.

An element of circularity exists in the use of vocabulary to determine sources. On the basis of various occurrences a term may be viewed as typical of a particular source-document. A further occurrence of the same word

---

[28] The only other OT occurrence of his phrase is Joshua 22:5, where the text is alluding back to Moses' exhortation to the Israelites.

[29] Driver, *Introduction*, 82, 119.

[30] Cf. J. Skinner, *Genesis* (2nd edn.; ICC; Edinburgh: T. & T. Clark, 1930), 289.

may come in a passage that on other grounds might be thought to belong to a different source. In such a situation, the verse or phrase containing the term is likely to be viewed as an interpolation, and the word retained as a criterion for source analysis. However, it would surely be much more appropriate to conclude that in these circumstances the term should not be used for source analysis; the one passage in question may indicate that the term is not unique to one source.

These observations draw attention briefly to the practical difficulties inherent in trying to recover the source-documents of the Pentateuch on the basis of distinctive vocabulary. Given the special significance of the divine names in this regard, we shall consider them in more detail.

2.8. The Divine Names in Genesis

The divine names have been widely acknowledged as one of the main criteria for the source analysis of the Pentateuch, although strictly speaking, as we shall observe, their use should be confined to the whole of Genesis and the first few chapters of Exodus. Their significance is underlined by the fact that two of the Pentateuchal sources are designated after them, the Yahwistic (J) and the Elohistic (E). With good reason Redford remarks that this criterion 'has become virtually an article of faith among biblical scholars'.[31]

Evidence supporting the claim that the peculiar arrangement of the divine names in Genesis is due to sources is drawn from a few significant passages: Genesis 4:26; Exodus 3:5–15; 6:3. Of these, Exodus 6:3, which is assigned to the Priestly Writer, is generally understood to state that the patriarchs Abraham, Isaac and Jacob did not know God by the name Yahweh: 'I appeared to Abraham, to Isaac and to Jacob as El Shaddai, but by my name Yahweh I did not made myself known to them.' Although it is not expressed explicitly, Exodus 3:13–15, ascribed to E, may imply that the name Yahweh was only first revealed to Moses. Thus, in the early chapters of Exodus the E and P sources apparently affirm that the patriarchs of Genesis were not familiar with the divine epithet Yahweh. This, it is suggested, is supported by the observation that 'Yahweh' never appears in the E and P material preserved in Genesis. In marked contrast, the J source introduces the name Yahweh right at the beginning of Genesis, and the importance of the name is indicated in Genesis 4:26: 'At that time men began to call on the name of Yahweh.' Only by dividing Genesis into sources, so it is argued, is it possible

---

[31] D.B. Redford, *A Study of the Biblical Story of Joseph (Genesis 37–50)* (VTS 20; Leiden: Brill, 1970), 108.

to reconcile the apparently conflicting statements found in Exodus 6:3 and Genesis 4:26.[32]

This interpretation of the evidence, however, creates an intriguing problem. Since the time of Wellhausen it has been customary to view J as the oldest of the Pentateuchal sources. Yet, if J existed prior to E and P, why did these later sources state that the patriarchs did not know the name Yahweh? Were the authors of E and P not already aware of the fact that the patriarchs knew God as Yahweh? In its present form, the Documentary Hypothesis offers no satisfactory explanation for this problem.

Although doubts have been expressed in the past about the validity of the criterion of divine names,[33] it is still widely viewed as an important guide to the sources underlying the Pentateuch, and especially the book of Genesis. Nevertheless, it is now acknowledged that a purely 'mechanical application' of this criterion is unsatisfactory.[34] This is so for a number of reasons:

- Whereas Yahweh is a personal name, Elohim is a common noun. While there are many occasions in Genesis were it is possible to interchange these terms, there are contexts which permit only the use of Elohim as a common noun meaning 'deity'.[35]
- There are some obvious instances where the use of a particular divine name is determined by the context. For example, in Genesis 3:1–5 the serpent and the woman use the designation Elohim, rather than Yahweh Elohim, which is used elsewhere throughout Genesis 2:4–3:24. As his adversary, it is hardly surprising that the serpent avoids using God's personal name Yahweh.
- 'The name for God is not as stringent a criterion for J as it is for P (or E).'[36] Given that in E and P the divine name Yahweh was first revealed to Moses, we would clearly not expect to find 'Yahweh' appearing in E or P

---

[32] For an outline of various attempts to harmonise the Exodus statements about the origin of the name Yahweh with the presence of the epithet in Genesis, see G.H. Parke-Taylor, *Yahweh: The Divine Name in the Bible* (Waterloo, Ontario: Wilfrid Laurier University Press, 1975), 18–62. The difficulties presented by Exodus 6:3 are discussed in T.D. Alexander, *Abraham in the Negev: A Source-critical investigation of Genesis 20:1–22:19* (Carlisle: Paternoster, 1997), 90–101.

[33] E.g. U. Cassuto, *The Documentary Hypothesis* (Jerusalem: Magnes Press, 1961), 15–41; M.H. Segal, 'El, Elohim, Yhwh in the Bible', *JQR* 46 (1955), 89–115.

[34] C. Westermann, *Genesis 1-11. A Commentary* (trans. John J. Scullion; London/Minneapolis: SPCK/Augsburg, 1984), 579; cf. R.N. Whybray, *The Making of the Pentateuch: A Methodological Study* (JSOTSS 53; Sheffield: Sheffield Academic, 1987), 63–72.

[35] E.g. Genesis 9:26; 17:7, 8; 24:3, 7, 12, 27, 42, 48; 26:24; 27:20; 28:13 (x2), 21; 31:5, 19, 29, 30, 32, 34, 35, 42 (x2), 53 (x2); 32:10 (x2); 33:20; 35:2, 4; 43:23 (x2); 46:1, 3; 50:17.

[36] Westermann, *Genesis 1–11*, 579.

passages occurring in Genesis. There is, however, no reason why Yahweh should not appear in E or P narratives describing events after the revelation of this new name to Moses; indeed, we would expect this to be the case. Similarly, there is no reason why the epithet Elohim may not be present in any J passage.[37] Thus, strictly speaking, in Genesis only the presence of 'Yahweh' in a text can be viewed as a decisive indicator for source analysis; the presence of Elohim in a particular verse does not automatically require that it should be assigned to either E or P.

- An examination of biblical material outside Genesis reveals that 'variation in the name for God is certainly possible in a literary unity'.[38] The presence of both divine names in a single passage does not necessarily imply that two separate accounts have been integrated together. It is possible for one author to use both divine epithets.

- We should be alert to the possibility that the biblical texts may have been modified as a result of editorial activity. Thus, for example, J. Skinner, supporting the Documentary Hypothesis, argues that the presence of Yahweh in Genesis 22:11, 14; 28:21 and 31:49 is 'due to the intentional action of a redactor'.[39]

- It is not inconceivable that in some instances a divine name was changed merely by accident in the transmission of the Genesis text. We cannot be completely certain that the Masoretic Text preserves accurately the arrangement of the divine names following the amalgamation of the supposed sources J, E and P. This possibility is supported by the different textual traditions found in the Samaritan Pentateuch and the Septuagint.[40]

All these observations underline the danger of adopting a purely mechanical application of the divine names criterion for source analysis.

In spite of these difficulties, the idea that Genesis is comprised of sources that use different divine names still attracts support, and many scholars

---

[37] Cf. Skinner, *Genesis*, l–li.

[38] Westermann, *Genesis 1–11*, 579; cf. Segal, 'El, Elohim and Yhwh', 94–7; Whybray, *Making of the Pentateuch*, 67–8.

[39] Skinner, *Genesis*, l–li. See also the suggestion of G.J. Wenham, 'The Religion of the Patriarchs', in A.R. Millard and D.J. Wiseman (eds.), *Essays on the Patriarchal Narratives* (Leicester: IVP, 1980), 157–88, that the name Yahweh was inserted into the Genesis material by a Yahwistic redactor. For a critique of Wenham's position, see Alexander, *Abraham in the Negev*, 93–6.

[40] For a fuller discussion of the textual evidence, see J. Skinner, *The Divine Names in Genesis* (London: Hodder & Stoughton, 1914). The SP differs from MT in some nine cases (7:1, 9; 14:22; 20:18; 28:4; 31:7, 9, 16a; 35:9b). The LXX manuscripts preserve over 60 readings where the divine names differ from the MT.

appear content to accept the Documentary Hypothesis explanation for the distribution of the divine epithets in Genesis. As Westermann observes, 'none of the attempts to explain the variation in the name for God in another way have [sic] so far led to any convincing result'.[41] While this may be so, the criterion of divine names cannot, in the light of the facts observed above, be relied upon to provide a definitive source analysis of Genesis.

2.9. Doublets

Alongside vocabulary, the source analysis of the Pentateuch has relied heavily upon the idea that the text contains duplicate accounts of the same events, often described as 'doublets'. These fall into two main types.

1. The same event may be described in two quite separate episodes. Thus, for example, there are two accounts of Abraham pretending that his wife is his sister (Gen. 12:10–20; 20:1–18; a similar incident involving Isaac comes in Gen. 26:1–11). In each episode Sarah is taken by a foreign ruler and only after divine intervention is returned to Abraham. According to the Documentary Hypothesis, Genesis 12:10–20 represents J's version of this event, and Genesis 20:1–18 is E's version.
2. Some doublets involve a single episode which is dissected into two separate accounts. Thus, for example, it is argued that the Flood Narrative in Genesis 6–9 is an amalgam of two versions, one deriving from J and the other from P. The existence of doublets is an important factor in support of the Documentary Hypothesis, for they indicate that the different source-documents used in the composition of the Pentateuch parallel each other in terms of contents.

Space does not permit a detailed critique of all the supposed doublets found within the Pentateuch.[42] It is the present writer's experience that under close inspection many of these doublets do not support the existence of once independent, parallel sources.[43] Thus, for example, the account of Sarah's abduction by Abimelech in Genesis 20 presupposes that the reader is already familiar with a similar incident that has occurred previously. Without a prior knowledge of the events described in Genesis 12:11–15, it is impossible to

---

[41] Westermann, *Genesis 1–11*, 578.

[42] For a fuller list of 'doublets' of both types, see R.E. Friedman, 'Torah (Pentateuch)', *ABD* 6:609.

[43] For a much fuller discussion of the main doublets found within the Abraham narrative in Genesis 11:27–25:11, see Alexander, *Abraham in the Negev*, 32–69.

make sense of Genesis 21:2. This strongly suggests that the account in Genesis 20 was composed as part of a document that already contained the material in Genesis 12:10–20 (or something very similar). This observation argues against a *documentary* solution to the presence of these two incidents in Genesis; possibly Genesis 20 was composed as a supplement to an already existing document. When, however, all the source-analysis criteria are considered in Genesis 12:10–20 and 20:1–18, it is highly likely that the same writer composed both episodes.[44]

The issues involved in determining the presence of true doublets within the Pentateuch are complex. Occasionally the arguments are so finely balanced that it is difficult to be confident that parallel source-documents exist. This is certainly the case with regard to the Flood Narrative.[45]

In the preceding paragraphs we have focused on distinctive vocabulary and doublets. While these represent the mainstays of the Documentary Hypothesis, other criteria are often discussed (e.g. contradictions; theological outlook). The latter, however, are of much less importance in terms of supporting the Documentary Hypothesis, for they do not automatically support the existence of parallel source-documents. It should also be noted that these other criteria were recognised only after the various sources were isolated using distinctive vocabulary and doublets.[46]

2.10. Implications for the History of Israelite Religion

An important aspect of the Documentary Hypothesis is the impact that it has had upon the study of Israelite religion. No longer was the Pentateuch viewed as providing evidence of religious practices dating from before the period of the monarchy. Rather it consisted of four source-documents, J, E, D and P, dated respectively to the tenth/ninth, ninth/eighth, seventh and sixth/fifth centuries BC. Since each source supposedly provided a snapshot of the religious customs being practised at the time of its composition, it was possible by comparing them to see how Israelite religion evolved from the

---

[44] See Alexander, *Abraham in the Negev*, 32–51.

[45] The arguments for and against the source-analysis of the Flood Narrative are debated in a series of articles by Wenham and Emerton: cf. G.J. Wenham, 'The Coherence of the Flood Narrative', *VT* 28 (1978), 336–48; J.A. Emerton, 'An Examination of Some Attempts to Defend the Unity of the Flood Narrative in Genesis', *VT* 37 (1987), 401–20; and *VT* 38 (1988), 1–21; Wenham, 'Method in Pentateuchal Source Criticism', *VT* 41 (1991), 84–109.

[46] For a much fuller critique of the criteria used in support of the Documentary Hypothesis, see Whybray, *Making of the Pentateuch*, 43–131.

tenth century through to the fifth century BC.[47] The impact of this development can be seen, for example, in the modern assessment of the history of Passover.[48]

By comparing Exodus 23:15–16 and Exodus 34:18–22 (both J) with Deuteronomy 16:1–17 (D) Wellhausen concluded that in ancient Israel there were three main feasts: Unleavened Bread, Weeks and Tabernacles/Booths.[49] On the basis of their earliest titles (Unleavened Bread, Harvest and Ingathering, as reflected in Ex. 23 and 34) they were clearly agricultural in origin, probably taken over by the Israelites from the Canaanites. Furthermore, because the J sections of the Pentateuch never mention it, the Passover could not have existed when J was composed.[50] Wellhausen then suggested, on the basis of Deuteronomy 16:1–8 (D), that the Passover and the Feast of Unleavened Bread were amalgamated about the time of Josiah's reforms in 621 BC. Prior to this they were totally unconnected. Subsequent developments, as revealed in the Priestly Writer's portrayal of the Passover (as found in Ex. 12:1–20, 28, 43–49, 13:1–2; Lev. 23:5–8; Num. 9:1–14; 28:16–25), confirmed this major innovation.[51] By concluding that the Passover and the Feast of Unleavened Bread were unrelated prior to about 620 BC, Wellhausen overturned the long-standing tradition, highlighted especially in Exodus 12–13, that both originated as commemorations of the Israelite exodus from Egypt. So cogent were his arguments for the original independence of the Passover and Unleavened Bread that Wellhausen's work heralded a new era in the study of the early history of these sacred feasts.

If the Passover was unconnected to the Feast of Unleavened Bread prior to the time of Josiah, how did it originate and what form did it take? For his part, Wellhausen suggested that the Passover developed in a pastoral, rather than an agricultural setting, as the offering of the first fruits of sheep and cattle.[52] Expressing gratitude to God for fruitful flocks and herds, it was the oldest of the feasts and was not tied to any particular time in the year. Although the offering

---

[47] For this reason Wellhausen's influential study was entitled, *Prolegomena to the History of Israel*.

[48] For a fuller discussion, see T.D. Alexander, 'The Passover Sacrifice', in R.T. Beckwith and M. Selman (eds.), *Sacrifice in the Bible* (Carlisle/Grand Rapids: Paternoster/Baker, 1995), 1–24.

[49] *Prolegomena*, 83–120.

[50] To support this idea Wellhausen, *Prolegomena*, 85, n.1, emends the expression ḥag happā saḥ 'feast of the passover' in Exodus 34:25, to ḥaggi 'my feast' on the basis of Exodus 23:18.

[51] E.g. the precise dating of the Passover; more exact specifications regarding the offerings.

[52] The inadequacy of this reconstruction is highlighted by M. Haran, 'The Passover Sacrifice', in *Studies in the Religion of Ancient Israel* (VTS 22; Leiden: Brill, 1972), 94–5.

of first fruits originated in Israel's nomadic past, it was only rarely observed during the early monarchy; hence it is not mentioned in the Book of the Covenant (Ex. 22:29–30). It was revived in Judah after the fall of the northern kingdom in 721 BC, to be amalgamated almost a century later with the Feast of Unleavened Bread. Only at this stage was the name *pesaḥ* 'Passover' introduced.

Other writers, accepting the validity of Wellhausen's general approach, revised substantially his picture of the Passover's origin. G.B. Gray sought to isolate various ancient features of the Passover by focusing on its later customs.[53] He concluded that the Passover was originally observed by nomadic Israelites on the night of the full moon nearest the Spring Equinox. In its earliest form it consisted of a sacrificial meal in which the entire victim was eaten raw, with the blood still in it.[54] This custom was later modified; the victim was now cooked and its blood smeared on the doorposts. The blood ritual had an apotropaic purpose; it was intended to protect those within from some power outside by providing a 're-inforced closed door'. With the centralisation of sacrificial worship in Jerusalem in 620 BC, the practice of smearing the blood on the door was abandoned; the sacrificial meal alone continued to be observed.

According to R. de Vaux, the Passover began as the springtime sacrifice of a young animal, not necessarily the firstborn, by nomadic or semi-nomadic shepherds in order to guarantee the prosperity of the flock.[55] It occurred prior to the tribal migration, and required neither a priest nor an altar. An important feature of the feast, which took place at the full moon, was the smearing of blood on the tent poles in order to drive away evil powers. Various features of the later Passover celebration reflect its nomadic origin:

---

[53] *Sacrifice in the Old Testament: Its Theory and Practice* (Oxford: Clarendon Press, 1925), 337–82.

[54] Gray, *Sacrifice*, 368, observes that in Exodus 12:9 and 12:46 it is forbidden to eat the victim raw, or to break any of its bones. He concludes, 'A legal prohibition is commonly directed against what is, or has been, actual practice. It has therefore been inferred that at one time the Paschal victim was eaten raw, and that the bones, having been broken and pounded for the purpose, were eaten as well as the flesh.'

[55] R. de Vaux, *Ancient Israel: Its Life and Institutions* (2nd edn.; London: Darton, Longman & Todd, 1965), 484–93. He appears to follow L. Rost's comparative study of the customs of nomadic Arabs, 'Weidewechsel und altisraelitischer Festkalender', *ZDPV* 66 (1943), 205–16; reprinted in L. Rost, *Das kleine Credo und andere Studien zum AT* (Heidelberg: Quelle & Meyer, 1965), 101–12. B.N. Wambacq has queried the relevance of Rost's study; see 'Les origines de la *Pesaḥ* israélite', *Biblica* 57 (1976), 206–24. In particular he notes that the blood rite among nomadic Arabs concerns their arrival and settlement in a new location, whereas the Passover ritual in Exodus 12 focuses on the Israelites' departure from Egypt.

The victim was roasted over a fire without any kitchen utensils; it was eaten with unleavened bread (which is still the normal bread of Bedouin to-day), and with bitter herbs (which does not mean vegetables grown in the garden, but the desert plants which Bedouin pick to season their food). The ritual prescribed that those eating it should have their belts already fastened, sandals on their feet (as if they were going to make a long journey on foot), and a shepherd's stick in one hand.[56]

Before the Israelite settlement of Canaan, the Passover was a common feast celebrated at the central sanctuary of the tribal federation. With the decentralisation of cultic worship, after Israel's occupation of Canaan, it became a family feast. Much later, as a result of Josiah's decision to have all cultic worship centralised in Jerusalem, it reverted to a common feast.

Recently, the speculative nature of such histories has been highlighted by J. Van Seters. On methodological grounds he rejects these attempts to reconstruction the Passover's origin through either the backward projection of later features or the use of comparative customs.

For all its ingenious reconstructions the disadvantages of the traditio-historical method are considerable. Since it speculates about the shape of the pre-literate tradition its theories cannot be falsified by an appeal to the present texts. There is also no way to make any judgment between radically different proposals and thus theories about the cult have greatly proliferated. Furthermore, those who follow this method have never demonstrated by comparative literature that tradition-history is anything but a completely artificial construction of biblical scholars.[57]

Because they cannot be substantiated, traditio-historical theories about the Passover's origin must be treated with the utmost caution. They clearly do not provide a very secure foundation upon which to base our investigation of the sacrificial nature of the Passover. (For a fuller discussion of the traditio-historical method, see 3.3 and 3.4)

Although Van Seters affirms emphatically the priority of source analysis for uncovering the true history of the Passover, he rejects Wellhausen's approach on a number of specific points.

1. He is convinced that the J material should be dated to the period of the exile, making D the earliest source, with J coming midway between D and P.
2. Whereas Wellhausen maintained that the Passover and the Feast of Unleavened Bread were first amalgamated in Deuteronomy 16, Van Seters views all the references to Unleavened Bread in Deuteronomy 16 as later additions.

---

[56] De Vaux, *Ancient Israel*, 489.

[57] J. Van Seters, 'The Place of the Yahwist in the History of Passover and Massot', *ZAW* 95 (1983), 169–70.

3. He supports the view of J. Halbe that the Feast of Unleavened Bread did not originate as an ancient Canaanite agricultural festival.[58] Rather, he dates it to the exilic period when the eating of the Passover sacrifice could no longer be observed due to the destruction of the temple; the eating of unleavened bread became the basis of a substitute festival.
4. He reassigns some of the material in Exodus 12–13 to different sources; 12:29–39 and 13:3–16 come from J; the remaining verses (12:1–28 and 13:1–2) are the product of P.[59]

In the light of these considerations, Van Seters proposes the following reconstruction of the Passover's history. The Passover, as reflected in the earliest source D, was a one-day festival in the spring at a local sanctuary. After the slaughter of an animal from the flock or herd there was a meal, eaten at night without unleavened bread. D restricted the celebration of the festival to a central sanctuary, and introduced the idea that it was a commemoration of the exodus. About a century and a half later, with the destruction of the temple, it was no longer possible to celebrate the Passover. As a result, J instituted the Feast of Unleavened Bread as a substitute. However, this new feast lasted for a week, and prominence was given to the eating of unleavened bread, the one significant element retained from the Passover celebration. With the restoration of the temple after the exile further modifications occurred, as witnessed in P. The revived Passover celebration was combined with the Feast of Unleavened Bread. This, however, presented a problem for Jews living in the Diaspora. How could they, far removed from the sanctuary, participate in the new combined feast? To resolve the problem each household was sanctified by means of a blood rite: 'A small animal could be slaughtered as a sacrifice, its blood used to purify the house, and the animal cooked in such a way as to resemble an offering by fire.'[60] To legitimise this

---

[58] J. Halbe, 'Erwägungen zu Ursprung und Wesen des Massotfestes', *ZAW* 87 (1975), 325–34. Among the reasons listed by Halbe, the following are the most convincing: (a) the month of Abib (March-April) is too early for a harvest festival; (b) it is strange that a harvest celebration should be marked by the eating of unleavened bread; (c) a seven-day festival is hardly likely to have occurred at the beginning of the harvest; (d) a special reason, the exodus from Egypt, has to be provided for celebrating the Feast of Unleavened Bread; this is not so for the true harvest feasts of Harvest (Weeks) and Ingathering (Tabernacles/Booths).

[59] Van Seters' source analysis may be compared with the more traditional position adopted by Driver, *Introduction*, 28. He assigns Exodus 12:1–20, 28, 37a, 40–51; 13:1–2 to P, Exodus 12:29–30 to J, Exodus 12:31–36, 37b–39, 42a to E, and Exodus 12:21–27; 13:3–16 to JE.

[60] Van Seters, 'The Place of the Yahwist', 180–1.

activity the Priestly Writer created the aetiology of the blood rite of the exodus story.[61]

The contrasting proposals of Wellhausen and Van Seters highlight the variety of reconstructions which are possible for the history of the Passover. Their differing conclusions depend heavily upon the source analysis of the relevant Pentateuchal passages and their dating in relation to one another. Since space does not permit us to critique in detail here these differing views of Passover, several observations must suffice.

First, at the present time the whole question of the source analysis of the Pentateuch is in a state of flux. As we shall discover in chapter 3, the once assured results of the Documentary Hypothesis no longer enjoy widespread acceptance. Recent studies have challenged both the validity of the criteria used to distinguish sources and the order in which they should be dated. In the light of these developments, we should be wary of reconstructing the history of the Passover on the basis of source-critical theories which lack widespread support.

Secondly, in the past it has generally been assumed that if a Pentateuchal source shows no knowledge of a custom or practice, that feature did not exist when the source was composed. Yet, conclusions drawn from the silence of the text may prove unwarranted. Two factors make this likely. On the one hand, some passages about the Passover are exceptionally brief (e.g. Ex. 34:25; Lev. 23:5; Num. 28:16). The absence of particular details may be due entirely to the succinct nature of the material.[62] On the other hand, if two sources have been combined, specific details in one source may be omitted for editorial reasons.[63] This is especially relevant regarding the narrative in Exodus 12–13, which is generally taken to be comprised of two, if not more, sources. Little allowance is made for the fact that the editor(s) who combined

---

[61] This proposal raises a number of problems. The smearing of blood on the doorposts is mentioned only in connection with the original Passover night in Egypt. There is no hint that the blood was used in this way during subsequent commemorations of the Passover. In view of the uniqueness of the original occasion, the Exodus narrative hardly provides a suitable aetiology for justifying the adoption of this practice on future occasions. Furthermore, would the Priestly Writer have supported a practice which involved the offering of sacrifices by non-priests? Finally, Van Seters offers no evidence of it having been practised in the exilic or post-exilic period, and no explanation as to why it ceased, presumably soon afterwards, to be observed.

[62] This difficulty is not helped when scholars deliberately remove evidence from a passage on the basis that it is a later interpolation.

[63] The source analysis of the Flood Narrative in Genesis 6–9 illustrates this possibility. Although the Yahwistic material contains no reference to the building of the ark, it clearly presupposes that one was constructed. If the present account is the product of J and P material having been combined, the editor has adopted the P version of the ark's construction in preference to that of J.

the supposed sources may have deliberately omitted details already present in one source in favour of parallel details found in another of the sources. For example, while J alone mentions the use of a basin for catching the blood and of hyssop for smearing it on the doorposts (Ex. 12:21–27), we should not suppose that P's silence about these matters means that he had no knowledge of them. We must allow for the possibility that some material became redundant when the sources were combined.[64] Unfortunately, we have no way of knowing how little or how much material has been lost in the editorial process.

In the light of these observations, it is apparent that the task of reconstructing the history of the Passover will continue to present a major challenge, even if scholars arrive at a new consensus regarding the source analysis of the Pentateuch. Two factors, however, suggest that greater reliability should be placed upon the present synchronic account of the Passover's history.

First, almost every passage which refers to the Passover associates it with either the Feast of Unleavened Bread or with the eating of unleavened bread.[65] Although Wellhausen and Van Seters maintain that the two feasts were originally unconnected in J and D respectively, their arguments are not convincing. M. Haran has demonstrated, *contra* Wellhausen, that J knew of both feasts, and there is no reason to delete the term *pesaḥ* 'Passover' in Exodus 34:25.[66] Nor is it necessary to remove, as Van Seters suggests, all references to Unleavened Bread in Deuteronomy 16.[67] Given the unanimity of the biblical tradition, there are surely good grounds for believing that both feasts were united from their inception. The evidence to the contrary is not compelling.

---

[64] As Haran, 'Passover Sacrifice', 88, observes, 'The J passage (Exod. xii 21–27) in no way contradicts the description given in P ... Both refer to the same happening, only neither of them embraces all the details, which means that they actually complement each other.' Indeed, such is the unity of the present narrative that Van Seters assigns all of Exodus 12:1–28 to P.

[65] Only two passages mention the Passover without making any reference to unleavened bread: Numbers 33:3, a brief chronological remark, and 2 Kings. 23:21–23, a short description of the Passover celebrated by Josiah. Passover and the Feast of Unleavened Bread are linked in Exodus 12:1–13:16; 23:15–18; 34:18–25; Leviticus 23:5–6; Deuteronomy 16:1–16; 2 Chronicles 30:1–21; 35:1–19; Ezra 6:19–22. Passover and the eating of unleavened bread are associated in Exodus 12:1–13:16; 23:18; 34:25; Numbers 9:2–14; 28:16–17; Deuteronomy 16:1–8; Joshua 5:10–11; Ezekiel 45:21.

[66] 'Passover Sacrifice', 96–101.

[67] Cf. J.G. McConville, *Law and Theology in Deuteronomy* (JSOTSS 33; Sheffield: JSOT Press, 1984), 99–123; Alexander, 'The Passover Sacrifice', 11–4.

Secondly, all the Pentateuchal sources link the Passover with the Israelite exodus.[68] The evidence does not support the assumption that later writers created a historical aetiology. No alternative explanation for the designation *pesah* 'Passover' has gained widespread support, and although scholars have expressed reservations concerning the explanation given in Exodus 12–13, it is by far the most suitable.[69]

2.11. Conclusion

In the opening section of this chapter we surveyed the chain of developments that led to the formulation of the Documentary Hypothesis towards the end of the nineteenth century. We next considered the two main criteria used to isolate the source-documents thought to underlie the Pentateuch, focusing in particular on the divine names. Finally, we observed how the Documentary Hypothesis has had a telling impact upon the history of Israelite religion, radically challenging the traditional understanding of the Pentateuch. Only a limited critique of various aspects of the Documentary Hypothesis has been offered here. In chapter 4 we shall observe more recent developments, some of which have seriously questioned the validity of the Documentary Hypothesis. Before doing so, it is necessary to consider the impact of both form and traditio-historical criticism upon the study of the Pentateuch.

---

[68] Among all the references to the Passover in the Pentateuch, only in Leviticus 23:5–6 is there no mention of the exodus. Apart from Exodus 12:1–13:16, the two events are linked together in Exodus 23:15; 34:18; Numbers 9:1; 33:3; Deuteronomy 16:1, 3, 6.

[69] H.-J. Kraus, *Worship in Israel: A Cultic History of the Old Testament* (Oxford: Basil Blackwell, 1966), 45–6; cf. J.B. Segal, *The Hebrew Passover From the Earliest Times to AD 70* (London Oriental Series 12; London: Oxford University Press, 1963), 95–101.

3

Going Behind the Documents

Following the widespread acceptance of the Documentary Hypothesis as *the* definitive explanation for the source-documents underlying the Pentateuch, a few scholars began towards the end of the nineteenth century to consider the pre-literary stage in the growth of the Pentateuch. This led to the development of two new methods of studying the OT texts: form criticism and traditio-historical criticism. Of significance is the fact that these methods sought to move backwards from written texts to oral accounts. This, however, compared with source criticism, involves a greater degree of speculation, for we can never expect to recover the original oral forms of the Pentateuchal materials. The best we could perhaps hope for is a written transcript of an oral presentation and even this is unlikely to be totally accurate.

Of these two methods, form criticism was the first to be developed in detail, although, as we shall see below, the origins of both methods may be traced back to one scholar, Hermann Gunkel.

3.1. Form Criticism

The scholar identified with pioneering form criticism is Hermann Gunkel. He sought to go beyond the work of earlier source critics by examining the development of the Israelite traditions in their oral stage. To achieve this he introduced a method of research now generally known as form criticism (*Formgeschichte*), although Gunkel himself referred to it as *Gattungsforschung* (research into literary types) or *Literaturgeschichte* (history of literature).

In his approach Gunkel broke free from the limits imposed by the older source-critical method which had restricted scholars to examining the growth of the Pentateuch at the purely literary level. Stressing the part played by oral transmission, Gunkel sought to write a history of the pre-literary development of the traditions underlying the Pentateuch, and in particular the book of Genesis.

According to Gunkel, it is possible to observe in Genesis different types or forms of material: aetiological stories describing how a custom or institution came into being; cultic legends explaining the origin of a sanctuary; ethnological legends outlining the relationship between different groups of people; etymological stories setting out how a person or place received its name. Gunkel believed that many of these were much older than the literary sources in which they are preserved. As a result, Gunkel was able to move back behind the documentary sources which comprise the Pentateuch. Moreover, Gunkel maintained that each type or form of material originated from a particular life setting (*Sitz im Leben*) in ancient Israelite society, which when analysed pointed towards an oral rather than a literary origin.

In his commentary on Genesis,[1] first published in 1901, Gunkel set out his reasons for believing that the narratives in Genesis had originally circulated orally. First, he noted that the book of Genesis consists of numerous episodes, which appear to have been collected together to form a longer narrative. Secondly, he argued that these episodes represented short, separate stories which he called *Sagen* (legends, fables, myths, tales; sing. *Sage*). In Gunkel's opinion, any piece of narrative that belonged to the category of *Sage* must have been transmitted orally. Three important features distinguished a *Sage* from other forms: (a) unlike real 'history' (*Geschichte*), a *Sage* has a poetic tone; (b) a *Sage* recounts supernatural or incredible events; (c) the subject matter of a *Sage* differs from that found in historiography; whereas, for example, the former may focus on family affairs, the latter is interested in national events. As these features reveal, Gunkel distinguished *Sagen* from 'history'. He believed that within an ancient society storytelling initially involved the use of *Sagen*, short oral accounts, and only later did this primitive form develop into 'history' writing. While the material compiled in Genesis belongs to the earliest period within the evolution of Israelite society, the books of Samuel and Kings, for example, reflect a much later phase. This distinction between *Sagen* and 'history' confirmed for Gunkel his belief that the material in Genesis originated orally.

Gunkel, however, not only argued that Genesis was composed of short episodes that had once circulated orally; he also sought to date the individual episodes. S.M. Warner summarises well Gunkel's approach:

> His [Gunkel's] argument was simple. The more primitive (ancient) a society was, the less moral, ethical, and spiritual awareness it would possess. Thus, for example, he believed that the older stories, lacking in religious sophistication, had a 'naive' (p. L) way of mixing the religious and profane elements within their narratives, while later stories emphasized only the religious element. He similarly thought that all those

---

[1] *Genesis: übersetz und erklärt* (3rd edn.;Göttingen: Vandenhoeck & Ruprecht, 1910); ET, based on 3rd ed., *Genesis* (Macon: Mercer University Press, 1997).

stories about the patriarchs which revealed them as flesh and blood people, warts and all, had to be earlier than those which emphasized only their religious qualities (p. LI). He also believed that the way in which the patriarchal stories depicted theophanic events could be used as an indicator of their age (p. XLII). Later, more sophisticated people would take offence at any story which could take seriously the idea that a deity would reveal itself in the flesh. In the same way the age of the narrative could be revealed from the extent to which it dissociated the deity from its sanctuary. Older stories could only depict a deity with influence in the area immediately surrounding its sanctuary. Later stories allowed a deity a far greater freedom of movement and influence (pp. XLII–XLIII).[2]

In both his general approach and in his dating of the individual episodes, Gunkel relied heavily upon a developmental theory of history in which things evolve from being simple and primitive to being complex and sophisticated. As Warner observes, the fallacy of such a contrast between primitive and modern man has been noted by those engaged in the study of 'primitive' societies in Africa and elsewhere; even so-called 'primitive' peoples have very elaborate and involved societies. As regards Genesis, the narrative techniques used in the writing of the book reflect the work of an author (or authors) who employed well-developed literary skills.[3] It is a mistake, therefore, to think of the material in Genesis as 'primitive'.

Fundamental to Gunkel's approach is the belief that the episodes in Genesis were composed orally. While this assumption is commonly made, it remains to be clearly demonstrated. In spite of attempts to define the nature of oral material, we have no way of showing that even one episode in Genesis was composed orally. As Warner observes:

> At present we see no reason to assume that the narratives of Genesis bear any close resemblance to orally transmitted data at all. If biblical scholars wish to argue such a thesis, they must develop new criteria with which to establish it.[4]

Warner's comments highlight one of the main unresolved issues as regards the study of the Pentateuch. Our knowledge of the oral stage is likely to remain minimal for years to come, and theories based upon it rest upon uncertain foundations.[5]

In time, Gunkel's form-critical approach was adopted and developed by other scholars, mainly in Germany. Albrecht Alt produced influential studies

---

[2] S.M. Warner, 'Primitive Saga Men', *VT* 29 (1979), 329.

[3] E.g. M.A. Fishbane, 'Composition and Structure in the Jacob Cycle (Gen. 25:19–35:22)', *JJS* 26 (1975), 15–38.

[4] Warner, 'Primitive Saga Men', 335.

[5] For a fuller critique of form criticism, see Whybray, *Making of the Pentateuch*, 133–85.

on the religion of the patriarchs[6] and Israelite law.[7] In the former he sought to explain the evolution of Israelite religion prior to the time of the monarchy, and in the latter he distinguished between two main types of law found in the Pentateuch; casuistic (If a man …) and apodictic (Thou shalt [not] …). Alt's approach had a profound influence on two of his students, Gerhard von Rad and Martin Noth, both of whom became leading exponents of the traditio-historical method.

3.2. Traditio-historical Criticism

We have already noted how source criticism seeks to determine the documents underlying the present text of the Pentateuch, and form criticism concentrates on the initial oral stage of the individual episodes. Traditio-historical criticism attempts to explain what happened between these two stages. It aims to account for the process by which the once independent oral episodes were united together to form those documents which, according to the Documentary Hypothesis, comprise the Pentateuch.

The origins of traditio-historical criticism can be traced back to Gunkel, particularly to his views on how the book of Genesis developed from once independent oral stories.[8] While Gunkel acknowledged that the different types of material found in Genesis originally existed as independent oral stories, he also proposed that during the oral stage of transmission some of them were collected together to form larger units. Consequently, he suggested that it was possible to uncover in Genesis 'cycles of legends' (*Sagenkränze*). Gunkel drew attention to several examples of such cycles. Once originally independent stories about Abraham and Lot were brought together at the oral stage to form a longer account comprising various episodes. Two similar 'cycles of legends' were composed using stories about Jacob-Esau and Jacob-Laban. As a further development, these two cycles were combined to form a single Jacob-Esau-Laban cycle. Gunkel also proposed that the Joseph story in Genesis 37–50 was another example of a cycle of legends, although he noted that in this case the episodes making up the cycle were less self-contained. As a result, he classified the Joseph Story as a *novelle*.

---

[6] *Der Gott der Väter* (Stuttgart, 1929); reprinted in *Kleine Schriften zur Geschichte des Volkes Israels I* (München: C.H. Beck'sche, 1953), 1–78. ET in *Essays on Old Testament History and Religion* (Oxford: Blackwell, 1966). For a helpful summary of Alt's views on early Israelite religion, see Nicholson, *The Pentateuch*, 54–8.

[7] *Die Ursprünge des israelitischen Recht*, 1934; reprinted in *Kleine Schriften zur Geschichte des Volkes Israels I* (München: Beck'sche, 1953). ET in *Essays on Old Testament History and Religion* (Oxford: Blackwell, 1966), 80–132.

[8] Nicholson, *The Pentateuch*, 31–43.

An important implication of Gunkel's approach was that he came to view the sources J and E as collections of oral material. Consequently, it was no longer appropriate to think of Yahwist and Elohist as 'authors'; they were merely collectors, who brought together material that was not entirely homogeneous.[9]

Gunkel's views on traditio-historical criticism did not immediately gain the same recognition as his form-critical ideas. It was to be some years before traditio-historical criticism emerged as a separate method and even then the shadow of form criticism was present.

Although presented as a form-critical study, von Rad's book, *Das formgeschichtliche Problem des Hexateuch*,[10] was influential in establishing the importance of the traditio-historical method. Von Rad suggested that J was composed along the lines of an outline of Israel's history contained in early credal forms used in cultic celebrations. Examples of these early credos are preserved in Deuteronomy 6:20–24; 26:5b–9 and Joshua 24:2b–13. Von Rad isolated in these credos three main themes: (a) Aramaean origin; (b) rescue from Egypt; (c) possession of the land. According to von Rad, these credos were first used in cultic worship related to the Festival of Weeks held at Gilgal during the initial period of Israel's settlement in Canaan. As such they celebrated the gift of land to the Israelites.

For von Rad's thesis to be valid these credos must have existed prior to the composition of J. However, the evidence points in the opposite direction. In each instance the credo occurs in a passage which is normally dated later than J. As Nicholson rightly observes, 'such brief recapitulations of the story of Israel's origins probably stand much more towards the end of the development of the Pentateuch than at its beginnings'.[11] It is, therefore, impossible to prove that J was based on such credal confessions.

In a similar fashion, von Rad argued that the tradition of theophany and covenant making at Sinai, recorded in Exodus 19–24 and the book of Deuteronomy, originated from a festival held in the autumn at Shechem, an important cultic centre in the pre-monarchic period. Associating this autumnal festival with the feast of Tabernacles, von Rad maintained that its origin was to be clearly distinguished from that of the credos linked to Gilgal.

Having argued for separate origins for the traditions associated with Gilgal and Shechem, von Rad proceeded to suggest that these were subsequently

---

[9] In marked contrast, Gunkel viewed P as an 'author' who clearly shaped into his own mould any traditional material that he received.

[10] (BWANT 24; Stuttgart: W. Kohlhammer, 1938); ET, *The Problem of the Hexateuch and Other Essays* (Edinburgh: Oliver & Boyd, 1966), 1–77.

[11] Nicholson, *The Pentateuch*, 89; for a fuller discussion, see E.W. Nicholson, *Exodus and Sinai in History and Tradition* (Oxford: Oxford University Press, 1973), 20–6.

combined by an author and theologian of some genius to form J.[12] While von Rad followed others in assigning authorship to the Yahwist, he viewed him as much more than a collector or editor of existing stories. Although the Yahwist drew on existing traditions, he gave them a totally new dimension by creating a larger, unified picture of divine activity which was no longer directly tied to cultic institutions.

One further aspect of von Rad's approach should be noted. Whereas scholars of the 'Wellhausenian school' were strongly inclined to date the origin of J to the middle of the ninth century BC, von Rad argued that the Yahwist was dated earlier, to the period of David. In the context of the nation being unified under David and taking possession of the land, the Yahwist was enabled to develop his distinctive understanding of God and create the J document in the latter part of the tenth century BC.[13]

Von Rad's approach was developed more fully by Noth in his study, *A History of Pentateuchal Traditions*.[14] Noth presented his aim as follows:

> The chief task … is to ascertain the *basic themes* from which the totality of the transmitted Pentateuch developed, to uncover their roots, to investigate how they were replenished with individual materials, to pursue their connections with each other, and to assess their significance.[15]

In order to determine the history of the traditions used in the Pentateuch Noth accepted the usual source analysis of the Documentary Hypothesis. However, he proposed that on account of the similarities between J and E they must have derived from a common origin or *Grundlage* 'foundation' (G). Where J and E contain similar elements it is possible to trace the influence of G.

Noth modified von Rad's position by arguing that five major themes could be uncovered in J:

1. Guidance out of Egypt.
2. Guidance into the arable land.
3. Promise to the patriarchs.

---

[12] In addition to the traditions associated with Gilgal and Shechem, von Rad believed that various other originally independent traditions were also taken over by the Yahwist and used in the composition of J. These included: episodes from the primaeval history in Genesis 1–11; much of the patriarchal material in Genesis 12–50; the exodus account in Exodus 1–15; the Balaam story in Numbers 22–24.

[13] For a fuller discussion of von Rad, see Nicholson, *The Pentateuch*, 63–74.

[14] *Überlieferungsgeschichte des Pentateuch* (Stuttgart: W. Kohlhammer, 1948); ET *A History of Pentateuchal Traditions* (Englewood Cliffs, New Jersey: Prentice-Hall, 1972).

[15] Noth, *A History of Pentateuchal Traditions*, 3.

4. Guidance in the wilderness.
5. Revelation at Sinai.

Noth proposed that these themes were brought together to form the framework of J. Various factors suggested that the themes were originally unconnected. For example, the theme of 'guidance out of Egypt' presupposes entry into the land of Canaan from the west. In contrast, 'guidance into the arable land' assumes that the land of Canaan is invaded from the east. According to Noth these two themes arose in different groups of people.

Although Noth viewed these five themes as having circulated independently, he believed that they were united at an early stage in Israel's history when the separate tribes joined together in what Noth described as an *amphictyony*. This term is used to describe an association of twelve (or six) tribes in ancient Greece and Italy who met at a central shrine for worship. The tribes had the responsibility of maintaining the shrine and did so on a monthly or bi-monthly rota. Noth suggested that the Israelite tribes were associated in the same way around a central shrine, and that this bound them together. After the amphictyony was formed the distinctive traditions of the separate tribes were combined together to form the five main themes which comprised the *Grundlage* (G).

Various assumptions underlie Noth's approach. He assumes that the bulk of the Pentateuch originally circulated orally. He also accepts the source analysis of the Pentateuch as proposed in the Documentary Hypothesis. As we have noted both of these are currently disputed issues.

Noth also assumes that the earliest narrative traditions were short and concise; later traditions did not exhibit the same brevity of form. Thus, for example, he views Genesis 24 as late due to its discursive style. Again, this is an assumption which modern scholars reject. Length cannot be a guide to age. Unfortunately, Noth's whole approach relies heavily upon his being able to distinguish early from late traditions.

Another of Noth's assumptions is worth mentioning. He believes that in the process of oral transmission stories may change their main characters. In particular, less well-known individuals may be replaced by better-known figures. This idea lies at the very heart of Noth's view of Moses. Although Moses is the main character in the books of Exodus to Deuteronomy, Noth maintains that he had no connection with the stories when they were first told, and that he was only introduced at a later stage. He argues, for example, that Moses did not appear in the earliest traditions about the Israelites coming out of Egypt as recorded in the first half of the book of Exodus. In the earliest traditions it was the elders (cf. Ex. 3:16, 18; 4:29) and foremen (Ex. 5:6–19) who negotiated with Pharaoh. To support this thesis, Noth holds that Exodus 5:3–19 represents the most original tradition concerning the departure of the Israelites from Egypt. Since Moses does not appear in this scene (v. 4, which mentions Moses, is designated a later insertion) Noth concludes that he had no part in the earliest tradition of the people leaving Egypt. Similarly, in the making of the covenant at Sinai, the presence of Moses was not part of the original tradition. Here also Moses has been introduced in place of the elders of the people. Noth offers no detailed arguments as to why Moses was introduced into these traditions. He merely assumes that this was the process by which the traditions developed. Finally, we should note that for Noth the most authentic element concerning Moses was the account of his burial. [16]

Whereas in Germany scholars like von Rad and Noth developed their form and traditio-historical criticism within the framework of the Documentary Hypothesis, a different approach was adopted in Scandinavia. The origins of this alternative approach can be traced back to the studies of S. Mowinckel on the Psalms,[17] H.S. Nyberg's emphasis on the importance of oral transmission prior to the exile,[18] and the negative reaction of P. Volz[19] and J. Pedersen[20] to the Documentary Hypothesis. By combining the views of these various scholars a new methodology for the study of the Pentateuch suggested itself, the leading exponent being I. Engnell.[21]

While Engnell referred to his approach as the traditio-historical method (*tradition-historisk metod*) on account of similarities with the *überlieferungsgeschichtliche Methode* used in Germany, it is important to note that the two approaches are not identical.[22] Engnell rejected the idea that one could discover separate literary sources underlying the present text. He maintained that a Priestly Writer who drew on both pre-exilic and post-exilic material composed Genesis to Numbers. By rejecting the possibility of pre-exilic literary sources Engnell was obliged to dismiss the Documentary Hypothesis. Oral strata replaced literary sources.

The attempts of Engnell and other Scandinavian scholars to dismiss the usual source analysis of the Pentateuch by emphasising the oral transmission of

---

[16] For a fuller critique of Noth's work, see Whybray, *Making of the Pentateuch*, 185–98.

[17] *Psalmenstudien II. Das Thronbesteigungsfest Jahwäs und der Ursprung der Eschatologie* (Kristiania: J. Dybwad, 1922); *Psalmenstudien III. Kultprophetie und prophetische Psalem* (Kristiania: J. Dybwad, 1923).

[18] *Studien zum Hoseabuche* (Uppsala: A.B. Lundequistska, 1935).

[19] *Der Elohist als Erzähler: Ein Irrweg der Pentateuchkritik?* (BZAW 63; Giessen: A. Töpelmann, 1933).

[20] 'Die Auffassung vom Alten Testament', *ZAW* 49 (1931), 161–81; in this article Pedersen expressed his rejection of the Documentary Hypothesis; cf. 'Passahfest und Passahlegende', *ZAW* 52 (1934), 161–75.

[21] *Gamla Testamentet I* (Stockholm: Svenska kyrkans diakonistyrelses, 1945); *idem* 'Methodological Aspects of Old Testament Study', *VTS* 7 (1960), 13–30.

[22] Cf. R. Rendtorff, 'Traditio-historical Method and the Documentary Hypothesis', *Proceedings of the World Congress of Jewish Studies* 5 (1969), 5–6.

the traditions have gained little support. However, the oral versus written distinction continues to influence some source-critical studies.[23]

3.3. The Limitations of Traditio-historical Criticism Illustrated

Traditio-historical criticism seeks to recover the process of composition which lies behind the source-documents. Since extra-biblical texts provide no direct evidence, scholars have had to reconstruct this process from the text of the Pentateuch as finally composed. This, however, opens the door to a wide variety of theories. Something of this may be observed by considering how several prominent scholars have approached the short passage in Genesis 14:18–20 featuring Abraham's encounter with Melchizedek.[24]

The following observations are normally made regarding Genesis 14. (a) It is generally accepted that the chapter as a whole does not come from one of the main source-documents, J, E, D or P; there are no clear criteria by which to identify it with one of these sources. (b) The style of verses 1–11 differs somewhat from that found in verses 12–24. (c) Abraham's meeting with the king of Sodom is interrupted by the unexpected arrival of the previously unmentioned king of Salem, Melchizedek. This has led many scholars to suggest that verses 18–20 are a later addition to the text, verse 17 having originally been followed directly by verse 21.

To explain the make-up of the chapter, C. Westermann suggests that the three sections come from separate periods in Israel's history.[25] Section 1 (vv. 1–11 [12]) is analogous to ancient near eastern accounts of military successes. Section 2 (vv. 12–17, 21–24) is a narrative of liberation, similar to those found in the book of Judges, in which a hero rescues people from foreign oppressors. Section 3 (vv. 18–20) comes from the time of the first temple (i.e. before 587 BC) and was told to encourage the bringing of tithes to Jerusalem. In support of this, Westermann observes that (a) Salem is another designation for Jerusalem (see Ps. 76:3 – a psalm of Zion), and (b) the name Melchizedek resembles that of Zadok, a high priest in the time of king David (cf. e.g. 2 Sam. 15:24–29).

---

[23] Cf. J. Van Seters, *Abraham in History and Tradition* (New Haven/London: Yale University Press, 1975).

[24] The discussion which follows relies heavily upon, J.G. McConville, 'Abraham and Melchizedek: Horizons in Genesis 14', in R.S. Hess, P.E. Satterthwaite and G.J. Wenham (eds.), *He Swore an Oath: Biblical Themes from Genesis 20–50* (2nd edn.; Grand Rapids/Carlisle: Baker/Paternoster, 1994), 93–118.

[25] Westermann, *Genesis 12-36. A Commentary* (trans. John J. Scullion; London/Minneapolis. SPCK/Augsburg, 1985), 198–9.

Westermann dates the final form of the story to the post-exilic period due to the elevation of Abraham to the position of a world figure; this conforms to a pattern found in the books of Judith and Daniel.

In his reading of Genesis 14, J.A. Emerton links Melchizedek with David and sees the insertion of verses 18–20 as designed to support the claim of David to rule over the Israelites and other peoples of Canaan.[26] Like Melchizedek, David is king over Jerusalem. Emerton, however, rejects links between Melchizedek and Zadok. He also rejects the suggestion that the purpose of the narrative was to encourage the bringing of tithes to Jerusalem.

A third approach is offered by J. Van Seters.[27] He dates the Melchizedek incident to the post-exilic period to a time when the priesthood of the second temple aspired to royal office. He finds evidence for this in the claim of the Hasmonaeans to be both kings and 'high priests of God Most High'.

J.G. McConville provides a helpful critique of these three views.[28] As regards the purposed analogies for the first two sections of Genesis 14, McConville highlights the inadequacy of the parallels suggested. The campaign account cannot be easily identified with a specific form of ancient near eastern material. The proposal that the second section resembles hero-liberation accounts found in the Book of Judges is also questionable. The similarities are very superficial and Abraham's actions do not parallel those of judges like Gideon or Samson. Moreover, the Genesis context presents Abraham as a figure of some standing, and it is not surprising to find him having contact with kings (cf. Gen. 12:10–20; 20:1–18; 21:22–34); elsewhere the inhabitants of Hebron call him a 'prince of God' (Gen. 23:6).

Regarding Genesis 14:18–20 McConville rejects the traditio-historical explanations of Westermann, Emerton and Van Seters. The post-exilic setting suggested by Van Seters is highly unlikely. Would a post-exilic author introduce a tradition about an ancient Canaanite priest-king in order to support the claims of Jewish priests? Westermann's proposal that the narrative encouraged the bringing of tithes to Jerusalem is not really appropriate. Likewise, Emerton's suggestion that it was intended to justify David's rule over both Israelites and non-Israelites is also dubious; David is more likely to be associated with the warrior Abraham than Melchizedek.

Adopting a different approach to Genesis 14 McConville makes the following observations:

1. In Genesis Abraham is commonly portrayed as a figure of some importance. Outside Genesis 14, he encounters foreign rulers: Pharaoh of Egypt and

---

[26] Emerton, 'The Riddle of Genesis xiv', *VT* 21 (1971), 403–39.

[27] Van Seters, *Abraham in History and Tradition*, 296–308.

[28] McConville, 'Abraham and Melchizedek', 93–118.

Abimelech of Gerar. The inhabitants of Hebron also acknowledge his special status. It is not surprising, therefore, that in Genesis 14 he should have dealings with two other kings, the kings of Salem and Sodom.

2. He notes the importance of Genesis 14 in the development of the Lot/Sodom motif which is prominent in Genesis 13 and 18–19.

3. He argues that the Melchizedek incident, while interrupting the narrative flow of Genesis 14, is not an intrusion. Various links exist with the surrounding text. Melchizedek knows that Abraham has won a victory (v. 20). Abraham's refusal to be made rich by the king of Sodom (v. 23) involves a word play with the term for 'tithe' in verse 20. When Abraham refers to 'Yahweh, El-Elyon, creator of heaven and earth', he echoes the expression used by Melchizedek in verse 19.

On the basis of these observations McConville proceeds to ask what effect the inclusion of the Melchizedek incident has on our reading of the chapter. He observes that Abraham's meetings with the kings of Salem and Sodom provide two contrasting pictures of how Abraham might take possession of the land of Canaan. With the king of Sodom the emphasis is upon human strength; it is through the exercise of military power that one comes to possess what belongs to others. The king of Salem, however, gives a very different answer. Abraham's victory is a gift from God (v. 20). By giving a tenth of the booty to Melchizedek Abraham acknowledges the truthfulness of what he has said. Abraham underlines this by refusing to accept anything from the king of Sodom. Thus, the Melchizedek incident is significant for it implies that Abraham will receive the land as a gift from God, and not by using his military muscle.

Several general comments may be made in the light of the preceding discussion. First, by its very nature traditio-historical criticism may give rise to conflicting theories concerning the process by which a text was composed. This underlines the speculative nature of traditio-historical criticism. Secondly, in the past many scholars have been quick to offer traditio-historical explanations for features in the text which they have been unable to explain by other means. While traditio-historical reconstructions may occasionally appear to solve perceived difficulties within a text, we should always be alert to the possibility that other explanations may yet be forthcoming. As we have observed with regard to Genesis 14:18–20, the synchronic reading proposed by McConville makes excellent sense of the text as it stands, without recourse to a traditio-historical reconstruction.

4

The Documentary Hypothesis Under Threat

The Documentary Hypothesis dominated the source criticism of the Pentateuch throughout most of the twentieth century. For many scholars the theory has been so convincing that it is merely assumed and used as the basic for further research on other issues. Some scholars, however, have continued to investigate the literary origins of the Pentateuch and have, as a result, proposed modifications of different kinds. Others, however, have rejected completely the Documentary Hypothesis. We shall now consider these modifications and rejections.

4.1. Modifications to the Documentary Hypothesis

Given the complex nature of the Documentary Hypothesis it is hardly surprising that various modifications to it have been proposed during the last hundred years. To a large extent these have arisen out of more detailed investigations of the individual sources and their relationship to one another. Even among those who accept the basic tenets of the Documentary Hypothesis there are many differences of opinion; for example, it is common for scholars to disagree over the assignment of individual verses or passages to a particular source. No attempt shall be made here to explore all these differences. Rather, we shall focus on some of the more significant ways in which some scholars have sought to modify the Documentary Hypothesis.

4.1.1 The J source[1]

Once it was accepted that the Pentateuch was composed of four main sources, and the extent of these sources agreed upon, it was only natural that questions

---

[1] A fuller survey of the J source is provided by A. de Pury, 'Yahwist ("J") Source', *ABD* 6:1012–20.

should be asked about the composition of the individual sources. Wellhausen himself drew attention to this question by noting that in the early chapters of Genesis J displayed inconsistencies.[2] This suggested that J was composite in nature, and if this were so, then it ought to be possible to determine the sources underlying it. (Similar views were expressed by Wellhausen about E and P.) A variety of studies have focused on the composite nature of J.

In 1883 K. Budde in his *Die Biblische Urgeschichte (Gen. 1–12, 5)*[3] argued that the J material in the early chapters of Genesis consisted of two documents, J^1 (tenth century BC) and J^2 (later ninth or possibly eighth century BC), which were combined by a Yahwistic editor in the eighth century BC. Budde's views were extended in 1885 by C. Brunston to include the whole of the Pentateuch.[4] Gunkel also maintained that the J material was composite.[5] However, he limited his views to the Primaeval History[6] and the Abraham narratives. Whereas in the Primaeval History J was comprised of two documents, J^e and J^j, in the Abraham narratives J consisted of two collections of traditions, J^a and J^b, which originated from the regions of Hebron and Beersheba respectively.[7] On the relationship of these latter two traditions Gunkel held that J^b supplemented J^a.

In 1912 R. Smend, in his *Die Erzählung des Hexateuch auf ihre Quellen untersucht*,[8] gave fuller expression to the view that the Hexateuch contained not one but two J documents, J^1 and J^2, which were the oldest sources used in the compilation of the Hexateuch; he placed the documents in the sequence J^1, J^2, E, D, P. Support for Smend's approach came from O. Eissfeldt who reverted to the idea of two J documents combined by a later editor.[9] Eissfeldt, however, referred to J^1 as the 'Lay source' (*Laienquelle*) which he denoted by the symbol L; as the name suggests this source has little interest in cultic or priestly affairs. Having designated J^1 as L, Eissfeldt was able to label J^2 as J; G. Fohrer followed

---

[2] *Die Composition des Hexateuchs und der historischen Bücher des Alten Testament* (Berlin: G. Reimer, 1899); first published as 'Die Composition des Hexateuchs', *Jahrbücher für Deutsche Theologie* 21 (1876), 392–450, 531–602; and *Jahrbücher für Deutsche Theologie* 22 (1877), 407–79.

[3] (Giessen: J. Ricker, 1883).

[4] 'Les deux Jehovistes', *Revue de Theologie et de Philosophie*, 18 (1885), 5–34, 499–528, 602–37.

[5] *Genesis übersetzt und erklärt*.

[6] The term 'Primaeval History' is often used to describe the material in Genesis 1:1–11:26.

[7] Skinner, *Genesis*, 240–2, followed the view of Gunkel, but labelled the sources J^h and J^b.

[8] (Berlin: G. Reimer, 1912).

[9] *Hexateuch Synopse* (Leipzig: J.C. Hinrich, 1922); support came also from W. Eichrodt, *Die Quellen der Genesis von neuem untersucht* (Giessen: A. Topelmann, 1916).

the position advocated by Eissfeldt.[10] However, Fohrer rejected the designation 'Lay source' because he considered the document to have a theology as developed as J or E. Instead, he referred to it as the Nomadic source (*Nomadenquelle*) N. Since Fohrer dated it later than J, but earlier than E, the sequence of the sources became J, N, E, D, P. R. Kilian has also advocated the view that J is not completely homogeneous.[11] In a detailed investigation of the pre-priestly Abraham traditions Kilian sought to demonstrate that the author of J employed both written and oral sources which he shaped according to his own theological outlook. Other scholars who oppose the concept of a single J source will be considered later in this chapter (see sections 2.1 and 2.2). Yet, while some scholars discovered sources underlying J, it must be recognised that the majority of scholars continued to view J as a unified source.[12]

Although Wellhausen argued that J was the earliest of the four main sources, he remained somewhat vague regarding the nature and date of J. While he believed that J was an author (*Schriftsteller*), Gunkel, subsequently, proposed that J was merely a collector and editor of existing traditions. It was left to von Rad to propose that J was a theologian of some brilliance who, during the 'golden age' of Solomon (c. 950–930 BC), produced a history of Israel which included the following elements: primaeval history, patriarchal stories, Joseph, Moses, exodus, Sinai, and conquest. While von Rad saw J as extending into the book of Joshua, Noth believed that the final part of J was lost when the Tetrateuch ('four-volumes'; i.e. Genesis to Numbers) was linked to the Deuteronomistic History (see 4.3). Although Noth modified aspects of von Rad's approach (see 3.2), he strongly supported a tenth century BC date for the composition of J. The significance of J as the earliest biblical writer of importance is developed in a number of recent works.[13]

Since 1970 there has been a sustained attempt to dissociate J from the Solomonic 'enlightenment'. H.H. Schmid suggested that various features pointed to a date for J well after the time of Solomon: various J texts display

---

[10] *Überlieferung und Geschichte des Exodus* (Berlin: A. Topelmann, 1964); *Introduction to the Old Testament* (London: SPCK, 1970).

[11] *Die vorpriesterlichen Abrahamsüberlieferungen* (BBB 24; Bonn: Hanstein, 1966).

[12] Driver, *Introduction*, 116–26, provides a description of the vocabulary, style and grammar of J. For a discussion of the theology of J, see H.W. Wolff, 'The Kerygma of the Yahwist', *Int* 20 (1966), 131–58; P.F. Ellis, *The Yahwist. The Bible's First Theologian* (London: G. Chapman, 1969); W. Brueggemann and H.W. Wolff, *The Vitality of Old Testament Traditions* (Atlanta: John Knox, 1975).

[13] Cf. R.E. Friedman, *Who Wrote the Bible?* (Englewood Cliffs, NJ: Prentice Hall, 1987); R. Coote and D. Ord, *The Bible's First Historian: From Eden to the Court of David with the Yahwist* (Philadelphia: Fortress, 1989).

Deuteronomistic ideas; J reflects a time of national crisis, not success.[14] On the basis of a detailed study of the Abraham narrative Van Seters also argued that J should be dated later. It is noteworthy, however, that his late J is not completely identical in content to the J source of the Documentary Hypothesis. (Van Seters' approach is discussed more fully in 2.1.) According to Van Seters, J is to be dated to the exilic period, being post-Deuteronomistic, but pre-Priestly. The idea of dating J late is also advocated by M. Rose who argues that J was composed as a 'prologue' to the Deuteronomistic History (Deuteronomy-Kings).[15] Rose maintains that various J texts show signs of having been composed after the corresponding episodes in the Deuteronomistic History. It must be recognised, however, that these proposals to date J late are not entirely homogeneous. Moreover, they require that the Documentary Hypothesis be substantially revised.

4.1.2. The E source

Of the various documents believed to underlie the Pentateuch, the source E has probably received the least attention from scholars. However, various writers have considered in detail the extent and nature of E, and its relationship to J. Prior to 1890 Kuenen had already suggested that E was composite in character.[16] He proposed that E comprised two documents, E^1 and E^2. E^1 originated in the northern kingdom during the eighth century BC. A century later E^1 underwent a revision in the southern kingdom and was expanded by the inclusion of new material, E^2. C.H. Cornill[17] and O. Procksch[18] subsequently adopted Kuenen's position. Generally, however, scholars have rejected the view that E is composite in character.

In 1930 Sigmund Mowinckel questioned the concept of an independent E document.[19] Instead, he viewed E as supplementing and expanding earlier traditions. Later, in *The Two Sources of the Pre-deuteronomic Primeval History (JE) in Gen i–xi*,[20] Mowinckel proposed that the pre-P material in Genesis 1–11 was

---

[14] *Der sogennante Jahwist: Beobachtungen und Fragen zur Pentateuchforschung* (Zürich: Theologischer Verlag, 1976).

[15] *Deuteronomist und Jahwist: Untersuchungen zu den Berührungspunkten beider Literaturwerke* (ATANT 67; Zurich: Theologischer Verlag, 1981).

[16] *An Historico-critical Inquiry into the Origin and Composition of the Hexateuch* (London: Macmillan, 1886) 248–62.

[17] *Einleitung in das Alte Testament* (2nd edn.; Freiburg: Mohr, 1892).

[18] *Das nordhebräische Sagenbuch. Die Elohimquelle* (Leipzig: J.C. Hinrichs, 1906).

[19] 'Der Ursprung der Bil'amsage', *ZAW* 48 (1930), 233–71.

[20] (Oslo: J. Dybwad, 1937).

composite, and identified the sources as J and E.[21] Prior to this most scholars had maintained that there was no E material in Genesis before chapter 15. Mowinckel subsequently revised his opinions on the extent of E and suggested that while it was present to a limited extent in the Pentateuch, it was absent from the primaeval history, the Jacob and Joseph stories and Exodus 1–15.[22] Rather than refer to JE, Mowinckel spoke of J^v (J *variatus*) because he regarded J as having been supplemented by material which had circulated mostly in oral form.

Another major challenge to the existence of an independent E document came from P. Volz and W. Rudolph. In a joint study on Genesis, *Der Elohist als Erzähler: Ein Irrweg der Pentateuchkritik?*[23] Volz and Rudolph questioned the existence of a continuous E document. Examining the first thirty-five chapters of Genesis, Volz concluded that there was a basic J narrative, mainly a collection of earlier traditions, which was subsequently expanded by E and P material. According to Volz, neither E nor P had existed as independent documents, a conclusion supported by the lack of substantial narrative material from these sources. Volz also assigned to J sections that had previously been designated E or P, e.g. Genesis 22–23. Rudolph, concentrating on the Joseph narrative, concluded that there was no need to posit an independent E document for this part of Genesis. He rejected the criterion of divine names by arguing that whereas the author used Yahweh in narrating the story, his characters used El-Shaddai and Elohim when speaking in Palestine and Egypt respectively. In a subsequent work on the books of Exodus to Joshua, Rudolph again challenged the idea of a continuous independent E document.[24]

More recently the existence of a parallel E source in the Joseph narrative has come under attack from various scholars. R.N. Whybray has argued (a) that the obvious literary qualities of the narrative cannot be adequately explained by supposing that the final account was produced by the conflation of two earlier parallel sources, and (b) that von Rad's dating of the story to the early monarchy excludes the possibility of two sources being combined together.[25] This latter argument presupposes an acceptance of von Rad's

---

[21] G. Hölscher, *Die Anfänge der hebräischen Geschichtsschreibung* (Heidelberg: C. Winter, 1942), followed Mowinckel in suggesting that E occurred in the primeval history.

[22] 'Erwägung zur Pentateuch Quellenfrage', *Norsk Theologisk Tidsskrift* 65 (1964), 1–138; cf. *Tetrateuch-Pentateuch-Hexateuch* (BZAW 90; Berlin: A. Töpelmann, 1964).

[23] (BZAW 63; Giessen: A. Töpelmann, 1933).

[24] *Der 'Elohist' von Exodus bis Josua* (BZAW 68; Berlin: A. Töpelmann, 1938).

[25] 'The Joseph Story and Pentateuchal Criticism', *VT* 18 (1968), 522–8. Whybray restricts himself to discussing the position adopted by G. von Rad, 'The Joseph Narrative and Ancient Wisdom', in *Problem of the Hexateuch*; first published as 'Josephsgeschichte und ältere Chokma', *VTS* 3 (1953), 120–7; cf. von Rad, *Die Josephsgeschichte* (Biblische

contention that the Joseph story is an example of wisdom literature, a view not accepted by all scholars.[26]

In his book, *A Study of the Biblical Story of Joseph (Genesis 37–50)*, D.B. Redford investigates the Joseph story in considerable detail. Demonstrating the literary qualities of the narrative, he argues, like Whybray, against dividing the account into separate J and E sources. Nevertheless, Redford does discover two sources underlying the present story. He suggests that an original 'Reuben'-version of the Joseph story was subsequently expanded by a 'Judah'-version. However, he rejects emphatically the idea that this 'Judah'-version existed as an independent account paralleling the 'Reuben'-version.

G.W. Coats has also subjected the Joseph story to a thorough investigation in his monograph *From Canaan to Egypt: Structural and Theological Context of the Joseph Story*.[27] Like Redford and Whybray, he questions the traditional source analysis of the story. However, he is much more emphatic than Redford in asserting the unity of the narrative. Redford's suggestion that a later author expanded the story is rejected. For Coats, the Joseph story is an 'artistic master-piece'. On the question of authorship and date Coats remains cautiously undecided, although he does not exclude the possibility that the Yahwist composed the story during the time of Solomon.

Another recent objector to the concept of a parallel E narrative source is C. Westermann. In his massive commentary on Genesis,[28] he argues that E never existed as a separate source in the Abraham narrative. Yet, although Westermann rejects the idea of an E document, he accepts that other traditions apart from J and P were incorporated into the final form of the Abraham narrative. Thus, he views Genesis 20:1–18 and 21:22–34 as supplements to the main J narrative.

In spite of a growing body of opinion against viewing E as an independent source paralleling J, various scholars still defend the traditional Documentary Hypothesis understanding of E. A.W. Jenks rejects the suggestion that E narratives were produced as 'deliberate corrective supplements to J'.[29] R.E. Friedman

---

[25] (*continued*) Studien 5; Neukirchen: Buchhandlung des Erziehungsvereins, 1954). Von Rad considered the Joseph narrative, which he termed a 'novel', to be an example of wisdom literature from the period of the early monarchy.

[26] Cf. J.L. Crenshaw, 'Method in Determining Wisdom Influence upon "Historical" Literature', *JBL* 88 (1969), 129–42; Redford, *Joseph*, 100–5; G.W. Coats, 'The Joseph Story and Ancient Wisdom: a Reappraisal', *CBQ* 35 (1973), 285–97. Whereas Crenshaw and Redford reject von Rad's position, Coats favours a wisdom background for Genesis 39–41, which he terms a 'political legend'.

[27] (CBQM 4; Washington: Catholic Biblical Association of America, 1976); cf. Coats, 'Redactional Unity in Genesis 37–50', *JBL* 93 (1974), 15–21.

[28] *Genesis: A Commentary* (3 vols.; Minneapolis/London: Augsburg/SPCK, 1984–87).

[29] A.W. Jenks, 'Elohist', *ABD* 2:479.

offers support for the view that E was once an independent source.[30] He argues that (a) during the process of being combined with J, much of the beginning of E was lost, and (b) some E material in the books of Exodus to Numbers has been wrongly assigned to other sources, especially J. A consequence of these factors is that E has mistakenly been perceived as shorter and more fragmentary than J. Friedman concludes that 'E is a well-represented source, originally continuous prior to its being combined with J, and that E and J are approximately equal in quantity of text now preserved in the Pentateuch.'[31]

From this brief survey it is obvious that scholarly opinion is divided over the extent and nature of the E source. While some scholars still maintain the traditional Documentary Hypothesis view of E as a continuous literary source paralleling J, there are a growing number who question the validity of this position.

4.1.3. The D source

In many ways the D source stands apart from J, E, and P. Whereas the latter sources are found running throughout the books of Genesis to Numbers (and possibly also in Joshua according to some early source critics), D is confined largely to the book of Deuteronomy. R.E. Friedman, for example, observes that 'the joining of D with JEP required little more than moving the accounts of the promoting of Joshua and the death of Moses to the end of Deuteronomy'.[32]

While the early proponents of the Documentary Hypothesis suggested that the book of Joshua ought to be considered in conjunction with the Pentateuch, Noth challenged this view in 1943. He proposed that the book of Deuteronomy was the first part of a larger literary work, which included the books of Joshua, Judges, Samuel and Kings. Noth designated this account of Israel's time in Canaan a 'Deuteronomic History'; subsequent writers have preferred the title 'Deuteronomistic History', retaining the term 'Deuteronomic' for the book of Deuteronomy itself. According to Noth, an exilic author (i.e. the Deuteronomist) took over an already existing law-code (most, but not all, of the book of Deuteronomy) which had been composed in the time of Josiah; here Noth adopts the Documentary Hypothesis dating of the D source. Adding a historical introduction (Deut. 1:1–3:29) to the Deuteronomic law-code, the Deuteronomist created the opening book of his History. Since the Deuteronomistic History concludes with the account of king Jehoiachin's release from prison in 562 BC (2 Kgs. 25:27–30), the whole work must have been composed shortly after this date. Noth proposed that this 'History' was originally unconnected to the books of Genesis to

---

[30] 'Torah (Pentateuch)', *ABD* 4:619; *idem, Who Wrote the Bible?*
[31] 'Torah (Pentateuch)', *ABD* 4:619.
[32] Ibid., 618.

Numbers. With the widespread acceptance of Noth's theory of a Deuteronomistic History, it became appropriate to speak of a Tetrateuch, rather than a Pentateuch. As a result, recent research on Deuteronomy has tended to focus mainly on its relationship to the books that come after it, rather than those that come before it.[33]

Noth's idea of a 'historian' who penned the books of Deuteronomy to Kings is taken up by Van Seters. In his study, *In Search of History: Historiography in the Ancient World and the Origins of Biblical Historical History*,[34] Van Seters argues that the Deuteronomistic Historian may be best compared with the Greek historians of the Persian period. However, Van Seters differs from Noth in two significant ways. First, he believes that the Deuteronomistic Historian did not incorporate earlier compositions into his work, but, with little recourse to existing sources, relied mainly upon his own imagination. Secondly, he argues that J was composed after the Deuteronomistic History, an idea that has found support with a number of other scholars.[35]

Schmid[36] and Rendtorff have also argued that the books of Genesis to Numbers are influenced by Deuteronomic/Deuteronomistic thinking. Indeed, Rendtorff goes some way to arguing that the final redaction of the Pentateuch was 'deuteronomically stamped', although he acknowledges that 'criteria for what is "deuteronomic" … have not yet been adequately worked out'.[37] T.B. Dozeman[38] and W. Johnstone[39] have expressed somewhat similar views regarding the book of

---

[33] For a review of modern approaches to the Deuteronomistic History, see S.L. McKenzie, 'Deuteronomistic History', *ABD* 2:160–8; J.G. McConville, *Grace in the End: a Study of Deuteronomic Theology* (Carlisle: Paternoster Press, 1993); *idem*, 'The Old Testament Historical Books in Modern Scholarship', *Them* 22.3 (1997), 3–13.

[34] (New Haven: Yale University Press, 1983).

[35] Cf. A.D.H. Mayes, *The Story of Israel between Settlement and Exile: A Redactional Study of the Deuteronomistic History* (London: SCM, 1983), 141; Whybray, *Making of the Pentateuch*, 225; Blenkinsopp, *The Pentateuch*, 233–7; E.T. Mullen, *Ethnic Myths and Pentateuchal Foundations: A New Approach to the Formation of the Pentateuch* (SBL Semeia Studies; Atlanta: Scholars Press, 1997), 317–8. Van Seters develops this further in his books, *Prologue to History: The Yahwist as Historian in Genesis* (Louisville: Westminster/ John Knox, 1992) and *The Life of Moses: The Yahwist as Historian in Exodus–Numbers* (Louisville: Westminster/John Knox, 1994).

[36] *Der sogennante Jahwist.*

[37] *The Problem of the Process of Transmission in the Pentateuch* (JSOTSS 89; Sheffield: JSOT Press, 1990), 197.

[38] *God on the Mountain: A Study of Redaction, Theology and Canon in Exodus 19–24* (SBLMS, 37; Atlanta: Scholars Press, 1989), 37–86.

[39] *Exodus* (OT Guides; Sheffield: JSOT Press, 1990), 75–86; cf. *idem*, 'Reactivating the Chronicles Analogy in Pentateuchal Studies, with Special Reference to the Sinai Pericope in Exodus', *ZAW* 99 (1987), 16–37; *idem*, 'The Decalogue and the Redaction of the Sinai Pericope in Exodus', *ZAW* 100 (1988), 361–85.

Exodus; both suggest that there is evidence of a major Deuteronomistic redaction in Exodus, although they believe, unlike Rendtorff, that this was followed by a further Priestly redaction. Blum also notes Deuteronomistic influence in the composition of Exodus.[40]

In spite of growing support (a) for finding Deuteronomic/Deuteronomistic influence in the Tetrateuch, and (b) for dating the composition of the Tetrateuch after the Deuteronomistic History, the issue is far from settled, with other scholars noting that many passages in Deuteronomy display clear signs of having been composed in the light of material found elsewhere in Genesis to Numbers. Thus, for example, M. Weinfeld argues that the Deuteronomic version of the Decalogue is based upon that found in Exodus 20, and Deuteronomy 7 presupposes Exodus 23:23–33.[41] Consideration must also be given to the views of those who argue that P must be dated earlier than D (see next section). J. Milgrom, for example, notes that D is often dependent upon P, but P is never dependent upon D.[42]

4.1.4 The P source

The P source has also come under close scrutiny in ways that resemble closely the discussion over the extent and nature of the E source. In 1924 M.R.H. Löhr argued that P never existed as an independent document.[43] Reverting to a type of fragmentary hypothesis, Löhr suggested that Ezra and his companions combined together various collections of narratives and laws to form the Pentateuch as we now have it. His position found support in the later work of Volz who also denied the existence of a separate P document.[44]

Von Rad discussed the unity of the P material in detail in his book, *Die Priesterschrift im Hexateuch literarisch untersucht und theologisch gewertet.*[45] He proposed that P consisted of two parallel narrative strands, P^a and P^b, and an independent work comprising genealogical lists (*Toledothbuch*). Although P^b had a greater interest in priestly affairs than the less complex P^a, both works were sufficiently similar to allow themselves to be easily combined together. This view, however, has received little support.

---

[40] *Studien zur Komposition des Pentateuch* (BZAW 189; Berlin: W. de Gruyter, 1990).

[41] *Deuteronomy 1–11* (AB 5; New York: Doubleday, 1991), 242–319, 367; cf. R.G. Kratz, 'Der Dekalog im Exodusbuch', *VT* 44 (1994), 205–38.

[42] *Leviticus 1–16: A New Translation with Introduction and Commentary* (AB 3A; New York: Doubleday, 1991) (AB 3A; New York: Doubleday, 1991), 9–13.

[43] *Untersuchungen zum Hexateuchproblem: Der Priesterkodex in der Genesis* (BZAW 38; Giessen: A. Töpelmann, 1924).

[44] *Der Elohist als Erzähler: Ein Irrweg der Pentateuchkritik?*

[45] (BWANT IV. 13; Stuttgart: W. Kohlhammer, 1934).

I. Engnell has also questioned the existence of P as an independent document.[46] He preferred to consider P as a compiler and editor of the books Genesis to Numbers. Although Noth agreed with Engnell that P ended in Numbers and not in Joshua as some scholars maintained, he accepted the traditional position that P was originally a separate document.[47] For Noth, P was a narrative history into which collections of laws and cultic regulations were later inserted.[48]

Support for Engnell's view that P never existed as an independent document has come from F.M. Cross. In an essay entitled 'The Priestly Work',[49] Cross concludes that, 'the Priestly strata of the Tetrateuch never existed as an independent narrative document'.[50] He proposes that towards the end of the exile the Epic (JE) tradition was expanded by a Priestly editor, or possibly a narrow Priestly school, to provide 'the Tetrateuch in its penultimate form'. According to Cross, the lack of substantial P narratives throughout the Tetrateuch casts serious doubt upon the idea that P first circulated as an independent narrative document; what we know of P points to it being merely a revision and expansion of earlier material. R. Rendtorff adopts a similar position, arguing that the P material never formed an independent source, but was employed by a redactor to combine together various traditions.[51]

As regards the legislative material associated with P, it has become widely accepted that Leviticus 17–26 represents a separate source, designated the *Heiligkeitsgesetz* 'Holiness Code' (H).[52] While early critics believed that H was taken over by the Priestly Writer and incorporated into his work, Milgrom and I. Knohl have recently argued that P existed prior to H.[53]

---

[46] *Gamla Testamentet. En traditionshistorisk inledning* (Vol. 1; Stockholm: Svenska kyrkans diakonistyreles bokförlag, 1945); cf. 'The Pentateuch', in J.T. Willis et al (eds.), *Critical Essays on the Old Testament* (London: SPCK, 1970), 50–67.

[47] *Überlieferungsgeschichte des Pentateuch* Stuttgart: W. Kohlhammer, 1948; ET *A History of Pentateuchal Traditions.*

[48] In Leviticus Noth assigned only chapters 8–10 to the original P narrative. He regarded the Holiness Code (chs. 17–26) as a later insertion into P. P is also limited to Genesis-Numbers by A. Bentzen, *An Introduction to the Old Testament* (7th edn.; Copenhagen: G.E.C. Gad, 1967), 271.

[49] In *Canaanite Myth and Hebrew Epic* (Cambridge, MA: Harvard University Press, 1973), 293–325.

[50] Ibid., 324.

[51] Rendtorff, *Problem of the Process of Transmission.*

[52] This title was first proposed by A. Klostermann in 1893 and is now commonly used. For a survey of recent research on the Holiness Code, see the relevant article by H.T.C. Sun in *ABD* 3, 254–7.

[53] Milgrom, *Leviticus 1–16*, 3–51; idem, 'Priestly ("P") Source', *ABD* 5:454–61; I. Knohl, *The Sanctuary of Silence: The Priestly Torah and the Holiness School* (Minneapolis: Fortress Press, 1995). Note, however, the proposal of Rendtorff ('Two Kinds of P?

Apart from difficulties over defining the exact nature of P, attention has also focused on the dating of the source. While most scholars have been content to accept a post-exilic date for P, allowing for the possible incorporation of some pre-exilic material, a growing number have attempted to date P considerably earlier. Y. Kaufmann argued at length in a series of articles and books that P was earlier than D and not later, as Wellhausen maintained.[54] Substantial support for dating P early has come from A. Hurvitz who has compared in detail the 'instructional' vocabulary of P with that of the exilic book of Ezekiel;[55] differences suggest that P must be dated to the pre-exilic period. In the recent studies of Milgrom and Knohl these observations are developed further; H is dated towards the end of the eighth century BC, with P having been composed no later that 750 BC.[56] The impact of these new developments can be observed in the article by Friedman on 'Torah (Pentateuch)' in the *Anchor Bible Dictionary*. While in every other respect Friedman follows the Documentary Hypothesis as formulated a century ago, he dates P prior to D.[57]

---

[53] *(continued)* Some Reflections on the Occasion of the Publishing of Jacob Milgrom's Commentary on Leviticus 1–16', *JSOT* 60 [1993], 75–81) that the cultic material assigned to P should be distinguished from the narrative material normally associated with the same source, and the response of Milgrom ('Response to Rolf Rendtorff', *JSOT* 60 [1993], 83–85).

[54] 'Probleme der israelitisch-jüdischen Religionsgeschichte', *ZAW* 48 (1930), 23–43; *ZAW* 51 (1933), 35–47; *twldwt h'mwnh hyśr'lyt* (Tel-Aviv, 1937–1957). The first seven volumes of this eight volume work were condensed and translated into English by M. Greenberg in a book entitled *The Religion of Israel* (Chicago: University of Chicago Press, 1960). Kaufmann's views exercised a considerable influence on subsequent Jewish scholarship; cf. S. Sandmel, *The Hebrew Scripture* (New York: Knopf, 1963); M. Weinfeld, *Deuteronomy and the Deuteronomic School* (Oxford: Clarendon, 1972). M. Haran, *Temples and Temple-Service in Ancient Israel* (Oxford: Clarendon Press, 1978); *idem*, 'Behind the Scenes of History: Determining the Date of the Priestly Source', *JBL* 100 (1981), 321–33. A late date for P is also rejected by S.R. Külling, *Zur Datierung der 'Genesis-P-Stüke'* (Kampen: J.H. Kok, 1964). As early as 1886, A. Dillmann, *Die Bücher Numeri, Deuteronomium und Josua* (Leipzig: Hirzel, 1886²), 593–690, defended the idea that P was earlier than D.

[55] A. Hurvitz 'The Evidence of Language in Dating the Priestly Code', *RB* 81 (1974), 24–56; *idem*, *A Linguistic Study of the Relationship between the Priestly Source and the Book of Ezekiel* (CahRB 20; Paris: J. Gabalda, 1982); *idem*, 'Dating the Priestly Source in Light of the Historical Study of Biblical Hebrew a Century after Wellhausen', *BZAW* 100 (1988), 88–99. For a recent critique of Hurvitz, see J. Blenkinsopp, 'An Assessment of the Alleged Pre-Exilic Date of the Priestly Material in the Pentateuch', *ZAW* 108 (1996), 495–518; cf. M.S. Smith and E.M. Bloch-Smith, *The Pilgrimage Pattern in Exodus* (JSOTSS 239; Sheffield: Sheffield Academic Press, 1997), 165–71.

[56] See note 53 above.

[57] See also Friedman, *Who Wrote the Bible?*

With all these proposed alterations to the Documentary Hypothesis, we must wait and see what their impact will be upon the scholarly consensus that develops during the next two decades. Alongside these modifications, however, scholars will also have to evaluate other recent developments which challenge strongly the very validity of the Documentary Hypothesis.

4.2. Alternatives to the Documentary Hypothesis

The past hundred years have also witnessed a variety of studies critical of the Documentary Hypothesis. Initially, many of these originated from scholars, who, as a result of their conservative theological convictions, were hostile to a theory which challenged the long-standing tradition of Mosaic authorship of the Pentateuch.[58] These attacks on the Documentary Hypothesis tended to be ignored or dismissed by the majority of biblical scholars. However, as time has progressed an increasing number of 'mainstream' scholars have joined this chorus of dissent. As a consequence during recent decades criticisms of the Documentary Hypothesis have been taken more seriously. Recent critics cannot all be dismissed as being theologically motivated in their opposition to the Documentary Hypothesis.

4.2.1 *Winnett, Wagner, Redford and Van Seters*

There have been few sustained attempts to produce an alternative source analysis for the Pentateuch. However, during the past fifty years a small group of North American scholars have proposed a new approach to the composition of the Pentateuch, focusing in particular on the book of Genesis. These scholars are F.V. Winnett, and his students, N.E. Wagner, D.B. Redford and J. Van Seters.

In 1949 Winnett suggested that the books of Exodus and Numbers formed one source, the Mosaic Tradition, which was subsequently revised by P.[59] Since this source originated in the Northern Kingdom, Winnett, somewhat reluctantly, designated it J. Instead of four main sources in the Pentateuch he discovered only three: J, D, P. Later, Winnett developed his views on Genesis in an article entitled 'Re-examining the Foundation'.[60] In this he divided Genesis into three main sections: the primaeval history, the patriarchal narratives and the Joseph story. Following an opinion first

---

[58] For a brief survey, see Alexander, *Abraham in the Negev*, 17–20.
[59] *The Mosaic Tradition* (Toronto: Toronto University Press, 1949).
[60] *JBL* 84 (1965), 1–19.

expressed by J. Morgenstern,[61] he dated the J material of the primaeval history to the early post-exilic period. In the Abraham cycle Winnett, developing a suggestion of S. Sandmel,[62] argued that E supplemented the J material in order to create a more favourable impression of Abraham. Viewed in this light, E could never have existed as an independent, parallel account of the life of Abraham. Winnett then proceeded to question the usual source analysis of the Jacob narrative, and concluded that the evidence in favour of an extensive E version of the story was extremely weak. As for J, Winnett believed that one could detect the use of both early and late material in its composition. To explain this, he suggested that an Abraham-Jacob cultic document (K) underwent two official revisions; the first of these was by E, and the second by 'Late J' who developed significantly the divine promises. In the Joseph story Winnett argued that a basic E story was supplemented by J material. These J additions, however, did not form part of a larger J narrative, but were merely a retelling of part of the E narrative. Winnett linked these J supplements with the J material of the primaeval history and the J revision of the patriarchal narratives. However, he believed that the basic E Joseph story differed markedly from the E supplements to the patriarchal narratives, and so must be viewed as having different origins.

Wagner also offered an analysis of the patriarchal narratives along the lines suggested by Winnett.[63] For the Abraham narrative (Genesis 11:26–25:18) he concluded that the material usually assigned to J consisted of a basic J narrative that was later supplemented by a compiler E. This expansion by E occurred during the time of Jeremiah and Ezekiel. Finally, C, who developed the theme of divine promises to the patriarch, supplemented the JE narrative. After considering Genesis 25:19–36:43 Wagner observed that the basic J narrative about Jacob appeared to have an Israelite origin, whereas the primary J material about Abraham came from Judah. He concluded that two J authors were responsible for these differences: J^a (Abraham) and J^j (Jacob). Wagner also maintained that there was no trace of E in Genesis 25:19–36:43. J^j, unlike J^a, was expanded only by C, a Judaean author from the sixth century BC who was responsible for the pre-P form of Genesis. Finally, about 400 BC, P supplemented C's work to produce the present book of Genesis.

---

[61] 'The Mythological Background of Psalm 82', *HUCA* 14 (1939), 29–126.

[62] 'The Haggada Within Scripture', *JBL* 80 (1961), 105–22. Sandmel rejects the idea of an ancient unified J document.

[63] *A Literary Analysis of Genesis 12–36* (PhD thesis; Toronto: University of Toronto Press, 1965); cf. *idem*, 'Pentateuchal Criticism: No Clear Future', *Canadian Journal of Theology* 13 (1967), 225–32; *idem*, 'Abraham and David?' in J.W. Wevers and D.B. Redford (eds.) *Studies on the Palestinian World* (Toronto: University of Toronto Press, 1972), 117–40.

Wagner's approach to Genesis 12–36 was extended by Redford, another of Winnett's students, to embrace the Joseph narrative (see 4.1.2). He cautiously suggested that the final redaction of the Joseph Story (his 'Judah'-version) might be equated with Winnett's 'Late J' or Wagner's source C.

By far the most significant attempt to produce a new source analysis for part of Genesis comes from Van Seters in his book *Abraham in History and Tradition*. Through an investigation of the relationship between the wife/sister incidents in Genesis 12, 20 and 26, Van Seters concludes that there were three important stages in the development of the Abraham cycle. Genesis 12:10–20 originally formed part of a pre-Yahwistic first stage which consisted of three episodes linked by a brief framework.[64] To this was added Genesis 20:1–17; 21:25–26, 28–31a, which Van Seters labels as a pre-Yahwistic second stage and equates with the source E. This material constituted a single unified story, originally following immediately after the account of Abraham's stay in Egypt (12:10–13:1). The third stage in the growth of the Abraham cycle involved the Yahwist (J) who added (a) brief secondary additions to the earlier material,[65] and (b) larger episodic units[66] which 'were skilfully incorporated into the older literary work with some new arrangement of the materials'.[67] The Yahwist's work was later supplemented by the Priestly author (P) who incorporated certain genealogical and chronological material,[68] as well as chapters 17 and 23. Van Seters identifies this as the fourth stage of development. The fifth and final stage in the growth of the Abraham cycle, the post-Priestly stage, occurred when chapter 14 was incorporated into the overall narrative. Concerning the dating of these various stages, Van Seters argues that the important Yahwistic stage occurred during the time of the exile. Significantly, Van Seters adopts a supplementary approach towards the composition of the Abraham cycle; rather than being composed of continuous parallel documents, it consists of one basic narrative supplemented by later additions.

Van Seters has supported his dating of J to the exilic period in subsequent writing.[69] In general his approach has been to reject the existence of pre-exilic sources while proposing that the Yahwist created the Tetrateuch largely from his own imagination (see section 3.1.3).

---

[64] Genesis 12:1, 4a, 6a, 7, 10–20; 13:1–2, 18; 16:1–3a, 4–9, 11ab, 12; 18:1a, 10–14; 21:2, 6–7; however, all references to Lot were added at a later stage.

[65] Genesis 12:2–3, 6b, 8–9; 16:7b, 10, 11c, 13–14; 20:1a; 21:1.

[66] Genesis 13:3–5, 7–17; 15; 18:1b–9, 18:15–19:38; 21:8–24, 27, 31b–34; 22; 24; 25:1–6, 11; (ch. 26).

[67] Van Seters, *Abraham in History and Tradition*, 313.

[68] Genesis 11:26–32; 12:4b–5; 13:6; 16:3b, 15–16; 21:3–5; 25:7–10.

[69] *Prologue to History* and *The Life of Moses*.

4.2.2 *Rendtorff and Blum*

In 1969 R. Rendtorff drew attention to what he perceived to be an irreconcilable conflict between the Documentary Hypothesis and more recent developments in form and traditio-historical criticism.[70] In particular, he argued that the existence of a continuous J or E document in Genesis is excluded by the observation that there are within Genesis larger independent, literary units, such as the Joseph Story, the Jacob-Esau cycle and the Jacob-Laban cycle, that were produced by different 'authors'.

More recently Rendtorff has renewed his attack on the Documentary Hypothesis in his book *The Problem of the Process of Transmission in the Pentateuch.*[71] Building on a number of important observations, Rendtorff contends that the time has now come to abandon the Documentary Hypothesis as the best way of explaining the composition of the Pentateuch. Various factors lead him to this conclusion. First, a survey of the relevant literature reveals that there is considerable disagreement among scholars regarding the precise formulation of the Documentary Hypothesis. What is often assumed to be a scholarly consensus is far from such, and the existence of diverse opinions clearly challenges the validity of the entire theory. Secondly, traditio-historical investigations of the Pentateuch have suggested that it is composed of a number of larger units which originally existed independently of each other (e.g. the primaeval history; the patriarchal narratives; the account of the exodus from Egypt; the Sinai passage; Israel's stay in the desert; the occupation of the land). Rendtorff believes that it is impossible to reconcile the existence of these larger units with the concept of continuous documents that extend throughout the Pentateuch. Thirdly, it is impossible to reconstruct from the material assigned to the Yahwistic and Priestly writers continuous, coherent documents. Fourthly, there are inconsistencies in the use of linguistic criteria to assign material to a particular source. Various words and expressions generally taken to be typical of one source may also occur in passages assigned to one of the other sources. Fifthly, it is questionable whether material as disparate in form as, for example, Genesis 12:10–20 ('brief' narrative style), 24:1–67 ('detailed' narrative style) and the Joseph Story ('novellistic' style) could have originated from the same source. Form-critical considerations would suggest that these passages derive from different settings and, therefore, cannot be the product of a single author. Yet, all three narratives are normally assigned to J. In the light of these differing arguments Rendtorff views the Documentary Hypothesis as untenable.

---

[70] Rendtorff, 'Traditio-Historical Method', 5–11.

[71] Cf. his 'The "Yahwist" as Theologian? The Dilemma of Pentateuchal Criticism', *JSOT* 3 (1977), 2–10.

While rejecting the idea that continuous parallel documents were used to compose the Pentateuch, Rendtorff offers an alternative explanation. Focusing on the divine promises found in Genesis 12–50, he concludes that it is possible to detect the redactional stages by which the patriarchal stories involving Abraham, Isaac, Jacob and Joseph were united. He argues, for example, that one can discern different redactional phases on the basis of the expressions: 'to you'; 'to you and your descendants'; 'to your descendants'.[72] Yet, although Rendtorff's analysis of the divine promises is very detailed, and his reconstruction of the redactional process closely reasoned, the whole approach rests upon the highly questionable assumption that minor variations within the divine promise speeches reflect different stages of composition. Nowhere, however, does he allow for the possibility that these variations may have arisen due to factors other than editorial reworking. In many instances it is possible that minor differences are little more than stylistic variations of expression, a natural feature of everyday speech. Consequently, reservations must be expressed about the basis for Rendtorff's reconstruction of the editorial process by which the patriarchal stories were united.

Although Rendtorff's critique of the Documentary Hypothesis is trenchant, especially his arguments against the existence of continuous documents extending throughout the Pentateuch, a word of caution must be expressed. Rendtorff places considerable weight on the traditio-historical observation that the Pentateuch consists of larger units. However, he does not discuss the extent and content of these units; their general existence is assumed rather than proved. Furthermore, the supposition that they were originally independent requires investigation. Not only are some of the units more closely linked than Rendtorff allows, but it is also apparent that later units pre-suppose in a variety of ways the existence of earlier units (e.g. Exodus 1–14 assumes a knowledge of the events recorded in the concluding chapters of Genesis in order to explain why the Israelites are in Egypt).

Rendtorff's rejection of the existence of J and E is developed further by one of his students, E. Blum, in a lengthy study entitled *Die Komposition der Vätergeschichte*.[73] Focusing on Genesis 12–50, Blum argues for a process of composition that differs significantly from that proposed under the Documentary Hypothesis. In essence, he rejects the existence of parallel sources in favour of a supplementary approach. Starting with material drawn from Genesis 25–33 Blum uncovers a story about Jacob (*Jakoberzählung*; 25:9–34; 27–33) which focuses on the importance of Bethel as a cultic centre and the theme of reconciliation between brothers. According to Blum, this narrative was composed in the northern kingdom to address the political situation that

---

[72] Rendtorff, *Problem of the Process of Transmission*, 55–84.
[73] (WMANT 57; Neukirchen-Vluyn: Neukirchener, 1984).

existed in the time of Jeroboam I following the break up of the Solomonic kingdom. Sometime later, before the downfall of the northern kingdom, the *Jakoberzählung* was expanded by the addition of the Joseph story to form the *Jakobgeschichte* ('the history of Jacob'; most, but not all, of Gen. 25–50), a biography of Jacob from birth to death. Subsequently, a Judaean author who wished to emphasise the importance of Judah further expanded this narrative; as a result chapters 34, 38 and 49, as well as 35:21–22a, were added.

After the collapse of the northern kingdom, the *Jakobgeschichte* was yet again expanded, this time by adding the Abraham-Lot story (Gen. 13, 18–19). This new document, which was centred upon the divine promises found in 13:14–17 and 28:13–15, formed the first patriarchal history or *Vätergeschichte* (Vg^1). A new version of this history (Vg^2) was produced during the Babylonian Exile; built around the divine speeches in 12:1–3; 26:2–3; 31:11, 13 and 46:1–5a, Vg^2 focused on the topics of nationhood, territory and blessing. Other material reflecting a similar outlook was also added at this stage (i.e. 12:6–9, 10–20; 16; 21:8–21; 22; 26).

In the post-exilic period an important redaction occurred at the hands of a Deuteronomistic editor who, apart from adding chapters 15 and 24, linked the patriarchal history to the rest of the Pentateuch. This was then followed by another revision, undertaken by a Priestly writer, which involved as regards the book of Genesis the creation of the *tôlĕdot* framework and the inclusion of various other texts (e.g. Gen. 17). While links with the Documentary Hypothesis are observable, particularly as regards the final stages of this process, Blum's reconstruction of the way in which the patriarchal narratives developed represents a major break with past approaches.

To his credit, Blum seeks to uncover the process of composition by undertaking a detailed study of the text itself; in so doing he avoids the more speculative type of traditio-historical research undertaken by Noth. His approach, however, like that of Wellhausen, assumes that early and late material can be distinguished with considerable certainty, and this in spite of the material having gone through a number of significant redactional stages. Finally, as regards the Abraham narrative, Blum relies heavily upon Rendtorff's analysis of the divine promises, which, as we have noted above, rests upon highly questionable premises.[74]

---

[74] Regarding this Van Seters rightly observes, 'Rendtorff had concluded (to my mind on dubious grounds) that Genesis 13:14–17 contained the earliest form of the land promise theme. This is what really dictates Blum's choice of the Abraham-Lot stories as the earliest level of the Abraham tradition. Rendtorff's complex scheme of promises development governs the other levels of Blum's composition history as well. But if one cannot accept the arguments for a multiplicity of levels in the non-priestly promise texts, then the whole scheme may be reconstructed in quite a different way' ('Review of E. Blum, *Die Komposition der Vätergeschichte*', *JBL* 105 [1986], 707).

Blum's observations of the patriarchal history have been extended to include the rest of the Pentateuch in his more recent study, *Studien zur Komposition des Pentateuch*.[75] Abandoning the Documentary Hypothesis model, Blum argues that the Pentateuch underwent two major stages in its composition. The first of these, D-Komposition (K^D), was undertaken by editors influenced by the Deuteronomistic History in the early post-exilic period. These editors integrated together two blocks of already existing material: an earlier form of Genesis 12–50 dating from the exilic period and a 'Life of Moses' which included much of the material presently in Exodus to Numbers. The process of integrating these two blocks of material involved the creation, by the K^D editors, of the promise texts in Genesis.[76] The importance of these promise texts is underlined by the fact that Blum views K^D as having started with Genesis 12:1–3. A second stage took place when Priestly writers reworked K^D; not surprisingly Blum designates this final redactional stage P-Komposition (K^P). With this final redaction the primaeval history of Genesis 1–11 was added, creating the Pentateuch as we now know it.

Central to Blum's approach is the idea that the Pentateuchal materials came into being through a number of distinctive stages: early written traditions, Deuteronomy, the Deuteronomistic History, K^D and, finally, K^P. Fundamental to the ordering of these is the idea that K^D was composed after the Deuteronomistic History. While this general idea finds support among some scholars, it has also invited serious criticism.[77] Although the issue of the relationship between the Tetrateuch and the Deuteronomistic History will continue to figure prominently in future scholarly discussion, the weight of evidence seems to argue strongly against Blum's approach.[78]

4.2.3 Whybray

In his book *The Making of the Pentateuch: A Methodological Study*,[79] R.N. Whybray provides one of the most recent, detailed assessments of the Documentary Hypothesis.[80] Focusing principally on the narrative sections of

---

[75] (BZAW 189; Berlin: W. de Gruyter, 1990).

[76] Genesis 15; 22:15–18; 24:7; 26:3b–5, 24; cf. Exodus 13:5, 11; 32:13; 33:1; Numbers 11:12; 14:16, 23.

[77] For example, Nicholson, *The Pentateuch*, 194, comments, 'the evidence does not support the notion of a systematic Deuteronomistic editing of the Tetrateuch, much less the view that the first Tetrateuch was the work of a Deuteronomistic author'.

[78] See, for example, the discussion of Deuteronomistic influence in the composition of Exodus 19–24 in chapter 5.

[79] (JSOTSS 53; Sheffield: JSOT Press, 1987).

[80] *Making of the Pentateuch*, 130.

the Pentateuch, he evaluates (a) the presuppositions underlying the theory (i.e. philosophical and religio-historical; linguistic; literary; cultural); (b) the criteria used to distinguish the different documentary sources (i.e. language and style; repetitions, duplications and contradictions; differences of culture, religion and theology); (c) the application of the criteria; and (d) the role of the redactors.

Among the more telling of Whybray's criticisms of the Documentary Hypothesis may be listed the following:

1. Proponents of the Documentary Hypothesis assume 'a consistency in the avoidance of repetitions and contradictions which is unparalleled in ancient literature (and even in modern fiction), and which ignores the possibility of the deliberate use of such features for aesthetic and literary purposes'.[81]
2. The Documentary Hypothesis often breaks up narratives into different sources, destroying their literary and aesthetic qualities, while at the same time creating texts which lack such qualities.
3. Variations in language and style need not result solely from the existence of different sources. They may arise equally well from 'differences of subject-matter requiring special or distinctive vocabulary, alternations of vocabulary introduced for literary reasons, and unconscious variation of vocabulary'.[82]
4. There is inadequate evidence to support 'the presence *throughout* each of the documents of a single style, purpose and point of view or theology, and of an unbroken narrative thread'.[83]

While others have already noted many of the shortcomings of the Documentary Hypothesis highlighted by Whybray, his work is noteworthy for two reasons. First, his rejection of the Documentary Hypothesis is not motivated by an underlying theological conservatism. Indeed, he concludes that the narrative sections of the Pentateuch were probably composed in the sixth century by a single author who, while drawing upon some recent traditions, relied mainly upon his own imagination.[84] Secondly, Whybray offers a generally comprehensive assessment of the Documentary Hypothesis. While some issues are dealt with briefly, he demonstrates that the Documentary Hypothesis rests on unacceptable presuppositions, inadequate criteria for distinguishing the different sources, and a method of literary composition for which there is no analogy elsewhere.

---

[81] Ibid.

[82] Ibid.

[83] Whybray briefly restates this position in his more recent book, *An Introduction to the Pentateuch* (Grand Rapids: Eerdmans, 1995).

[84] See Nicholson, *The Pentateuch*.

Although Whybray's criticism of the Documentary Hypothesis is compelling, he nowhere attempts to demonstrate the literary unity of the Pentateuch by a detailed exposition of the entire text, or even part of it. Thus, while he may have gone some way to demolishing the idea that the Pentateuch was composed of continuous, parallel documents, his study does not exclude the possibility of either a fragmentary or supplementary explanation for the composition of the Pentateuch.

4.3. Conclusion

As we move into a new millennium there can be little doubt that Pentateuchal criticism is in something of a crisis. The opponents of the Documentary Hypothesis are no longer limited to those of a conservative theological outlook. While some scholars remain committed to the basic concept of the Documentary Hypothesis, others seek to modify it substantially, and still others are willing to approach afresh the whole issue of the composition of the Pentateuch. As Whybray has recently remarked:

> There is at the present moment no consensus whatever about when, why, how, and through whom the Pentateuch reached its present form, and opinions about the dates of composition of its various parts differ by more than five hundred years.[85]

---

[85] *An Introduction to the Pentateuch*, 12–3.

5

The Sinai Narrative – A Test Case

As we have observed in the preceding chapter, recent developments in Pentateuchal Criticism have challenged the validity of the Documentary Hypothesis, prompting a variety of alternative approaches. Among these newer developments has arisen the idea that the material in the books of Genesis to Numbers underwent several redactional stages, one of which resembles the literary style of the writer(s) responsible for the Deuteronomistic History (i.e. the books of Deuteronomy to Kings).[1] As a result, some scholars now argue that the books of Genesis to Numbers were composed to form a prologue to the Deuteronomistic History.

In the light of these developments, we shall examine afresh in this chapter the composition of the Sinai Narrative in Exodus 19:1–24:11. This provides us with an opportunity (a) to test the validity of the Documentary Hypothesis as applied to a particular text, and (b) to evaluate claims of Deuteronomistic influence in the composition of Genesis to Numbers. Not only does Exodus 19–24 lend itself well to both of these issues, but it also merits attention because scholarly efforts to uncover the source(s) of these chapters have proved less than satisfactory. As J.I. Durham observes:

> Though many helpful observations may be harvested from the critical work of more than a century, the sum total of that work is a clear assertion that no literary solution to this complex narrative has been found, with more than a hint that none is likely to be found.[2]

Although Durham's assessment reflects well the current state of play regarding Exodus 19:1–24:11, there are perhaps grounds for hoping that a new approach, freed from some of the constraints of previous studies, may yet yield a better understanding of the process by which these chapters were composed. It will be argued below that Exodus 19:1–24:11 displays greater signs of

---

[1] See section 1.3, chapter 4.
[2] *Exodus* (Waco: Word, 1984), 259.

literary unity than has been recognised in the past, the key to this resting in the narrative framework which surrounds the divine speeches in Exodus 19:3–6 and 20:22–24:2.

5.1. The Narrative Framework of the Divine Speeches in 19:3–6 and 20:22–24:2

As presently constituted Exodus 19:1–24:11 describes the ratification of a covenant between Yahweh and the Israelites, involving a divine theophany at Mount Sinai. Central to these events are a number of important divine speeches. While the best known of these is the Ten Commandments or Decalogue (Ex. 20:2–17), we shall focus initially on the addresses in Exodus 19:3–6 and 20:22–24:2. As D. Patrick has observed, these latter speeches, in spite of their very differing lengths, share a common narrative framework.[3] Expanding slightly upon Patrick's observations, the parallels between Exodus 19:2b–8a and 20:21–24:3 are set out in Table A.

Among the most striking aspects of these parallels are the following. A contrast is made between Moses' ascent to Yahweh (Ex. 19:3; 20:21) and the people remaining at the foot of the mountain (Ex. 19:2b; 20:21).[4] After Moses separates from the Israelites, Yahweh takes the initiative and speaks to him (Ex. 19:3; 20:22). Each speech begins with the expression, 'This is what you are to say', emphasising that Moses is to convey Yahweh's remarks to the people 'word for word'.[5] In both instances Yahweh's opening words for the Israelites are, 'YOU yourselves have seen'; these introduce brief comments about prior divine activities witnessed by the people. Later, after hearing what Yahweh has to say, Moses returns and, as instructed, reports all that he has been told (Ex. 19:7; 24:3). Finally, the people respond positively, affirming their willingness to do all that Yahweh has said (Ex. 19:8; 24:3; cf. 24:7). Although minor variations in wording exist, the strong similarities between the narrative frameworks and the introductory words of the divine speeches in Exodus 19:3–6 and 20:22–24:2 suggest common authorship.[6] We shall return later to the issue of the identity of this author.

---

[3] 'The Covenant Code Source', *VT* 27 (1977) 145–57; cf. *idem, Old Testament Law* (London; SCM, 1986), 64.

[4] In both cases this contrast is marked by a break in the *vav*-consecutive sequence of the Hebrew text, and by naming the subject, Moses, prior to a perfect verb.

[5] B. Jacob, *Exodus* (Hoboken, NJ: Ktav, 1992), 525.

[6] While a later author could have modelled the narrative framework and opening words of one divine speech upon an already existing account, it is much more likely that a single author was responsible for composing both.

Table A

Exodus 19:2b–8a	Exodus 20:21–24:3
{2b} There Israel camped in front of the mountain. {3} But Moses went up to God,	{20:21} The people remained at a distance, but Moses approached the thick darkness where God was.
and the LORD called to him from the mountain, saying,	{20:22} Then the LORD said to Moses,
"This is what you shall say to the house of Jacob and what you shall tell the children of Israel:	"This is what you are to say to the children of Israel:
{4} 'YOU[7] yourselves have seen what I did to Egypt, and how I carried YOU on eagles' wings and brought you to myself...	'YOU yourselves have seen that I have spoken to YOU from heaven:...
The main part of the divine speech.	*The main part of the divine speech.*
{7} So Moses came and summoned the elders of the people and put before them all these words which the LORD had commanded him.	{24:3} So Moses came and told the people all the LORD's words and all the laws.
{8} The people replied all together, "All that the LORD has said we will do."	All the people replied with one voice, "All the words that the LORD has said we will do."

While Yahweh's words in Exodus 19:3–6 are normally assigned to the same source as the narrative that follows in verses 7–8,[8] source critics have generally not observed any connections between the speech in Exodus 20:22–24:2 and its narrative framework. Since the time of Wellhausen, Exodus 20:22–23:33 has generally been viewed as coming from an independent source,[9] having

---

[7] 'YOU' is used here to indicate the use of the second person plural in the Hebrew text: 'you' translates the second person singular.

[8] The source analysis of Exodus 19 will be discussed later.

[9] It is not possible to consider here the process by which Exodus 20:22–23:33 was composed. For four recent, but differing approaches, see E. Otto, *Wandel der Rechtsbegründungen in der Gesellschaftsgeschichte des Antiken Israel: Eine Rechtsgeschichte des "Bundesbuches" Ex XX 22–XXIII 13* (Leiden: Brill, 1988); L. Schwienhorst-Schönberger, *Das Bundesbuch [Ex 20, 22–23, 33]* (Berlin: W. de Gruyter, 1990); Y. Osumi, *Die Kompositionsgeschichte des Bundesbuches Exodus 20, 22b–23, 33* (Göttingen: Vanderhoeck & Ruprecht, 1991); J.M. Sprinkle, *'The Book of the Covenant': A Literary Approach* (JSOTSS 174; Sheffield: JSOT Press, 1994).

nothing in common with Exodus 24:1–11. In the light of this, and given that the parallels noted above include only the very opening words of Yahweh's speech (i.e. Ex. 20:22), can other evidence be found to link 20:22–23:33 with 24:1–11?

To address this question, some general observations must be made briefly regarding the content and structure of the speech in Exodus 20:22–24:2. As it stands, Yahweh's address to Moses falls into a number of distinct sections:[10]

20:22–26   instructions concerning the making of cultic objects

21:1–22:20   regulatory principles (*mišpāṭîm* [mishpāṭîm])

22:21–23:9   moral imperatives

23:10–19   instructions concerning the Sabbath and religious festivals

23:20–33   promises and warning concerning the land of Canaan

24:1–2   instructions for Moses and other individuals to come up to Yahweh

On the basis of content and form, the boundaries between these sections are relatively clear. The reference to *mišpāṭîm* (regulations) in 21:1 introduces the material in 22:2–23:19, setting 20:22–26 apart as the first unit in the speech. A new section comes in 22:20–23:9, framed by 22:20 and 23:9, which together form an *inclusio*;[11] this section consists of exhortations concerned mainly with protecting the weaker members of society and safeguarding the judicial system. Exodus 23:10–19 consists of cultic instructions relating to the Sabbath and festivals; this material is bound together by the use of the numbers 'six' (vv. 10, 12) and 'three' (vv. 14, 17). The next section, 23:20–33, is distinguished from the rest by both its paraenetic style and subject matter; directions are given as to how the Israelites must behave in order to be assured of Yahweh's help in taking possession of the land of Canaan. Finally, 24:1–2 is set apart from the rest of the address by the inclusion of the brief narrative comment, 'and to Moses he said'. For the purpose of this present study, detailed attention will be given to 20:22–26 and 24:1–2, since both passages provide evidence linking the divine speech to 24:3–11.

Although it is often suggested that the so-called 'altar laws' (Ex. 20:22–26) have been separated from 22:17–23:19 by the later insertion of the *mišpāṭîm* in 21:1–22:16, a number of factors support the originality of the present

---

[10] Patrick, *Old Testament Law*, 63–96.

[11] An *inclusio* is a literary device whereby a section of material is framed by using similar expressions as the beginning and end. In this instance, the text repeats comments about not ill-treating aliens because the Israelites were themselves aliens in Egypt.

arrangement. First, the prohibition against making idols and the instructions for building altars both focus on the important subject of how God's presence is to be experienced by the Israelites in the future. Yahweh's blessing will come to the people when they worship him through the offering of sacrifices on altars, but not through the construction of golden or silver images. Since the whole thrust of the Sinai covenant is the establishment of a special relationship between God and the Israelites, through which the people will continue to know and experience the divine presence, these instructions form an appropriate introduction to the covenant document. Secondly, the directions concerning the building of altars relate in a direct way to the ratification of the covenant in Exodus 24:3–11. The narrative in Exodus 24 describes the construction of an altar and the making of whole-burnt offerings and fellowship offerings, the two types of sacrifices specified in 20:24. While there are prior references in Genesis and Exodus to the building of altars and the making of sacrifices, Exodus 20:24 and 24:4–5 are the first passages in the Pentateuch to mention side-by-side both whole-burnt offerings and fellowship offerings. Thirdly, the prohibition in Exodus 20:23 against having gods of either gold or silver takes on a special significance in the light of the 'golden calf' incident recorded later in Exodus 32:1–6. Close parallels exist between the ratification of the covenant in Exodus 24 and the account of its undoing in Exodus 32.[12] Both passages describe the making of an altar (Ex. 24:4; 32:5), the sacrificing of whole-burnt offerings and fellowship offerings (Ex. 24:5; 32:6), and the people eating and drinking in Yahweh's real or supposed presence (Ex. 24:11; 32:6). Moreover, in Exodus 'gods of gold' are mentioned only in 20:23; 32:4, 31. All of these observations suggest that Exodus 20:22–26 is integrated more fully into the Sinai narrative than is usually supposed. Further evidence in support of this is provided below.

As regards Exodus 24:1–2, there has been a strong tendency to discuss these verses apart from Exodus 20:22–23:33. However, verses 1–2 are obviously intended to be understood as a continuation of the preceding divine speech. Unfortunately, the present chapter division exacerbates the apparent break between 23:33 and 24:1. The continuity between 23:33 and 24:1 is immediately evident from the fact that the identity of the speaker is not specified; it is assumed that he has already been introduced (cf. Ex. 20:22). B.S. Childs rightly observes that Exodus 24:1 forms an unusual opening,[13] for it marks not the beginning of a new episode, but merely a minor break in the divine speech which commences in Exodus 20:22. Through the inclusion of the brief narrative comment at the start of verse 1, Yahweh's concluding words

[12] Cf. A. Phillips, 'A fresh look at the Sinai pericope', *VT* 34 (1984), 51.
[13] *Exodus* (OTL; London: SCM, 1974), 499–500.

to Moses are deliberately set apart from what has gone before. Whereas the content of Exodus 20:22–23:33 concerns all the Israelites (cf. Ex. 20:22), the instructions addressed to Moses in Exodus 24:1–2 relate only to him and a selected group of Israelite leaders.[14]

By viewing Exodus 24:1–2 as the conclusion to Yahweh's speech to Moses, the structure of Exodus 24:1–11 becomes much clearer and shows signs of careful composition. This is evident from the way in which the overall structure of the divine speech in Exodus 20:22–24:2 is reflected in the events described in Exodus 24:3–11. After returning to the people, Moses reports 'all Yahweh's words and regulatory principles' (Ex. 24:3), fulfilling the instruction given to him in 20:22. Moses then records this material in writing.[15] The next day he constructs an altar and oversees the offering of whole-burnt offerings and fellowship offerings (Ex. 24:4–5), activities that parallel in a striking way the instructions given in 20:24–26. Moses then reads to the Israelites the 'Book of the Covenant' (presumably the contents of Ex. 20:23–23:33) before sealing the covenant by sprinkling blood upon the people (Ex. 24:7–8). Finally, in obedience to Yahweh's concluding instructions (Ex. 24:1–2), Moses and the elders ascend the mountain, bringing the covenant ratification ceremony to an end by eating and drinking in Yahweh's presence (Ex. 24:9–11). These parallels between the lengthy divine speech (Ex. 20:22–24:2) and the subsequent account of the covenant being ratified (Ex. 24:3–11), in conjunction with our earlier observations concerning the narrative framework in 20:21–22 and 24:3, suggest that the narrative from 20:21 to 24:11 has been skilfully constructed.

Before leaving Exodus 24:1–11, it should be noted that previous attempts to uncover the sources underlying this section have not proved particularly satisfactory. In general there has been a trend towards finding in these verses two, or even three, distinctive sources, but no consensus exists. Noth attributes verses 1–2, 9–11 to E, verses 1–2 having undergone further redactional changes, with verses 3–8 originating from a once independent 'Book of the Covenant' source.[16] In marked contrast, J.P. Hyatt assigns verses 1–2, 9–11 to J, verses 3, 4b–6, 8 to E, and verses 4a, 7 to a Deuteronomistic redactor.[17] Childs assigns verses 3–8 to E,

---

[14] Childs, *Exodus*, 502–4; Durham, *Exodus*, 342–43. Although the 3rd person references to Yahweh in Ex. 24:1–2 might suggest that the speaker is someone other that Yahweh (cf. M. Noth, *Exodus* [OTL; London: SCM, 1962], 196–7), it is not uncommon within the Sinai narrative for God to refer to himself in this way (e.g. Ex. 19:21–22, 24; 20:7, 10–11).

[15] Since the 'regulatory principles' make up only part of Exodus 20:22–24:2, the expression 'all Yahweh's words' probably refers here to the remaining sections of the Book of the Covenant and not the Decalogue.

[16] *Exodus*, 194–9.

[17] *Exodus*, 254–7.

with the surrounding verses lacking any clear criteria by which their source(s) may be determined.[18]

While diverging over the precise identity of the sources in Exodus 24:1–11, critical scholars generally agree that verses 1–2, 9–11 differ in origin from verses 3–8. This belief rests largely on the fact that the former verses record both a command for Moses and others to ascend to Yahweh (vv. 1–2) and its fulfilment (vv. 9–11), whereas the latter verses focus on a covenant ratification ceremony. Consequently, while acknowledging the lack of decisive criteria for source analysis, Childs, through recourse to the pre-literary stage, concludes that verses 3–8 go back to an oral account of a 'covenant renewal ceremony', whereas verses 1–2, 9–11 reflect 'a covenant meal following a theophany'.[19] Although this proposal neatly circumvents the inadequacy of the criteria for source analysis, it is entirely speculative.

Support for the unity of Exodus 24:1–11 may be deduced from Deuteronomy 27:1–8 which contains instructions for the renewing of the covenant at Mount Ebal (cf. Jos. 8:30–35). Deuteronomy 27:1–8 describes a series of closely related activities: the recording of the covenant obligations; the building of a stone altar without using iron tools (cf. Ex. 20:25); the offering of whole-burnt offerings and fellowship offerings; eating in the presence of the LORD. From a form-critical perspective, these features obviously comprise a covenant ratification ceremony. Significantly, the same elements come in Exodus 24:1–11, taken as a whole.[20] Moreover, as Childs observes, 'the covenant meal [Ex. xxiv 9–11] is now seen as a culmination of the rite in 3–8, and not as a rival ceremony'.[21] Since taken together verses 1–2, 9–11 and verses 3–8 form a coherent account, no justification exists for maintaining that more than one source is present in Exodus 24:1–11.

---

[18] *Exodus*, 500–2.

[19] *Exodus*, 501.

[20] While clear parallels exist between Exodus 24:3–11 and Deuteronomy 27:1–8, the ratification of the covenant at Mount Sinai represents a unique occasion; future covenant ceremonies take place (a) after the construction of the tabernacle, and (b) within the promised land. Thus, in Exodus 24:3–11 Moses and the seventy elders ascend Mount Sinai in order to eat and drink in Yahweh's presence; when the covenant is later renewed at Mount Ebal, the people, having been instructed to eat and rejoice in 'the presence of Yahweh' (Deut. 27:7), gather around 'the ark of the covenant of Yahweh', the symbol of God's presence in their midst (Jos. 8:33). Similarly, whereas Moses records the terms of the covenant in a scroll, elsewhere they are inscribed on large stones coated with plaster (cf. Deut. 27:2, 4; Jos. 8:32). The use of different writing materials is explicable in terms of the Israelites' location. A scroll enables the details of the covenant obligations to be transported to the land of Canaan. These variations between the Sinai covenant and later renewals are explicable, therefore, in terms of the differing settings in which the covenant ratification ceremonies occur.

[21] *Exodus*, 502.

5.2. Exodus 20:22 and the Decalogue

Thus far we have argued that the divine speeches in Exodus 19:3–6 and 20:22–24:2, together with the narratives immediately surrounding them (Ex. 19:2a, 7–8a; 20:21; 24:3–11), display evidence of having been constructed as a unified work. Central to our argument have been the parallels noted in Table A, especially the similar introductions to the two divine addresses. We must turn now to consider the relationship between the proclamation of the Decalogue (Ex. 20:1–17) and Yahweh's speech in Exodus 20:22–24:2.

As we have already noted briefly, a common element in Exodus 19:3 and 20:22 is the expression, 'YOU yourselves have seen'. In both speeches this phrase draws attention to divine activities witnessed by all the Israelites personally. Exodus 19:3 refers to the deliverance of the people from Egypt and their journey to Mount Sinai; significantly, Exodus 20:22 focuses not on the exodus from Egypt but on the fact that Yahweh has spoken to the Israelites 'from heaven'. In view of the parallels between the introductions to the two speeches, this latter activity is obviously presented as being comparable to the divine rescue of the Israelites from slavery in Egypt. The mention of Yahweh speaking 'from heaven' must refer to the giving of the Decalogue (Ex. 20:1–17), for all the other divine speeches recorded in Exodus 19–24 are mediated through Moses to the Israelites. This indicates that the author who penned Exodus 20:22 had already incorporated Exodus 20:1–17 (or its equivalent) into his composition.

Exodus 20:22 also provides further evidence supporting the present location of Exodus 20:18–21 after the Decalogue. If Yahweh has indeed spoken directly to the Israelites, as he claims, why does he now in verse 20 instruct Moses to convey his words to the people? The obvious answer to this question comes in 20:18–21 which records how the people, out of fear, no longer desire that Yahweh should address them directly. Consequently, they ask Moses to act once more as Yahweh's spokesman. A careful reading of Exodus 20:22 suggests strongly that it was penned as the sequel to Exodus 20:1–21.

Since Exodus 20:22 both presupposes a speech uttered directly by Yahweh to the people, and introduces a divine address delivered via Moses, there seems every reason to believe that the Decalogue and the Book of the Covenant were incorporated into the Sinai narrative by the author responsible for composing the narrative frameworks that presently surround the divine speeches in Exodus 19:3–6 and 20:22–24:2.

5.3. Deuteronomistic Redaction and the Sinai Narrative

Several recent studies have already drawn attention to the importance of Exodus 20:22 for understanding the process by which the Sinai narrative was composed, although differing somewhat in their conclusions. The two earliest studies both appeared in volume 27 of *VT*, the first by Patrick[22] and the second by E.W. Nicholson.[23] While these originated independently of each other, their findings are taken up and developed at some length by Phillips in *VT* 34.[24]

Patrick draws attention, as we have noted above, to the common authorship of Exodus 19:3b–8, 20:22–23, 24:3–8, which was 'composed for the purpose of setting the [Covenant] Code in the context of the revelation at Sinai'.[25] According to Patrick, this independent source was inserted into E before the latter was combined with J. While acknowledging 'points of contact' between the narrative framework of the Covenant Code and Deuteronomy/Deuteronomistic literature, Patrick sees the latter as having been influenced by the former, and not vice versa.

Approaching Exodus 20:22–23 from a different perspective, Nicholson finds in the reference to Yahweh speaking from heaven evidence of a Deuteronomistic redaction of the Sinai narrative which involved the interpolation of both the Decalogue and Exodus 20:22–23. Taking as his starting point the tradition in Deuteronomy 4–5 concerning the 'Decalogue as God's direct address to Israel', and similarities between Exodus 20:23 and Deuteronomy 4:16–28, he argues that Exodus 20:1–17, 22–23 was composed after Deuteronomy 4:1–40, and added by a Deuteronomistic redactor to an existing version of the Sinai narrative, which already included the Book of the Covenant.

Responding to Nicholson's discussion, Phillips highlights a number of factors that argue against Exodus 20:1–17, 22–23 coming from a Deuteronomistic redactor. In particular, he observes that the Deuteronomic version of the Decalogue 'shows clear signs of having been altered from the Exodus version in order to comply with Deuteronomic legal concerns'.[26] Consequently, he favours a pre-Deuteronomic date for the redaction of the Sinai narrative. Moreover, he maintains that Exodus 20:24–26 ought to be included in any discussion of Exodus 20:22–23, the former being relocated and placed alongside Exodus 20:22–23 when these verses, with the rest of the Book of the Covenant, were inserted into the Sinai narrative. Significantly, Phillips argues that Exodus 20:22–26 reflects 'a purification of Israel's sanctuaries to a much simpler and primitive form', and derives 'from a pre-Deuteronomic attempt to reform Israel's worship'.[27] Phillips dates these reforms to the time of Hezekiah (cf. 2 Kgs. 18:4) and gives to those

---

[22] 'The Covenant Code Source', 145–57.
[23] 'The Decalogue as the Direct Address of God', *VT* 27 (1977), 422–33.
[24] 'A Fresh Look at the Sinai Pericope: Part I', *VT* 34 (1984), 39–52; 'Part II', *VT* 34 (1984), 282–94.
[25] 'The Covenant Code Source', 156.
[26] 'A Fresh Look at the Sinai Pericope: Part I', 43–4.
[27] 'A Fresh Look at the Sinai Pericope: Part I', 41.

responsible for redacting the Sinai narrative the label Proto-Deuteronomists. These theologians introduce for the first time the concept of the Decalogue being spoken by Yahweh from heaven, although, according to Phillips, they did not see this as having any theological significance.[28]

The arguments presented by both Patrick and Phillips against a Deuteronomistic redaction of the Sinai narrative are more convincing than those offered by Nicholson in favour of such, and several recent studies have also come out strongly in support of the priority of the Exodus version of the Decalogue.[29] Yet, while Phillips' case for a pre-Deuteronomistic redaction is skilfully argued, two major modifications are necessary. The first of these concerns the dating of this redaction to the time of Hezekiah, and its description as Proto-Deuteronomic. The second involves a more radical assessment of the redactional process which Phillips believes took place.

As regards the dating of the redaction involving Exodus 20:22, Phillips, like Patrick, is undoubtedly correct in placing this prior to the composition of Deuteronomy. However, by labelling the redaction Proto-Deuteronomic and locating it in the time of Hezekiah, he obviously implies that those responsible were not far removed from the Deuteronomic activities normally associated with king Josiah (2 Kgs. 22–23). Yet, one major factor suggests that this redaction of the Sinai narrative took place at a much earlier time.

An important component of Phillips' discussion is the present location of material concerning idols and altars at the very start of the Book of the Covenant. For Phillips the prominence given to these ideas in Exodus 20:23–26 reflects a concern to purify Israelite sanctuaries, as occurred in the time of Hezekiah. However, he fails to observe the close link, noted above, that exists between 20:24–26 and the preliminary activities concerned with the ratification of the covenant in 24:4–5. This connection has important implications for dating the redaction, for Phillips himself views Exodus 24:4–6, 8 as reflecting 'an early covenant ritual which must pre-date the monarchy'.[30]

---

[28] In passing it should be noted that Phillips views Exodus 20:18–21 as originally having come immediately after Exodus 19:19, with the Decalogue following both of these passages. The Proto-Deuteronomists were also responsible for inserting the Book of the Covenant into the Sinai narrative, as well as introducing Exodus 32–34.

[29] Cf. Weinfeld, *Deuteronomy 1–11*, 242–319; R.G. Kratz, 'Der Dekalog im Exodusbuch', *VT* 44 (1994), 205–38.

[30] 'A Fresh Look at the Sinai Pericope: Part II', 285. In addition to the reference to 'young men', Phillips (p. 285) notes that D.J. McCarthy, 'b'rît in Old Testament History and Theology', *Bib* 53 (1972), 117, describes the phrase 'blood of the covenant' as 'very un-Deuteronomic'. Interestingly, Phillips (p. 285) also draws attention to the fact that E.W. Nicholson, 'The Interpretation of Exodus xxiv 9–11', *VT* 24 (1974), 77–97, dates Exodus 24:1–2, 9–11 as 'pre-Yahwistic'.

Taken together, Exodus 20:23–26 and 24:4–6, 8 display no awareness of either a special priesthood or a central sanctuary. Indeed, this material implies that any Israelite could build an altar and offer whole-burnt offerings and fellowship offerings to Yahweh.[31] Such an outlook can hardly come from theologians who, as Phillips' designation Proto-Deuteronomic implies, were the immediate predecessors to a reform movement which favoured the restriction of worship to a central sanctuary. Both the content of Exodus 20:23–26 and the prominence given to these verses suggests a much earlier date of composition than that advocated by Phillips.[32] In the light of this, the term Proto-Deuteronomic seems inappropriate.

The second aspect of Phillips' approach which requires modification is the issue of the nature and extent of the redaction associated with Exodus 20:22. This issue is not really addressed by Phillips who tends to work within the framework established by Nicholson. However, once the existence of Deuteronomic/Deuteronomistic material within the Sinai narrative is rejected in favour of the Sinai narrative having been composed prior to Deuteronomy, the presence of redactional activity within Exodus 19–24 can no longer be automatically assumed. Unfortunately, Phillips fails to appreciate the implications of his own re-dating of the supposed redactional material and continues to assume that the narrative framework associated with Exodus 20:22 originates from an editor who modified an earlier version of the Sinai narrative. Yet, once Deuteronomic/Deuteronomistic influence is rejected, the redactional nature of Exodus 20:22 and the verses associated with it must be demonstrated afresh; it cannot be merely assumed.

---

[31] In support of this it is noteworthy (a) that no special skills are required to construct the altar, which can be made from easily found materials, and (b) that the reason given for the prohibition against steps leading up to an altar in 20:26 would not apply to Aaronic priests who were expected to wear undergarments (Ex. 28:42–43). Furthermore, the fact that these instructions are expressed in the second person singular suggests that they were intended for all the Israelites and not merely a selected few.

[32] Further evidence, in keeping with an earlier date for this redaction of the Sinai narrative, comes in a study on the dating of the Book of the Covenant by J. W. Marshall, *Israel and the Book of the Covenant: An Anthropological Approach to Biblical Law* (Atlanta: Scholars Press, 1993). While it is clear that an early date for the Book of the Covenant does not automatically mean an early date for the redaction of the Sinai narrative, the redaction cannot be dated prior to the composition of the Book of the Covenant. By dating the Book of the Covenant to the pre-monarchic period, Marshall's study leaves open the possibility of an early redaction. A similar argument may be applied as regards the dating of the Decalogue, for its existence is presupposed by Exodus 20:22. However, the very nature of the Decalogue makes it exceptionally difficult to date.

At this stage it is necessary to bring into consideration Exodus 19:2b–8, which, as we noted at the start of our study, parallels closely the narrative framework surrounding the divine speech in Exodus 20:22–24:2. If Phillips is correct in finding evidence of redactional activity in 20:22–26, this ought to be reflected also in 19:2b–8. Unfortunately, Phillips pays little attention to the source analysis of 19:2b–8.

5.4. The Source Analysis of Exodus 19

As the Sinai narrative comes to us, Exodus 19:2b–8 introduces the account of the theophany that dominates Exodus 19:1–25. Any attempt to understand the process by which 19:2b–8 was composed must take into consideration the whole chapter. For convenience we shall examine 19:1–15 and 19:16–25 separately, observing the natural break in the narrative that comes between verses 15 and 16.

Since the end of the nineteenth century scholars interested in the source analysis of Exodus 19:1–15 have tended to assign verses 3b–8 to a Deuteronomic editor, and verses 1–2a to P, with the remaining verses (verses 2b, 9–15) being attributed to J and E, the precise allocation of these latter verses being uncertain. While this analysis has been widely followed, its tentative nature is demonstrated by Van Seters who suggests that verses 2–11, 13a–15 originate from J (as he understands it) and verses 1, 12–13a from P.[33]

Exodus 19:1–2a, which provides the chronological and geographical settings for the events narrated in 19:1–15, is normally assigned to P. Whereas the initial verse dates the arrival of the Israelites at Sinai in relation to their departure from Egypt, verse 2 picks up the itinerary of the Israelites' journey by noting briefly their progress from the last named campsite at Rephidim (17:1; cf. 17:8). Since each verse performs a different function, there is no reason to view them as coming from separate sources (*contra*, on the one hand, Van Seters[34] who views the chronological statement of verse 1 as an addition from P, and, on the other hand, Durham[35] who considers verse 2 to have been inserted later). Under the Documentary Hypothesis, chronological notices are normally attributed to P. However, the formula in Exodus 19:1 is unique, the date being reckoned in terms of the time elapsed since the departure of the Israelites from Egypt, and not from the start of the calendar year as is

---

[33] 'Comparing Scripture with Scripture: Some Observations on the Sinai Pericope in Exodus 19–24', in G.M. Tucker, D.L. Petersen and R.R. Wilson (eds.), *Canon, Theology, and Old Testament Interpretation* (Philadelphia: Fortress Press, 1988), 112–4.

[34] Ibid., 112.

[35] *Exodus*, 261.

normally the case.[36] Given the distinctiveness of the chronological formula in verse 1, little weight should be assigned to it as a criterion for ascribing the origin of this verse to P.[37]

In spite of widespread support for finding Deuteronomic influence in Exodus 19:3b–8, none of the terms used to describe Israel's future status is found in exactly the same form in Deuteronomy. This is especially true of the expressions 'kingdom of priests' and 'holy nation' which occur only here in the whole of the OT. Although the term *sĕgullâ* 'treasured possession' is found in Deuteronomy 7:6; 14:2; 26:18, it comes in the distinctive expression '*am sĕgullâ* 'treasured people'. Even the comment about God carrying the Israelites on 'eagles' wings' (v. 4) is sufficiently different from that used in Deuteronomy 32:10–12 to suggest that they are not necessarily the product of a single author. Given the lack of clearly identifiable Deuteronomic language in verses 3b–8, the possibility of an alternative origin for these verses should not be dismissed.[38] This is supported by three further observations. First, as the Sinai narrative stands, verses 3b–8a perform an important function, establishing at the outset the Israelites' willingness to accept Yahweh's covenant. In spite of suggestions to the contrary, verses 3–8a are an integral part of the present section and there is no reason to view them as secondary. The divine speech is merely an invitation to enter into a covenant relationship and as such lacks a detailed presentation of the obligations that the Israelites were expected to keep.[39] Secondly, the parallels (noted above) between the introductions to the divine speeches in Exodus 19:3–6 and 20:22–24:2, and their narrative settings, suggest that the source analysis of Exodus 19:3b–8 cannot be decided in isolation. Significantly, however, the narrative framework surrounding Exodus 20:22–24:2 displays no obvious Deuteronomic characteristics. Thirdly, Weinfeld observes that Deuteronomy 7:6 is 'dependent on Exodus 19:5–6'.[40] These observations suggest that any similarities between Exodus 19:2b–8 and Deuteronomy are best explained by maintaining the priority of the Exodus material, rather than vice versa.

The account of Moses' return to Yahweh (verse 8b) and his subsequent reporting of the people's reply (v. 9c), clearly presuppose the events of verses 3–8a. Having received a favourable response, Yahweh instructs Moses regarding the

---

[36] Within the context of the book of Exodus as a whole the phrase, 'In the third month of the Israelites' going out from Egypt', must refer to (the day of) the third new moon since the Passover; this would then be the first day of the fourth month of the year, since the Passover took place on the fourteenth day of the first month (Ex. 12:2–6).

[37] Cf. Rendtorff, *Problem of the Process of Transmission*, 157–63.

[38] Cf. Patrick, 'The Covenant Code Source', 145–57, esp. 154–6.

[39] Cf. Ibid., 148–9.

[40] Weinfeld, *Deuteronomy 1–11*, 367. According to Weinfeld, Deuteronomy 7 presupposes also Exodus 23:23–33.

preparations necessary for the theophany which will occur prior to the sealing of the covenant (Ex. 19:10–13). The detailing of these preparations is clearly contingent upon the people having expressed their willingness to accept their role as outlined in Exodus 19:4–6. While verses 8b–15 have usually been assigned to J and E, no consensus has emerged regarding individual verses. As they stand verses 8b–15 form a coherent account and there is no need to attribute the material to two or more sources.[41] Moreover, these verses build well upon verses 3–8a, suggesting that they should all be assigned to the same source.

The second half of Exodus 19 falls into two main scenes: verses 16–19 are a vivid description of the divine theophany as observed by the people from below the mountain; verses 20–25 record a brief conversation between Yahweh and Moses that takes place at the top of the mountain. Both scenes build upon verses 1–15. The chronological notice in verse 16, referring to 'the third day', not only marks the beginning of a new episode, but immediately links this section to the preceding (cf. vv. 11, 15) by indicating that God's promise to come to Moses (verse 9) is about to be fulfilled. Similarly, Moses' reply in verse 23 clearly presupposes God's earlier instructions in verses 10–13.

As regards the source analysis of this section, only a very general consensus exists, with verses 16–20, 25 being assigned between J and E, and verses 21–24 being viewed as a later addition. Thus, Noth attributes verses 16aά, 18, 20 to J, and verses 16aβb, 17, 19 to E, with verses 21–25 being 'secondary additions'.[42] Hyatt assigns verses 16a, 18 to J, and verses 16b–17, 19, 25 to E, with verses 20–24 coming from the 'J supplementer'.[43] The uncertainty of this analysis is highlighted by Van Seters' willingness to attribute verses 16–19 to J and verses 20–25 to P.[44] While some scholars[45] find two separate accounts of a divine theophany here – a thunderstorm and a volcanic eruption – this is quite unnecessary. As Durham observes:

> The storm and fire imagery of vv. 16–19a is one part of an attempt to describe the indescribable experience of the coming of Yahweh. It is language recurrent in OT theophany accounts, and language rooted in Canaanite descriptions of the arrival of deity.[46]

---

[41] The general assumption, fostered especially by the Documentary Hypothesis, that parallel sources extend throughout most of the Pentateuch has tended to drive the quest for finding at least two sources in many passages.

[42] *Exodus*, 154–60.

[43] *Exodus*, 199–203.

[44] 'Comparing Scripture with Scripture', 113–14.

[45] E.g. M.L. Newman, *The People of the Covenant* (Nashville: Abingdon, 1962), 39–51; J.K. Kuntz, *The Self-Revelation of God* (Philadelphia: Westminster, 1967), 72–100.

[46] *Exodus*, 270; cf. R.J. Clifford, *The Cosmic Mountain in Canaan and the Old Testament*, (Cambridge, MA: Harvard University Press, 1972), 107–20; J.J. Niehaus, *God at Sinai* (Grand Rapids: Zondervan, 1995), 17–141.

Given the coherence of verses 16–19 and the lack of decisive criteria for distinguishing between J and E, there seems no reason to posit here two sources. Finally, since verses 16–19 presuppose the preceding episode, there is every reason to assign Exodus 19:1–19 to a single source.

This leaves the issue of the source analysis of Exodus 19:20–25 to be resolved. These verses form a coherent scene that is framed by comments about Moses ascending (verse 20) and descending (verse 25) the mountain. The unit forms a neat palistrophe:

A   Moses goes up   (v. 20)
    B   Yahweh speaks to Moses   (vv. 21–22)
        C   Moses replies   (v. 23)
    B´   Yahweh speaks to Moses   (v. 24)
A´   Moses goes down   (v. 25)

These verses, however, are widely viewed as a later insertion, interrupting the climax of the theophany and containing material that appears somewhat secondary to the account of Exodus 19. Why, it may be asked, should Moses at this stage be called up the mountain again, and why does God warn him yet again concerning the people coming up? To these questions may be added the following observations:

(a) Verses 20–25 contain no mention of the various signs of the theophany (e.g. cloud, lightning, fire) found in verses 16–19.
(b) The dialogue between Yahweh and Moses appears to be concerned with preparations for the theophany.
(c) According to Van Seters, 'there is no public legitimization of Moses as suggested in verse 9 as the point of Moses' role in the theophany, only a reprimand'.[47]
(d) The warning that the people are not to approach the mountain in verses 21–22 seems to be at odds with the later reaction of the people in standing at a distance in Exodus 20:18–21.[48]
(e) Noth[49] and Hyatt[50] suggest that Exodus 20:18–21 forms a better sequel to verses 16–19, with both Exodus 19:20–25 and 20:1–17 being considered to be later additions to the narrative. Rejecting the idea that the Decalogue is a later insertion, Durham views only Exodus 19:19b–25 as secondary, Exodus 20:1 being the natural sequel to 19:19a.[51]

---

[47] 'Comparing Scripture with Scripture', 113.
[48] Cf. G.C. Chirichigno, 'The Narrative Structure of Exodus 19–24', *Bib* 68 (1987), 472.
[49] *Exodus*, 168.
[50] *Exodus*, 217.
[51] *Exodus*, 283, 302.

These arguments in favour of the secondary nature of Exodus 19:20–25 must be weighed against a number of considerations that support the originality of this passage.

(a) Verses 20–25 presuppose knowledge of Yahweh's earlier instructions to Moses concerning the preparations necessary for the theophany; Moses' reply in verse 23 obviously alludes to the divine commands in verses 10–13. This indicates that verses 20–25 are unlikely to have had an independent existence outside their present context; they only make sense in the light of verses 9–15.

(b) Verses 20–25 are linked to the earlier part of Exodus 19 by two important motifs. First, Moses' mediating role in verses 20–25 is in keeping with God's earlier remarks in verse 9, which assume that Moses will continue to convey Yahweh's instructions to the Israelites. Verses 20–25 provide (*contra* Van Seters) a public legitimisation of Moses' role. Secondly, the dominant issue in the dialogue between Yahweh and Moses is the holiness of the mountain. Remarkably, while the theme of holiness is prominent in verses 10–15, it is completely absent from the description of the theophany in verses 16–19. Without verses 20–25 the narrative contains no mention of the mountain becoming holy as a result of Yahweh's presence.[52] Since the holiness of the mountain cannot be perceived by ordinary senses – in Exodus 3:4 Moses has to be told that the ground is holy – it is not surprising that Exodus 19:16–19 make no mention of the mountain's holy state. Verses 20–25 clearly complement the description of the theophany by focusing on the motif of holiness. The complementary nature of the two scenes probably also explains why verses 20–25 contain no reference to the signs of the theophany. Whereas the first scene abounds in narrative details and records no direct speech, the second has a bare minimum of narrative details and consists mainly of dialogue. This, however, does not necessarily mean that verses 16–19 and 20–25 come from different sources.

(c) The dialogue in verses 20–25 highlights another theme that lies at the very heart of the covenant relationship being established at Sinai. This concerns the obedience of the people. By commanding Moses to warn the Israelites against ascending the mountain, God implies that some of them at least tend towards disobedience rather than compliance. This will be highlighted later when they construct the golden calf (Ex. 32:1–8). God's warning in verses 20–25 casts a dark shadow across the positive response of the people in verse 8.

---

[52] This would be a remarkable omission in the light of the way Exodus 19 parallels the earlier theophany in Exodus 3:1–4:17.

(d) While the divine commands in verses 20–25 clearly echo those of verses 10–13, an important difference is introduced regarding the way in which those who transgress the boundary around the mountain will be punished. Whereas in verses 10–13 Moses is ordered to put to death by stoning or shooting those who touch the mountain, in verses 20–25 it is Yahweh himself who will 'break out' against anyone coming up the mountain. Since Yahweh will now punish any transgressors, this suggests that he has descended upon the mountain. Prior to the theophany, the responsibility for punishment rests with Moses and the people.

In the light of these considerations, the case for viewing Exodus 19:20–25 as secondary is not as strong as often suggested, and several recent commentators lean towards this conclusion. Childs suggests that verses 20–25 are a fitting part of the narrative, focusing on the preparations necessary 'for the deliverance of the law'.[53] In a similar vein, Fretheim appears to accept that verses 20–25 are an integral part of Exodus 19, forming 'an interlude between 19:19 and 20:1'.[54]

The preceding discussion highlights the ambiguous nature of scholarly attempts to uncover the sources underlying Exodus 19:1–25. In spite of frequent assertions to the contrary, the narrative displays substantial unity, and, but for an *a priori* belief that parallel sources were combined to form much of the Pentateuch, there is little evidence to suggest that the present narrative was composed through either several sources being combined or an early text being expanded by later redactional activity. As the chapter stands it may be read as a continuous account, with later verses building upon those which have gone before. Consequently, since the divine speech in Exodus 19:3–6 and its narrative framework (Ex. 19:2b, 7–8) cannot be excised from its present context without destroying the whole account, Exodus 19:2b–8 argues against, rather than for, the occurrence of redactional activity in the composition of the Sinai narrative.

5.5. Conclusion

At the outset of our investigation into the sources underlying Exodus 19:1–24:11 we observed the remarkable similarities between the narrative sections framing the divine speeches in Exodus 19:3–6 and 20:22–24:2. These, together with the parallels between Yahweh's speech in Exodus 20:22–24:2 and the following episode in 24:3–11, suggest that 20:21–24:11 was composed

---

[53] *Exodus*, 370.

[54] T.E. Fretheim, *Exodus* (Louisville: John Knox, 1991), 219–20.

by a single author.[55] Building on this, we proceeded to observe that Exodus 20:22 presupposes the direct proclamation of the Decalogue by Yahweh to the Israelites in 20:1–17 and the subsequent short episode in 20:18–21. Next, in the light of the parallels between the narrative frameworks surrounding the divine speeches in Exodus 19:3–6 and 20:22–24:2, we turned to consider the composition of Exodus 19. No evidence of redactional activity was found in connection with Exodus 19:2b–8. Rather, the whole of Exodus 19 displays signs of having been composed as a unified account.

These observations suggest that the narrative framework surrounding the divine speeches in Exodus 19:3–6 and 20:22–24:2 comes from the author who shaped the entire Sinai narrative in 19:1–24:11. As regards the composition of the Decalogue and the Book of the Covenant, this author may have taken over existing material. However, if he did so, he fully incorporated these two blocks of material into this account. Consequently, in spite of numerous statements to the contrary, the Sinai narrative in Exodus 19:1–24:11 appears to have been skilfully composed. As regards the date of composition, the limited evidence considered above indicates (a) that Exodus 19:1–24:11 already existed before the book of Deuteronomy was composed, and (b) that it could have been penned as early as the pre-monarchic period.

In spite of its restricted scope, the preceding discussion has important implications for current developments in Pentateuchal criticism. First, our study of the Sinai narrative provides no evidence to support the existence of the sources associated with the Documentary Hypothesis. While previous writers have sought to analyse the text on the basis of the criteria relating to the sources, J, E, D and P, this approach has failed to provide a consensus. Moreover, adherence to the Documentary Hypothesis has prevented scholars from observing the main compositional features of the text. These, as we have observed, suggest that a single author has skilfully composed the entire narrative. Secondly, while links have been observed with the book of Deuteronomy, these are best explained in terms of the priority of the Sinai narrative. Our analysis of the Sinai narrative showed there is no evidence of a Deuteronomistic revision having occurred; everything points towards Deuteronomy having been influenced by Exodus 19–24. On the basis of the Sinai narrative, there is no reason to suppose that the books of Genesis to Numbers were penned as a prologue to an already existing Deuteronomistic History.

---

[55] In saying this, it must be acknowledged that no evidence has been presented regarding Exodus 21:1–23:33. Our concern, however, is primarily with the composition of the narrative within which the Book of the Covenant is placed. A detailed discussion of the process by which the Book of the Covenant was composed would require much more space than is currently available, as evidenced by the various works cited in note 9, p.64.

6

The Future of Pentateuchal Studies

6.1. Looking to the Future

At this stage there is no telling how Pentateuchal studies will develop. Without new evidence, possibly from yet to be discovered extra-biblical sources, it is highly unlikely that biblical scholars will be able to uncover with any certainty the process by which the Pentateuch was created.[1] For the present we can but hope that contemporary scholars will learn from the shortcomings of their predecessors, and be more willing to acknowledge the tentative nature of their theories regarding how the Pentateuch came into being.

In this regard it is enlightening to consider the ongoing debate regarding the composition of the Synoptic Gospels. Even when NT scholars have the opportunity of comparing three similar and closely related texts, major and minor differences of opinion still exist as to how these texts were composed. If such is the case when we have a number of texts to compare, what would the situation be like if only one text were extant? Would, for example, NT scholars using only Matthew's Gospel have arrived at a solution similar to that proposed by proponents of Markan priority? Probably not. If doubts continue to exist over the composition of the Gospels, how can OT scholars with any confidence delineate correctly the sources underlying the books of the Pentateuch? Surely, the time has arrived to acknowledge seriously the limitations of source and form criticism and to avoid the construction of theories regarding the development of Israelite history and religion which rest primarily on the supposed sources of the Pentateuch.

As regards future developments, the following issues ought to receive consideration:

1. Since the introduction of source criticism in the mid-eighteenth century, the study of the Pentateuch has been dominated by diachronic considerations.

---

[1] For a detailed discussion of the problems surrounding the source analysis of Genesis 20–22, see Alexander, *Abraham in the Negev*.

As a result, considerable effort has been expended first on trying to explain how the Pentateuch was composed and then on applying these results to shed new light on the history of Israelite religion. The diachronic methods have had such a bewitching effect that scholars, by and large, have ignored completely a synchronic reading of the text. Indeed, many scholars find it difficult to read the Pentateuch as a unified continuous narrative. Moreover, the impression is strongly given that such a reading is not merely naive, but involves reverting from a two-dimensional view of the text to a one-dimensional view. However, as we have observed, the diachronic methods are not completely satisfactory, and their hypothetical results possibly provide no better a picture of Israelite history and religion than that available from a synchronic reading of the Pentateuch. The time has come to take more seriously a synchronic approach, especially given recent progress in understanding how biblical narratives are constructed.[2]

2. The issue of historical accuracy must remain open. Various studies have rightly highlighted the inadequacy of some attempts to support an early date for parts of the Pentateuch.[3] While this has had the effect of increasing historical scepticism towards the books of Genesis to Deuteronomy, it ought to be recognised that the dismissal of poor arguments for the historicity of these books does not prove that the Pentateuch records fiction rather than fact. Unfortunately, many scholars have become so acclimatised to dating the Pentateuchal material in the monarchic or post-monarchic periods that attempts to date it earlier are generally dismissed without being given adequate consideration. Moreover, the nature of the material in Genesis to Deuteronomy makes it highly unlikely that we shall find reports of these events in the relatively few contemporary non-biblical documents which have so far been uncovered by archaeologists. For example, the biblical narrative places the patriarchs in approximately the twenty-first to nineteenth centuries BC and portrays them as semi-nomadic herdsmen who

---

[2] Cf. e.g. J. Licht, *Storytelling in the Bible* (Jerusalem: Magnes, 1978); R. Alter, *The Art of Biblical Narrative* (New York: Basic Books, 1981); M. Sternberg, *The Poetics of Biblical Narrative: Ideological Literature and the Drama of Reading* (Indianapolis: Indiana University Press, 1985); S. Bar-Efrat, *Narrative Art in the Bible* (Sheffield: Almond, 1989); H.C. Brichto, *Toward a Grammar of Biblical Poetics* (Oxford: Oxford University Press, 1992); D.M. Gunn and D.N. Fewell, *Narrative in the Hebrew Bible* (Oxford: Oxford University Press, 1993).

[3] E.g. T.L. Thompson, *The Historicity of the Patriarchal Narratives* (BZAW 133; Berlin: de Gruyter, 1974); J. Van Seters, *Abraham in History and Tradition*. See also the series of articles in A.R. Millard and D.J. Wiseman (eds.), *Essays on the Patriarchal Narratives* (Leicester: IVP, 1980), and more recently G.J. Wenham, *Genesis 16–50* (Dallas: Word, 1994), xx–xxviii.

may have engaged in limited agriculture. After almost four millennia there is little reason to expect that we shall uncover archaeological evidence that relates directly to their existence. In these circumstances, 'absence of evidence is no evidence of absence'. Unfortunately, some scholars exploit for their own reasons the inadequacy of the very limited evidence that is available. Such an approach is ultimately as defective as that which claims more than the available evidence supports.[4]

3. In spite of the long-standing tradition that the first five books of the Bible belong together, it needs to be recognised that they are intimately connected to the books which follow them. As they stand, the books of Genesis to Kings form a continuous narrative. This is apparent from both the overall picture provided and the way in which individual books are linked together. Viewed as a whole, Genesis to Kings records selected events from the creation of the earth to the demise of the Davidic monarchy at the time of the Babylonian exile. Later books in the sequence presuppose that the reader is already familiar with those that have gone before. For example, the introductory verses of Exodus assume a knowledge of the Joseph story. References to the deaths of Moses and Joshua at the very start of the books of Joshua and Judges respectively serve the purpose of linking these books with those immediately preceding.[5] Whatever the prior oral and/or literary history of the individual books it is obvious that they have been deliberately linked together to form a continuous narrative. On the basis of content and language, we may with reasonable confidence assume that all this material was brought together to form this continuous narrative shortly after 562 BC, the date of Jehoiachin's release from prison in Babylon (2 Kgs. 25:27–30).[6] Given the unity of Genesis to Kings, the composition of the Pentateuch must be discussed in conjunction with that of the books of Joshua to Kings.[7] This, however, does not imply that the contents of the Pentateuch only came into being during the exilic period.

[4] A very helpful discussion of the whole subject of biblical historiography is provided by V.P. Long, *The Art of Biblical History* (Leicester: Apollos, 1994).

[5] Many more examples could be added to this short list.

[6] For a recent defence of this dating based on linguistic considerations, see A. Hurvitz, 'The Historical Quest for "Ancient Israel" and the Linguistic Evidence of the Hebrew Bible: Some Methodological Observations', *VT* 47 (1997), 301–15.

[7] Cf. J.G. McConville, 'The Old Testament Historical Books in Modern Scholarship', *Them* 22 (1997), 3–13; cf. C. Westermann, *Die Geschichtsbücher des Alten Testaments: gab es ein deuteronomistisches Geschichtswerk?* (Theologische Bücherei 87 AT; Gütersloh: Chr. Kaiser, 1994). Westermann argues that there was a pre-Deuteronomistic narrative extending from Exodus to Kings which associated the beginning of the nation's history with the exodus from Egypt.

6.2. Why was the Pentateuch Composed?

While scholars have expended considerable energy in seeking to determine the origins of the Pentateuch, it has to be acknowledged that they have tended to ignore the question, why was the Pentateuch composed? Yet, this question is as important as the issue of how the Pentateuch came into being. The 'why' question is also likely to be of greater interest to those who seek to read the Pentateuch from a theological perspective. What follows is a tentative step towards addressing this issue afresh.

As we have observed the Pentateuch cannot be easily separated from the books of Joshua to Kings. While Noth's theory of a Deuteronomistic History is not without problems, it highlights the close links that exist between the book of Deuteronomy and those books that come after it. Unfortunately, OT scholars rarely read and comment on the books of Genesis to Kings as a unified narrative; attention is usually given to either the Tetrateuch/Pentateuch or the Deuteronomistic History. Those who do comment on Genesis to Kings as a whole are inclined to describe it as a record of the history of the people of Israel. This is implied by R.N. Whybray who remarks that the Pentateuch is 'a history of the origins of the people of Israel, prefaced by an account of the origins of the world', which may have been intended as a 'supplement (i.e. a prologue) to the work of the Deuteronomistic Historian, which dealt with the more recent period of the national history'.[8] According to C. Houtman, Genesis to Kings 'presents itself as a description of Israel's history from the perspective of its calling and its continual unfaithfulness'.[9] E.T. Mullen has recently proposed that the Tetrateuch was composed as a prologue to the Deuteronomistic History in order to provide 'a narrative foundation for the reformulation and maintenance of "Israelite" ethnic and national identity in the Second Temple period'.[10]

The idea that the books of Genesis to Kings were brought together to provide an account of Israel's history seems an obvious explanation for their redactional unity. Beginning in Genesis we trace the growth of Israel from the initial call of Abraham through to the establishment of his descendants as a nation in the land of Canaan. Years of struggle and frustration eventually give way to a time of stability and splendour during the reigns of David and Solomon. Thereafter, the nation's history is marked by decline, leading eventually to the overthrow of the kingdom of Judah at the hands of the Babylonians.

---

[8] Whybray, *Making of the Pentateuch*, 242.

[9] C. Houtman, 'The Pentateuch', in A.S. van der Woude (ed.), *The World of the Old Testament* (Vol. 2; Grand Rapids: Eerdmans, 1989), 200.

[10] *Ethnic Myths and Pentateuchal Foundations*, 327.

Central to the development of the theme of nationhood in Genesis to Kings are the divine promises announced to Abraham (strictly speaking Abram) in Genesis 12:1–3. These play a major role in linking together the books of Genesis to Kings by setting the agenda for most of what follows. Summoning Abraham to leave his family and homeland, the LORD promises, 'I will make you into a great nation' (Gen. 12:2). Several chapters later this promise of nationhood is developed more fully and confirmed by a covenant that focuses on two areas: numerous descendants (Gen. 15:1–6) and land (Gen. 15:7–21).

The divine promise of land is renewed with Abraham's immediate descendants, Isaac and Jacob (cf. Gen. 26:3; 28:13; 35:12; cf. 28:4; 48:4; 50:24). In Exodus God's promise of land to Abraham, Isaac and Jacob is mentioned on various occasions (Gen. 2:24; 6:4, 5; 13:11; 33:11; cf. Lev. 26:42; Deut. 34:4) and there are several allusions to the covenant of Genesis 15 (Ex. 3:8, 17; 13:5; 23:23; 33:2; in these passages the peoples of Genesis 15:19–21 are named; cf. Deut. 1:7; 7:1; 20:17). In the light of the specific references to slavery and release in Genesis 15:13–14, it is hardly surprising that this covenant features prominently in Exodus. Indeed, God's deliverance of the Israelites from Egypt is directly linked in Exodus 2:24 to his covenant with Abraham. Later, after the Israelites are punished for making the golden calf, the renewal of the Sinai covenant is once again based on the promises made to Abraham, Isaac and Jacob concerning land (cf. Ex. 32:13). Preparations for taking possession of the land are prominent in the book of Numbers. Occupation is delayed, however, through the unbelief and rebellion of the people. Nevertheless, after the death of all the adult Israelites who left Egypt, excluding Joshua and Caleb, the imminent fulfilment of the promise of land is anticipated in the later chapters of Numbers and the book of Deuteronomy. The books of Joshua, Judges and Samuel, up to the reigns of David and Solomon, record the gradual completion of this process.

The promise of land and its fulfilment is clearly important in the books of Genesis to Samuel. The same is true as regards the promise of descendants, the other aspect of becoming a great nation. A recurring theme in the patriarchal narratives is God's role in overcoming the barrenness of the matriarchs, Sarah, Rebekah and Rachel (Gen. 21:1; 25:21; 30:22–24). In the opening chapter of Exodus the remarkable increase of the Israelites causes resentment in Egypt and leads to the repressive policy of the Pharaoh (Ex. 1:6–10). Later, as the Israelites prepare to enter the land of Canaan, Moses acknowledges that the promise of Genesis 15:5 has been fulfilled: 'The LORD your God has increased your numbers so that today you are as many as the stars of the sky' (Deut. 1:10; cf. 10:22; 28:62; Neh. 9:23). While the topic of population growth is less prominent in the books of Joshua to Kings, it is specifically noted that during the reign of Solomon

'the people of Judah and Israel were as numerous as the sand on the seashore'
(1 Kgs. 4:20; cf. 2 Sam. 17:11).

Whereas the books of Genesis to Samuel describe the gradual fulfilment of
the divine promise of nationhood to Abraham, Kings charts the reversal of
this process. Beginning with Solomon the narrative describes how the failure
of both monarchy and people leads to the loss of territory and the deportation
of many citizens. Of significance is the fact that these later events are anticipated even before the Israelites enter the promised land (cf. Deut. 28:64–68;
30:1, 4). However, there are indications that the loss of land and population
is not the final chapter in God's dealings with Israel (cf. Deut. 30:1–5; 1 Kgs.
8:46–51).

This brief survey reveals that the theme of nationhood plays a major role in
linking together the books of Genesis to Kings. While in no way wishing to
diminish the importance of this theme, it is paralleled by another concept
which is as important, if not more so, for understanding the redactional unity
of the books of Genesis to Kings. This parallel theme concerns a king through
whom the nations of the earth will be blessed.

While scholars have long recognised the importance of the promise of
nationhood in Genesis, they have failed, by and large, to observe that Genesis
also focuses on a divinely promised royal 'seed'. This failure results, in part at
least, from a general tendency to neglect the final form of Genesis in favour of
source and form critical approaches. When, however, Genesis is viewed as a
literary unity, there can be little doubt that it is especially interested in
pointing towards the coming of a unique king. Viewed against this background, the theme of kingship in the books of Exodus to Kings takes on a
new dimension.

Although the promise of nationhood (i.e. land and descendants) is a central
feature of the patriarchal narratives in Genesis, it is not the only promise highlighted. The LORD says to Abraham:

> Leave your country, your people and your father's household and go to the land
> I will show you, so that I may make you into a great nation and bless you and make
> your name great. Be a blessing, so that I may bless those who bless you, and curse the
> one who disdains you, and so that all the families of the ground may be blessed
> through you (Gen. 12:1–3; my translation).

This statement falls naturally into two halves, each introduced by an
imperative. Whereas the first part focuses primarily on the promise of nationhood, the second centres chiefly on the blessing of others. The entire speech
comes to a climax in the statement: 'so that all the families of the ground may
be blessed through you'. The promise that Abraham will become a 'great
nation' is of secondary importance to God's principal desire to bless all the

families of the ground.[11] Thus, the primary motive behind the call of Abraham is God's intention to bless, rather than curse, humanity. By commanding him to leave his homeland and be a blessing, God places the onus on Abraham to obey in order that the promises concerning nationhood and blessing may be fulfilled.

As we have already observed, the fulfilment of the promise of nationhood is later guaranteed through the divine covenant made with Abraham in Genesis 15. A further covenant is introduced in Genesis 17.[12] Most commentators, unfortunately, focus on the sign of the covenant, circumcision, without noting that the essence of this covenant lies in the promise that Abraham will be the 'father of many nations' (Gen. 17:4–5). Since this promise is later associated with Sarah – 'she will be the mother of nations' (Gen. 17:16) – it is unlikely that it includes the nations descended from Abraham through his relationships with Hagar (cf. Gen. 17:20) and Keturah (Gen. 25:1–4). The OT, however, is remarkably silent concerning the idea that Abraham would be the biological ancestor of different nations. In the light of this, we should observe that the Hebrew word *'āb* (*'āv*) 'father' is sometimes 'used of a variety of social roles that carried authority or exercised a protective or caring function. It could be used of a prophet (2 Kgs. 6:21), priest (Judg. 18:19), king (1 Sam. 24:11), or governor (Isa. 22:20–21).'[13] By taking *'āb* in this non-biological sense, we may understand Genesis 17:4–5 as stating that Abraham will be the 'father of many nations' not because these nations are his physical descendants but because he will be for them a channel of divine blessing.[14] As N.M. Sarna observes, the phrase 'father of many nations' 'has a more universal application in that a large

---

[11] On the importance of the promise of blessing, see V.P. Hamilton, 'Genesis: Theology of', *NIDOTTE*, 4:667; P.R. Williamson, *Abraham, Israel and the Nations: the Patriarchal Promise and its Covenantal Development in Genesis* (JSOTSS 315; Sheffield: Sheffield Academic Press, 2000), 217–59.

[12] While the covenant of Genesis 15 focuses primarily on nationhood (land and descendants), the covenant in Genesis 17 highlights Abraham's special status as regards the nations. Unfortunately, biblical scholars have tended to blur the differences between these two covenants, some viewing them as parallel accounts of the same covenant, preserved in different sources. For a fuller discussion of the Abraham narrative, see chapter twelve and the recent study by Williamson, *Abraham, Israel and the Nations*.

[13] C.J.H. Wright, 'אָב (*'āb*)', *NIDOTTE*, 1:219.

[14] This understanding of 'father' is probably reflected in the unusual comment that Joseph was 'father to Pharaoh' (Gen. 45:8). Furthermore, when God blesses Jacob in Genesis 35:11, echoing an earlier blessing by Isaac upon Jacob (Gen. 28:3), a distinction is drawn between 'a nation' and 'a community of nations' coming from him. The implication would seem to be that whereas many nations will be closely associated with him, only one nation will be directly descended from him.

segment of humanity looks upon Abraham as its spiritual father'.[15] This non-biological understanding of *'āb* 'father' is supported by the fact that Abraham is instructed to circumcise those who are not his offspring; this includes those born in his 'household or bought with money from a foreigner' (Gen. 17:12–13). This suggests that circumcision, and the covenant associated with it, was never intended to be a sign of racial purity. Later in Genesis the men of Shechem undergo circumcision in order to establish a bond of kinship with Abraham's descendants (Gen. 34:14–17). This makes their subsequent slaughter by Simeon and Levi all the more reprehensible.

Although all the male members of Abraham's household are circumcised, including Ishmael, the LORD emphasises that the covenant will be established with Isaac, and him alone (Gen. 17:19, 21). The uniqueness of Isaac's position regarding this covenant is underlined by the exclusion of Ishmael even though he is also circumcised.[16] This introduces an important distinction between those who may enjoy the benefits of this covenant and the one through whom the covenant will be established. Whereas the former includes all who are circumcised, the latter appears to be restricted to a single line of descendants. On this we shall have more to say below.

The Abraham narrative moves towards an important climax in Genesis 22. After testing Abraham's obedience by demanding that he sacrifice his much loved son, Isaac, the episode concludes with a divine oath (Gen. 22:16–18). This oath corresponds closely with the initial divine speech in Genesis 12:1–3, framing the main section of the Abraham narrative, and possibly also marks the ratification of the covenant announced in Genesis 17.[17] As it stands, the LORD's proclamation to Abraham falls into two distinctive parts; whereas the first half affirms that Abraham's 'seed' will become very numerous, the second half asserts that Abraham's 'seed' will defeat his enemies and mediate blessing to the nations of the earth. While each half of the oath refers to 'seed', syntactical considerations strongly suggest that in the second half, in contrast to the first, the term 'seed' denotes a single descendant of Abraham.[18]

---

[15] N.M. Sarna, *Genesis* (The JPS Torah Commentary; Philadelphia: Jewish Publication Society, 1989), 124.

[16] Cf. Genesis 21:12. A similar pattern may be observed concerning Esau and Jacob. The covenant is established with Jacob, but not Esau. The importance of Abraham, Isaac and Jacob as successive recipients of the divine covenant is reflected in the way that they are mentioned together in later passages.

[17] See T.D. Alexander, 'Genesis 22 and the Covenant of Circumcision', *JSOT* 25 (1983), 17–22; Williamson, *Abraham, Israel and the Nations*, 234–59.

[18] See T.D. Alexander, 'Further Observations on the Term "Seed" in Genesis', *TynBul* 48 (1997), 363–7; this builds on J. Collins, 'A Syntactical Note (Genesis 3:15): Is the Woman's Seed Singular or Plural?' *TynBul* 48 (1997), 139–48.

In other words, God swears that the nations will be blessed through one of Abraham's descendants rather than through all of them collectively. Moreover, this individual will be victorious over his enemies.[19]

This emphasis upon a single descendant takes on special significance when viewed against the whole of Genesis. Several distinctive literary features reveal that the book of Genesis traces the development of a unique line of 'seed' beginning with Adam and ending with Jacob/Israel and his twelve sons.[20] One of these features is the *tôlĕdot* formulae ('These are the generations of ...'),[21] which, in part, functions like the zoom lens on a camera by focusing attention on a single individual and his immediate descendants. Used in conjunction with the linear genealogies found in Genesis 5 and 11, the *tôlĕdot* formulae enable the Genesis narrative to follow the progress of a unique family line which includes Enoch, Methuselah, Noah, Abraham, Isaac and Jacob.

Linked to the *tôlĕdot* formulae in terms of purpose is the Hebrew word *zera'* 'seed' which is used in Genesis as a keyword; it occurs throughout Genesis 59 times compared to 170 times in the rest of the OT. Genesis draws attention to the existence of a distinctive line of 'seed' which begins with Seth, the third born son to Adam and Eve (cf. Gen. 4:25), and concludes by highlighting in particular the importance of both Perez, the son born as a result of Judah's unusual relationship with Tamar (Gen. 38:27–29), and Ephraim, the younger of Joseph's two sons (Gen. 48:1–22).[22] Throughout Genesis, and especially in the patriarchal narratives, special care is taken to establish the identity of those who belong to this line of seed; occasionally this results in a first-born son being passed over in favour of a younger sibling.[23]

When due attention is given to the *tôlĕdot* formulae and the keyword *zera'*, it becomes evident that the book of Genesis in its final form anticipates the coming of a royal saviour through whom God's blessing will be mediated to all the nations of the earth.[24] The existence of such an individual is first intimated in Genesis 3:14–15 when the LORD God comments to the serpent:

---

[19] These ideas are developed in Psalm 72 which clearly associated the blessing of the nations with the universal rule of a future Davidic king.

[20] See T.D. Alexander, 'From Adam to Judah: the Significance of the Family Tree in Genesis', *EvQ* 61 (1989), 5–19; *idem* 'Genealogies, Seed and the Compositional Unity of Genesis', *TynBul* 44 (1993), 255–270. These ideas are developed more fully in chapter 8.

[21] Genesis 2:4; 5:1; 6:9; 10:1; 11:10, 27; 25:12, 19; 36:1, 9; 37:2.

[22] See chapter 9 for a fuller discussion of the significance of the terms *tôlĕdot* and *zera'* in Genesis.

[23] Seth takes priority over Cain (Gen. 5:3), Isaac over Ishmael (Gen. 21:12), Jacob over Esau (Gen. 27:36).

[24] A fuller discussion of this comes in chapters 9 and 10.

Cursed are you above all the livestock and all the wild animals! You will crawl on your belly and you will eat dust all the days of your life. And I will put enmity between you and the woman, and between your seed and her seed; he will crush your head, and you will strike his heel (NIV translation, altered slightly).

Although modern trends in OT scholarship have led many writers to reject the idea that the 'seed of the woman' refers to an individual, the case for such an interpretation remains strong,[25] especially if one takes into account Collins' recent observations on the syntax of Genesis 3:15.[26] While Genesis 3:15 does not explicitly state that this individual will be of royal status, W. Wifall notes interesting links with various expressions found in 'royal' Psalms, and these he takes as indicating a Davidic or royal background to Genesis 3:15.[27]

The linear genealogies in Genesis 5 and 11 trace the 'seed of the woman' to Abraham, through whom God promises to bless all the families of the ground (Gen. 12:1–3). This same promise probably underlies the covenant of circumcision and the idea that Abraham will be the 'father of many nations'. Although this covenant is made first with Abraham, it is clearly orientated towards the future. The LORD states that it will be established with Abraham's 'seed' 'for the generations to come' (Gen. 17:7). Furthermore, the establishment of the covenant is linked specifically to Isaac. Later, as we have already observed, the LORD swears an oath to Abraham, presumably in Isaac's presence, that all the nations of the earth will be blessed through his 'seed' (Gen. 22:18). The fulfilment of this divine oath, which is unique within the Pentateuch, also lies in the future.

The Abraham narrative clearly builds on the divine promise given in Genesis 3:15 regarding the 'seed of the woman' overcoming the 'seed of the serpent'. The motif of blessing which is very prominent in Genesis 12:1–3 stands in marked contrast to that of cursing which dominates the divine judgements announced in Genesis 3. In addition, the 'royal' nature of the line of

---

[25] Cf. T.D. Alexander, 'Messianic Ideology in the Book of Genesis', in P.E. Satterthwaite, R.S. Hess and G.J. Wenham (eds.) *The Lord's Anointed: Interpretation of Old Testament Messianic Texts* (Grand Rapids/Carlisle: Baker/Paternoster, 1995), 27–32.

[26] Collins, 'A Syntactical Note (Genesis 3:15)'.

[27] According to W. Wifall, 'David is addressed as God's "anointed" or "messiah" (Ps. 89:21, 39; 2 Sam. 22:51) whose "seed" will endure forever under God's favor (Ps. 89:5, 30, 37). As Yahweh has crushed the ancient serpent "Rahab" (Ps. 89:11), so now David and his sons will crush their enemies in the dust beneath their feet (Ps. 89:24; 2 Sam. 22:37–43) ... In Psalm 72:9, the foes of the Davidic king are described as "bowing down before him" and "licking the dust." In the familiar "messianic" Psalms, God is described as having placed "all things under his feet" (Ps. 8:6) and will make "your enemies your footstool" (Ps. 110:1)'; see 'Gen 3:15 – A Protevangelium?' *CBQ* 36 (1974), 363.

seed becomes more explicit within the Abraham story. At the outset this is reflected in the promise that Abraham's name will 'become great'.[28] Although he is nowhere designated a king, Abraham is presented in various episodes as enjoying a status similar to that of contemporary monarchs (Gen. 14:1–24; 21:22–34; 23:6). Furthermore, the LORD specifically promises Abraham that 'kings will come from you' (Gen. 17:6; cf. 17:16).

The theme of royalty is less evident in Genesis 25–36. Isaac, like his father Abraham, enters into a covenant with Abimelech, king of Gerar (Gen. 26:26–31). Upon his return from Paddan Aram, Jacob receives the divine promise that 'kings will come from your body' (Gen. 35:11). The existence of a future monarchy in Israel is also suggested by the brief comment in Genesis 36:31: 'These were the kings who reigned in Edom before any Israelite king reigned.'

In marked contrast, kingship is important in the account of Joseph's life, being the dominant motif in the two dreams which he experiences (Gen. 37:5–11). Although his brothers, filled with jealousy and hatred, remark, 'Do you intend to reign over us? Will you actually rule us?' Joseph's father 'kept the matter in mind'. In spite of the brothers' attempt to rid themselves of Joseph, he later emerges from an Egyptian prison to become second only to Pharaoh in authority over the kingdom of Egypt (Gen. 41:39–43). Ironically, when some years later Joseph's older brothers travel to Egypt, the narrative records how they bow before him with their faces to the ground (Gen. 42:6). In due course, however, Joseph reveals his identity to them, and remarks how God has made him 'father to Pharaoh, lord of his entire household and ruler of all Egypt' (Gen. 45:8; cf. 45:9, 26).

In the light of Genesis as a whole, Joseph clearly plays a major role by being one of the 'first-born' through whom God's blessing is imparted to others.[29] The importance of his family line is further underlined when Joseph brings his two sons, Manasseh and Ephraim, to the elderly and frail Jacob in order to have them blessed. As has happened previously in Genesis, the younger of the two boys, Ephraim, receives the superior blessing, in this way confirming the importance of his family line for the fulfilment of God's purposes. Later, when the Israelites come to take possession of the promised land, it is an Ephraimite, Joshua, who successfully leads the twelve tribes across the Jordan to their new home.[30]

---

[28] Cf. Wenham, *Genesis 1–15*, 275–6; V.P. Hamilton, *The Book of Genesis: Chapters 1–17* (NICOT; Grand Rapids: Eerdmans, 1990), 372–3.

[29] On the status of Joseph as Jacob's first-born, see chapter 9.

[30] Although Joshua is never given the title of king, it is interesting to observe that his success as a leader is directly associated with his obedience to the 'Book of the Law' (Jos. 1:8). According to Deuteronomy 17:18–19, the king was expected to 'write for himself on a scroll a copy of this law' and 'to read it all the days of his life'.

Although the account of Joseph's life dominates Genesis 37–50, when in old age Jacob gathers his sons around him to tell them what will happen in days to come (cf. Gen. 49:1), kingship appears to be associated with the descendants of Judah (cf. Gen. 49:8–12), and not Joseph (cf. Gen. 49:22–26). While the poetic language of Genesis 49 makes it possible for differing interpretations to be placed upon Jacob's remarks, viewed against the background of Genesis as a whole, these verses clearly point to a powerful future ruler to whom the nations will submit in obedience.[31]

In the light of this the earlier description of the birth of Judah's son, Perez, takes on added significance. Recorded in Genesis 38, the story of Judah's unseemly relationship with Tamar interrupts unexpectedly the account of Joseph's arrival in Egypt. Not only does Genesis 38 divert attention away from Joseph, but also, significantly, it picks up on the important theme of the continuation of the family line.[32] Remarkably, the story concludes with a brief description of the birth of twins, during which the younger, Perez, breaks out in front of the first-born, Zerah (Gen. 38:28–30). Taking into account the location and central theme of Genesis 38, the symbolism of this birth account should not be overlooked, especially given, as we shall observe below, the much later divine rejection of the line of Joseph–Ephraim in favour of the line of Judah.

The account of the Israelites' divine deliverance from bondage in Egypt and their journey towards the promised land dominates the books of Exodus to Deuteronomy. While the theme of kingship surfaces only rarely in these books (e.g. Num. 24:17–19; Deut. 17:14–20), it becomes much more prominent in Joshua and Judges. These books anticipate the establishment of a monarchy in Israel by focusing on the divine provision of spirit-empowered deliverers. Although those appointed by God as leaders fulfil many of the tasks of a king, they are prohibited from creating royal dynasties, as highlighted in the story of Gideon's son, Abimelech (Judg. 9:1–57). The picture in Judges of ever increasing moral and spiritual decline comes to a climax in the final four chapters of the book. These are framed by the significant refrain, 'in those days Israel had no king; everyone did as he saw fit' (Judg. 17:6; 21:25; cf. 18:1; 19:1).

Although the books of Genesis and Joshua give prominence of the line of Joseph, traced through Ephraim, thereafter things appear to fall apart for the Ephraimites. As the book of Judges reveals, during the time of Jephthah, the Ephraimites not only fail to take the lead in delivering the Israelites from their

---

[31] Cf. Alexander, 'Messianic Ideology in the Book of Genesis', 32–7. In passing, we should observe that the reign of this destined king will be marked by a time of abundant fruitfulness, a sign of divine blessing.

[32] This is developed more fully in chapter 8.

enemies, but they also aggressively oppose others who do so successfully (Judg. 12:1–7). As a consequence, 42,000 Ephraimites are slaughtered at the fords of the Jordan.

The eventual rejection by God of Ephraim as the anticipated royal line comes to the fore in the early chapters of Samuel. Here the narrative focuses on events associated with the temple at Shiloh in the region of Ephraim, describing how God distances himself from the hereditary priesthood associated with the sanctuary. The final stage, in what appears to have been a long process, comes when the ark of the covenant is taken in battle by the Philistines. The significance of this event is poignantly captured by the dying remarks of Eli's daughter-in-law when she names her son Ichabod because, 'The glory has departed from Israel' (1 Sam. 4:21).

Although 1 Samuel goes on to describe the appointment of Saul as the first king of Israel, due to his own shortcomings, he is soon replaced by David, the youngest son of Jesse, a descendant of Judah.[33] When David is eventually enthroned as king over all Israel, he establishes Jerusalem as his capital and in due course brings there the ark of the covenant. This event, among other things, confirms God's choice of David as king. Soon afterwards the LORD makes a covenant with David in which he promises to establish David's dynasty for ever (2 Sam. 7).

The reign of David's son Solomon provides an interesting picture of the kind of rule which God intends to establish through the promised 'seed' of Abraham. Under Solomon the people experience peace, justice and prosperity. Unfortunately, Solomon fails to remain loyal to the LORD and the kingdom is partitioned following his death, with the house of David keeping control of only the region of Judah. Throughout the book of Kings God's promise to establish David's dynasty for ever stands in tension with his warning that he will punish the disobedience of David's ancestors. Eventually, Kings records the destruction of the Jerusalem temple and the removal of king Jehoiachin to Babylon. While this marks the end of the Davidic dynasty's rule over Jerusalem, the final episode in the book of Kings focuses on the release of Jehoiachin from prison, an event that clearly symbolises the possibility of the throne being restored to David's line.

The preceding survey reveals, if somewhat sketchily, that within the books of Genesis to 2 Kings the divine promise of a royal saviour plays a more important role than the promise of nationhood.[34] Yet, in spite of this, the

---

[33] The significance of David's ancestry for the fulfilment of the divine promises announced in Genesis is highlighted in the book of Ruth; cf. E.H. Merrill, 'The Book of Ruth: Narration and Shared Themes', *BS* 142 (1985), 130–9.

[34] Although the promises of nationhood and royal saviour are distinctive, it would be a mistake to divorce them from each other.

pledge of a royal saviour remains unfulfilled by the end of Kings. Nevertheless, some progress towards fulfilment occurs as the line of 'seed' introduced in Genesis is traced through to the creation of the Davidic dynasty. Furthermore, following the establishment of David as king over Israel, God makes a covenant with him confirming that through his lineage the nations of the earth will be blessed (2 Sam. 7:5–16; 1 Chr. 17:4–14).[35] As the book of Kings reveals, however, the cumulative disobedience of David's descendants appears to thwart the fulfilment of God's promise to bless the nations. There are, however, strong indications in Kings that the removal of the house of David from the throne in Jerusalem is not the end of the story. Although God punishes with complete justification the sins of David's descendants, the hope remains that there will yet be a 'son of David' through whom the nations will experience God's favour.[36]

Since the books of Genesis to Kings, as a coherent narrative, cannot have existed prior to the exilic period, the events of the exile may well have been catalytic in bringing these books together into a continuous account. This does not automatically mean, however, that the tradition of a divinely promised royal saviour originated after 587 BC. The eighth-century prophets were already familiar with this idea, as reflected, for example, in the final chapter of Amos and in Isaiah 7–11. From a different perspective, it is worth observing that it would require an author of exceptional genius and religious optimism to compose these books *ab initio* after the demise of the Davidic monarchy and the destruction of the temple in Jerusalem.

Viewed from this perspective the books of Genesis to Kings take on a new dimension in terms of their importance for understanding the development of messianic ideology within the OT. For the Christian this is important in the light of NT claims that the coming of Jesus Christ fulfils what is written in the Law of Moses, the Prophets and the Psalms (e.g. Lk. 24:44; cf. Mt. 5:17; Lk. 24:27). Although human curiosity will undoubtedly prompt scholars to ask how the Pentateuch was composed, it is vitally important that we should

---

[35] For a fuller discussion of the Davidic covenant and in particular the expression 'and this is the law of mankind' (2 Sam. 7:19), see T.E. McComiskey, *The Covenants of Promise: A Theology of Old Testament Covenants* (Grand Rapids: Baker, 1985), 21–35. O.P. Robertson, *The Christ of the Covenants* (Phillipsburg, NJ: Presbyterian and Reformed, 1980), 33–4, notes that the bringing of the ark to Jerusalem is linked by David to the covenant promised to Abraham (1 Chr. 16:15–18). Further links between David and Abraham are discussed by R.E. Clements, *Abraham and David: Genesis XV and Its Meaning for Israelite Tradition* (Studies in Biblical Theology; 2nd Series 5; London: SCM, 1967).

[36] This hope is articulated in many of the prophetic books of the OT. Cf. T.D. Alexander, *The Servant King: the Bible's Portrait of the Messiah* (Leicester: IVP, 1998), 89–120.

not lose sight of the question, why was the Pentateuch composed? While the 'how' question is never likely to be answered with complete certainty, the 'why' question directs us to the one who is the source of all true knowledge.

Part 2
The Main Themes of the Pentateuch

7

An Overview of the Pentateuch

Before embarking on a fuller study of the individual books which compose the Pentateuch, it may be helpful to provide a brief overview of the whole, highlighting in the process those themes which will be examined in more detail in subsequent chapters.

As presently constituted the Pentateuch consists of five books which have been composed in the light of each other to form a single unit. Various factors reveal the interdependence of the individual books. Primary among these is the plot which begins in Genesis and flows logically through to the end of Deuteronomy. Certain threads run through this plot uniting the different books. For example, Genesis introduces the idea that the land of Canaan is promised to the descendants of Abraham, Isaac and Jacob. The fulfilment of this promise sets the agenda for the books of Exodus to Deuteronomy, and beyond. Although the land is promised to Abraham, Isaac and Jacob, it is anticipated that their descendants will only take possession of it following a long stay in Egypt (Gen. 15:13–16). Thus, the Joseph story records how the early Israelites leave Canaan to settle temporarily in Egypt. Here, however, as the opening chapters of Exodus reveal, the Egyptians enslave the Israelites, until, through divine intervention, the Israelites are enabled to flee the country. Their subsequent journey through the wilderness towards Canaan is narrated in Exodus, Leviticus and Numbers. The account of this journey ends in Deuteronomy with the people located on the plains of Moab east of the Jordan. Central to the account of the Israelites' divine rescue from Egypt is the figure of Moses, with the opening chapters of Exodus describing his birth and the final chapter of Deuteronomy recording his death.[1]

Apart from threads which run through a number of books, adjacent books are also linked closely together. For example, Genesis concludes with Joseph making the sons of Jacob swear that they will carry his bones up from Egypt (Gen. 50:25); the exact fulfilment of this request is picked up in Exodus 13:19.

---

[1] In the light of the importance of Moses it is hardly surprising that an early and enduring title for the Pentateuch has been 'The Books of Moses'.

Whereas instructions for the setting apart of priests are given in Exodus 29, the account of their appointment comes later in Leviticus 9. While Numbers 20:12 anticipates the death of Moses outside the promised land, the account of this happening comes in Deuteronomy 34.

Even Genesis, which is generally viewed as being quite different in character from the remaining books of the Pentateuch, is clearly integrated into the overall plot. Apart from the promises to the patriarchs which are very significant, the whole of the Joseph story provides an essential link between the stories of Abraham, Isaac and Jacob living in Canaan and the account of their descendants being rescued from Egypt. In the light of these observations it is important not to dismiss lightly the present unity of the Pentateuch. Although the books of Genesis to Deuteronomy are made up of very diverse components, which may superficially give the impression of disunity, someone has skilfully brought them together to form a narrative that exhibits considerable unity. In its present form the Pentateuch is clearly a unified work.

The basic plot of the Pentateuch may be outlined as follows. At the outset human beings are created in order to enjoy a special relationship with God and to exercise authority on his behalf over the earth. However, the disobedience of Adam and Eve alienates them from God, and as a result they are punished through divine curses and expelled from Eden. While the early chapters of Genesis concentrate mainly on the terrible consequences of these initial developments, the rest of Genesis, from chapter 12 onwards, moves forward with the hope that humanity may yet be reconciled to God.

Central to this hope of reconciliation are the divine promises made to Abraham. The importance of these should not be underestimated; they set the agenda for all that follows in the rest of the Pentateuch and beyond. From a careful study of the Abraham narrative it is clear that there are two main dimensions to these promises. First, there is the promise that through the 'seed' of Abraham 'all nations on earth will be blessed' (Gen. 22:18). Although of primary importance for reversing the consequences of what took place in the Garden of Eden, this promise remains unfulfilled by the conclusion of the Pentateuch. Within Genesis this promise is specifically linked to a future royal lineage which will be descended from Abraham, in the first instance, through his great-grandson, Joseph. This line is subsequently traced via Ephraim to Joshua. However, as we shall observe in chapter 8, Genesis appears to anticipate that the future monarchy associated with Joseph-Ephraim will be replaced by one that will come from the line of Judah through his son Perez.

The other divine promises to Abraham centre on the establishment of a great nation. These promises generally emphasise two aspects of this: descendants and land. God guarantees Abraham through a special covenant that his descendants will be given the land of Canaan some four centuries later

(Gen. 15). For this promise of nationhood to be fulfilled various developments must occur and these are recorded in the rest of the Pentateuch. Interestingly, however, the promise of nationhood, like the promise of blessing for the nations of the earth, remains unrealised by the end of Deuteronomy.

The promises of blessing and nationhood are closely linked. The blessing of the nations can only occur after the promise of nationhood has been fulfilled and a monarchy is created. This explains why the Pentateuch concentrates on the establishment of Abraham's descendants as a nation in the land of Canaan. Indeed, because so much attention is given in the Pentateuch to it, this latter promise tends to overshadow the promise of blessing for the nations through a royal descendant of Abraham.

The setting apart of Israel as a nation distinct from all others dominates the books of Exodus to Deuteronomy. The primary purpose behind this is that Israel should be an example of how true communion with the LORD may be achieved; God expects Israel to be 'a kingdom of priests and a holy nation' (Ex. 19:6). At the heart of this is the idea that Israel will exercise a mediatorial role between God and other peoples. Consequently, the Pentateuch anticipates in part a return to the kind of divine/human relationship enjoyed in Eden, with the Israelites living in harmony with the LORD on land blessed by him. Yet, although God comes to dwell in the midst of Israel, the people still do not experience the same intimate communion with him that Adam and Eve originally enjoyed. While the making of the Sinai covenant and the building of the tabernacle bring about an important advance in God's relationship with one section of humanity, this does not give the Israelites immediate and unhindered access to the divine presence. Barriers still exist between God and the people. Only Moses enjoys what might be described as intimate contact with God, but even this is limited. Thus, God's relationship with Israel as a people merely anticipated that which is yet to come in conjunction with the blessing of the nations of the earth.

Another aspect of Israel's mediatorial role is that she should exemplify the kind of righteousness required by God. To this end she is to be a holy nation governed by God's decrees and laws. The importance of this is highlighted in the covenant obligations given first at Sinai and repeated later on the plains of Moab. Israel as a nation is expected to reflect God's holy and perfect nature to the other nations of the earth.

Although the Pentateuch emphasises that the Israelites are especially privileged by the fact that the LORD has revealed himself to them through signs and wonders in Egypt and then later through verbal communication at Sinai, it also highlights their waywardness by failing to trust and obey God completely. In spite of all that he does for them, their shortcomings are a recurring feature of the narrative in Exodus to Numbers. Moreover, even as they stand poised to possess the promised land, the LORD reminds them that, although they will initially enjoy his blessing, they will eventually be unfaithful and, as a result, be exiled from the land. No longer will they know God's presence in their midst.

This latter observation highlights another important idea within the Pentateuch. The enjoyment of the benefits of the divine promises is linked to a trust in God's ability to fulfil them. Faith in God marked by obedience is highlighted in a variety of ways, both positively and negatively. The absence of faith was responsible for the disobedience of Adam and Eve in the Garden of Eden. Faith was central to the life of Abraham, who is presented as a model for others to follow. Similarly, it was important in the experience of the Israelites in the wilderness. Here, however, it is their frequent lack of faith that is highlighted. Later, in Deuteronomy, Moses encouraged the people to trust and obey the LORD in order that they might take possession of the promised land. While the benefits of the divine promises may be forfeited temporarily due to human failure, the promises will ultimately be realised because they originate with God.

Although the Pentateuch gives a very distinctive history of the world from its creation to the arrival of the Israelites on the borders of Canaan, it is much more than a history of what has taken place. The divine promises of blessing and nationhood, which are so important to the development of the plot, remain unfulfilled by the end of Deuteronomy. As a result, the Pentateuch is orientated towards the future. What will become of these promises? To answer this we must look beyond the concluding chapters of Deuteronomy.[2] As it stands, the Pentateuch is an unfinished story.

---

[2] In the light of this observation it is important to note that the books of Joshua to 2 Kings provide a vital sequel to the Pentateuch. See T.D. Alexander, 'Genesis to Kings', in *NDBT*, 115–20.

8

The Royal Lineage in Genesis

8.1. Summary

The book of Genesis has been carefully composed to focus on a unique family line, starting with Adam and continuing down to the twelve sons of Jacob. This line of 'seed' includes various individuals who all enjoyed a very special relationship with God: Noah, Abraham, Isaac, Jacob and Joseph. Genesis anticipates that the descendants of this line will become very numerous and that a royal dynasty will arise from the descendants of Abraham. While this future dynasty is associated initially with Joseph and his son Ephraim, it is also linked in a very subtle way to Judah and his son Perez.

8.2. Introduction

For many readers Genesis is a collection of unconnected stories, interrupted here and there by apparently irrelevant genealogies. Yet the present text has been carefully shaped to highlight the importance of a family lineage that begins with Adam and is traced through to the sons of Jacob. To appreciate this we shall consider first the overall structure of the book and the function of the various genealogies found within it. Next, we shall examine briefly the concept of 'seed' and observe how Genesis deliberately focuses on a single line of descendants. Finally, we shall draw some conclusions about the nature of this special lineage.

8.3. The Structure of Genesis

A quick survey reveals that Genesis consists of narrative sections that are linked together by genealogies. Interestingly, many of these narrative sections and genealogies are introduced by similar headings; these occur in 2:4; 5:1; 6:9; 10:1; 11:10, 27; 25:12, 19; 36:1, 9; 37:2. The common element in all of these headings is the Hebrew word *tôlĕdot* which is translated in the NIV as 'account'.[1] The word itself is associated with 'giving birth' and when linked to a person or object refers to what that person or object produces. For example, the initial words of 11:27 could be translated, 'And these were born of Terah'; the NIV has 'This is the account of Terah'.

The *tôlĕdot* headings serve two functions. First, they are like chapter or section headings in modern books. Some of them introduce major narrative sections, indicating a new stage in the development of the plot. These major sections deal mainly with the lives of Adam, Noah, Abraham, Jacob and Joseph, and they are introduced by the headings in 2:4, 6:9, 11:27, 25:19 and 37:2 respectively. The other *tôlĕdot* headings introduce either linear genealogies (see Diagram A) which list descendants who belong to the central family line (5:1; 11:10), or segmented genealogies (see Diagram B) which provide details about family members of some of the minor participants in Genesis (10:1; 25:12; 36:1, 9). To ensure that the main line of descent is clearly established, segmented genealogies are never used; only linear genealogies are employed (5:1–32; 11:10–26).

Second, the *tôlĕdot* headings function like a zoom lens on a camera. They focus the reader's attention on a particular individual and his immediate children. This enables the author of Genesis to trace the fortunes of the main family line without having to follow in detail the lives of all other relatives. In this way Genesis highlights the importance of the lineage which, beginning with Adam, is traced through Adam's youngest son Seth to Noah, the father of Shem, Ham and Japheth. The next stage of the line takes us from Shem to Terah, the father of Abraham, Nahor and Haran. We then move from Abraham to Isaac, from Isaac to Jacob, and, finally, to Jacob's twelve sons.

Diagram A

A linear genealogy

M gave birth to N	M
	|
N gave birth to O	N
	|
O gave birth to P	O
	|
	P

---

[1] In Genesis the term *tôlĕdot* is used elsewhere only in 10:32 and 25:13.

Diagram B

A segmented genealogy

A gave birth to B, C, D
B gave birth to E, F, G
C gave birth to H, I, J
D gave birth to K, L, M

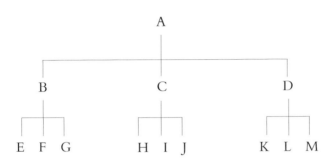

8.4. The Chosen 'Seed'

Closely linked to the genealogical structure of Genesis is the frequent use of the Hebrew word *zera'* which is perhaps best translated as 'seed'. Unfortunately, the NIV translates *zera'* using a variety of terms – the most common being 'descendants', 'offspring', 'seed', 'children', 'family', 'grain', 'semen', 'line', 'people'. For this reason the importance of the concept of 'seed' in Genesis is easily missed. *Zera'* is a keyword, however, occurring 59 times in Genesis compared to 170 times in the rest of the Old Testament.[2]

Several factors are worth noting briefly about the use of the term 'seed' in Genesis. (a) The Hebrew word *zera'*, like the English word 'sheep', can be either singular or plural; it may denote a single seed or many seeds. An example of the former comes in 21:13 where Ishmael is described as Abraham's 'seed'. On the other hand, in 28:14 *zera'* refers to the 'seed' (descendants) of Jacob 'who will be like the dust of the earth'. (b) 'Seed'

---

[2] These statistics exclude the one occurrence of the Aramaic word *zera'* in Daniel 2:43. In Genesis *zera'* comes in 1:11 (x2), 12 (x2), 29 (x2); 3:15 (x2); 4:25; 7:3; 8:22; 9:9; 12:7; 13:15, 16 (x2); 15:3, 5, 13, 18; 16:10; 17:7 (x2), 8, 9, 10, 12, 19; 19:32, 34; 21:12, 13; 22:17 (x2), 18; 24:7, 60; 26:3, 4 (x3); 28:4, 13, 14 (x2); 32:12; 35:12; 38:8, 9 (x2); 46:6, 7; 47:19, 23, 24; 48:4, 11, 19.

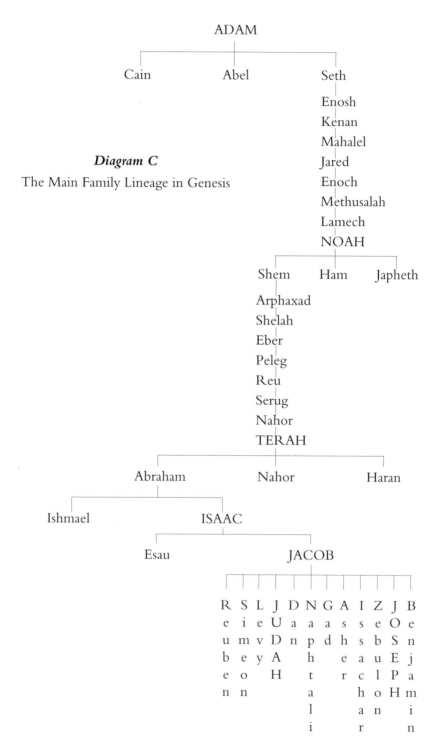

Diagram C

The Main Family Lineage in Genesis

ADAM

Cain   Abel   Seth

Enosh

Kenan

Mahalel

Jared

Enoch

Methusalah

Lamech

NOAH

Shem   Ham   Japheth

Arphaxad

Shelah

Eber

Peleg

Reu

Serug

Nahor

TERAH

Abraham   Nahor   Haran

Ishmael   ISAAC

Esau   JACOB

Reuben Simeon Levi Judah Dan Naphtali Gad Asher Issachar Zebulun Joseph Benjamin normally denotes an individual's natural child or children. When Eve gives birth to Seth, she comments, 'God has granted me another child (seed) in place of Abel, since Cain killed him' (4:25). In 15:3 Abraham laments the fact that although his heir is Eliezer of Damascus, he is not of his own seed; this reflects the fact that as yet Abraham and Sarah have no child of their own. (c) The Hebrew word *zera'* conveys the idea that there is a close resemblance between the 'seed' and that which has produced it. We see this underlying the comment that plants and trees are to produce seeds 'according to their various kinds' (1:11–12).

8.5. The Lineage of Adam

When Genesis is viewed as a whole it is very apparent that the genealogical structure and the concept of 'seed' are closely linked in order to highlight a single, distinctive, family lineage (see Diagram C). Moreover, although Genesis concludes by noting that the total seed of Jacob was reckoned as numbering seventy (46:6–27), within this group of seventy special attention is focused on the status given to the descendants of two of Jacob's sons, Joseph and Judah. As we shall observe below, although Joseph's younger son Ephraim receives the blessing of the first-born from his grandfather, Jacob (48:1–22), and is clearly viewed as the one through whom a royal line is anticipated, attention is also drawn to the future importance of Judah and his descendants (38:1–30; 49:8–12).

When we examine the nature of the main family lineage in Genesis various features are noteworthy. First, the lineage is always traced through male descendants, and all are clearly named.[3] Yet, while it might be expected that the line of 'seed' would always be traced through the eldest son, this is not so. In a number of instances a younger son is given priority over an older brother and, interestingly, on each occasion the text of Genesis suggests why this occurs. For killing his brother Abel, Cain, the first-born, is passed over in favour of Seth, the third-born (4:1–25). Although Ishmael is Abraham's first-born son, he is excluded from

---

[3] This does not necessarily imply that every generation is included in the record. R.R. Wilson, *Genealogy and History in the Biblical World* (Yale Near Eastern Researches 7; New Haven: Yale University Press, 1977), 133–4, notes that even in written genealogies there is a tendency to limit the maximum length of the lineage to ten generations, such as we have in Genesis 5 and 11. Consequently, it is not uncommon to find Near Eastern genealogies being modified by the addition and omission of names. Examples of this process of 'telescoping' are also to be found in the biblical texts (e.g. compare 1 Chr. 6:3–14 and Ezra 7:1–5; cf. W.H. Green, 'Primeval Chronology', *BS* 47 [1890], 285–303).

the line of 'seed' because he is the son of Sarah's Egyptian maidservant Hagar (16:1–16; 17:18–21; 21:9–20). As the God-given 'seed' of Abraham, Isaac enjoys priority over Ishmael. While Esau is born before Jacob, his secondary position to Jacob is divinely predicted prior to the birth of the twin boys (25:23). Furthermore, the narrator appears to justify this choice by highlighting Esau's attitude towards his birthright, which he sells to Jacob for a pot of red stew (25:29–34), and by the fact that he displeases his parents by marrying two Hittite women (26:34–35).

A more complex situation exists regarding the twelve sons of Jacob, where both Judah, the fourth-born, and Joseph, the eleventh-born son, are privileged before older brothers. Once again the Genesis narrative reveals that the eldest brothers, Reuben, Simeon and Levi, are excluded from enjoying their father's foremost blessing due to unseemly actions (see 35:22 and 34:25–30). From the outset of Genesis 37 Joseph is clearly presented as the one who is privileged by his father as the first-born (cf. 1 Chr. 5:1–2). The fact that he was Rachel's first child undoubtedly encouraged this. Later, Joseph's status as first-born is confirmed when Jacob gives the blessing of the first-born to Joseph's family by blessing his two sons Manasseh and Ephraim (48:1–22).[4] Remarkably, yet again in Genesis, a younger son, Ephraim, receives the superior blessing normally associated with the first-born.

While Joseph's position as the 'first-born' is assumed in the Genesis narrative, a subtle development occurs involving Judah. This centres chiefly around Genesis 38 which interrupts the Joseph story in order to focus attention on the 'seed' of Judah. The account of Judah's relationship with Tamar concludes by describing the birth of twins during which the younger boy, Perez, 'breaks out' in front of the 'first-born', Zerah. The significance of this event should not be overlooked in the light of the larger story which unfolds in the books of Genesis to Kings. Whereas the tribe of Ephraim is initially presented as the one from which Israel's leader will come, as reflected for example in the important role played by Joshua, the 'first-born' line of Ephraim is rejected in the time of Samuel and replaced by the line of David, from the tribe of Judah.[5]

---

[4] The status of Joseph as the first-born of Jacob's twelve sons is probably also reflected in the fact that 'Joseph', through the tribes of Ephraim and Manasseh, received a double portion of the land of Canaan when it was distributed among the tribes of Israel.

[5] Apart from the evidence derived from the book of Genesis, Psalm 78:59–72 provides a strong case for believing that a royal line descended from Joseph was divinely rejected in favour of a lineage associated with Judah. Interestingly, here, as in the books of Samuel, the rejection of Ephraim is linked to the demise of Shiloh as the central sanctuary, whereas the choice of David is associated with the divine decision to make Zion/Jerusalem the new location for God's sanctuary.

Secondly, it is noteworthy that the central family line exists due to the gracious activity of God. At the outset Eve recognises this following the birth of Seth: 'She named him Seth, saying, "God has granted me another child (seed) in place of Abel, since Cain killed him" ' (4:25). It is, however, in the lives of Abraham, Isaac and Jacob that we see most clearly God's role in sustaining the family line. In the account of Abraham's life one of the first details recorded is that 'Sarai was barren; she had no children' (11:30). As the Abraham story unfolds, God reiterates on various occasions that Sarah will indeed give birth to a son (17:16–21; 18:10–14), and this in spite of the fact that both Abraham and Sarah are well beyond the natural age of having children; Abraham is one hundred years old (17:17; 21:5) and Sarah ninety (17:17). When at last Sarah gives birth to Isaac, the text specifically states that this is due to divine intervention: 'Now the LORD was gracious to Sarah as he had said, and the LORD did for Sarah what he had promised' (21:1). A similar situation is recorded very briefly in 25:21 regarding Isaac and Rebekah: 'Isaac prayed to the LORD on behalf of his wife, because she was barren. The LORD answered his prayer, and his wife Rebekah became pregnant.' Remarkably, history repeats itself yet again in the case of Jacob, for we learn that his wife Rachel was also barren (29:31). When Rachel eventually gives birth to a child of her own, the narrative affirms God's part in this:

> Then God remembered Rachel; he listened to her and opened her womb. She became pregnant and gave birth to a son and said, 'God has taken away my disgrace.' She named him Joseph, and said, 'May the LORD add to me another son' (30:22–24).

All of these examples highlight that God is actively responsible for the continuation of the family line.

Thirdly, the Genesis narrative emphasises the existence of a special relationship between God and individual members of the main family line. We see this in a variety of ways. Sometimes it is highlighted in the briefest of comments. For example, we read that 'Enoch walked with God; then he was no more, because God took him away' (5:24). The *tôlĕdot* heading of Noah is immediately followed by the statement, 'Noah was a righteous man, blameless among the people of his time, and he walked with God' (6:9).[6] Elsewhere the

---

[6] The Hebrew original of the comments in 5:22, 24 and 6:9 that Enoch and Noah 'walked with God' uses a distinctive form of the verb 'to walk' – the *hitpa'el* form. The same form occurs elsewhere in Genesis in 3:8; 13:17; 17:1; 24:40; 48:15. Apart from 3:8, where God is the subject of the verb, and with the possible exception of 13:17, on all of these occasions the verb 'walk' denotes a special relationship with God. Sarna comments, 'this expression seems originally to have been a technical term for absolute loyalty to a king'; see *Genesis,* 123.

presence of a special relationship is revealed in considerably more detail. This is so in the longer accounts concerning Noah, Abraham, Isaac, Jacob and Joseph. In the cases of Noah and Abraham, God not only reveals future plans but also establishes eternal covenants through both of them. Isaac and Jacob also receive revelations from God confirming, in particular, promises which were previously made to Abraham. Although God never reveals himself directly to Joseph, he enables him to discern future events by interpreting dreams. Furthermore, the account of Joseph's time in Egypt highlights God's providential care of him.

While the members of the main family line enjoy God's favour and blessing, their faults and failures are never disguised. We see Noah becoming drunk (9:20–21), Abraham being less than fully truthful concerning his marriage to Sarah (12:10–13), and Jacob wilfully deceiving his father (27:1–40), to mention the more obvious shortcomings. Nevertheless, in spite of such faults, the members of the family line are viewed as more righteous than others. This is perhaps most evident in the case of Noah, who is introduced as 'a righteous man, blameless among the people of his time' (6:9) and who, with his family, is not condemned to destruction by the flood like all other human beings. Abraham's righteousness is highlighted in various ways. It is first mentioned specifically in 15:6 where the narrator comments that 'Abram believed the LORD, and he credited it to him as righteousness'. Later, the extent of Abraham's righteousness is revealed by his willingness to obey God and sacrifice his much-loved son, Isaac (22:1–19). Although, in comparison to the other patriarchs, relatively little information is given about Isaac, the fact that he clearly enjoyed God's favour suggests that he too was viewed as righteous (cf. 26:12–13, 23–24). Jacob's relationship with God develops over a long period of time, and while Genesis focuses initially on his deceptive behaviour (27:1–29), we see him eventually taking active steps to rid his household of foreign gods (35:1–5). Like Abraham and Isaac, Jacob too knows God's blessing. Furthermore, all three patriarchs actively worship God by building altars and offering sacrifices (12:7–8; 13:18; 22:9; 26:25; 35:1–7).

Fourthly, as noted above, the concept of 'seed' implies a resemblance between the 'seed' and the one who has produced it. In the context of Genesis this suggests that sons will resemble their fathers. The most obvious example of this comes in the record of Isaac's stay in the region of Gerar (26:1–35). Here Isaac's behaviour mirrors closely that of his father. Like Abraham, he pretends that his wife is his sister (26:1–11; cf. 12:10–20; 20:1–18), is involved in a dispute with the inhabitants of Gerar over the ownership of certain wells (26:17–25; cf. 21:22–34), and enters into a covenant with Abimelech (26:26–31; cf. 21:22–34). In a different way Jacob's sons resemble him in that they too knowingly deceive their father (27:1–29; 37:12–35). Significantly, those elder sons who are overlooked in favour of younger brothers generally exhibit behaviour which is not in keeping with that expected of the line of seed. For example, Reuben's affair with his father's concubine Bilhah (35:22; cf. 49:3–4) and the murderous actions of Simeon and Levi apparently exclude them from receiving the blessing of the first-born from their father, Jacob (34:1–31; cf. 49:5–7).

Members of the main family line are not the only ones in Genesis to share common features; the same is true of others. Cain's descendant Lamech repeats his murderous actions (4:19–24). Similarly, among the descendants of Ham, who sinned against his father Noah, we find listed the Canaanites (who include the inhabitants of Sodom and Gomorrah) and the Amorites (10:15–19), all of whom are viewed worthy of divine punishment (cf. 13:13; 15:16; 19:1–29).

Fifthly, there are strong grounds for believing that the main line of descent in Genesis is viewed as a royal lineage. This possibility is implied by the divine promise made to Abraham that 'kings will come from you' (17:6), echoed in a similar statement concerning Sarah that 'kings of peoples will come from her'(17:16). Moreover, although Abraham is never directly designated a king, he is sometimes portrayed as enjoying the status of a king. We see this in his defeat of the eastern kings in Genesis 14, in the desire of Abimelech, king of Gerar, to make a covenant with him (21:22–34), and, finally, in the title 'mighty prince' (literally, 'a prince of God') given to him by the Hittite inhabitants of Hebron (23:6).

While there are only a few allusions to kingship in Genesis 25–36, they are nevertheless noteworthy. Isaac's importance is reflected in Abimelech's wish to enter into a treaty with him (26:26–31), as he had previously done with Abraham. In a divine promise which echoes Genesis 17, Jacob is promised that 'kings will come from your body' (35:11). Finally, the brief comment in 36:31, 'These were the kings who reigned in Edom before any Israelite king reigned', indicates that whoever wrote this either anticipated or already knew of a royal dynasty within Israel.

The subject of kingship is prominent in the Joseph story. At the outset his brothers interpreted Joseph's first dream as implying that he will be a king: 'Do you intend to reign over us? Will you actually rule us?' (37:8). His second dream reinforces this idea (37:9–11), and later we witness the fulfilment when Joseph rises from the obscurity of an Egyptian prison to hold the office of governor of Egypt, second only to Pharaoh (41:39–43).

Although Joseph enjoys the spotlight in Genesis 37–50, it is noteworthy that of the other sons of Jacob most attention is focused on Judah.[7] This is particularly so in Genesis 38 where we have one of the more unusual episodes

---

[7] See 43:8–9; 44:16; 44:18–34; 46:28.

in the book. The inclusion of this story in Genesis can best be accounted for by noting that it focuses on Judah's reluctance, following the deaths of his sons Er and Onan, to allow Er's wife Tamar to marry Judah's third son Shelah in order to produce 'seed' and so maintain the family line. When Tamar eventually becomes pregnant by deceiving Judah, he is forced to acknowledge the righteousness of her actions (38:26). The account concludes by recording the birth of Perez (and his twin brother Zerah) from whom the royal line of David is descended.[8]

Judah's importance is further indicated by the special blessing which he receives from his father in 49:8–12. Without considering every aspect of this blessing, the following points are worth noting. (a) When compared with the other blessings pronounced by Jacob upon his sons, the length and content of Judah's blessing clearly suggests that he enjoyed a special relationship with his father. Only Joseph receives a comparable blessing. (b) Jacob states that Judah and his descendants will exercise leadership over his other brothers and their descendants (49:8). We see this especially in the comment that 'Your father's sons will bow down to you' (49:8) and in the reference to the sceptre and ruler's staff not departing from Judah (49:10). (c) Jacob anticipates that eventually there shall come in the royal line of Judah one to whom the nations will submit in obedience (49:10) and whose reign will be marked by prosperity and abundance (49:11). Such comments would clearly have been very important for the royal line of David, justifying their claim to rule over the whole of Israel.[9]

Sixthly, the 'seed' of the main family lineage is frequently associated with the divine promises which are an important feature of the patriarchal stories. Three aspects of these promises deserve special notice. (a) God promises the land of Canaan to the 'seed' of Abraham. This is mentioned specifically when

---

[8] There are interesting parallels between Genesis 38 and the book of Ruth which concludes by giving the genealogy of king David beginning with Perez the son of Tamar (Ruth 4:18–22). Although Tamar and Ruth are non-Israelites, they both play an active role in continuing the royal line. It is also interesting to observe that David names one of his daughters Tamar (2 Sam. 13:1). See Alexander, *The Servant King*, 49–54.

[9] In passing it is noteworthy that Genesis 1:28 indicates that human beings were created by God to rule over the earth. This being so, Adam is to be viewed as the first member of this royal line. However, not only was Adam a king, but he was also a priest (see chapter 9). In the light of this, the concept of priest-king takes on a special significance. In Genesis we encounter this unusual status in the figure of Melchizedek. Clearly it is implied that anyone who enjoys this particular status resembled Adam before he was expelled from the Garden of Eden. Later, the Israelites are called by the LORD to be a royal priesthood (Ex. 19:6).

Abraham first arrives in Canaan, 'To your seed I will give this land' (12:7), and repeated on various occasions to Abraham, Isaac and Jacob (13:15; 15:18; 17:8; 22:17; 26:3; 28:13; 35:12; cf. 24:7; 24:60; 28:4; 48:4). On the significance of these promises concerning land, see chapter 10. (b) It is frequently stressed that the 'seed' of Abraham will be very numerous. Different images are used to highlight the extent of the 'seed': the dust of the earth (13:16; 28:14), the stars of the heavens (15:5: 22:17; 26:4) and the sand of the seashore (22:17; 32:12). The fulfilment of the promise of numerous descendants, like that of land, clearly lies beyond the book of Genesis, indicating that it merely records the beginning of something which will only be completed later. Taken together these promises related to the creation of a 'great nation' (12:2).[10] (c) It is emphasised that through Abraham's 'seed' all nations on earth will be blessed (22:18; 26:4; 28:14). While this will be discussed more fully in the next chapter where we shall consider the theme of blessing in Genesis, it should be noted here that in this context the expression 'Abraham's seed' designates a single descendant. As we shall observe, Genesis anticipates that a royal descendant from Abraham will play an important role in bringing divine blessing to all the nations of the earth.

8.6. Conclusion

The entire book of Genesis is clearly composed around the history of a unique family line that enjoys a special relationship with God. With Abraham we are informed, on the one hand, that the 'seed' of this lineage will become very numerous and possess the land of Canaan, and, on the other hand, one particular line of 'seed' will establish a royal dynasty through which all the nations of the earth will be blessed. While this royal line is clearly linked to Joseph and Ephraim, Genesis anticipates that the line of Judah through Perez will replace this 'first-born' lineage. In this way Genesis focuses on both the birth of the nation of Israel and the early ancestry of a future monarchy. In that the nation and the king are of the 'seed' of Abraham, they share a common origin, and, as recipients of the divine promises, a common destiny. To the promises of blessing and land we shall turn next in chapters 9 and 10, respectively.

---

[10] The nature of this nation – holy and righteous – becomes a prominent theme in Exodus, Leviticus and Deuteronomy.

8.7. New Testament Connections

In the New Testament various passages relate directly or indirectly to the family lineage which we have noted in Genesis. By far the most important connection is that this special line of seed finds its fulfilment in Jesus Christ. Since Genesis anticipates a royal line of seed descended from Judah, it is easy to understand how Jesus, 'the son of David' (cf. Rom. 1:3; 2 Tim. 2:8), is linked to the 'seed' of Abraham. Paul explicitly states this in his Galatian letter: 'The promises were spoken to Abraham and to his seed. The Scripture does not say "and to seeds", meaning many people, but "and to your seed", meaning one person, who is Christ' (Gal. 3:16). The same idea probably underlies other New Testament passages which associate Abraham with David. For example, Matthew's genealogy of Jesus begins with Abraham and is traced downwards through David to Joseph (Mt. 1:1–17).[11] In Zechariah's song of praise the arrival of a saviour from the house of David is viewed as the fulfilment of the oath which God swore to Abraham (Lk. 1:68–75). In a slightly less obvious way the same link is found in Peter's speech in Acts 3:12–26. Here Peter explains that Jesus as the suffering Messiah fulfils God's promise to Abraham that through his 'seed' all peoples on earth will be blessed (cf. Acts 3:25–26).

Although the New Testament writers view Jesus as belonging to the line of Abraham/David, they reveal that he is much greater than either Abraham or David. John 8:52–58 and Matthew 22:41–46 record Jesus' own assessment that he is superior to Abraham and David respectively. A similar claim is also recorded regarding Jesus and Solomon in Matthew 12:42 (cf. Lk. 11:31). Further links between Jesus and the 'seed' of Abraham will be noted in chapters 10 and 12.

The special lineage in Genesis also appears in Paul's letters to the Romans and Galatians. In Romans 9 and Galatians 4 he draws an important distinction between 'natural children' and 'children of promise'. Using the Genesis stories concerning Ishmael/Isaac and Esau/Jacob he argues that 'not all who are descended from Israel are Israel. Nor because they are his descendants are they all Abraham's children' (Rom. 9:6–7). Paul is concerned to show that natural descent from Abraham is no guarantee of salvation. Thus he demonstrates from Genesis that although Ishmael and Esau are both descendants of Abraham, they are not part of the chosen line of 'seed'.

---

[11] Although the genealogy ends with Joseph, Matthew nowhere claims that Joseph is the natural father of Jesus; he merely observed that Joseph was married to Mary the mother of Jesus (Mt. 1:16). In keeping with this, the immediately following account is concerned to show that Joseph adopts Jesus as his son (Mt. 1:18–25).

Another element of Paul's discussion in Romans and Galatians is that the seed of Abraham should resemble him. We see this clearly in his comments in Galatians 3:6–7:

> Consider Abraham: 'He believed God, and it was credited to him as righteousness.' Understand, then, that those who believe are children of Abraham.

The same point underlies Paul's words in Romans 4:16–17:

> Therefore, the promise comes by faith, so that it may be by grace and may be guaranteed to all Abraham's offspring – not only to those who are of the law but also to those who are of the faith of Abraham. He is the father of us all. As it is written: 'I have made you a father of many nations.' He is our father in the sight of God, in whom he believed – the God who gives life to the dead and calls things that are not as though they were (Rom. 4:16–17).

In both these passages Paul argues that the true children of Abraham are those who, like Abraham, exercise faith. Consequently, descent from Abraham counts for nothing unless his natural descendants resemble him by being made righteous through faith. On this, we shall have more to say in chapter 12.

9

The Blessing of the Nations

9.1. Summary

Although the first chapter of Genesis affirms that human beings were created in the divine image and blessed by God, the subsequent disobedience of Adam and Eve in the Garden of Eden resulted in a series of divine curses that radically affected human existence. The tragic events that resulted from the broken relationship between God and humankind are highlighted in Genesis 4–11. After the division of humanity into different peoples and nations, Abraham is introduced as the one through whom God's blessing will once again extend to human beings. Genesis looks forward to all families and nations being blessed through Abraham and his 'seed'.

9.2. Introduction

Blessing and cursing are important concepts in the book of Genesis. This is reflected by the fact that the Hebrew verbs for 'blessing' (*brk*) and 'cursing' (*'rr*) occur 73 and 9 times respectively. Normally in Genesis blessing is associated with God's favour and cursing with his disfavour. In order to be blessed the recipient must be at harmony with the donor. Consequently, God's blessing extends only to those who seek to be righteous; the wicked are under his curse.

Genesis presents a picture of changing human fortunes. When God created the first generation of human beings they enjoyed his favour and were blessed by him (1:28). Soon this situation was disrupted by events which took place in the Garden of Eden. For disobeying God's command not to eat from the tree of the knowledge of good and evil, Adam and Eve were divinely punished through various curses. Some of the immediate consequences are described in Genesis 4–11. Here we observe the total destruction of the human race, apart from Noah and his family and, later, the division of human beings into different nations. Whereas the accounts of the flood and of the tower of Babel highlight the disastrous consequences of evoking God's displeasure, with the call of Abraham in Genesis 12 the way begins to open up for human beings to once more enjoy God's favour. Significantly, as illustrated in the record of the lives of Jacob and Joseph, God's blessing is mediated through the 'first-born seed' descended from Abraham.

9.3. Creator and Creation in Harmony

The opening section of the book of Genesis describes how God created the heavens and the earth. It stresses the ease with which everything was made, and that nothing happened by chance; everything was made according to design. By merely speaking, God created time in the form of 'day' and 'night' (1:3–5). Next he made three distinctive regions, the sky (1:6–8), the land and the seas (1:9–11), and placed in each as appropriate plants (1:11–13), stars and planets (1:14–19), fish and birds (1:20–23), living creatures (1:24–26) and human beings (1:27–31). God's final verdict that everything 'was very good' (1:31) echoes a common refrain in the chapter, 'God said that (it) was good' (1:4, 10, 12, 18, 21, 25). With remarkable brevity and skill the narrator conveys a picture of total harmony between God, the creator, and the world, his creation.

The creation of human beings comes as the climax to God's creative activity: 'So God created man in his own image, in the image of God he created him, male and female he created them' (1:27). This comment is immediately followed by the remark that 'God blessed them and said to them, "Be fruitful and increase in number; fill the earth and subdue it. Rule over the fish of the sea and the birds of the air and over every living creature that moves on the ground" ' (1:28). Unlike all other creatures, human beings alone enjoyed the privilege of being made in the divine image and having a special relationship with God. Moreover, blessed by God they were to increase numerically and rule over the earth as his representatives.

Although God's creative activity ends on the sixth day, the account of creation concludes by focusing on the seventh day in which God rested from all work (2:1–3). Of significance is the comment, 'God blessed the seventh day and made it holy, because on it he rested from all the work of creating that he had done' (2:3). The seventh day is set apart from all the other days of the week because rest is viewed as the climax of the work pattern established by God. As reflected in God's own experience, the opportunity to rest, having completed one's work, is a sacred blessing.

9.4. In the Garden of Eden

The account of creation in 1:1–2:3 is followed by a second in 2:4–25. Whereas the first account gives a cosmic picture of God's activity, the second is much more down to earth, portraying God as the one who personally moulds the man from clay and breathes life into him (2:7).[1] The narrative also reveals that God provides the right environment for the man (2:8–17) and a suitable companion (2:18–25). Although the two accounts of humanity's creation differ in style, they complement each other, both emphasising the special relationship which existed between the LORD God and the first man and woman.

Unfortunately, the harmony of creation was soon broken by the serpent, who persuaded the woman, and, through her, the man, to disobey God's command by eating 'from the tree of the knowledge of good and evil' (2:17). Although few details are given, the narrative makes clear that eating from this tree radically changed the man and the woman. Only at this stage do they become conscious of their own nakedness.

When the LORD God next visited the garden, the man and the woman were unable to hide what had taken place. Aware of their actions, God pronounced judgement on all the participants. No longer did God's blessing favour the man and the woman; now they had to endure the consequences of his displeasure. As a result of their broken relationship with God, Adam and Eve were expelled from Eden.

The contents of God's pronouncements against the serpent, the woman and the man are significant. Regarding the serpent he states:

> Because you have done this, 'Cursed are you above all the livestock and all the wild animals! You will crawl on your belly and you will eat dust all the days of your life. And I will put enmity between you and the woman and between your offspring (seed) and hers (her seed); he will crush your head, and you will strike his heel' (3:14–15).

Of particular interest here is the comment about the enmity which will exist between the 'seed' of the serpent and the 'seed' of the woman. Unfortunately, most commentators miss the obvious connection which exists between this reference to 'seed' and the fact that Genesis highlights a particular line of 'seed' (see chapter 8). The implication is surely that the divine pronouncement against the serpent will be fulfilled through the divinely chosen family lineage.[2]

God's judgement upon the woman is directed against two important aspects of her life: her ability to produce children and her relationship to her husband:

---

[1] By placing these two accounts side by side, the divine attributes of transcendence and immanence are given equal weight and presented in a manner that highlights their importance while avoiding confusion.

[2] See pages 120–7.

> I will greatly increase your pains in childbearing; with pain you will give birth to children. Your desire will be for your husband, and he will rule over you (3:16).

Since in the future every birth will be accomplished only through pain, this pronouncement reverses in part God's initial blessing that human beings should be fruitful and increase in number (1:28).

The man's punishment is also designed to cause him maximum discomfort.

> Cursed is the ground because of you; through painful toil you will eat of it all the days of your life. It will produce thorns and thistles for you, and you will eat the plants of the field. By the sweat of your brow you will eat your food until you return to the ground, since from it you were taken; for dust you are and to dust you will return (3:17–19).

Whereas God had intended the man's work to be a responsibility under-taken with joy and satisfaction, it now becomes hard labour. On the basis of 2:7 it is obvious that the LORD God intended there to be a close and harmonious relationship between the man and the ground; this is evident in the Hebrew original where the words for 'man' and 'ground', 'ādām and 'ādāmâ respectively, are very similar.[3] By disrupting the man's relationship with the ground God ensured that humanity was not able to enjoy, like their creator, rest from labour.

The story of the fall brings to a bitter end the harmony that was the hallmark of God's creative activity. We witness in particular a breakdown in relations between animals and human beings, between men and women, and, most importantly of all, between God and humanity. Genesis 3 describes dramatic changes to the created world. Human beings no longer know God's blessing, but must now come to terms with his displeasure. The final act of judgement is the expulsion of the man and woman from Eden. Not only are they prevented from eating of the tree of life (3:22), they are also expelled from the place where they have enjoyed a close relationship with God. As we shall observe below, Genesis 4–11 focuses mainly on the terrible consequences of humanity's initial disobedience and provides a grim picture of what life was like without God's blessing. Only with the call of Abraham in 12:1–3 do we begin to see a brighter prospect with some human beings once again experiencing divine blessing in their lives.

---

[3] We shall have more to say about the theme of 'land' in chapter 10.

9.5. Outside Eden

After the departure of Adam and Eve from the Garden of Eden, the next episode in Genesis focuses on the murder of Abel by his brother Cain. Because Abel enjoyed God's favour, Cain became jealous and killed him. As punishment, Cain was cursed by God; the ground 'will no longer yield its crops' for him and he will become a 'restless wanderer on the earth' (4:11–12). This marks an extension of the curse imposed upon Cain's parents in Eden and highlights the fact that every unrighteous action alienates humankind further from the ground, making it even more difficult to cultivate food and so experience divinely intended rest.

The Genesis story reveals that God's curse upon the ground brought increased pain for humankind. Lamech particularly highlighted this in a brief comment concerning his son Noah. He named him Noah because, 'he will comfort us in the labour and painful toil of our hands caused by the ground the LORD has cursed' (5:29). Interestingly, when the earth is recreated after the flood Noah is described as 'a man of the soil (ground)' (9:20), implying that he enjoyed greater harmony with the ground than his immediate forefathers.

The concept of curse underlies the entire story of the flood. God's decision to wipe humankind from the face of the earth is motivated by the fact that he 'saw how great man's wickedness on the earth had become, and that every inclination of the thoughts of his heart was only evil all the time' (6:5). However, Noah finds favour in God's eyes and, together with some of his family, is spared from destruction. When Noah disembarks from the ark and offers sacrifices to God, the LORD remarks, 'Never again will I curse the ground because of man, even though every inclination of his heart is evil from childhood' (8:21). The curse mentioned here is not the one pronounced in the Garden of Eden. Rather it refers to the flood. The continued existence of 'thorns and thistles' and the necessity for humankind to toil with sweat indicate that the original divine curse on the ground has not been cancelled. Here God promises that he will never again send another flood upon the earth.[4] Later this is confirmed in the covenant outlined in 9:8–17.

In passing we should note that the story of the flood exhibits close parallels with the initial account of creation. The rising of the waters marks a return to the chaos that existed at the beginning of creation (7:11–24; cf. 1:2). Later, the dry land emerges from the waters (8:1–14; cf. 1:9–10). Finally, God's blessing of Noah and his sons in 9:1 echoes closely 1:28: 'Be fruitful and increase in number and fill the earth.' Yet, although these parallels suggest that the flood

---

[4] The syntax of the Hebrew original indicates that God promises here not to add to the curse pronounced against the ground in 3:17. Furthermore, the Hebrew word for 'curse' in 8:21 comes from a different root to that used in 3:17.

story should be understood as marking the re-creation of the earth, it is apparent that human nature was not renewed. We see this reflected in God's comments in 8:21 and 9:6 which draw attention respectively to the evil inclination of the human heart and the likelihood that murders will still occur.

The topic of blessing is prominent in 9:20–29. Here the narrative focuses on the contrasting actions of Ham and his brothers Shem and Japheth towards their father Noah. Whereas Ham looks 'upon his father's nakedness', Shem and Japheth take great care to cover it without seeing it. When Noah awakes he pronounces a curse upon Ham's son Canaan but blesses Shem and Japheth. Of significance is the fact that this is the first occasion in Genesis when a human being pronounces a blessing or a curse; previously it was always God who blessed or cursed. Yet, in cursing Canaan and blessing Shem and Japheth, Noah's words obviously carry divine authority. For the first time we meet something which is repeated later in Genesis: those within the chosen line of 'seed' are divinely empowered to bless or curse others.

Noah's speeches highlight another important motif in the book of Genesis; this concerns the descendants of Canaan and Shem. Whereas Canaan's descendants are destined to a future of servitude (9:25), Noah indicates that the line of Shem will enjoy a special relationship with God (9:26–27). Later, we see God promising to Abraham, a descendant of Shem, that he and his descendants will take possession of the land occupied by the descendants of Canaan (15:18–21).[5] Noah also predicts that Japheth will be blessed through having a close relationship with Shem.

Although blessing or cursing is not mentioned explicitly in the story of the tower of Babel, it is clear from the conclusion that the creation of different languages and the scattering of the peoples over the whole earth represent further divine curses upon the human race. God's punishment is intended to prevent human beings working together in harmony.

The picture of human existence under God's curse, in Genesis 3–11, contrasts sharply with the initial account of the divine creation and blessing of humankind. The narrator, however, makes it very evident that God's displeasure is not arbitrary but is in proportion to the extent of human wickedness. Yet, although Genesis 3–11 concentrate on the divine punishment of wicked human beings, the narrative reveals here and there that God still displays mercy in the face of unrighteous behaviour. We see this in the clothing of Adam and Eve (3:21), the placing of a mark on Cain (4:13–15), the saving of Noah and his family from the flood (6:8–8:19), and the making of

---

[5] Among the various nations listed in 15:19–21, the following are named as descendants of Canaan in 10:15–18: Hittites, Amorites, Canaanites, Girgashites and Jebusites. Furthermore, 10:19 draws attention to the fact that the borders of the Canaanite clans reached as far as Sodom and Gomorrah (cf. 14:1–24; 18:16–29).

an eternal covenant with every living creature (9:1–17). Significantly, the remaining chapters of Genesis develop further the possibility that human beings may once again know God's blessing in their lives.

9.6. Abraham and the Blessing of the Nations

The *tôlĕdot* heading in 11:27 introduces a new section in Genesis which concludes in 25:11. The central character of these chapters is Abraham and there is good reason to view him as the most important human participant in the whole of Genesis. After some brief preliminary details in 11:27–32, the account of his life begins with a short but highly significant divine speech that marks the beginning of a major new stage in God's relationship with human beings. At the heart of this speech is God's desire to bless humanity and so reverse the negative effects of the divine curses under which they live. The LORD says to Abraham,

> Leave your country, your people and your father's household and go to the land I will show you, so that I may make you into a great nation and bless you and make your name great. Be a blessing, so that I may bless those who bless you, and curse the one who disdains you, and so that all the families of the ground may be blessed through you (12:1–3; my translation).[6]

A number of points are noteworthy. First, the fulfilment of the promises listed here is conditional on Abraham's obedience. He is commanded by God to leave the security of his own country, people and family, and 'be a blessing'. Since the divine curses are due to human disobedience, it is hardly surprising that God expects Abraham to be obedient before blessing him. Secondly, the promise that Abraham will become a great nation implies that he will have numerous descendants who will possess their own land. While the fulfilment of this lies in the distant future, it is important to observe that at the outset major barriers stand in the way: Abraham has neither children nor land. Thirdly, the reference to 'a great name' alludes back to the story of the tower of Babel and possibly also to the 'men of renown' mentioned in 6:4. Whereas the people of Babel tried to establish a 'name' for themselves without God's help (11:4), the LORD will make Abraham famous. Fourthly, God promises that

---

[6] Two aspects of the translation adopted here require comment. First, the imperative form *wĕhyeh* (*vĕhyeh*) 'be' in 12:2d is maintained; NIV reads 'and you will be a blessing'. Second, special consideration has been given to the fact that the imperatives 'go' and 'be a blessing' are both followed by cohortatives. In such contexts the cohortative normally expresses purpose or result. To highlight this syntactic arrangement, the imperatives 'go' and 'be a blessing' are followed by 'so that'.

those who 'disdain' Abraham will be divinely 'cursed'. Implicit in this is a guarantee of protection for Abraham and victory over his enemies. The wording of the Hebrew original possibly also indicates that whereas a few will disdain Abraham, a majority will bless him. Fifthly, the climax of the passage comes in the concluding words that 'through you all the families of the earth will find blessing'. Here we meet for the first time an idea that is prominent in the rest of Genesis. Through Abraham and, as we shall observe below, his 'seed', God's blessing will be mediated to humanity. Sixthly, underlying the fulfilment of all these promises is the establishment of a special relationship between God and Abraham on account of which Abraham will be blessed.[7] The promises will be fulfilled as a result of divine blessing.

The theme of blessing is also prominent in the divine oath in 22:16–18 which marks the conclusion to the main part of the Abraham narrative.[8] Here the LORD declares to Abraham,

> I swear by myself, declares the LORD, that because you have done this and have not withheld your son, your only son, I will surely bless you and make your descendants [seed] as numerous as the stars in the sky and as the sand on the seashore. Your descendants [seed] will take possession of the cities [gate] of their [his] enemies, and through your offspring [seed] all nations on earth will be blessed, because you have obeyed me (22:16–18).

Although the wording here differs from that found in 12:1–3, the same basic ideas underlie both speeches. Yet, whereas 12:1–3 marks the beginning of the Abraham story, the divine oath in 22:16–18 comes at the climax and looks beyond Abraham to his 'seed'. Unfortunately, the identity of this 'seed' is not easy to determine. While the first mention of 'seed' denotes 'descendants' in the plural, the remaining references are ambiguous and could refer either to many descendants or to a single descendant. This latter possibility, however, is favoured by the syntax of the Hebrew text and is in keeping with the overall aim of Genesis to highlight a royal lineage.[9]

---

[7] Abraham is later designated the friend of God in 2 Chronicles 20:7; Isaiah 41:8.

[8] The Abraham narrative falls into two sections separated by a brief genealogy in 22:20–24. The main narrative is 11:27–22:19, with 23:1–25:11 forming an appendix. The divine speeches in 12:1–3 and 22:16–18, which come at the beginning and end of the main section, form what is known technically as an *inclusio*, marking the boundaries of the narrative. Whereas the promises in 12:1–3 are conditional on Abraham obeying God, the oath in 22:16–18 comes as a reward for Abraham's obedience, confirming the fulfilment of the earlier divine promises. For a fuller discussion, see chapter 11.

[9] See Alexander, 'Further Observations of the Term "Seed"', 363–7.

All of the material in the Abraham story relates in one way or another to the promises highlighted in the opening verses of Genesis 12 and so to the theme of blessing. Whereas some episodes focus on Abraham and his descendants possessing the land of Canaan (e.g. 13:1–18; 15:7–21), others are concerned with his lack of a son and the establishment of Isaac as his legitimate heir (e.g. 15:1–6; 16:1–18:15; 20:1–21:21). Inter-linked with these episodes are passages that reflect the fulfilment of God's promise that those who bless Abraham will know God's favour and those who act against Abraham will experience God's displeasure. On the one hand, Pharaoh and Abimelech are divinely punished for taking Sarah (12:17; 20:18), and the eastern kings are defeated when Abraham rescues Lot (14:1–16). On the other hand, Melchizedek blesses Abraham and receives in return a tenth of everything captured from the eastern kings (14:18–20). Much later we learn that Abimelech enters into a covenant with Abraham in order to ensure his own prosperity (21:22–34). Finally, to underline that the divine promises to Abraham have indeed been fulfilled, in so far as this is possible during his lifetime, Genesis 24 begins with the comment, 'The LORD had blessed him (Abraham) in every way' (24:1; cf. 24:35).

9.7. Blessing in the Remainder of Genesis

The theme of blessing, which is so important in the Abraham story, continues to play a major role in the remaining chapters of Genesis. Among the different aspects of blessing introduced in the Abraham narrative, which are continued and developed, the following are the most important.

First, God's blessing is closely associated with prosperity. This figures prominently in a number of episodes in the Abraham narrative. When Abraham returns from Egypt we read of a conflict between the servants of Abraham and Lot due to the fact that both men have become very wealthy (13:2, 5; cf. 12:16). Later, after rescuing Lot from the eastern kings, Abraham refuses to take anything from the king of Sodom lest he should claim to have made Abraham rich (14:21–23; cf. 15:1 which links Abraham's reward to the LORD). In Genesis 24 Abraham's servant not only presents valuable gifts to Rebekah and her family (24:22, 53), but also directly associates his master's prosperity with the LORD's blessing: 'The LORD has blessed my master abundantly, and he has become wealthy. He has given him sheep and cattle, silver and gold, menservants and maidservants, and camels and donkeys' (24:35). In the same context we may observe that Laban likewise links wealth with divine blessing (24:29–31).

Prosperity is also linked to blessing in the accounts concerning Isaac, Jacob and Joseph. Although it is only mentioned briefly, the narrator emphasises that

Isaac's great wealth was due to God's blessing (26:12–13). While Jacob fled to Paddan Aram with few possessions, as a result of God's blessing, he returned to Canaan a very rich man (30:43; 32:3–21), and this in spite of attempts by his uncle Laban to limit his wealth (31:6–9). The story of Joseph also revolves around the idea that it is through God's blessing that he prospered in Egypt. Although he began life there as a slave (39:1–6), and later was imprisoned unjustly (39:6–23), he eventually became governor of the country second only to Pharaoh (41:39–43). Throughout the patriarchal stories prosperity is closely tied to divine blessing.[10]

Secondly, God's blessing is also associated with fertility. We see this in Genesis 1 where the first reference to God blessing the man and the woman is directly followed by the command, 'Be fruitful and increase in number' (1:28). This close association of blessing and fertility is echoed later in 9:1: 'Then God blessed Noah and his sons, saying to them, "Be fruitful and increase in number and fill the earth."' The same phrases are used when first Isaac and then God bless Jacob in 28:3 and 35:11 respectively (cf. 48:4). In the Abraham story the lack of fertility is the setting against which the LORD promises that Abraham will become a great nation. Thereafter we have frequent reminders that the 'seed' of Abraham will be as numerous as the dust of the earth (13:16; 28:14), the stars of the heavens (15:5: 22:17; 26:4) and the sand of the seashore (22:17; 32:12). The topic of fertility is also prominent in the story of Jacob where it dominates the competitive relationship between Leah and Rachel (29:31–30:24) and, on a different level, the relationship between Jacob and Laban (30:25–43). Here also fertility is linked to divine blessing (cf. 29:32–33; 30:6, 17–18, 20, 22–24, 27–30). Throughout Genesis the ability to reproduce is viewed as a sign of divine blessing.[11]

Thirdly, and most importantly of all, the power to mediate God's blessing to others is passed on through the chosen line of patriarchs. This is highlighted in Genesis in two different ways: through God renewing his special relationship with the head of each generation, and through a unique blessing which each father bestows on his 'first-born' son.

In the patriarchal stories the LORD renews his special relationship with the head of the chosen family in each generation. The promises associated with God's desire to bless Abraham in 12:1–3, and later confirmed by oath in 22:16–18, are passed on to his first-born 'seed'. When Isaac is faced with a famine in the land of Canaan, the LORD appears to him and says,

---

[10] The idea that God blesses the righteous materially is important in the Old Testament. However, it needs to be remembered that the Old Testament counter-balances this belief by teaching that the righteous may suffer (e.g. the story of Job) and that the wicked may prosper (e.g. Ps. 49).

[11] The reference to the rapid increase of the Israelites in Exodus 1:7 provides an important link between the books of Genesis and Exodus.

Do not go down to Egypt; live in the land where I tell you to live. Stay in this land for a while, and I will be with you and bless you. For to you and your descendants I will give all these lands and will confirm the oath I swore to your father Abraham. I will make your descendants [seed] as numerous as the stars in the sky and will give them [your seed] all these lands, and through your offspring [seed] all nations on earth will be blessed, because Abraham obeyed me and kept my requirements, my commands, my decrees and my laws (26:2–5).

Much of this speech echoes 22:16–18, highlighting Abraham's willingness to obey God. In this way God encourages Isaac to obey him. As in 12:1–3, God's blessing through the fulfilment of the divine promises is dependent upon Isaac obeying him and remaining in Canaan. Interestingly, Genesis 26, which is the only chapter to focus exclusively on Isaac, contains three explicit references to God blessing him (26:12, 24, 29).

The story of Jacob also includes a divine speech containing promises regarding numerous descendants, possession of the land, and the blessing of all peoples on earth. It occurs when Jacob is fleeing to Paddan Aram in order to escape from his brother Esau. God says,

I am the LORD, the God of your father Abraham and the God of Isaac. I will give you and your descendants [seed] the land on which you are lying. Your descendants [seed] will be like the dust of the earth, and you will spread out to the west and to the east, and to the north and to the south. All peoples on earth will be blessed through you and your offspring [seed]. I am with you and will watch over you wherever you go, and I will bring you back to this land. I will not leave you until I have done what I have promised you (28:13–15).

Although it is not mentioned specifically, the contents of the speech, which resemble very closely earlier divine statements, clearly imply that God will bless Jacob. In response, Jacob vows that if God will indeed protect him and bring him back safely to his father's house, 'then the LORD will be my God and this stone that I have set up as a pillar will be God's house, and of all that you give me I will give you a tenth' (28:21–22). When many years later Jacob returns from Paddan Aram, God appears to him again and, blessing him (35:9), states,

I am God Almighty; be fruitful and increase in number. A nation and a community of nations will come from you, and kings will come from your body. The land I gave to Abraham and Isaac I also give to you, and I will give this land to your descendants after you (35:11–12; cf. 48:3–4).

Here God confirms Jacob as the heir to the covenant earlier established with Abraham and Isaac.

In the light of these divine speeches it is apparent that Abraham, Isaac and Jacob all enjoy the same privileged relationship with the LORD. While Abraham and Isaac have other children, they are not part of the chosen lineage and so do not have the same unique relationship with God.[12]

As a result of this special relationship the patriarchs are able to mediate God's blessing to others. This blessing, however, is in direct proportion to how the patriarchs and their 'seed' are treated by others. Apart from the examples in the Abraham story considered above, the stories of Jacob and Joseph contain further illustrations. Laban learns by divination that the LORD has blessed him because of Jacob (30:27). Potiphar and his household prosper on account of Joseph (39:2–6), as does the prison warder (39:20–23). Later, following Joseph's appointment as governor over Egypt, not only is the entire nation enabled to survive a seven-year famine (47:13–26), but other nations also benefit from his wise leadership (41:56–57). Finally, it should be noted that when Pharaoh offers Joseph's relatives 'the best part of the land' (47:6), Jacob blesses him (47:7–10).

The other way in which the Genesis narrative reveals that the power to bless others is granted to succeeding patriarchs is through the paternal blessing of the first-born. Clearly, it was the custom that the first-born son should receive from his father a special blessing that gave him privileges not enjoyed by other sons. This idea lies at the heart of the account of Jacob deceiving his father Isaac in order to obtain the blessing about to be given to Esau (27:1–40). So important is this blessing to Jacob that he is prepared to face both his father's displeasure, should he be found out (27:11–12), and his brother's anger at being deprived of what by custom was rightfully his (cf. 27:41). Although Isaac becomes fully aware that Jacob has deceived him, he subsequently blesses him again before sending him to find a wife in Paddan Aram.[13] This suggests that Isaac willingly accepts what has happened (28:1–5).[14]

---

[12] This is highlighted, for example, in Genesis 17 where God explicitly states that the covenant will be established through Isaac and not Ishmael (17:19–21). Although Ishmael is here blessed by God (17:20), he does not enjoy the same standing as Isaac.

[13] Interestingly, this blessing echoes 1:22, 28; 9:1, 7.

[14] While some readers may feel that, by deceiving his father and stealing his brother's blessing, Jacob acts immorally, various details in the narrative suggest that Jacob's actions are pardoned, at least in part, by the narrator. First, it is emphasised that Rebekah not only instigates the deception (27:5–10) but also states that she will accept full responsibility should the deception be discovered (27:13). Secondly, the narrator appears critical of Isaac for allowing his appetite for wild game to influence his attitude towards Esau (25:28). By favouring Esau, Isaac seemingly ignores the implications of the divine statement made prior to the birth of the twin boys that Esau will be sub-servient to Jacob (25:23). Thirdly, the concluding comments of Genesis 26, that Esau's

The subject of paternal blessing also figures prominently in Genesis 48 and 49. In the first of these we have the account of how Jacob blesses Joseph's two sons, Manasseh and Ephraim. Not only does Jacob deliberately give the younger son Ephraim the superior blessing (48:17–20), but also Ephraim receives the rights of the first-born that should have gone to his father's older brother Reuben (cf. 1 Chr. 5:1). This event established the tradition that through the tribe of Ephraim God would create a royal dynasty. Undoubtedly this idea influenced later developments, especially the choice of Joshua as a leader and the importance of Shiloh as the location for the central sanctuary. All this changed, however, when God later chose David and Jerusalem (Ps. 78:59–72).

In Genesis 49 we have a long list of pronouncements that Jacob makes regarding his twelve sons. The narrator's comment in 49:28 indicates that these are given in the context of Jacob blessing his sons, with each one receiving 'the blessing appropriate to him'. Clearly, the content of these blessings reflects Jacob's attitude towards each son. Without examining them in detail, it is significant that the pronouncements concerning the eldest brothers Reuben, Simeon and Levi are all negative, whereas those given to Judah and Joseph are very favourable. In the light of the special interest that Genesis has in the theme of blessing, Jacob's comments about Joseph are noteworthy:

> Joseph is a fruitful vine, a fruitful vine near a spring, whose branches climb over a wall. With bitterness archers attacked him; they shot at him with hostility. But his bow remained steady, his strong arms stayed supple, because of the hand of the Mighty One of Jacob, because of the Shepherd, the Rock of Israel, because of your father's God, who helps you, because of the Almighty, who blesses you with blessings of the heavens above, blessings of the deep that lies below, blessings of the breast and womb. Your father's blessings are greater than the blessings of the ancient mountains, than the bounty of the age-old hills. Let all these rest on the head of Joseph, on the brow of the prince among his brothers (Gen. 49:22–26).

Here, as in Genesis 48, we encounter the idea of blessing coming through Joseph's descendants. Yet, while Joseph is associated with blessing, it is noteworthy that that when Jacob blesses Judah he comments that 'the sceptre will not depart from Judah' and that one of his descendants will enjoy 'the obedience of the nations' (49:10). Although it is not explicitly stated that the nations will be blessed as a result, in the light of Genesis as a whole, this is possibly implied.

---

[14] (*continued*) wives were a source of grief to Isaac and Rebekah (26:34–35), together with the earlier story of Esau selling his birthright for some stew (25:29–34), suggest that Esau is not worthy of the special paternal blessing. In the light of these factors, all the family members share responsibility for Jacob's deception.

By highlighting the patriarchs' special relationship with God and their ability to impart a unique blessing to one of their sons, Genesis draws attention to the privileged position of the 'seed' of the chosen lineage. As a result, the expectation is created that through a future royal descendant all the nations of the earth will be blessed.

9.8. Conclusion

As a whole the book of Genesis records three important phases regarding the theme of divine blessing. At the outset all of creation, including especially humanity, experiences God's favour. However, as a result of the disobedience of Adam and Eve, a significant reversal occurs with human beings and the rest of creation coming under God's curse. The tragic consequences of this are noted throughout the rest of Genesis. However, at the beginning of the Abraham narrative God not only promises to bless Abraham but also through him to bless all the families of the earth. The remaining episodes of the patriarchal narratives focus on this latter promise by linking it to the first-born/ royal 'seed' of Abraham. Although none of them is biologically the first-born, Isaac, Jacob and Joseph are all treated as such and through them blessing is imparted to others. While Joseph stands out in Genesis as the one who comes closest to fulfilling the divine promise of international blessing, the ultimate fulfilment of God's promise to bless all the nations of the earth through the 'seed' of Abraham still lies in the future. Genesis thus establishes the concept that through a (royal) 'first-born' descendant of Abraham, God's blessing will be imparted to the nations of the earth.

9.9. New Testament Connections

The most obvious allusions in the New Testament to the theme of blessing in Genesis come in Acts 3:25–26 and Galatians 3:14 In the first of these passages Peter suggests that Jesus Christ is the one through whom God's blessing will come to others.

> And you are heirs of the prophets and of the covenant God made with your fathers. He said to Abraham, 'Through your offspring all peoples on earth will be blessed.' When God raised up his servant, he sent him first to you to bless you by turning each of you from your wicked ways (Acts 3:25–26).

Paul makes the very same point in Galatians: 'He redeemed us in order that the blessing given to Abraham might come to the Gentiles through Christ Jesus ...'

(Gal. 3:14). In both of these contexts Jesus Christ, the 'seed' of Abraham, is the one in whom the divine promise that all peoples of earth will be blessed is fulfilled. The same idea is also prominent in Romans 15:8–12, although the concept of blessing is not mentioned specifically. With these passages one might also include Romans 4:6–9. While Paul does not specifically mention the text of Genesis in these verses, his brief comment regarding divine blessing, based on Psalm 32:1–2, comes in the context of his argument that Abraham is the father of those who have faith, both Jews and Gentiles.

Other passages which may allude indirectly to the concept of blessing highlighted in Genesis include Elizabeth's reaction to Mary in Luke 1:42–45, and the beatitudes of Jesus in Matthew 5:3–12 and Luke 6:20–26.

10

Paradise Lost

10.1. Summary

The motif of 'land' is important in Genesis due to the special relationship which God establishes between the first man and the ground; a relationship reflected in their respective names 'ādām and 'ādāmâ. At harmony with God, each is dependent upon the other. However, when the first human couple disobeyed the LORD God and ate of the forbidden fruit, two important consequences followed. First, their relationship with the ground was severely affected; no longer did the earth give willingly of its bounty to satisfy their needs. Secondly, they were expelled from Eden and so deprived of a unique environment in which to commune with God. With every subsequent unrighteous act humankind was further alienated from the earth. The accounts of Cain killing Abel, Noah and the flood, and the tower of Babel all reveal the increasing tension which existed between humanity and the earth. In each episode divine judgement comes in the form of exile and alienation from the earth. Against this background the divine gift of land to Abraham is significant. It is indicative of Abraham's positive relationship with the LORD and anticipates the divine presence in the midst of the nation of Israel.

10.2. Introduction

A careful reading of Genesis reveals that the concept of land figures prominently in the thinking of the author. From the initial creation of the dry land through to Joseph's desire that his bones be buried in the land promised by God to Abraham, Isaac and Jacob, there is hardly an episode in the entire book which does not in one way or another mention land. While not all references to land are to be viewed as equally important, it is clear that the relationship between human beings and the earth is of major interest to the author.

Before looking at the theme of land in Genesis it may be helpful to observe briefly that in the Hebrew text three different terms are used for 'land'. By far the most common is the word *'eres* (*'erets*) which comes 312 times in Genesis. Usually *'eres* (*'erets*) denotes either the earth as a whole (e.g. 1:1, 10, 26) or a particular country (e.g. 12:1, 5). The term *'ādāmâ* occurs 43 times and normally means 'ground' or 'soil' (e.g. 2:5, 7, 19). The third term is *śādēh*, which comes approximately 50 times in Genesis and usually refers to wide-open spaces; it is often translated 'field' (e.g. 2:19, 20). Although it is possible to view each term as having distinctive aspects, they may on occasions be used to denote the same thing.[1]

10.3. The Creation of the Earth

The opening chapter of Genesis establishes the nature of the earth's relationship to both God and humanity. Of fundamental importance is the belief that the earth is created by God; by merely speaking he brings order to that which is 'formless and empty' (1:2). With the creation of the dry land, God establishes three distinct realms: 'sky', 'land' and 'seas' (1:6–10). Of these the most important is the land. Unlike the sky and the seas, the land plays an active role in God's creative activity. It is divinely commanded to produce both vegetation (1:11–12) and living creatures (1:24). Having created the earth, God delegates authority to human beings to govern it and its creatures (cf. 1:28).

Complementing Genesis 1, the account in 2:4–25 develops more fully the close relationship which exists between the man and the ground. First, the man is actually made from the ground: 'the LORD God formed the man from the dust of the ground and breathed into his nostrils the breath of life, and the man became a living being' (2:7). Secondly, in the Hebrew original the terms for 'man' and 'ground' are very similar; they are respectively *'ādām* and *'ādāmâ*.[2] This unique relationship between the first man and the ground is further emphasised when the LORD God places him in the Garden of Eden with responsibility 'to work it and take care of it' (2:15). Here the man is

---

[1] An interesting example of this comes in the Abraham narrative. The expression 'all peoples on earth' (lit. 'families of the ground') in Genesis 12:3 is later replaced by the expression 'all nations on earth' (18:18; 22:18). No essential difference in meaning is meant. However, in 12:3 the emphasis is upon the oneness of all human beings in that they have a common origin, the dust of the ground. The expression in 18:18 and 22:18 highlights the idea that the earth consists of different nations. The switch from the former expression to the latter may be due to the fact that the fulfilment of the divine promise that the nations will be blessed is linked to the creation of Israel as a nation.

[2] In English we might capture the connection between the terms *'ādām* and *'ādāmâ* by translating them as 'earthling' and 'earth' respectively.

portrayed as a tenant placed in charge of his master's garden, and, with one exception, permitted to enjoy freely all of its produce (2:16–17). Thus, Genesis 1–2 highlights the special relationship that exists between God, humanity and the land/ground. Human beings are charged by God to exercise authority over the earth, and the earth is divinely empowered to produce food in abundance for humankind. Dependent upon each other, humanity and the earth are both accountable to God.

4. The Garden of Eden as Sanctuary

In Genesis 2–3 the Garden of Eden functions as the meeting place between the LORD God and the first human couple. Interesting parallels exist between Eden and the later sanctuaries, in particular the tabernacle and Jerusalem temple.[3]

1. The LORD God walks in Eden as he later does in the tabernacle (3:8; cf. Lev. 26:12; Deut. 23:15; 2 Sam. 7:6–7).
2. Eden and the later sanctuaries are entered from the east and guarded by cherubim (3:24; Ex. 25:18–22; 26:31; 1 Kgs. 6:23–29).
3. The tabernacle menorah (or lampstand) possibly symbolises the tree of life (2:9 3:22; cf. Ex. 25:31–35).
4. The pair of Hebrew verbs in God's command to the man 'to work it (the Garden) and take care of it' (2:15) are only used in combination elsewhere in the Pentateuch of the duties of the Levites in the sanctuary (cf. Num. 3:7–8; 8:26; 18:5–6).[4]
5. The river flowing from Eden (2:10) is reminiscent of Ezekiel 47:1–12 which envisages a river flowing from a future Jerusalem temple and bringing life to the Dead Sea.
6. Finally, gold and onyx which are mentioned in 2:11–12 are used extensively to decorate the later sanctuaries and priestly garments (e.g. Ex. 25:7, 11, 17, 31).[5] Gold in particular is associated with the divine presence.

Since Eden is a paradise where divinity and humanity enjoy each other's presence, it is hardly surprising that it becomes a prototype for later sanctuaries. Although human beings enjoy close fellowship with God within the tabernacle and

---

[3] These parallels are set out by G.J. Wenham in his article, 'Sanctuary Symbolism in the Garden of Eden Story', *Proceedings of the World Congress of Jewish Studies* 9 (1986), 19–25.

[4] *'ābad ('āvad)* 'to serve', 'to till'; *šāmar (shāmar)* 'to keep', 'to observe'.

[5] There are about one hundred references to gold and seven to onyx in the Exodus account of the building of the tabernacle.

Jerusalem temple, direct access into God's immediate presence is limited to once a year and then only for the high priest.[6] However, within Eden the first man and woman have the unique privilege of being able to relate to God face to face without fear or shame. Against this background the account of their disobedience is even more tragic.

10.5. Expelled from Eden

The harmony of Eden ends when the man and the woman knowingly disobey God and eat from the tree of the knowledge of good and evil (3:1–13; cf. 2:16–17). Two consequences are significant regarding the subject of land. First, God curses the ground because of Adam's disobedience (3:17–19). No longer is the ground divinely empowered to produce food in abundance. Man must work by the sweat of his brow in order to eat. Furthermore, his task is made more difficult because the ground 'will produce thorns and thistles' (3:18). No longer is the man at harmony with the ground from which he was taken and upon which he depends for food.

Secondly, the man and the woman are banished from the Garden of Eden (3:23). Like a landlord expelling an unsatisfactory tenant, God ousts them from Eden. The reason for their expulsion is recorded by the narrator: 'He must not be allowed to reach out his hand and take also from the tree of life and eat, and live for ever' (3:22). Separated from the tree of life, each human will experience death, the divine punishment for eating from the tree of the knowledge of good and evil (2:17). To ensure that human beings may not return to Eden, God places 'cherubim and a flaming sword flashing back and forth to guard the way to the tree of life' (3:24). Expelled from Eden, Adam and Eve will no longer enjoy the intimacy of God's presence. While this does not mark the end of God's relationship with humanity, it does indicate a dramatic change. The special relationship that was established at creation will only exist with those to whom God now makes himself known. No longer will humanity automatically have a personal knowledge of God. Thus, as a result of human disobedience the initial harmony of creation between God, humanity and the land is replaced by alienation.

10.6. Cain – a Restless Wanderer on the Earth

The relationship between human beings and the ground is important in the story of Cain killing his brother Abel. Initially, Cain is described as one who

---

[6] See chapter 14.

'worked the soil (ground)' (4:2). When, out of jealousy, he kills his brother, the LORD God confronts him regarding his crime. The relationship between Cain's action and the ground is highlighted in God's speech:

> What have you done? Listen! Your brother's blood cries out to me from the ground. Now you are under a curse and driven from the ground, which opened its mouth to receive your brother's blood from your hand. When you work the ground, it will no longer yield its crop for you. You will be a restless wanderer on the earth (4:10–12).

Whereas Adam's punishment resulted in the ground being difficult to toil, Cain is actually 'driven from the ground' and forced to become a restless wanderer. He must also go out from the LORD's presence (4:14, 16). Alienated from both God and the ground, Cain's punishment resembles that of his parents.

Two points are worth underlining from the story of Cain killing Abel. First, the narrative highlights the continuing relationship between humanity and the ground. Cain's actions have a direct bearing upon the ground; it is stained by Abel's blood. Secondly, each unrighteous action increases humanity's alienation from the ground. The ground, which was to nourish humankind, is now the agent of divine punishment. The natural environment no longer automatically favours humanity as God intended; it is now hostile and the degree of this hostility is determined in some measure by the extent of human unrighteousness.

10.7. The Flood Narrative

The subject of land is prominent in the account of Noah's rescue from the flood. It first appears in the naming of Noah by his father Lamech: 'When Lamech had lived 182 years, he had a son. He named him Noah and said, "He will comfort us in the labour and painful toil of our hands caused by the ground the LORD has cursed"' (5:28–29).[7]

Here Noah is presented as the one who will bring relief to those already heavily burdened by the task of working the ground. Behind this comment is the hope that Noah will reverse the ever-worsening relationship between humanity and the ground.

God's decision to send a flood that will destroy all living creatures is clearly linked to the wickedness of humankind (cf. 6:5).

---

[7] Although the name Noah is probably linked etymologically to the Hebrew verb *nûaḥ* (*nûakh*) meaning 'to rest', it also sounds like the Hebrew verb *niḥām* (*nikhām*) 'to comfort'.

Now the earth was corrupt in God's sight and was full of violence. God saw how corrupt the earth had become, for all the people on earth had corrupted their ways. So God said to Noah, 'I am going to put an end to all people, for the earth is filled with violence because of them. I am surely going to destroy both them and the earth' (6:11–13).

Once again we see how the continual violence of humanity has a direct bearing upon the earth. Through the shedding of innocent blood the ground is polluted, reducing its fertility. Consequently, the task of toiling the ground had become almost unbearable by the time of Noah.

The flood narrative in 6:9–9:19 exhibits close parallels with Genesis 1. The description of the floodwaters gradually covering the entire earth, including the highest mountains, portrays a return to the earth's original state prior to the separation of the land and seas (cf. 1:9–10). With the retreat of the floodwaters and Noah's departure from the ark, we have the re-creation of the earth.[8] Consequently, those who emerge from the ark now inhabit ground which has been cleansed from the pollution caused by unrighteous behaviour. Yet, although the earth has been recreated, the same is not true of human nature, for, as God comments, 'every inclination of his (man's) heart is evil from childhood' (8:21). Nevertheless, God promises that he will never again 'curse the ground because of man' (8:21) by sending another flood.[9] This is subsequently confirmed in the covenant outlined in 9:8–17.

---

[8] According to G.V. Smith, the flood narrative echoes the initial account of creation in the following ways:

> When Genesis 1 and 2 are compared with 8 and 9, one begins to perceive the extent to which the author uses repeated phrases and ideas to build the structural relationships within the units. The following relationships are found: (a) Since man could not live on the earth when it was covered with water in chaps. 1 and 8, a subsiding of the water and separation of the land from the water took place, allowing the dry land to appear (1:9–10; 8:1–13); (b) 'birds and animals and every creeping thing that creeps on the earth' are brought forth to 'swarm upon the earth' in 1:20–21, 24–25 and 8:17–19; (c) God establishes the days and seasons in 1:14–18 and 8:22; (d) God's blessing rests upon the animals as he commands them to 'be fruitful and multiply on the earth' in both 1:22 and 8:17; (e) man is brought forth and he receives the blessing of God: 'Be fruitful and multiply and fill the earth' in 1:28 and 9:1, 7; (f) Man is given dominion over the animal kingdom in 1:28 and 9:2; (g) God provides food for man in 1:29–30 and 9:3 (this latter regulation makes a direct reference back to the previous passage when it includes the statement, 'As I have given the green plant'); and (h) in 9:6 the writer quotes from 1:26–27 concerning the image of God in man. The author repeatedly emphasises the fact that the world is beginning again with a fresh start. But Noah does not return to the paradise of Adam, for the significant difference is that 'the intent of man's heart is evil' (Gen 8:21) ('Structure and Purpose in Genesis 1–11', *JETS* 20 [1977], 310–1).

[9] As we have noted in chapter 9, this refers to the flood.

Prior to the flood the shedding of innocent blood polluted the ground, decreasing significantly its fertility. In 9:1–7 God issues certain instructions which are intended to prevent the earth from being contaminated in the future. These focus on the 'lifeblood' of both animal and humans which must be treated with due respect.

10.8. Noah, a Man of the Soil

The episode following the account of the flood begins by describing Noah as a 'man of the soil (ground)' (9:20) and focuses briefly on his ability to cultivate a vineyard that produces an abundant crop. This part of the story is clearly intended to highlight the dramatic change which has occurred as a result of the flood. Whereas the ground's fertility was severely limited before the flood, now it produces abundantly. In this we see the fulfilment of Lamech's comments regarding Noah in 5:29.

10.9. The Table of Nations

The Table of Nations in Genesis 10 outlines where the descendants of Noah gradually settle.[10] Of particular note are the details concerning Canaan and his sons; 10:15–18 provides a detailed list of the various people descended from Canaan, and 10:19 describes the borders of Canaan. These details are significant in the light of later events in Genesis, when Abraham is promised by God possession of the land of Canaan (cf. 15:18–21). This development clearly builds upon the blessing which Noah pronounces upon Shem which contrasts sharply with the curse upon Canaan (9:25–27).

10.10. The Tower of Babel

The incident involving the tower of Babel centres on humanity's desire to dwell together in one place and through co-operation to make a name for

---

[10] Because it indicates that the descendants of Noah were divided into different clan and nations, each with it own language, the material in Genesis 10 ought to come after the account of the tower of Babel (11:1–9); 10:25 probably alludes to the creation of different nations, speaking different languages. The writer of Genesis may have felt it inappropriate to place the Table of Nations between 11:1–9 and 11:10–26, since this would bring into immediate proximity two quite different types of genealogy, both concerning the descendants of Shem.

themselves (11:4). However, God views with displeasure their activities, especially their desire to build a city with a tower that reaches to the heavens. Consequently, he prevents them from continuing their construction by confusing their language and scattering them over the face of the whole earth (11:9). Humanity is thus 'exiled' by the LORD and hindered from establishing a community that might challenge his authority over the earth.

10.11. The Abraham Narrative

As we have previously noted, the Abraham narrative marks an important turning point in the book of Genesis. This is certainly true as regards the subject of land. Whereas the early chapters of Genesis are dominated by accounts of human disobedience resulting in exile, one of the main themes of the story of Abraham is God's gift of land to Abraham and his descendants.

Several factors are significant regarding God's promise of the land of Canaan to Abraham. First, it is conditional upon Abraham's obedience to God. At the very outset Abraham must obey the LORD's call to leave his own land and go to a new land (12:1). Implicit in this divine command, and in the associated promise that God will make Abraham 'into a great nation' (12:2), is the idea that God will give Abraham a new land. The identity of this land is soon revealed as Canaan (12:5–7), and, in spite of the fact that it is already occupied by the Canaanites (12:6), the LORD confirms that Abraham's descendants will possess it. Later, in the account of the separation of Abraham and Lot, the promise of land is stated in more detail (cf. 13:14–17). These initial promises, however, are given added weight by the covenant which God makes with Abraham in 15:7–21.[11] This covenant is linked to Abraham being credited as righteous on account of his faith. Whereas the early chapters of Genesis focus on the loss of land as a result of disobedience, Abraham is portrayed as gaining the land due to obedience and trust in God.

Secondly, God informs Abraham that his descendants will only occupy the land of Canaan after a period of over four hundred years (15:13–14). The announcement of this delay has important implications for the rest of the Pentateuch. Although Genesis records that Abraham and Isaac live within the borders of Canaan, the concluding chapters describe how Jacob and his family leave Canaan to dwell in Egypt. The remaining books of the Pentateuch focus on the future exodus of the Israelites from Egypt and various developments that occur prior to their taking possession of the promised land.

---

[11] Although further references to the land occur in the Abraham narrative (e.g. 17:8; 22:17), the covenant in Genesis 15 marks a climax as regards land.

Thirdly, although Abraham is divinely promised the land of Canaan, various peoples already occupy the land. This naturally raises the question, how can God give to Abraham land that is already owned by others? The author of Genesis, however, answers this question indirectly by indicating that the inhabitants of Canaan are unworthy occupants of the land. We first encounter this idea prior to the Abraham narrative itself in 9:20–29. Here attention is drawn to the unrighteous behaviour of Ham and the resulting curse upon his son Canaan. Implicit in this is the idea that the descendants of Canaan may behave like their forefather Ham. The identity of these descendants is provided in 10:15–18, along with details of the land occupied by them (10:19).

> Canaan was the father of Sidon his firstborn, and of the Hittites, Jebusites, Amorites, Girgashites, Hivites, Arkites, Sinites, Arvadites, Zemarites and Hamathites. Later the Canaanite clans scattered and the borders of Canaan reached from Sidon towards Gerar as far as Gaza, and then towards Sodom, Gomorrah, Admah, and Zeboiim, as far as Lasha (10:15–19).

Within the Abraham story itself various passages draw attention to the unrighteous nature of the descendants of Ham. In 13:13 the narrator comments, 'Now the men of Sodom were wicked and were sinning greatly against the LORD.' This negative view of the Canaanite inhabitants of Sodom is reflected in Abraham's attitude towards the king of Sodom (14:21–24), especially when compared with his reaction to Melchizedek king of Salem (14:18–20). In the light of these passages the later account of the destruction of Sodom and Gomorrah in Genesis 19 is hardly surprising; indeed it is anticipated in 13:10. God's comment in 18:20–21 about the sin of Sodom and Gomorrah is confirmed by the events surrounding the visit of the two angels in Genesis 19. Significantly, the sexual nature of the sin of the men of Sodom is reminiscent of the unrighteous action of their ancestor Ham. Another reference to the sin of Ham's descendants comes in 15:16. Here God indicates that Abraham's descendants will return to the land of Canaan in the fourth generation, 'for the sin of the Amorites has not yet reached its full measure'. Since the early chapters of Genesis have established the idea that unrighteous behaviour results in exile from the land, there can be little doubt that the present inhabitants of Canaan will be dispossessed due to their sin. The later conquest of the land by the Israelites is thus understood as an act of divine judgement upon those already living there.[12]

Fourthly, although Abraham is divinely promised that his descendants will only take possession of the land of Canaan several centuries later, by

---

[12] The same principle was later applied on different occasions to the inhabitants of the northern kingdom of Israel and the southern kingdom of Judah.

allowing Abraham to buy the cave of Machpelah in Ephron's field, the Hittites of Hebron acknowledged Abraham's right to be an inhabitant of Canaan (23:1–20). Moreover, because the land was bought for the purpose of being a burial place, this guaranteed Abraham's descendants a permanent right of ownership. Although the divine promise of the land would only be fulfilled in the future, Abraham witnessed the beginning of the process.

10.12. The Jacob Story

The story of Jacob revolves around his temporary exile in the region of Paddan Aram caused when he deceives his father into giving him the first-born blessing. In spite of his deceitful behaviour Jacob receives various assurances regarding the land of Canaan. The first comes from his father in 28:4. Although Isaac encourages Jacob to leave Canaan in order to find a wife, he prays that God Almighty will bless him: 'May he give you and your descendants the blessing given to Abraham, so that you may take possession of the land where you now live as an alien, the land God gave to Abraham' (28:4).

Next, just as Jacob is about to depart from Canaan God reassures him regarding the land through a dream at Bethel:

> I am the LORD, the God of your father Abraham and the God of Isaac. I will give you and your descendants the land on which you are lying. Your descendants will be like the dust of the earth, and you will spread out to the west and to the east, to the north and to the south. All peoples on earth will be blessed through you and your offspring. I am with you and will watch over you wherever you go, and I will bring you back to this land. I will not leave you until I have done what I have promised you (28:13–15).

Although Jacob must flee from Canaan on account of Esau, the narrative anticipates his future return. Much later the divine promise of land is again repeated to Jacob (35:11–12).

The turning point in Jacob's exile in Paddan Aram comes when the LORD says to him, 'Go back to the land of your fathers and to your relatives, and I will be with you' (31:3). With this assurance Jacob prepares to return to Canaan. While he had arrived in Paddan Aram alone, he leaves with a large family and numerous possessions. In spite of all that the LORD has done for him in Paddam Aram, Jacob is still very conscious of the reason for his exile there. Consequently, on returning to the borders of Canaan he makes preparations for his encounter with Esau (32:1–21). Interestingly, just as Jacob experienced the LORD's presence when he left Canaan (28:10–22), so once again he has a dramatic meeting with the LORD as he is about to re-enter the land (32:22–32). By locating these theophanies on the border of Canaan, the narrative draws attention to the importance of the land.

The reconciliation between Jacob and Esau not only brings to an end the conflict which had separated them for years (33:1–16) but also results in Jacob settling in the land of Canaan (33:17–20). Esau, however, eventually settles outside Canaan in the land of Seir (33:16; 36:6–8). Remarkably, this parting of the brothers echoes the earlier separation of Abraham and Lot; Jacob and Esau agree to dwell in different regions because the land is not able to support all of their livestock (36:7–8; cf. 13:5–18). As a result only Jacob is left dwelling in the land of Canaan.

10.13. The Joseph Story

The final quarter of Genesis revolves around the character of Joseph and tells of his role in bringing the descendants of Abraham out of Canaan and into Egypt. Given God's comments to Abraham that 'your descendants will be strangers in a country not their own, and they will be enslaved and ill-treated four hundred years' (15:13), the Joseph story provides an essential link between the Abraham and Jacob narratives and the later account of the exodus from Egypt. The overall plot of the Pentateuch requires a transition from Canaan to Egypt.

Several features of the Joseph story invite further comments as regards the topic of land. First, it is interesting to observe that it is a famine in Canaan that brings the brothers of Joseph back into contact with him in Egypt. Throughout Genesis famines are associated with God's curse upon the earth; they reflect the absence of divine blessing and highlight the lack of harmony that ought to exist between human beings and the ground. But for the preparations made by Joseph, the effects of this famine would have been much more terrible.

Secondly, given Jacob's own experience of having been exiled from Canaan in Paddan Aram, it is not surprising that he is somewhat reluctant to leave Canaan again. He only goes when the LORD intervenes and commands him to do so:

> Do not be afraid to go down to Egypt, for I will make you into a great nation there. I will go down to Egypt with you, and I will surely bring you back again. And Joseph's own hand will close your eyes (46:3–4).

Jacob's reluctance to go to Egypt should be viewed against other episodes in Genesis. Earlier, during a famine in Canaan, Abraham had gone down to Egypt (12:10–20). However, his experience there had placed in jeopardy the fulfilment of the divine promises. Later, when another famine occurred in the land of Canaan, Isaac was specifically commanded by God not to go down into Egypt (26:1–2). In the light of these events, Jacob may have felt strongly inclined to remain in Canaan.

Thirdly, although the movement in the Joseph story is from Canaan to Egypt, there are various indications that this was not to be a permanent move. This is reflected, for example, in God's words to Jacob: 'I will surely bring you back again' (46:4). The Israelites' attachment to Canaan is also reflected in the events surrounding the death of Jacob. After his death, Jacob's embalmed body is transported back to Canaan to be buried in the cave at Machpelah alongside the bodies of Abraham and Isaac (49:29–50:14). Later, Joseph makes a similar request that his bones should be carried up from Egypt to Canaan (50:24–25). Significantly, Joseph does not expect this to happen immediately after his death, as with his father, but thinks in terms of this being done when God comes to the aid of the Israelites (cf. Ex. 13:19). Thus, although Genesis ends with the account of Joseph's death, there is an expectation of things yet to come; the Israelites shall one day return to the promised land.

10.14. Conclusion

Genesis emphasises throughout the close relationship that human beings have with the ground. The basis for this interdependence is explained in the account of creation where the first man, Adam (*'ādām*), is created from the dust of the ground (*'ādāmâ*). Unfortunately, although God initially blesses the relationship between humanity and the earth, the disobedience of Adam and Eve in the Garden of Eden leads to a dramatic reversal of this situation. Moreover, Adam and Eve are exiled from Eden ending the intimate relationship that they enjoyed there with the LORD. Later, through the promises given to Abraham, the restoration of divine blessing becomes a possibility. This, however, will only be fully achieved when all the families of the ground are blessed. In the meantime Abraham is assured that, as part of the process by which the nations shall be blessed, his descendants will possess the land of Canaan. For them Canaan will resemble in part the Garden of Eden; there the people will enjoy a special communion with God surrounded by signs of God's blessing upon the land.[13]

---

[13] For a fuller discussion of the implications of this, see T.D. Alexander, 'Beyond Borders: The Wider Dimensions of Land' in P. Johnston and P. Walker (eds.), *The Land of Promise: Biblical, Theological and Contemporary Perspectives* (Leicester: Apollos, 2000), 35–50.

10.15. New Testament Connections

The NT develops the concept of land in ways that are both similar and
dissimilar to those found in Genesis. In order to appreciate the reason for this it
is important to note that in Genesis the theme of land comes in two different
contexts. First, it is used in the context of humanity as a whole. All human
beings must daily confront the reality that nature is under God's curse due to
humanity's disobedience from Adam and Eve onwards. The NT makes clear
that nature, like all believers, awaits redemption from the bondage of decay
(Rom. 8:19–25). For Paul, the reconciliation of all things to God is achieved
by Jesus Christ 'through his blood, shed on the cross' (Col. 1:20; cf. 2 Cor.
5:17–21; Eph. 1:7–10). Significantly, Paul views Christ not only as the one
responsible for the restoration of harmony within the cosmos, but as the
creator of all things in the first instance (Col. 1:15–17; cf. 1 Cor. 8:6).

The climax of the re-creation process is the appearance of a new heaven
and a new earth where God and human beings live together in harmony
(Rev. 21:1). Although this is portrayed in Revelation 21:1–22:5 in terms of
'the Holy City, the new Jerusalem, coming down out of heaven from God'
(Rev. 21:2), it is also viewed as a return to Eden. Various factors suggest this,
the most significant being the reference to the 'tree of life' (Rev. 22:2; cf. Gen.
2:9; 3:22, 24) and the comment that 'no longer will there be any curse'
(Rev. 22:3). However, whereas Eden is presented as 'prime development
land', the 'new Jerusalem' is a fully developed city.

For the author of Hebrews the goal of God's redemptive activity for
humanity is expressed in terms of rest (Heb. 4:1–11). Two related ideas are
developed. First, this rest resembles that which God enjoyed following the
creation of the heavens and the earth (Gen. 2:2–3) and which humanity lost
as a result of the disruption of creation following the disobedience of Adam
and Eve. Secondly, the ancient Israelites due to their disobedience failed to
obtain such rest when they took possession of the land of Canaan. However,
the opportunity to enter into God's rest still exists for those who believe
the gospel.

The second context in which land is used in an important way in Genesis
has to do with the establishment of Abraham's descendants as a nation in the
land of Canaan. With the introduction of a new covenant embracing all
nations, it is hardly surprising that the NT plays down the importance of Israel
as a nation. Israel's role in God's purposes has now dramatically changed and, as
a consequence, it is no longer important that Israel should possess the land of
Canaan. Whereas the Sinai Covenant centred on one nation, the New
Covenant is international in its scope. Although the promise of land to
Abraham in Genesis is generally stated in terms of the land of Canaan
(Gen. 12:7; 13:14–17; 15:18–21; 17:8), there are indications that for the

nations to be blessed, Abraham's 'seed' would exercise authority over the entire earth (49:10; cf. 22:17; Ps. 2:8; Mic. 5:2–5). In the light of this movement from one nation, Israel, to all nations, it is hardly surprising that there is a similar shift from thinking in terms of one land to the whole world. This, for example, is reflected in Paul's treatment of the fifth commandment, to honour your father and mother, in Ephesians 6:2–3. Whereas in the original context of Exodus 19:12 and Deuteronomy 5:16 the commandment includes the promise of long life as regards possession of the land of Canaan, in Ephesians Paul expands this to include the whole earth.

11

By Faith Abraham ...

11.1. Summary

The Abraham story (Gen. 11:27–25:11) forms the heart of the book of Genesis. At the outset Abraham is the recipient of major divine promises (12:1–3) with the fulfilment of these being linked to Abraham's obedience to God. As the narrative develops special attention is drawn to the fact that Abraham's faith in God is credited to him as righteousness (15:6). In response God covenants unconditionally to give Abraham's descendants the land of Canaan (15:18–21). Later God initiates a second covenant which differs from the first in two main ways: (a) it guarantees that Abraham will be the 'father' of many nations who will be blessed through him and his 'seed', and (b) in order for the covenant to be established Abraham must remain loyal and obedient to God. This second covenant is later established by divine oath when Abraham displays total trust in God through his willingness to sacrifice his son Isaac (22:16–18). The entire narrative highlights Abraham's faith in God as he awaits the fulfilment of the initial divine promises.

11.2. Introduction

In terms of the number of chapters given over to him Abraham is clearly the most important of all the human characters in Genesis. Moreover, his life marks an important watershed in God's relationship with human beings. Although there are in Genesis 3–11 indications that divine mercy will triumph over the consequences of the fall, it is with Abraham that a clearer picture begins to emerge. The divine promises associated with his call (12:1–3) reveal that he is to play a central role in restoring humanity's broken relationship with God.

11.3. Overview of the Abraham Narrative

The Abraham narrative falls into two sections separated by a brief genealogy in 22:20–24; the main section consists of 11:27–22:19, with 23:1–25:11 forming an appendix. Running through the main section are the three closely inter-twined themes of seed, land and blessing.

Within the Abraham narrative the theme of seed centres on the divine assurance that Abraham will have many descendants. The initial promises that Abraham will become a 'great nation' (12:2) and that his 'seed' will possess the land of Canaan (12:7) are set against the background of Sarah's inability to have children (11:30). Later, after the LORD assures Abraham that he will have a son of his own and many descendants (15:1–5), Sarah persuades him to have a child by her maidservant Hagar (16:1–4).[1] By naming him, Abraham claims Ishmael as his own (16:15). Afterwards, however, God reveals on two separate occasions that Sarah will indeed have a son who will be Abraham's true heir (17:15–21; 18:9–15). Eventually, Sarah gives birth to Isaac (21:1–7), and he is established as Abraham's heir through the divinely approved departure of Hagar and Ishmael (21:8–21). Thus Isaac's birth marks the first step towards the fulfilment of the divine promise that Abraham will become a 'great nation' and have numerous descendants.

The second theme in the Abraham narrative concerns land. Initially God commands Abraham to leave his own land and 'go to the land I will show you' (12:1). Although it is not mentioned specifically that Abraham will possess this land, the promise that he will become a 'great nation' (12:2) implies that his descendants will possess it; the Hebrew term *gôy* 'nation' denotes people inhabiting a specific geographical location and forming a political unit. Thus when Abraham first arrives in Canaan, the LORD promises, 'To your offspring (seed) I will give this land' (12:7). Later, following the separation of Lot from Abraham, God repeats this promise, emphasising the extent of the land to be possessed by Abraham's descendants (13:14–17).[2] The topic of land reappears in 15:7–21 where the idea is introduced that Abraham's descendants will only take possession of the land of Canaan after a period of four hundred years during which they will be slaves in another country (15:13–14). This revelation of a delay regarding the acquisition of the land probably explains why the promise of land, which is very prominent in Genesis 12–15, is mentioned less frequently in the remaining chapters of the Abraham narrative (cf. 17:8; 22:17). Although later episodes highlight Abraham's acquisition of a well at Beersheba and a tomb at

---

[1]   It was a custom in the ancient Near East that the maidservant of a barren wife might act as a surrogate mother.

[2]   Although Abraham is mentioned as possessing the land, there is no suggestion that the present inhabitants of the land will be dispossessed during Abraham's lifetime.

Hebron, these mark only the beginning of the process by which God will fulfil his promise to Abraham regarding nationhood.

The third main strand in the Abraham narrative is, as we have already noted in chapter 9, the idea that Abraham and his 'seed' will be a source of divine blessing, or possibly cursing, for others. This is highlighted in both the initial call of Abraham and the concluding oath in 22:16–18. Although various episodes reflect in part the divine blessing or cursing of others (e.g. the visit to Egypt [12:10–20], the abduction of Lot by the eastern kings [14:1–24], the rescue of Lot from Sodom [18:16–19:29], the abduction of Sarah by Abimelech [20:1–18] and the treaty between Abimelech and Abraham [21:22–34]), it is clear that, like the promise of nationhood, the promise of God's blessing upon all the families of the earth will only be fulfilled in the future (cf. 22:18).

This brief survey of the themes of seed, land and blessing establishes their presence within Genesis 12–25. To explore further how they are developed within the Abraham narrative we shall examine in more detail the initial call of Abraham in 12:1–3, the covenants in Genesis 15 and 17, and the divine oath in 22:16–18. This will enable us to have a clearer picture of how the overall narrative is structured.

11.4. The Divine Call of Abraham in Genesis 12:1–3

Within the context of the book of Genesis the divine speech in 12:1–3 is very important. It marks the beginning of a new stage in God's relationship with humanity, and sets the agenda for the entire Abraham story, and beyond, introducing those themes which will be developed in the subsequent narrative.

> The LORD says to Abraham, Leave your country, your people and your father's household and go to the land I will show you, so that I may make you into a great nation and bless you and make your name great. Be a blessing, so that I may bless those who bless you, and curse the one who disdains you, and so that all the families of the ground may be blessed through you (12:1–3; my translation).

Two features of this speech are noteworthy in the present context. First, the fulfilment of the divine promises is conditional upon Abraham's obedience. By commanding him to leave his homeland and be a blessing, God places the onus on Abraham to obey in order that the promises concerning land, descendants and the blessing of others may be fulfilled.[3] Secondly, the climax

---

[3] As it stands the divine speech to Abraham falls naturally into two halves, each introduced by an imperative. Whereas the first half focuses on the promise of nationhood (i.e. land and descendants), the second centres on the blessing of others. As we shall observe below, this twofold division is reflected in the two covenants found in Genesis 15 and 17.

of the speech comes in the statement that 'through you all the families of the earth will find blessing'. The primary motive behind the call of Abraham is God's desire to bring blessing, rather than cursing, upon the nations of the earth. The promise that Abraham will become a great nation, implying both numerous seed and land, must be understood as being subservient to God's principal desire to bless all the families of the earth.[4]

Abraham's positive response to God's command is noted immediately, and his arrival in the land of Canaan is rewarded by the assurance that 'to your descendants (seed) I will give this land' (12:7). The subject of land dominates Genesis 13 where, following the separation of Lot and Abraham, God confirms that Abraham's many descendants will take possession of the land of Canaan (cf. 13:14–17). The promise of land then comes to an important climax in Genesis 15 with God covenanting to give Abraham's descendants the land 'from the river of Egypt to the great river, the Euphrates' (15:18).

11.5. The Unconditional Promissory Covenant of Genesis 15

Genesis 15 falls into two parts which have in common the subject of inheritance. Whereas verses 1–6 are concerned with Abraham's immediate and future heirs, verses 7–21 focus on what shall be inherited. God reassures Abraham that (a) he will have a son of his own from whom shall come numerous descendants, and (b) after several centuries these descendants will take possession of the land of Canaan. Interestingly, the two parts of the chapter parallel each other structurally. They both begin with a divine statement (15:1, 7) followed by a question from Abraham (15:2, 8). Next we have God's response involving an appropriate sign (15:4–5; 9–17),[5] and finally, a concluding comment by the narrator (15:6; 18–21).

Two elements in the chapter deserve special attention. First, verse 6 contains the observation that 'Abram believed the LORD, and he credited it to him as righteousness.' The rarity in Genesis of such comments by the

---

[4] The importance of the theme of blessing is underlined by the fivefold repetition of the Hebrew root *brk* 'to bless' in 12:2–3.

[5] The first sign, the stars in the heavens, conveys the vast number of Abraham's descendants. The second sign is more complex. Probably the sacrificial animals represent Abraham's descendants, the birds of prey are the Egyptians and 'the smoking brazier with a blazing torch' indicates God's presence. The sign thus looks forward to the release of the Israelites from slavery in Egypt and the subsequent presence of the LORD in their midst. After the exodus God's presence was indicated by the pillar of cloud by day and the pillar of fire by night (Ex. 13:21; 19:18; 20:18).

narrator makes them all the more important when they occur. Here Abraham is viewed as righteous in God's sight because he believes unreservedly that the LORD will fulfil his promise regarding a son and numerous descendants. Thus, Abraham is reckoned righteous on account of his faith in God's promise, rather than due to any deeds performed by him.

Secondly, the LORD makes a covenant with Abraham which affirms that his 'seed' will possess the land of Canaan. This marks the climax of the earlier divine promises regarding land and descendants found in 12:7 and 13:14–17. Several features of the covenant are worth noting:

1. It guarantees unconditionally what the LORD has stated to Abraham. Nowhere is it indicated that the fulfilment of the covenant is dependent upon the actions of either Abraham or his descendants; God covenants unreservedly to fulfil his promise that Abraham's descendants will possess the land of Canaan. For this reason it may be designated an unconditional promissory covenant.
2. The structure of the chapter suggests that there is a link between the making of the promissory covenant in verses 18–21 and the comment about Abraham believing God in verse 6. Because of the righteousness attributed to Abraham, God blesses Abraham by guaranteeing that the divine promises regarding descendants and land will be fulfilled.
3. The terms of the covenant mention only descendants and possession of the land; there is no reference to blessing being mediated to others. This omission is significant and is one of the main ways in which this covenant differs from that outlined in Genesis 17. The covenant in Genesis 15 guarantees only some of the divine promises mentioned in 12:1–3. For the remainder we must look ahead to Genesis 17.

11.6. The Eternal Covenant of Circumcision

The introduction of a second covenant in Genesis 17 is somewhat surprising. Why should God make another covenant with Abraham? To answer this, it is necessary to observe that the covenant in Genesis 17 differs in a number of important ways from that given in Genesis 15. First, it is a conditional covenant. Whereas the promissory covenant of Genesis 15 is unconditional, the establishment or ratification of the covenant of circumcision is dependent upon Abraham's continuing obedience to God. This is highlighted in the introduction to the covenant. After identifying himself as El Shaddai (God Almighty), the LORD says to Abraham, 'Walk before me and be blameless so that I may confirm my covenant between me and you and increase you greatly' (17:1–2; my translation). Unfortunately, many English translations fail to appreciate the distinctive syntax of the Hebrew original and so miss the important link which exists between the initial imperatives, 'Walk before me and be blameless', and the fact that these must be obeyed before the covenant will be established. The LORD will ratify the covenant only if Abraham walks before God and is blameless. Significantly, for the actual establishment of the covenant we must look to the divine oath which concludes the account of the testing of Abraham in Genesis 22.[6]

Secondly, the covenant of circumcision differs from the promissory covenant of Genesis 15 in that it is an eternal covenant. Whereas the covenant of Genesis 15 is a divine guarantee to Abraham that his descendants will possess the land of Canaan, the covenant of circumcision entails a continuing special relationship between God and Abraham's 'seed'. Although the covenant will embrace those who are not Abraham's natural children – others within his household, including foreigners, may be circumcised (17:12) – God makes it clear that his covenant is intimately linked to the chosen family line; it will be established with the promised 'seed' Isaac and not Ishmael (17:19–21).

Thirdly, whereas the emphasis in Genesis 15 is solely upon descendants and land, the covenant in Genesis 17 focuses primarily on Abraham as the father of many nations. God states,

> As for me, this is my covenant with you: You will be the father of many nations. No longer will you be called Abram; your name will be Abraham, for I have made you a father of many nations. I will make you very fruitful; I will make nations of you, and kings will come from you (17:4–6).

These words are echoed briefly regarding Sarah: 'I will bless her so that she will be the mother of nations; kings of peoples will come from her' (17:16). The mention of nations coming from Abraham and Sarah presents a problem if this is interpreted as referring only to those nations which are directly descended from both of them; strictly speaking, only the Israelites and Edomites come within this category.[7] However, it is likely that the concept of 'father' is not restricted here to actual physical descendants.[8] Rather, Abraham is the 'father' of all who are circumcised. Thus God instructs Abraham to circumcise not

---

[6] Although the covenant of circumcision is initiated in Genesis 17, it is only finally established in Genesis 22. A period of time must elapse between the initiation and the establishment of the covenant due to its conditional nature. What establishes the covenant is not the act of circumcision itself, but obedience to God.

[7] The Israelites and Edomites are descended from Jacob and Esau respectively. The Ishmaelites and Midianites are probably not to be included here because they are not descended from Sarah.

[8] See pp. 86–7.

merely his own family members but every male 'including those born in your household or bought with your money from a foreigner – those who are not your offspring (seed). Whether born in your household or bought with your money, they must be circumcised' (17:12–13).[9]

By changing Abram's name to Abraham, God underlines the importance of the fact that he will be the father of many nations. This occurs not because these nations are his natural descendants but because he is for them the channel of divine blessing. This understanding of 'father' is probably reflected in the unusual comment that Joseph 'was father to Pharaoh' (45:8). Furthermore, when God blesses Jacob in 35:11, echoing an earlier blessing by Isaac upon Jacob (28:3), a distinction is drawn between 'a nation' and 'a community of nations' coming from him. The implication would seem to be that whereas many nations will be closely associated with him, only one nation will be directly descended from him.[10]

In the light of the divine promises given in 12:1–3 it is clear that the covenants in Genesis 15 and 17 complement each other. Whereas Genesis 15 focuses on descendants and land, the emphasis in Genesis 17 is upon Abraham as the one who imparts God's blessing to others; in this capacity he is the father of many nations. This understanding of the covenant of circumcision is later reflected in the divine oath of Genesis 22 which establishes the covenant with Abraham.

11.7. The Divine Oath in Genesis 22:16–18

The divine speech in 22:16–18 forms a frame with Abraham's call in 12:1–3 and so brings to a conclusion the main section of the Abraham narrative. All that was promised conditionally in 12:1–3 is now guaranteed by divine oath:

> I swear by myself, declares the LORD, that because you have done this and have not withheld your son, your only son, I will surely bless you and make your descendants

---

[9] Those who were circumcised enjoyed a special relationship with each other. We witness evidence of this in Genesis 34 where the sons of Jacob promise Shechem and his father Hamor that if they are circumcised, 'Then we will give you our daughters and take your daughters for ourselves. We'll settle among you and become one people with you' (34:16). Against this background the killing by Simeon and Levi of all those who have just been circumcised is exceptionally repulsive to their father Jacob (34:24–31). What was intended by God to be a symbol of family solidarity is misused for the destruction of others.

[10] The same idea of blessing being mediated to others may underlie Noah's comments regarding the relationship between Japheth and Shem: 'May God extend the territory of Japheth; may Japheth live in the tents of Shem ...' (9:27).

[seed] as numerous as the stars in the sky and as the sand on the seashore. Your descendants [seed] will take possession of the cities [gate] of their [his] enemies, and through your offspring [seed] all nations on earth will be blessed, because you have obeyed me (22:16–18).

This oath not only signals the end of the main section of the Abraham narrative, but also establishes the covenant of circumcision promised in Genesis 17. By demonstrating his obedience to God, even to the point of being willing to sacrifice his only son, Abraham fulfils the conditions laid down in 17:1; he shows beyond doubt his willingness to walk before God and be blameless.

Evidence supporting the idea that Genesis 22 should be linked to the covenant of circumcision in Genesis 17 may be deduced by considering the account of the covenant with Noah in Genesis 6–9.[11] An analysis of this earlier covenant reveals that it has the following structure:

1. The promise of a covenant (6:18).
2. The obligations of the covenant (6:14–16, 19–21; 7:1–3).
3. The fulfilment of the obligations (6:22; 7:5).
4. The sacrifice of a burnt offering (8:20).
5. The establishment of the covenant (9:9–17).

Remarkably, the same structure emerges if Genesis 17 and 22 are taken together. Chapter 17 records the promise of a covenant with Abraham,

---

[11]   Six important parallels can be observed between the two covenants.
       First, both covenants are described as eternal or everlasting covenants, *běrit 'ôlām* (9:16; 17:7, 13, 19). Secondly, these covenants are accompanied by an appropriate sign. In the case of Noah it is the rainbow (9:12–14), and in the case of Abraham it is circumcision (17:11). The rainbow is related to rain which in turn would remind the people of the flood. Circumcision relates to the procreation of descendants which is a point of emphasis in the covenant of ch. 17. Thirdly, in both cases, the expressions used of the formation of the covenant are *hēqîm běrit* (9:9, 11, 17; 17:7, 19, 21) and *nātan běrit* (9:12; 17:2). Fourthly, the covenants in Genesis 9 and 17 are spoken of by God as 'between me and you' (9:12, 15; 17:2, 7). However, at the same time they also include the descendants of Noah and Abraham (9:9, 12; 17:7, 9). Fifthly, the benefit which each covenant brings for those with whom it is established is that they shall not be cut off (9:11; 17:14). Sixthly, the divine command in 17:1, 'Walk before me and be blameless,' resembles the description of Noah in 6:9, 'Blameless in his generation; Noah walked with God.' The word 'blameless', *tāmîm*, is found only on these two occasions in the whole of Genesis. This list of similarities highlights the close parallels that exist between the two covenants (Alexander, 'Genesis 22 and the Covenant of Circumcision', 19–20).

accompanied by certain obligations: Abraham is to walk before God and be blameless. While these are more general than those given to Noah, God later tests Abraham's obedience in a specific way; he demands that Abraham should offer up his only son Isaac as a burnt offering (22:2). In spite of the terrible consequences of killing his heir, Abraham displays his willingness to fulfil even the most testing of divine commands. After God's intervention and the deliverance of Isaac, Abraham offers up as a burnt offering a ram which has been unexpectedly provided.[12] Finally, God establishes the covenant with Abraham by swearing an oath (22:16–18).

By linking Genesis 17 and 22 new light may be shed on a number of issues. First, it is possible to account for the divine testing of Abraham. Through his obedience in Genesis 22 Abraham demonstrates his willingness to keep the conditions of the covenant laid out in 17:1. Secondly, the fact that the events of Genesis 22 are part of a conditional covenant explains why Abraham is considered in 22:16–18 and 26:2–5 to have merited by his obedience the divine guarantee of the promises concerning seed, land and the blessing of others. Thirdly, the oath in 22:16–18 forms a very fitting conclusion to the main section of the Abraham narrative. Although many scholars view verses 15–18 as a later addition to the original account of the testing of Abraham, the structure of the covenant requires the sacrifice of a burnt offering before God could confirm with an oath the earlier promises. Verses 15–18 are an integral and essential part not only of Genesis 22 but of the entire Abraham narrative.[13]

The divine oath in 22:16–18 not only embraces the contents of the earlier promissory covenant regarding many descendants and land but also includes the additional aspect that all nations will be blessed through Abraham's 'seed'. The mention of 'seed' is significant. Unfortunately, the identity of this 'seed' is not easy to determine. While the first mention of 'seed' denotes 'descendants' in the plural, the remaining references are ambiguous; they may refer either to many descendants or to a single descendant. This latter possibility deserves special consideration for four reasons. First, the syntax of the Hebrew supports strongly the idea that the 'seed' mentioned in verses 17b–18 is singular.[14] Secondly, the book of Genesis as a whole devotes considerable attention to tracing a line of 'seed' which, beginning with Adam and ending with Judah,

---

[12] It is noteworthy that in the whole of Genesis it is only here and in 8:20 that the term 'burnt offering' is used to designate a sacrifice.

[13] The proposal supported by various commentators that originally in verses 1–14 the sparing of Isaac was the reward for Abraham's obedience is surely inadequate. Had Abraham disobeyed the divine command and stayed at home, the life of Isaac would never have been placed in any danger. The sparing of Isaac is hardly a suitable reward for Abraham's obedience.

[14] See Alexander, 'Further Observations of the Term "Seed"', 363–7.

forms the early ancestry of the Davidic dynasty. Unfortunately, scholars generally overlook the importance of this single line of descendants. Thirdly, the Jacob and Joseph stories give prominence to the blessing which the patriarchs, as members of this family line, may bestow on others. Although Esau and Jacob are both the 'seed' of Isaac, it is clear that the brother who receives the father's blessing is favoured more than the other. Thus, it is Jacob who experiences God's blessing and is able to mediate it to others. Similarly, Joseph is undoubtedly favoured by his father Jacob who eventually imparts the blessing of the first-born to Joseph's son Ephraim (48:1–22). Significantly, Genesis focuses on the blessing which others receive through Jacob and Joseph. They alone are presented as the ones who may impart blessing to others. Although other 'seed' exist, the Genesis narrative usually associates the power to bless with those who receive the first-born blessing. Fourthly, in announcing the covenant of circumcision to Abraham, God emphasises the unique role of Isaac; it is with Isaac that the covenant will be established and not with Ishmael (17:19, 21). Given the limited interest which Genesis displays in the descendants of Ishmael, it seems logical to conclude that the 'seed' of Abraham mentioned in 22:18 does not include Ishmael and his descendants. For these reasons, the possibility exists that the final reference to 'seed' in 22:18 denotes a single descendant.

The covenants in Genesis 15 and 17 differ markedly.[15] Whereas Genesis 15 records an unconditional promissory covenant which does not necessarily entail an ongoing relationship between God and the descendants of Abraham, the covenant of circumcision is both conditional and eternal. Furthermore, while it is implied in Genesis 15 that Abraham's faith, credited as righteousness, is the catalyst for the making of the promissory covenant, the establishment of the covenant of circumcision rests on Abraham's obedience to God. As reflected in 26:2–5, Abraham's obedience is an important factor in the establishment of this eternal covenant.

11.8. Conclusion

Viewed as a whole, the Abraham narrative provides an interesting picture of the interplay between divine word and human faith and obedience. Initially, the LORD makes a series of promises, the fulfilment of which is conditional upon Abraham's obedience (12:1–3). As Abraham in faith obeys and journeys to Canaan, God declares that he shall have both land and descendants (12:7; 13:14–17). In time these statements are confirmed in a promissory covenant

---

[15] A full discussion of the relationship between Genesis 15 and 17 is provided by Williamson in *Abraham, Israel and the Nations*.

(15:18–21), which is linked to Abraham being credited as righteous on account of his faith (15:6). The narrative, however, does not conclude here; it goes on to highlight Abraham's continuing faith in and obedience to God, as revealed in the establishment of the eternal covenant of circumcision (17:1–27; 22:1–19), a covenant which focuses on the divine blessing that will come through Abraham and his 'seed' to all nations. From beginning to end, faith expressed in obedience is the hallmark of Abraham's relationship with the LORD.

Abraham's faith, however, is all the more remarkable when the following factors are also taken into account. First, it is clear that the divine promises concerning nationhood (i.e. seed and land) and the blessing of all the families of the earth will never be fulfilled in Abraham's lifetime; at the very most Abraham will only experience the first fruits of their fulfilment. Secondly, circumstances exist or develop which militate against the fulfilment of these promises. Sarah's barrenness is a major obstacle for much of the narrative, and even when all seems assured with the birth of Isaac, God himself places the future fulfilment of the promises in jeopardy by demanding that Abraham sacrifice Isaac. Yet, in spite of these factors Abraham displays a faith in God which in the book of Genesis is matched only by that of Noah.

11.9. New Testament Connections

There is little doubt that within the New Testament Epistles the most note-worthy aspect of Abraham's life is his faith. We see this very clearly in Hebrews 11 which provides a detailed list of those 'ancients' who were commended for having faith. Approximately one-third of the chapter is devoted to Abraham (Heb. 11:8–19), making him by far the most important person listed.[16] Fittingly, the author of Hebrews highlights Abraham's faith as an example of 'being sure of what we hope for and certain of what we do not see' (Heb. 11:1).

As regards Paul's understanding of Abraham, in Romans 4 and Galatians 3 the emphasis is clearly on the fact that, according to Genesis 15:6, Abraham was justified or made righteous by his faith and not by being circumcised and keeping the law.[17] For Paul, the sequence of events in the Abraham story is all-important. Since Abraham is credited as righteous prior to being circumcised, circumcision is not necessary in order for an individual to be reckoned righteous in God's eyes. He writes,

---

[16] Moses, who is next in importance, receives about half the space given to Abraham (cf. Heb. 11:23–28).
[17] Genesis 15:6 is quoted in Romans 4:3 and Galatians 3:6.

We have been saying that Abraham's faith was credited to him as righteousness. Under what circumstances was it credited? Was it after he was circumcised, or before? It was not after, but before! And he received the sign of circumcision, a seal of the righteousness that he had by faith while he was still uncircumcised. So then, he is the father of all who believe but have not been circumcised, in order that righteousness might be credited to them. And he is also the father of the circumcised who not only are circumcised but who also walk in the footsteps of the faith that our father Abraham had before he was circumcised (Rom. 4:9–12).

Here Paul stresses that Abraham is the father of those who have faith, whether they are his natural descendants or not (cf. Rom. 9:6–8). Thus he concludes that Jews and Gentiles can only be justified by faith.

A similar, but not identical, argument is advanced in Galatians 2:5–3:29 as Paul responds to those who emphasise the necessity of circumcision in order to be children of Abraham and hence recipients of the promises made to him. He writes: 'Consider Abraham: "He believed God, and it was credited to him as righteousness." Understand, then, that those who believe are children of Abraham' (Gal. 3:6–7). By stressing the importance of faith over against circumcision Paul concludes that it is not necessary for an individual to be circumcised in order to be a child of Abraham.

Paul, however, does not conclude his argument in Galatians at this point. He focuses on three further aspects of the Abraham narrative in order to drive home his case that the Gentiles are now the recipients of God's blessing. First, he sees in the justification of the Gentiles the fulfilment of the divine promise to Abraham that all nations would be blessed through him.

The Scripture foresaw that God would justify the Gentiles by faith, and announced the gospel in advance to Abraham: 'All nations will be blessed through you.' So those who have faith are blessed along with Abraham, the man of faith (Gal. 3:9).

By highlighting the importance which the Genesis narrative places on all nations being blessed through Abraham, Paul challenges the view of his opponents that God's blessing was only intended for the actual descendants of Abraham.

Secondly, Paul argues that the divine promises made to Abraham find their ultimate fulfilment in Jesus Christ. To arrive at this conclusion Paul focuses on the concept of 'seed'. He argues that the promises were given to Abraham and to his 'seed', implying one person, and that this 'seed' is Jesus Christ. Some biblical scholars conclude that while Paul adopts here a form of rabbinic exegesis which might have been practised by his Jewish contemporaries, his approach is clearly not in keeping with modern critical methods of exegesis. Unfortunately, these scholars have perhaps too readily dismissed Paul's interpretation without examining in detail how the term 'seed' is used in Genesis. As noted in chapter 9, the Hebrew word *zera'* 'seed' is clearly a keyword in Genesis and while it sometimes denotes a group it may also refer to a single individual (e.g. Gen. 4:25; 21:13). This latter possibility is significant, especially when we observe that the entire book of Genesis focuses on a particular line of seed which enjoyed a special relationship with God. Remarkably, Genesis devotes considerable attention, especially in the patriarchal stories, to identifying the seed of this special line. Furthermore, there are clear indications that this line of seed formed the early ancestry of the royal line of David. Apart from the reference to kings being descended from Abraham (17:6), Jacob's blessing of Judah in 49:8–12 indicates that royalty will come from the line of Judah. If Genesis as a whole focuses on a royal line of seed through which God will fulfil his promises to Abraham, then Paul's interpretation of the term *zera'* as referring to Jesus Christ is in keeping with the common NT understanding of Jesus as the Davidic Messiah. Thus, Paul affirms that it is only through faith in Jesus Christ, the 'seed' of Abraham, that Jews and Gentiles may now receive the blessing given to Abraham and become God's children.

Finally, Paul also argues in Galatians that the divine covenant made with Abraham takes precedence over the law given several centuries later at Mount Sinai. Whereas his opponents were advocating that believers must keep the law in order to be righteous, Paul responds by noting that the law, given later to fulfil a temporary role until Christ came, could never make anyone righteous since it merely indicated the righteousness required by God, not the means of achieving such righteousness. As such it underlined the necessity of becoming righteous through faith.

Since Paul uses the Abraham narrative in four distinctive ways in Galatians to challenge the view of his opponents that Gentile believers must be circumcised and obey the law of Moses in order to know God's salvation, it is apparent that his understanding of the gospel was heavily influenced by his reading of Genesis 12–25.

Abraham's faith is also discussed in James 2:20–24. Here, however, the context differs from that found in Romans and Galatians. Whereas Paul seeks to demonstrate the priority of faith over circumcision, James is concerned to clarify the nature of saving faith: 'What good is it, my brothers, if a man claims to have faith but has no deeds? Can such faith save him?' (Jas. 2:14) At the heart of James' discussion is the desire to show that true faith in God will exhibit itself in righteous actions. Thus he focuses on Abraham and in particular the offering of Isaac on the altar.

> Was not our ancestor Abraham considered righteous for what he did when he offered his son Isaac on the altar? You see that his faith and his actions were working together, and his faith was made complete by what he did. And the scripture was fulfilled that says, 'Abraham believed God, and it was credited to him as

righteousness,' and he was called God's friend. You see that a person is justified by what he does and not by faith alone (Jas. 2:21–24).

Here James reveals how faith in and obedience to God cannot be separated. While James accepts that Abraham was justified by faith, as stated in Genesis 15:6, he views the later actions of Abraham as visible expressions of his inner faith. Undoubtedly, he focuses on Genesis 22 because of the way in which Abraham is rewarded for his willingness to sacrifice Isaac. For James there can be no separation of faith and deeds. He views Abraham's actions in Genesis 22 as the fulfilment or culmination of what was stated in Genesis 15:6.

Although James writes 'that a person is justified by what he does and not by faith alone' (Jas. 2:24), it is clear from the context that he does not actually contradict what Paul has to say in Romans and Galatians. Both men were addressing different situations and therefore highlighted different aspects of Abraham's faith. On the one hand, Paul concentrated on Genesis 15:6 because he was responding either directly or indirectly to those who wished to emphasise the necessity of circumcision for salvation. On the other hand, James was concerned to show that Abraham's faith, by which he was justified, produced righteous actions. Thus, he writes, 'faith without deeds is dead' (Jas. 2:26). Undoubtedly, Paul and James would have agreed wholeheartedly with what the other had to say, given the different problems that confronted them.

The final New Testament passage to be considered briefly is Hebrews 6:13–18. It is included here not because it focuses on Abraham's faith, but because it draws attention to the oath which God made to Abraham in order to guarantee beyond doubt the fulfilment of the divine promise made to Abraham.

> Because God wanted to make the unchanging nature of his purpose very clear to the heirs of what was promised, he confirmed it with an oath. God did this so that, by two unchangeable things in which it is impossible for God to lie, we who have fled to take hold of the hope offered to us may be greatly encouraged (Heb. 6:17–18).

The oath mentioned here clearly refers to Genesis 22:16–18. By antici-pating the coming of a royal descendant of Abraham who will impart God's blessing to the nations, this oath is an important part of the NT understanding of Jesus Christ's mission.

12

Who is the LORD?

12.1. Summary

Exodus is essentially a book about knowing God through personal experience. The plot centres on the relationship which develops between the LORD God and the Israelites, from the dramatic meeting with Moses at the burning bush (3:1–4:17) to the glory of the LORD filling the tabernacle (40:34–38). Throughout Exodus God always takes the initiative, revealing himself not only through words, but also through signs and wonders. In differing ways he reveals his most significant attributes: his sovereign majesty; his holiness; his power to perform signs and wonders; his awesome glory; his righteousness; his compassion.

12.2. An Overview of Exodus

The book of Exodus continues the story of Genesis by tracing the destiny of the children of Jacob. Although Exodus itself forms a continuous account it may be divided into two parts, both focusing on the theme of knowing God. The first half of the book is dominated by the theme of coming to a personal knowledge of God. At the outset Moses encounters God at the burning bush, and in the ensuing conversation discovers much about God's nature, including his divine name, the LORD (3:1–4:17). The theme reappears when Pharaoh expresses his ignorance about the LORD: 'Who is the LORD, that I should obey him and let Israel go? I do not know the LORD and I will not let Israel go' (5:2). As the various signs and wonders unfold the Egyptians gradually come to acknowledge the LORD's sovereign power. When God finally lures Pharaoh and his army to their death in the Sea of Reeds it is with the expressed purpose that 'the Egyptians will know that I am the LORD' (14:4, 18). In celebration of their deliverance from Egypt the Israelites worship God in a dynamic song of praise that highlights their knowledge of him: 'Who among the gods is like you, O LORD? Who is like you – majestic in holiness, awesome in glory, working wonders?' (15:11).

The second half of Exodus develops further the theme of knowing God by focusing on the establishment of a special relationship between the LORD and the Israelites. To this end the narrative concentrates on two topics which receive extensive coverage, the making of a covenant and the construction of the tabernacle. The former of these, like the signing of a contract or the taking of marriage vows, sets out the conditions under which the Israelites must live in order to enjoy an ongoing relationship with God; these conditions are recorded in the Decalogue (20:3–17) and the Book of the Covenant (20:22–23:33). The people are required to reflect God's righteous and compassionate nature if they wish to experience his continued blessing and presence. Exodus records not only the establishment of the initial covenant agreement (Ex. 19–24), but also the events surrounding the making of the golden calf which almost brought the covenant relationship to an early and abrupt conclusion (Ex. 32–34). The construction of the tabernacle forms a natural sequel to the making of the divine covenant. Built according to divine instruction, the tabernacle becomes the focal point of the LORD's presence in the midst of the people, and reminds them, through its materials and structure, of God's sovereign, holy nature. Following the erection of the tabernacle, the LORD takes up residence in the midst of his people (40:34–38), bringing the book of Exodus to a fitting conclusion.

12.3. The Israelites in Egypt

The initial two chapters of Exodus record events which span a period of several centuries and form a bridge between the detailed account of the life of Joseph in Genesis 37–50 and the report of the Israelites' release from Egypt in Exodus 3–15. Not only do chapters 1–2 presuppose that the reader is already familiar with the book of Genesis, but they also continue an important trend in Genesis regarding how God is portrayed. Whereas Genesis begins with God as the central participant in the story, a change occurs throughout the book as God gradually retreats from the centre of the stage and adopts the role of an offstage director. We see this most clearly with Joseph, who, unlike his immediate ancestors, has no direct encounter with the LORD. Rather, God controls the destiny of both Joseph and his wider family without revealing himself directly. The opening two chapters of Exodus also convey the impression that God no longer reveals himself in person. The narrative highlights only his providential care as reflected in the case of the two midwives and inferred in the remarkable increase of the Israelites. Against this background the narrator's comments in 2:23–25 are significant. Although the Israelites may have felt that God was no longer concerned about them, such was not the case. God was well aware of their situation, and, when the time was right, he would act in a dramatic way to free them from oppression.

Special attention is also given in Exodus 2 to the events surrounding the early life of Moses and his later exile in Midian. By highlighting his remarkable deliverance from death at birth and the irony of his growing up within the household of Pharaoh, the narrative anticipates the important role which Moses will play within the rest of the book. Furthermore, the nature of this role is hinted at by his actions on behalf of those who are oppressed by others. With Moses' flight to Midian, the scene is set for God to reveal himself in a most remarkable way.

12.4. The LORD Reveals Himself to Moses

Although the reader is partially prepared for the encounter between God and Moses, it must have come as a surprise to Moses. Several elements of the meeting are worth noting briefly. First, Moses encounters God in a burning bush. Throughout Exodus the divine presence is frequently symbolised by fire and smoke (13:21, 22; 14:24; 19:18; 24:17; 40:38; cf. Lev. 9:24; 10:2; Num. 9:15, 16; 11:1–3; 14:14; Deut. 1:33; 4:11, 12, 15, 24, 33, 36; 5:4, 5, 22–26; 9:3, 10, 15; 10:4; 18:16). Secondly, Moses acknowledges God's holiness by removing his sandals; God must be approached with caution. The concept of divine holiness reappears in Exodus (and Leviticus) as a major theme.[1] Thirdly, having led his father-in-law's flock through the desert to Horeb (v. 1), Moses will later lead the Israelites to the same location (cf. 3:12; 19:1–2), where they also will witness God's holy presence revealed through fire.

Although God initially introduces himself to Moses as 'the God of your father, the God of Abraham, the God of Isaac and the God of Jacob' (3:6), the issue of his identity reappears in verses 13–15 when Moses inquires about his name. This request is important because the Israelites believed that an individual's nature was reflected in his or her name. In Genesis different aspects of God's nature are highlighted by the names used to designate him: *El Elyon* ('God Most High'; Gen. 14:18–20), *El Roi* ('God who sees me'; Gen. 16:13), *El Shaddai* ('God Almighty'; Gen. 17:1), *El Olam* ('God Everlasting'; Gen. 21:33). Here God introduces himself using the personal name 'Yahweh', translated in most English versions as 'the LORD' (3:15).[2] The Hebrew name

---

[1] See chapter 16.

[2] The English translation fails to convey the idea that the Hebrew *Yahweh* is a personal name. Due to the veneration of the divine name Yahweh, it became the practice of Jews to substitute the Hebrew word *'ădônāy* 'Lord' for the divine name; hence the English translation. When vowels were eventually added in the medieval period to the consonantal text of the Hebrew Bible, the vowels of *'ădônāy* were used in conjunction with the consonants YHWH. This in turn probably led to the name Yahweh being wrongly read as Jehovah.

'Yahweh' is closely related to the phrase in verse 14 which may be translated in a variety of ways: 'I AM WHO I AM,' 'I will be who I will be,' 'I will be what I was.' An abbreviated form of this phrase comes in the statement, 'I AM has sent me to you' (3:14). Unlike previous designations, the name Yahweh does not limit God's nature to any particular characteristic: he is what he is. Furthermore, his nature does not change. He is the God worshipped by earlier generations ('the God of Abraham, the God of Isaac and the God of Jacob') and generations yet to come ('this is my name for ever, the name by which I am to be remembered from generation to generation').

Apart from revealing his name, God also informed Moses that he was to return to Egypt and assemble the elders of Israel. Together they are to ask permission from Pharaoh to take the Israelites on a short three-day journey into the desert in order that they may worship their God (3:18). Pharaoh's reaction to this relatively minor demand will reveal his strong antagonism towards the Israelites. He will refuse to accommodate them, not because their request is excessive, but because of his own hardness of heart. The narrative in Exodus 7–15 reinforces this initial observation. Pharaoh will not change his mind 'unless a mighty hand compels him' (3:19). The influence of God's hand upon the Egyptians will be such that they will readily give of their possessions in order to see the Israelites leave Egypt. These gifts will compensate the Israelites for the suffering they have already endured.

In spite of the assurance of God's presence, Moses raises a problem. What if the Israelites do not believe him? How will he convince them that God has indeed appeared to him? In response God provides three signs which involve miraculous transformations: Moses' staff will become a snake (4:2–4); his hand will become leprous (4:6–7); Nile water will become blood (4:9). Moses witnesses for himself the first two of these signs. The third, at this stage, must be accepted by faith. Significantly, when all three are later shown to the Israelites they are convinced that God has indeed sent Moses (4:30–31).

When Moses first encounters Pharaoh, the Egyptian king displays his contempt towards Moses, Aaron and, especially, the LORD: 'Who is the LORD, that I should obey him and let Israel go? I do not know the LORD and I will not let Israel go' (5:2).[3] Although Pharaoh has no knowledge of the LORD, this will soon change dramatically. The motif of knowing the LORD recurs frequently throughout the following chapters (cf. 6:7; 7:5, 17; 8:10, 22; 9:14, 16, 29; 10:2; 14:4, 18). Having already revealed himself to Moses, Aaron and the Israelite elders, God will now reveal himself powerfully to Pharaoh and the Egyptians.

---

[3] Interestingly, the personal name of Pharaoh is never given. For the reader he is the unknown one.

A further divine speech to Moses in 6:28–7:7 also anticipates the 'miraculous signs and wonders' which are to dominate Exodus 7 to 14. Attention is drawn to the hardening of Pharaoh's heart and to the 'mighty acts of judgement' by which God will lead Israel out of Egypt. God declares that as a result 'the Egyptians will know that I am the LORD' (7:5). Thus the scene is set for the cycle of episodes which compose 7:8–14:31.

12.5. Signs and Wonders in Egypt

The Exodus narrative devotes considerable space to the account of the signs and wonders performed in Egypt. While they are often described as 'the ten plagues', this is not an entirely satisfactory designation. First, although the biblical text refers to a few of them individually as 'plagues'[4] (9:3, 14, 15; 11:1; cf. 8:2), as a whole they are more frequently designated 'signs' (7:3; 8:23; 10:1, 2) or 'wonders' (4:21; 7:3; 11:9, 10; cf. 'miracle' in 7:9).[5] Secondly, there are in fact eleven miraculous signs recorded in Exodus 7–12. The first of these, the episode of the staff becoming a snake (7:8–13), is generally not included in the list of 'plagues'. This was also the first sign which God gave Moses in order to convince the Israelites that the LORD had indeed appeared to him (4:2–5). The next sign which Moses performed before Pharaoh, turning water into blood (7:14–25), was also earlier used to demonstrate Moses' divine calling to the Israelites (4:8–9). Yet, whereas the Israelites believed Moses on account of these signs (4:30–31), Pharaoh paid no attention to them (7:13, 22); his own magicians were able to perform the same wonders (7:11, 22).

The individual accounts of the miraculous signs follow the same pattern, but with some variation to avoid monotony. Certain features are common to

---

[4] It should, however, be noted that in the NIV 'plague' translates various Hebrew words.

[5] It has been suggested that the plagues described in Exodus can be related to a series of natural phenomena which may have occurred in ancient Egypt. For example, the turning of the Nile waters to blood was due to an unusually high inundation of the river during the months of July and August. The river became 'blood-like' due to the presence of red earth carried in suspension from the basins of the Blue Nile and Atbara. Such an explanation, however, does not account for the presence of such 'blood' in wooden buckets and stone jars everywhere in Egypt (7:19). Nor does it explain either the earlier sign which Moses performed before the Israelites (4:30), or the activities of the Egyptian magicians (7:22). The text consistently emphasises the divine provenance of these events. This is indicated, for example, by the many references to Moses or Aaron stretching out their hands or a staff in order to bring about the different signs or wonders. Although some of these may be associated with natural phenomena, their occurrence is clearly attributed to divine intervention.

all eleven episodes. The report of each miraculous sign begins with the phrase, 'the LORD said to Moses' (7:8, 14; 8:1, 16, 20; 9:1, 8, 13; 10:1, 21; 11:1). The initiative for each sign rests with God, with every stage in the encounter between Moses and Pharaoh being divinely controlled. Each episode, echoing the predictions given in 4:21 and 7:3–4, concludes with an explicit reference to the hardening of Pharaoh's heart (7:13, 22; 8:15, 19, 32; 9:7, 12, 35; 10:20, 27; 11:10). The numerous references to the hardening of Pharaoh's heart underline the importance of this motif. The narrative describes this hardening in two ways. Whereas in the initial stages it is reported that Pharaoh hardened his own heart (7:13, 14, 22; 8:15, 19, 32; 9:34, 35), the narrative switches from this to state that the LORD hardened Pharaoh's heart (9:12; 10:20, 27; 11:10; 14:4, 8, 17), as predicted in 4:21 and 7:3. By describing the hardening of Pharaoh's heart in these ways, the narrative emphasises both the guilt of Pharaoh and the sovereignty of God.

The hardening of Pharaoh's heart stands in sharp contrast to other developments which occur in the narrative. Although the Egyptian magicians could initially duplicate the miraculous signs of Moses and Aaron, they soon reached the limit of their power and affirmed to Pharaoh, 'This is the finger of God' (8:19). Later, it is specifically noted that they 'could not stand before Moses because of the boils that were on them' (9:11). Similarly, Pharaoh's own officials were gradually persuaded of the LORD's power. When Moses predicted the 'worst hailstorm that has ever fallen on Egypt' (9:18), some of them took precautions against his threat (9:20). When Moses next warned of a plague of locusts, the officials urged Pharaoh to let the Israelites go (10:7; cf. 11:3).

While those around him gradually conceded to the LORD's power, Pharaoh remained stubbornly resistant. Nevertheless, even he was forced to make concessions as a result of the divine signs and wonders. Initially he was willing to let the people go on the condition that Moses prayed for the removal of the frogs (8:8). Next, while he desired that the Israelites should stay within Egypt, he was persuaded to let them go a little way into the desert (8:25–28). Although he actually stated after the hail that the people could go (9:28), this never happened. When Moses threatened an invasion of locusts, Pharaoh was prepared to allow the Israelite men, but not the women and children, to go and offer sacrifices to the LORD (10:8–11). Finally, he conceded that men, women and children could go, but not their flocks and herds (10:24). In spite of his apparent willingness to give way to Moses and Aaron in the face of further divine signs and wonders, Pharaoh persistently refused to let the people go.

The final demonstration of God's power to Pharaoh and the Egyptians involved the death of the male first-born. At this point the narrative expands to give a detailed account of the events surrounding the night on which the Israelites were delivered from Egypt. The occasion was so significant that it received a special name, the Passover, and was commemorated in various ways.[6] As a result of the death of all the male first-born in Egypt, Pharaoh was forced to recognise and concede to the power of the LORD. No longer could he deny any knowledge of the God who had demonstrated his existence by signs and wonders that surpassed anything the Egyptians had previously witnessed.

Although Pharaoh permitted the Israelites to leave Egypt after the death of the first-born, there was to be one further demonstration of the LORD's power. To achieve this, God delayed the Israelites' departure for Canaan, and they remained in Egypt on the western side of the Red Sea (cf. 13:18; 15:4). When Pharaoh and his army pursued their former slaves, the Israelites, believing themselves trapped, were terrified (14:10–12). However, by stretching out his staff Moses provided a safe escape route for the people through the divided waters of the sea. When the Egyptians followed, Moses again stretched out his hand over the sea, this time with tragic consequences for Pharaoh and his soldiers: 'not one of them survived' (14:28). Through repetition, verses 4 and 18 draw attention to the LORD's prime motive in destroying the Egyptian army: 'the Egyptians will know that I am the LORD'. Earlier Pharaoh had rejected Moses' request to let the people go by stating, 'Who is the LORD, that I should obey him and let Israel go' (5:2)? To his own peril he eventually discovered why the LORD should be obeyed. Interestingly, the narrative also highlights the changing attitude of the Israelites from unbelief and fear in the face of the Egyptian threat (14:10–12) to faith and trust in the light of the LORD's deliverance (14:31).

As a fitting conclusion to the preceding account of the divine deliverance of the enslaved Israelites from Egyptian control, the Exodus narrative records how Moses and the people celebrated in song the majesty and power of the LORD (15:1–18). Here the narrative switches from prose to poetry. The exalted language of the poetry conveys better than prose the thoughts and feelings of the Israelites as they worshipped the one who had taken pity upon them and rescued them from the tyrant's power. By rehearsing what has already been recorded in prose, the reader too is encouraged to participate in the celebrations of the Israelites. As the people responded in adoration and praise for what God had already done, they looked forward with confidence to the future. Thus their song concludes by focusing on what God has yet to accomplish on their behalf (15:13–18). In the light of past events and future expectation it is hardly surprising that at the end of this section we read of Miriam and all the women playing tambourines and dancing with joy.

---

[6] See chapter 13.

12.6. The Sinai Covenant

Following their divine rescue from Egypt the Israelites gradually proceeded to Mount Sinai in fulfilment of what God had earlier told Moses (cf. 3:12). Once there further developments occurred in their relationship with God. A special agreement or covenant was established between God and the Israelites, based on the principle that if the people obeyed God, then they would be his treasured possession. Instructions were given for the construction of a suitable dwelling place for the LORD which would be located in the middle of the Israelite camp. This would enable God to be visibly present among his people. As a result of these developments the people would have a more intimate knowledge of their God. No longer would he be a remote deity, but rather one to whom the people could physically draw near.

At Sinai God revealed himself in a new way to the Israelites. Three aspects of this revelation are significant. First, attention is drawn to the holiness of God's nature. We see this in the instructions given to Moses. The people must consecrate themselves, wash their clothes and abstain from sexual relations for three days (19:14–15). Furthermore, Moses must establish a boundary around the mountain in order to prevent the people from coming into direct contact with God; even the priests were subject to this constraint. As the ground near the burning bush was made holy by God's presence (3:5), so too was Mount Sinai (19:23). Secondly, God's presence, accompanied by thunder and lightning, fire and smoke, and the violent trembling of the mountain itself (19:16–19), was seen, heard and felt by all the people. Thirdly, God spoke directly to all those gathered at the foot of the mountain and declared the principal obligations to which they must adhere in order for the covenant relationship to be established (20:1–17). The effect of all this upon the people was such that they asked Moses to mediate with God on their behalf. Moses subsequently received further obligations concerning the covenant (21:1–23:33). Both sets of obligations reflected God's nature, especially his divine attributes of righteousness and compassion.[7]

Following the ratification of the Sinai covenant (24:3–8), Moses was summoned into God's presence in order to receive instructions for the building of a tent or tabernacle which would be God's dwelling place on earth. The special nature of this tent reflects certain aspects of God's character, in particular his sovereignty and holiness. The precious metals and bluish fabrics used in its construction are indicative of royalty, and the appointment of priests and the consecration of all the furnishings underline the holiness of God.[8]

While Moses was receiving God's instructions concerning the construction of the tabernacle, the people who remained at the foot of Sinai desired to have

---

[7] For a fuller discussion of the Sinai covenant, see chapter 14.
[8] For a fuller discussion of the tabernacle, see chapter 15.

a symbol of the LORD's presence. This resulted ironically in the making of a golden calf. Whereas the tabernacle, with it golden furnishings, portrayed the LORD as a royal personage, the golden calf, in marked contrast, represented him as a mere beast. Although the people offered sacrifices, their worship of the calf degraded the one who had delivered them from slavery in Egypt. Worship, to be true, must be based on a right perception of God. The book of Exodus emphasises the importance of knowing God as he truly is, and not as we imagine him to be.

Following the golden calf incident Moses asked to see God's glory (33:18). From the LORD's response it is clear that he equated his glory with 'all my goodness' (33:19). To assure Moses of his identity, God would proclaim his personal name, the LORD. Interestingly, when God had previously revealed his name to Moses, 'Moses hid his face, because he was afraid to look at God' (3:6). Now he displayed a greater confidence. Yet, although Moses was granted the opportunity to see God as no one else had done, even he could not look upon the divine face with immunity (33:20).

When God revealed himself to Moses on top of the mountain, he not only stressed his mercy and compassion, 'forgiving wickedness, rebellion and sin' (34:7; cf. 33:19), but also his justice, 'he does not leave the guilty unpunished' (34:7; cf. 32:34). The revelation of these divine characteristics to Moses was so significant that this passage is echoed on seven occasions in the Old Testament (Num. 14:18; Neh. 9:17; Ps. 86:15; 103:8; 145:8; Joel 2:13; Jon. 4:2). In this dramatic setting, we have stated verbally two of the most important characteristics of God's nature, mercy and justice, qualities which have already been revealed through his deliverance of the Israelites from Egypt.

Apart from this unique encounter with God on the mountain, Moses also communed with God on a regular basis by entering a tent which was pitched at some distance from the main encampment.[9] Given its specific function, this tent was known as the 'tent of meeting' (33:7).[10] Here Moses enjoyed a unique and personal relationship with God: 'The LORD would speak to Moses face to face, as a man speaks with his friend' (33:11). Although they were in close proximity to one another, even Moses the faithful servant was not permitted to look directly upon God; 33:9 implies that the tent curtain shielded Moses, who was within, from the LORD, who was without.

---

[9] The tenses of the Hebrew verbs in 33:7–11 and 34:33–35 indicate that these passages describe events which occurred on a regular basis.

[10] This tent of meeting should not be confused with the tabernacle, also known as the 'Tent of Meeting' (e.g. 40:2, 6), which was constructed only later (36:8–38) and which was pitched in the midst of the Israelite encampment (Num. 1:53; 2:2, 17). See chapter 15.

Remarkably, every time Moses met with God his face became radiant and remained so afterwards (34:29–35).[11]

When the tabernacle was finally erected a cloud covered it and the glory of the LORD filled it (40:34). God now dwelt in the midst of the people. The tabernacle became the 'Tent of Meeting' (40:35), replacing the tent used previously by Moses (cf. 33:7–11). Whereas Moses went inside the earlier tent and God remained outside (33:9), now God dwelt within the tent and Moses stayed outside (40:35). God's presence was visible to everyone through the cloud and fire which settled upon the tabernacle. From here he guided them on their journeys (40:36–38). Thus, Exodus comes to a dramatic conclusion by recording the arrival of the glorious presence of the sovereign God in the midst of his people Israel.

12.7. Conclusion

There can be little doubt that the most important theme running throughout the book of Exodus is that of knowing God. Not only does the text highlight the different ways in which God may reveal himself, but it also focuses on those attributes which lie at the very heart of his nature: his sovereign majesty, his holiness, his awesome glory, his power to perform wonders, his righteousness and his compassion.

12.8. New Testament Connections

Many of the theological ideas highlighted in the book of Exodus are also found in the NT. Those associated with the Passover, the Sinai covenant and the tabernacle will be considered in the next three chapters respectively. The themes of testing in the wilderness and God's remarkable provision for the people are dealt with in chapter 21. Here we shall focus briefly on a number of other ways in which the Exodus story is echoed in the NT.

The NT writers generally picture God in the same way as he is revealed in Exodus. Paul highlights the sovereign majesty of God when he refers to him as 'the King eternal' (1 Tim. 1:17) and 'the blessed and only Ruler, the King of kings and Lord of Lords, who alone is immortal and who lives in unapproachable light, whom no-one has seen or can see' (1 Tim. 6:15–16). Similarly, the

---

[11] Moses' radiant face set him apart from the rest of the people as God's messenger. When he communicated God's words to the people, he spoke with his face uncovered. At all other times he covered his face with a veil. In this way the Israelites were able to know when Moses spoke with divine authority and when he spoke on his own behalf.

author of Hebrews, quoting Deuteronomy 4:24, speaks of worshipping God 'with reverence and awe, for our "God is a consuming fire"' (12:28–29).

Of all the NT writings John's Gospel probably contains the broadest range of allusions to the exodus story. The following are the more obvious. First, the early chapters of Exodus and John's Gospel share a similar interest in 'signs'.[12] Apart from the resurrection, seven signs draw attention in John to the uniqueness of Jesus:

water to wine	2:2–11
healing of an official's son	4:46–54
healing of paralysed man	5:1–15
feeding of 5,000	6:1–14
walking on water	6:15–21
healing of blind man	9:1–41
raising of Lazarus	11:1–45

For the author of the Gospel these signs witness to Jesus' divine nature.

> Jesus did many other miraculous signs in the presence of his disciples, which are not recorded in this book. But these are written that you may believe that Jesus is the Christ, the Son of God, and that by believing you may have life in his name (Jn. 20:30–31).

While the 'signs' performed by Jesus are all positive in nature, in marked contract to the signs of 'judgement' in Exodus, it is surely noteworthy that the first and last signs in both books have much in common. The water into blood and the death of the first-born in Exodus are replaced in John's Gospel with 'signs' of hope: water into wine and the raising from death of the first-born.

Secondly, in marked contrast to the Synoptic Gospels, the Gospel of John focuses particular attention on various visits undertaken by Jesus to Jerusalem. Indeed, if we only had John's record we would be inclined to place most of Jesus' ministry in Jerusalem. Significantly, Jesus' visits to Jerusalem coincide with major Jewish festivals which celebrate the exodus from Egypt: Passover (2:13; 11:55); Tabernacles (7:2); a feast (5:1). Furthermore, in John's Gospel John the Baptist describes Jesus as 'the Lamb of God' (1:29; 1:36) and, perhaps most significantly of all, the crucifixion of Jesus occurs at the time of the Passover.[13]

Thirdly, another very distinctive feature of John's Gospel is the 'I am' sayings of Jesus.

---

[12] The Greek word *semeion* 'sign' is sometimes translated into English by 'miracle'.

[13] For further comments on the links between John's Gospel and the Passover, see chapter 13.

I am the bread of life (6:35).

I am the light of the world (8:12).

I am the door (10:7, 9).

I am the good shepherd (10:11).

I am the resurrection and the life (11:25).

I am the way, the truth and the life (14:6).

I am the true vine (15:1).

Jesus uses "I am" without a predicate on a number of other occasions (8:24, 28, 58; 13:19). Although the precise link between these 'I am' sayings and the book of Exodus is open to discussion,[14] it seems highly likely that the author of John's Gospel sees in them an allusion to Exodus 3:14: 'God said to Moses, "I AM WHO I AM. This is what you are to say to the Israelites: 'I AM has sent me to you.'"' (Ex. 3:14).

In the light of the other features which link John's Gospel with Exodus, we are probably intended to see in Jesus' statement, 'I am the light of the world; he who follows me will not walk in darkness, but will have the light of life …' (Jn. 8:12), a reference to the cloud of fire which guided the Israelites in the wilderness (Ex. 13:21–22; 14:19; 40:38). Elsewhere, Jesus clearly alludes to the manna which Israel ate in the wilderness when he comments, 'I am the bread which came down from heaven' (Jn. 6:41). Indeed, as we shall observe in chapter 21, John 6 is especially rich in allusions to the exodus experience of the Israelites.

Turning from John's Gospel, other NT links with Exodus exist. In his letter to the Romans, Paul refers briefly to the Exodus description of the divine hardening of Pharaoh's heart (Rom. 9:17). Focusing throughout Romans 9 on the sovereignty of God, Paul draws on various examples to highlight God's freedom to use individuals in a variety of ways for the outworking of his purposes.

With vivid imagery the author of Hebrews contrasts Mount Sinai with Mount Zion, the heavenly Jerusalem (cf. Heb. 12:22).

You have not come to a mountain that can be touched and that is burning with fire; to darkness, gloom and storm; to a trumpet blast or to such a voice speaking words that those who heard it begged that no further word be spoken to them, because

---

[14] Although some writers have connected Jesus' special use of the expression 'I am' with God's use of the same words in Exodus 3:14, it is possible that the 'I am' expressions in John's Gospel echo similar expressions in the book of Isaiah (especially 41:4; 43:10, 13, 25; 46:4; 48:12). However, given that the phrase 'I am' in Isaiah probably alludes back to Exodus 3:14, it is not completely inappropriate to observe a link between Jesus' use of 'I am' in John's Gospel and its use as a divine designation in Exodus 3:14.

they could not bear what was commanded: 'If even an animal touches the mountain, it must be stoned.' The sight was so terrifying that Moses said, 'I am trembling with fear.' But you have come to Mount Zion, to the heavenly Jerusalem, the city of the living God. You have come to thousands upon thousands of angels in joyful assembly, to the church of the firstborn, whose names are written in heaven. You have come to God, the judge of all men, to the spirits of righteous men made perfect, to Jesus the mediator of a new covenant, and to the sprinkled blood that speaks a better word than the blood of Abel (Heb. 12:18–24).

Whereas the ancient Israelites encountered God at an earthly mountain, those embraced by the new covenant receive 'a kingdom which cannot be shaken' (Heb. 12:28).

13

The Passover

13.1. Summary

The account of God's rescue of the Israelites comes to a climax in the killing of the Egyptian first-born males. To distinguish them from the Egyptians, God instructs the Israelites to follow a special ritual involving a sacrificial meal. As a result their houses were 'passed over' when the LORD struck down all the first-born in Egypt. Such was the importance of the occasion that later generations of Israelites were not to forget what the LORD had done in delivering their ancestors from slavery in Egypt. For the nation of Israel the Passover was the most significant redemptive event in their history.

13.2. Introduction

The account of the Passover in Exodus 12:1–13:16 forms the conclusion to the cycle of episodes that, beginning in 7:8, displays God's power over Pharaoh (7:8–11:10). Considerable attention is focused on the fulfilment of the divine pronouncement that 'every first-born son in Egypt will die' (11:5). The unique way in which the Israelite first-born are protected from death furnishes the designation for this remarkable occasion, 'the Passover' (cf. 12:11, 23, 27).

The narrator not only recounts the main events of the first Passover through a skilful use of dialogue, but by the same technique he also highlights how the Passover was to be remembered by subsequent generations of Israelites. First, they will celebrate for seven days annually the Feast of Unleavened Bread (12:14–20; 13:3–10). Several other references underline the close association between unleavened bread and the Passover (12:34, 39). Given their swift departure from Egypt, it was not possible for the Israelites to observe this feast until the first anniversary of the exodus (cf. Num. 9:1–14). Secondly, in conjunction with the Feast of Unleavened Bread, the Israelites were to commemorate the Passover through the eating of a year-old lamb or kid (12:24–27, 42–50).[1] Celebrated on the evening of the fourteenth day of the first month the Passover preceded the start of the Feast of Unleavened Bread which began on the fifteenth day and continued until the twenty-first day of the month (cf. 12:18). Thirdly, to commemorate the survival of their first-born sons, the Israelites were commanded to give the LORD all future firstborn sons and male animals (13:11–16). These various activities were an ongoing testimony to the fact that the LORD had brought them out of Egypt with his mighty hand (cf. 13:3, 9, 16).

13.3. The Account of the Passover

Exodus 12:1–28 is composed of two speeches containing instructions for the activities associated with the Passover. Although placed side by side the speeches were given days apart. The first speech (12:1–20) was delivered by God to Moses some time before the first Passover night; verse 3 records instructions concerning the selection of the Passover lamb or kid four days before the Passover was observed. In the second speech (12:21–27) Moses addressed the elders of Israel on the day of the Passover. Through these two speeches the narrator highlights the events leading up to the striking down of the Egyptian first-born at midnight on the fourteenth day of the month (12:29). Interestingly, both speeches conclude with comments drawing attention to future commemorations of the Passover (12:14–20; 24–27). Moreover, the second speech complements the first, providing additional information on various aspects of the Passover celebration. Since the reader is able to reconstruct the events that took place from the content of the two speeches, the author refrains from describing the fulfilment of the instructions; he merely comments, 'the Israelites did just what the LORD commanded Moses and Aaron' (12:28).

Various predictions made in 11:1–10 are fulfilled in 12:29–36. The LORD strikes down at midnight all the Egyptian first-born, causing the people to wail loudly (12:29–30; cf. 11:4–6).[2] After summoning Moses and Aaron for the final time, Pharaoh eventually permits the Israelites to leave unconditionally (12:31–32; cf. 11:1). As instructed in 11:2, the Israelites ask for and receive from the Egyptians 'articles of silver and gold' and 'clothing' (12:35). Because 'the LORD had made the Egyptians favourably disposed towards the people …

---

[1] The Hebrew word śeh denotes either a lamb or a goat. The mention of 'Passover lamb' in 1 Corinthians 5:7 is unfortunate. A more accurate translation of the verses is: 'For Christ, our Passover, has been sacrificed.'

[2] The precise identity of 'the destroyer' (12:23) is not revealed in Exodus. According to Psalm 78:49 this may refer to a 'band of destroying angels'.

they gave them what they asked for' (12:36; cf. 11:3). The plundering of Egypt is presented as retribution for the way in which the Egyptians treated the Israelites as slaves (cf. Gen. 15:14).

With Pharaoh's permission the Israelites begin their journey to freedom travelling from Rameses to Succoth (12:37–41). The haste of their departure is marked by the fact that they have time only to prepare bread made without yeast or leaven (12:39; cf. 12:11). At last, after 430 years, the people are enabled to leave Egypt as a result of the mighty wonders performed by the LORD.[3]

The account of the departure of the Israelites is interrupted by 12:42–50 which records 'regulations for the Passover'. Clearly these regulations applied to both the first Passover and later commemorations (cf. 12:42). The section ends by noting the obedience of the Israelites, with verse 50 corresponding closely to 12:28, possibly indicating that the instructions belong there chronologically. By ordering the material as he does, the narrator brings together in 12:42–13:16 the three ways in which the Israelites' deliverance from Egypt was to be celebrated: by re-enacting the Passover (12:43–49); by keeping the feast of Unleavened Bread (13:3–10); by consecrating every first-born male (13:11–16).

The narrative picks up in verse 51 where it left off in verse 41 by repeating various details (e.g. 'on that very day', 'divisions'; the NIV obscures somewhat the similarity between the two verses in the Hebrew text). On the day following the destruction of the Egyptian firstborn God announces to Moses that the Israelites must set apart as special 'the first offspring of every womb … whether man or animal' (13:1). Moses in turn expands upon this directive as he conveys it to the people (13:11–16). It is preceded, however, by instructions regarding the celebration of the feast of Unleavened Bread (13:3–10). Although Moses and Aaron were divinely instructed about this feast earlier (12:14–20), it is only now that the people learn of it. Moses' speech to the people in 13:3–16 falls neatly into two halves, which parallel each other closely. Both begin with references to the people taking possession of the land of Canaan in fulfilment of God's oath to their forefathers (13:5, 11). Next come instructions regarding the commemoration of the Israelites' deliverance from Egypt (13:6–7, 12–13), and the explanation of these activities to the children (13:8, 14–15). Finally, both halves are marked by similar endings, concluding with the comment that 'the LORD brought you out of Egypt with his mighty hand' (13:9; cf. v. 16).

---

[3] Genesis 15:13 refers to the descendants of Abraham being enslaved and ill-treated for 400 years (cf. Acts 7:6). The larger figure of 430 years probably includes the period of peace which they enjoyed after their initial arrival in Egypt.

13.4. The Purpose of the Passover Ritual

At the heart of the Passover ritual is the slaying of a lamb or kid, the smearing of its blood on the doorposts and the eating of its meat (12:6–11, 21–22). The details of the ritual parallel closely those relating to sacrifices and this is confirmed by the comment in 12:27, 'It is the Passover sacrifice to the LORD.' Yet, while resembling other sacrifices, the Passover ceremony is unique, reflecting its peculiar historical setting. Because it occurs prior to the establishment of the Aaronic priesthood (Lev. 8:1–9:24), Moses commands 'all the elders of Israel' to slaughter the Passover victims (12:21). Similarly, there is no reference to the central sanctuary which was first instituted after the exodus at Sinai (20:24–26; 24:4; 27:1–8). Whereas other sacrifices were normally offered up during daylight, the Passover is sacrificed at 'twilight' as this was the only convenient time due to the exploitation of the Israelites by the Egyptians. Finally, the timing of the Passover to the fourteenth day of the month coincides with the full moon, the most suitable night in the month for undertaking the activities associated with the exodus from Egypt.

Special attention is focused on the use made of the animal's blood: it is smeared on the sides and tops of the doorframe of the house (12:7, 22). Some scholars emphasise the apotropaic purpose of this action, designed to protect those within from hostile powers without (cf. 12:13, 23). Others suggest that the blood was used to purify the Israelite houses, a proposal supported by the mention of hyssop (12:22) which is elsewhere associated with ritual purification (e.g. Lev. 14:4, 6, 49, 51, 52; Num. 19:6, 18).

An equally important part of the Passover rite is the eating of the animal. Everyone in the Israelite community is to participate (12:47), and for each animal slaughtered there has to be an adequate number of people to eat all the meat. Special instructions are given concerning the cooking of the meat: the entire animal is roasted, not boiled (12:9); the meat must be eaten indoors and the animal's bones must not be broken (12:46). Any meat that remains to the morning must be burnt (12:10).

The description of the Passover meal parallels closely elements of the account of the consecration of the Aaronic priests in Exodus 29 and Leviticus 8. Here the slaughter of a ram together with the sprinkling of its blood and the eating of its meat form the main elements of a consecration ritual. Although there are differences of detail, these same elements underlie the Passover ritual. The sacrifice of the animal atones for the sin of the people, the blood smeared on the doorposts purifies those within, and the eating of the sacrificial meat consecrates those who consume it. By participating in the Passover ritual the people sanctify themselves as a nation holy to God (cf. 19:6).

13.5. Conclusion

The divine redemption of the Israelites from Egypt comes to a dramatic climax in the events associated with the Passover. Later generations were never to forget this unique event which signalled the beginning of the process by which the LORD established Israel as his holy people. The events and ideas associated with the Passover became a paradigm for later generations of God's redemptive activity.

13.6. New Testament Connections

The crucifixion of Jesus, the central redemptive event in the NT, is linked in various ways to the Passover, the most important redemptive event of the OT period. First, the Gospels all highlight the fact that the death of Jesus took place in Jerusalem when the Jews were commemorating the Passover by keeping the Feast of Unleavened Bread. Secondly, the Synoptic Gospels (Matthew, Mark and Luke) present the Last Supper as a Passover meal (Mt. 26:17; Mk. 14:12; Lk. 22:7–8), emphasising its importance and the special significance of Jesus' words and actions. This final meal of Jesus and his closest disciples is subsequently commemorated in the Lord's Supper (1 Cor. 11:23–33). Thirdly, the actual death of Jesus is linked to the offering up of the Passover sacrifice. John's Gospel alludes to this by observing that because Jesus' bones are not broken his death resembles that of the Passover sacrifice (Jn. 19:36; cf. Ex. 12:46). This connection is made even more explicit in 1 Corinthians 5:7: 'For Christ, our Passover, has been sacrificed.' Finally, although other interpretations are possible, 1 Peter 1:18–19 probably also associates the death of Jesus with the Passover sacrifice.

One particular difficulty must be noted regarding the NT association of the death of Jesus with the Passover. In the OT the Passover sacrifice was always offered up before the eating of the Passover meal. However, this pattern is reversed in the NT; the Passover meal is eaten on the evening prior to the crucifixion of Jesus. One solution has been to argue that the Last Supper was only a preparatory meal which took place on the evening before the real Passover celebration. Although this is a convenient explanation, the Synoptic Gospels emphasise to such an extent the preparations for this meal that it is difficult to imagine that it could be anything other than the Passover meal itself.

An alternative solution may lie in the observation that John does not explicitly say that Jesus was crucified at the very time when the Passover victims were being slaughtered at the temple. Perhaps John encountered no difficulty in the fact that Jesus was crucified the day after the other

Passover sacrifices. What mattered to John was the manner of his death, not the timing.[4]

By linking the crucifixion of Jesus to the Passover, the NT church drew attention to the redemptive nature of Jesus' death. Like the original Passover sacrifice, his death atoned for the sin of the people, his blood purified and cleansed, and his body sanctified those who ate it at the Lord's Supper.

---

[4] John may have believed that the timing of Jesus' death fulfilled accurately the OT regulations regarding the Passover sacrifice. He observes that the crucifixion took place on 'the day of Preparation of Passover Week' (19:14; cf. 19:31) and that the next day was to be a 'special Sabbath' (19:31). This special Sabbath clearly refers to the first day of the feast of Unleavened Bread. If we assume that this special Sabbath coincided with a normal Sabbath (i.e. it fell on a Saturday), then we may conclude that Jesus was crucified on the Friday preceding the beginning of the Feast of Unleavened Bread. Since in NT times the day was reckoned as beginning at sunset, the Friday evening marked the beginning of the first day of the feast of Unleavened Bread (that is, the fifteenth day of the month). If the Passover meal was eaten on the evening of the fourteenth day of the month, this would have been the Thursday evening (as implied in the Synoptic Gospels). For his part, John may have appreciated that the original instructions regarding the Passover assumed that the day began at sunrise. Consequently, the first day of Unleavened Bread commenced on the Saturday morning and not the Friday evening. This observation is based on the premise that the timing of the Passover celebration in the NT period differed from that intended in the original OT instructions due to an important change concerning the way in which the start of the day was reckoned. Whereas the OT Passover regulations presupposed that the day began at sunrise, from the sixth century BC onwards the Jews followed the Babylonian system of reckoning the day as beginning at sunset. In view of this, the Passover sacrifice ought on the basis of the OT regulations to have been offered up on Friday with the meal being eaten on the Friday evening. If John adopted this interpretation of the timing of Jesus' death, we may assume that Jesus and his disciples followed the custom of their day and ate the Passover on the Thursday evening. John, however, sees in the death of Jesus on the Friday an exact fulfilment of the Exodus instruction for celebrating the Passover.

14

The Covenant at Sinai

14.1. Summary

A formalising of the Israelites' relationship with God through a special agreement follows soon after their divine rescue from Egypt. This agreement, or covenant, sets out how the people must live in order to be a holy nation. Two sets of obligations are placed before the people. The Ten Commandments, which make up the principal obligations of the covenant, emphasise the importance of loving God and one's neighbour. A further document, the Book of the Covenant, contains more detailed obligations which take a number of forms: some are model laws which can be enforced by human courts; others are moral rules which emphasise exemplary behaviour, especially towards the weaker members of society; a further group of obligations focuses on religious duties. The principal and detailed obligations complement each other, setting out how God expects his people to live. Obedience will ensure God's blessing; disobedience will lead to punishment.

14.2. Introduction

At the heart of the book of Exodus is the establishment of a special covenant relationship between God and the Israelites. The basic form of this agreement is found in 19:4–6. If Israel, in the light of her divine deliverance from Egypt, will obey the LORD, then she will be his 'treasured possession ... a kingdom of priests and a holy nation'. As regards this covenant four factors are worth noting.

First, from beginning to end God takes the initiative in making the covenant. He is the one who rescues the Israelites from Egypt and leads them to Mount Sinai (cf. 19:4; 20:2). There he instructs Moses as to how the people must prepare themselves (19:10–13, 21–22). Following his dramatic arrival on Mount Sinai, God announces directly to the people the main conditions of the covenant; the Israelites do not negotiate. Throughout, God acts first and the people are invited to respond.

Secondly, God highlights Israel's special status: 'out of all nations you will be my treasured possession' (19:5). Furthermore, they will be 'a kingdom of priests and a holy nation' (19:6). The expression 'a kingdom of priests' can also be translated 'priestly kings', suggesting that the Israelites are to enjoy the privilege of being both priests and kings in their relationships with other peoples. This indicates the important role which Israel is to play in God's future plans. They are also to be a holy nation.[1] The implications of this are revealed in the obligations which God places before the people. In their daily lives they are to reflect God's righteous and loving nature.

Thirdly, the establishment of the covenant relationship is conditional upon Israel's obedience to God. After throwing off the yoke of Egyptian slavery, the Israelites must now obey a new sovereign. Obedience to God lies at the heart of the covenant relationship (cf. 19:8; 24:3, 7). However, obedience by itself does not create the special covenant relationship. Rather, it is a loving response to what God in his grace does first (cf. 20:6; 'those who love me and keep my commandments').

Fourthly, two sets of obligations are placed before the Israelites. The first set, the Ten Commandments (20:3–17), are announced directly to all the people by God. These are the main covenant obligations that the people must accept. Later, God gives through Moses further obligations that are recorded in a document known as the Book of the Covenant (20:23–23:33). The material in this document falls into different categories and consists of more specific obligations than those listed in the Ten Commandments. Both sets of obligations reveal how the Israelites must live in order to maintain their covenant relationship with God.

14.3. The Principal Covenant Obligations – the Ten Commandments (Ex. 20:1–17)

As the people stand in awe before Mount Sinai, they hear the very voice of God introducing himself to them: 'I am the LORD your God, who brought you out of Egypt, out of the land of slavery' (20:2; cf. Deut. 4:12–13; 5:4). There then follows a list of stipulations that form the basis of Israel's covenant relationship with God (20:3–17). These are later termed 'the ten words' (34:28; Deut. 4:13; 10:4), from which we derive the designations Decalogue or Ten Commandments. Their importance is further emphasised when God eventually inscribes them on two stone tablets (24:12; 31:18; 34:1, 28).

Strictly speaking, the Decalogue is not a collection of laws. Various factors set it apart from the other legal collections of the Pentateuch. First, it is spoken directly

---

[1] For a fuller treatment of the concept of holiness, see chapter 16.

by God to the people; at this stage Moses does not act as an intermediary (20:1, 19; cf. Deut. 4:12–13; 5:4–5, 22–27). Secondly, it alone is inscribed on stone tablets by the 'finger of God' (31:18; cf. 24:12; 32:15–16; 34:1, 28; Deut. 5:22). Moses writes down all the other regulations and instructions (24:4; 34:27–28). Thirdly, the Ten Commandments are not laws, since no punishments are listed. Although the second and fifth commandments appear to contain penalties, these are really 'motivation clauses' designed to promote the observance of the divine instructions. Fourthly, the language used in the Decalogue generally denotes broad concepts and lacks the kind of precision that one might expect from a legal document.[2] Finally, what human law court could begin to enforce the prohibition against coveting described in the tenth commandment?

The stipulations outlined by the LORD are to govern Israel's relationship with her God. These represent the principal requirements which God places upon the people of Israel for the establishment and maintenance of the divine/human covenant relationship. The covenant stipulations in Exodus 20 are listed in order of descending priority and focus on the Israelites' relationship to first the LORD and then other people. The people are to be single-minded in their devotion to the one who delivered them from Egypt; they are to worship only Yahweh (20:3). Furthermore, their social behaviour is to follow a pattern which places a high priority on the rights of the individual as regards life, marriage and possessions. They are to obey these commands out of love for God: 'who love me and keep my commands' (20:6).

First commandment 20:3

Sole allegiance to the LORD lies at the very heart of the covenant relationship. It is the foundation upon which everything else rests. The people were in practice to be monotheistic, worshipping only the LORD. As is made clear elsewhere in the Pentateuch, the worship of other deities was punishable by death (Num. 25:1–18; Deut. 13:1–18).

Second commandment 20:4–6

Unlike contemporary peoples, the Israelites were not to make or worship visual representations of their God. In both Egypt and Canaan, human and

---

[2] For this reason, attempts to define carefully the legal boundaries established by the Decalogue are fraught with problems. Anyone trying to decide precisely what is included and excluded by, for example, 'honouring parents' will never arrive at a satisfactory conclusion on the basis of the terminology used in the Decalogue. What we have here are broad principles.

animal forms played an important function in depicting the attributes of a deity. Any attempt on the part of the Israelites to represent the LORD using such images would produce a distorted picture of his true nature. However, in the ancient world the image played a more important role than merely being a representation of the deity. The image was understood to be the place where the deity would manifest himself. The book of Exodus, however, emphasises the LORD's self-disclosure through 'signs and wonders', theophanies and verbal communications, occasionally in combination. Furthermore, for the future God's presence among the Israelites is linked to the tabernacle or divine tent. Here, the LORD will manifest himself to the people through theophany and speech. Given these alternative modes of divine manifestation, images were both unnecessary and inappropriate. The incident of the golden calf in Exodus 32 reveals both the necessity of this prohibition, in the light of the people's desire to have some visual image of the LORD, and the serious consequences of disregarding it.

Third commandment 20:7

Whereas the second commandment prohibits visual representations of God, the third focuses on verbal representations. As a sign of their respect for God, the people were to exercise the greatest caution when talking about God or invoking his name. They were to say nothing that might detract from a true appreciation of his nature and character.

Fourth commandment 20:8–11

The people were to refrain from work on the seventh day, the Sabbath. According to 31:12–18 the Sabbath was the sign of the covenant relationship inaugurated at Sinai; as such it functioned like the earlier covenant sign of circumcision (Gen. 17:9–14). Anyone failing to observe the Sabbath showed their disdain for the special relationship established between the LORD and Israel.

Fifth commandment 20:12

The concept of honouring is usually associated with God or his representatives, prophets and kings. In all likelihood parents were envisaged as representing God to their children, the family unit being a miniature of the nation. Furthermore, in ancient Israel the extended family was important, and family heads played a significant role in communal matters. Any attempt to undermine their authority was an attack on the basic authority structure within the local community. The seriousness of this commandment is reflected in the fact that the death penalty was required for children who wilfully disrespected their parents (Ex. 21:15, 17). If children respect parents as authority figures within the family, then respect for authority figures within society at large will also follow.

Sixth commandment 20:13

This commandment, by prohibiting murder or manslaughter,[3] demonstrates the high priority which God places upon human life. No human being has the right to take another's life because each person is made in God's image (cf. Gen. 1:27; 9:6). In the Pentateuch the punishment for taking another's life is normally death, although different factors may be taken into account when determining the precise punishment. The commandment, however, does not include judicial executions for capital offences or legitimate deaths resulting from war, and it should also be noted that the OT laws draw a careful distinction between premeditated and accidental deaths. (See below, under 21:1–22:20, the section entitled 'The sanctity of life'.)

Seventh commandment 20:14

In God's order of priority, the sanctity of human life is followed by the importance of the marriage relationship. Adultery here means sexual relations between a married woman and a man who is not her husband. Those caught in adultery could be executed (Lev. 20:10; Deut. 22:22). Interestingly, relations between a married man and an unmarried woman do not qualify as adultery. Polygamy is not automatically excluded by this commandment, although in practice it was rare in OT times and is usually viewed as a source of trouble. Similarly, divorce was permitted, but not encouraged (cf. Deut. 24:1). As a whole the Bible reveals that God desires the establishment of harmonious marital relationships and that neither partner should do anything to undermine this.

Eighth commandment 20:15

The next principle to govern the Israelites' relationship with God was respect for the property of others. Any individual found guilty of dispossessing another

---

[3] The Hebrew term used, *rāṣaḥ* (*rātsakh*), refers to the killing of a person (but not animals). Given its use elsewhere in the OT, it is not possible to restrict its meaning to 'murder' (as in the NIV).

was punished in accordance with the value of what they stole and the injured party was suitably compensated. While other ancient Near Eastern cultures sometimes invoked the death penalty for theft, the Old Testament consistently rejects such a position, indicating clearly that God values human life and the marital relationship above property.

Ninth commandment 20:16

In the final two commandments we proceed from prohibitions involving actions to prohibitions involving words and thoughts respectively. This concludes the downward progression of priorities which we have observed. The ninth commandment emphasises the importance of truthfulness. While the prohibition against false testimony is primarily intended for a court of law, it may be extended to include any situation in which untrue words are used to harm another individual.

Tenth commandment 20:17

The final commandment forbids an individual coveting what belongs to another. Unlike all the other commands, it addresses specifically inner feelings and thoughts, such as envy or greed. If the Israelites were to enjoy a harmonious covenant relationship with God, every aspect of their lives must conform to his will. Outward adherence was insufficient; their inner selves had to be patterned according to the divine principles of morality found in the Ten Commandments.

14.4. The Detailed Covenant Obligations

Alongside the principal obligations of the Decalogue, God also gave through Moses other obligations which had to be observed. Later, Moses recorded everything that the LORD said in a document known appropriately as the Book of the Covenant (24:7; cf. 24:4). Possibly most, if not all, of this document is preserved in 20:23–23:33. As it stands it falls into five sections. The opening part focuses on issues to do with the divine presence and how the Israelites are to encounter God (20:23–26). Secondly, there is a long list of laws dealing with various aspects of social life (21:1–22:20). The next part consists of moral rules or requirements which highlight the exemplary behaviour God expects of his people, especially towards the underprivileged (22:21–23:9). Then there are instructions regarding the observance of the Sabbath and religious festivals (23:10–19). The final section outlines how God would act on behalf of the Israelites, enabling them to take possession of the land of Canaan (23:20–33).

In a book that underlines God's passionate concern for justice through his rescue of the Israelites from Egypt, it is hardly surprising that a similar concern for justice should dominate the covenant which he established with the Israelites. This is most apparent in the legal material and moral rules that form the second and third sections of the Book of the Covenant.

14.5. The Legal Material of the Book of the Covenant (Ex. 21:1–22:20)

The material that comprises this section probably represents only some of the statutes which formed part of ancient Israel's law. In all likelihood many of those included here have been selected because they parallel God's actions in rescuing the Israelites from slavery in Egypt. At the very outset the principle is established that slaves have the right to be set free after a fixed period of time (21:1–4); this implies that the Egyptians acted illegally in holding the Israelites as slaves for a long period of time. In contrast, the inclusion of the statutes concerning a slave who loves his master (21:5–6) and a female servant (21:7–11) are intended to highlight various aspects of Israel's covenant relationship with the LORD; the Israelites will serve the LORD because they love him; having chosen Israel God will remain faithful to them. A further group of laws draw attention to the necessity of compensation for those who have been physically injured (21:18–27). In particular, it is noted that any slave who suffers serious injury at the hand of his or her master is to be released immediately (21:26–27). In the light of Israel's harsh treatment in Egypt (cf. 2:11; 5:14–16) these laws justify indirectly the LORD's action in freeing the Israelites. Another set of laws focuses on the concept of restitution (22:1–15). Here also it is possible to see a connection with earlier comments about how the Israelites demanded articles of silver and gold and clothing from the Egyptians (3:21–22; 11:2; 12:35–36). These items compensated the Israelites for the way in which they had been exploited in Egypt.

Apart from their relevance in justifying prior events in the book of Exodus, the laws in this section are also significant because of the ideals and values which permeate them. In all likelihood they were given as model laws, providing guidance for situations not directly covered by them.[4] The following are the most noteworthy.

---

[4] This possibility is highlighted by the detailed study of Sprinkle, *The Book of the Covenant*.

14.6. Moral Symmetry

The biblical laws are based on the principle that the punishment should match the crime. This is stated most clearly in the well known, but generally misunderstood, 'law of talion': 'life for life, eye for eye, tooth for tooth, hand for hand, foot for foot, burn for burn, wound for wound, bruise for bruise' (21:23–25; cf. Lev. 24:17–21; Deut. 19:21). At first sight, the law of talion appears to be a rather barbaric way of ensuring justice. Yet, within the development of law in the ancient Near East it represented an important advance. In the earliest known collections of laws monetary fines were imposed in cases of assault and bodily injury. The weakness of such fines was that they failed to take into account an individual's ability to pay. (For an unemployed labourer a fine of a thousand pounds imposes great hardship; to a millionaire it is a mere trifle.) The law of talion removes all such discrepancies by ensuring that the punishment should be no less, or no more, than the crime demands.

The law of talion, however, was not necessarily applied literally. In the Book of the Covenant it is preceded by a case of wounding, the punishment for which is the cost of medical expenses and compensation for lost wages (21:18–19). Similarly, it is followed immediately by a law in which a servant is granted release as compensation for the loss of an eye or a tooth (21:26–27). Clearly, there was no literal application of the law of talion in these instances.

14.7. The Sanctity of Life

Many modern readers of the biblical laws are likely to be disturbed by the use of capital punishment for a variety of crimes, including murder, kidnapping, physical or verbal assaults against parents, sorcery, bestiality and idolatry (21:12–17; 22:18–20).[5] Against modern standards of justice this punishment appears extremely harsh. Nevertheless, it reflects the value which the Israelites placed upon individual human life, the hierarchical structure within the family, and the purity of worship. In the case of murder the death penalty is invoked, not out of indifference for human life, but rather because each human life is of tremendous value (cf. Gen. 9:6). A life for a life does not express vengefulness, but rather the idea that the only payment that can be

---

[5] Stoning was used as a common means of execution because it underlined that the whole community, without exception, was responsible for the judicial death of the criminal. Because of the serious consequences of their testimony in capital cases, the prosecution witnesses had to throw the first stones (Deut. 17:7).

made for the taking of a human life is a human life itself. This even applies to animals responsible for human deaths (21:28).[6]

The distinctiveness of the biblical laws is apparent when one compares the other ancient Near Eastern laws. In the earlier Laws of Hammurabi (c. 1750 BC), a murderer is required only to make financial compensation to the victim's family. This contrasts sharply with the biblical insistence of a life for a life. On the other hand, the non-biblical laws apply the death penalty to breaking and entering, looting at a fire and theft. These examples reveal that in other cultures financial loss was sometimes treated more seriously than loss of life. The biblical laws consistently emphasise that human life is of greater value than material possessions.

14.8. Moral Imperatives (Ex. 22:21–23:9)

The material in this passage is generally taken to be detailed statutes. However, a number of factors suggest that it should be distinguished from the model laws found in 21:1–22:20:

(a) The section is marked off from the surrounding material by the frame formed by 22:21 and 23:9. Both verses not only prohibit the mistreatment of aliens, but they also underline this by reminding the Israelites that they were once aliens in Egypt.
(b) The way in which the material is presented does not conform to the two distinctive forms used in 21:1–22:20; rather it is reminiscent of the form adopted in the Decalogue.
(c) Apart from the general comment in 22:24, 'I will kill you with the sword', no penalties enforceable by a human court are stipulated for breaking the rules outlined here.

---

[6] In the light of these observations, it might appear that Christians ought to support the death penalty for crimes like murder. However, other factors must be considered. First, the ancient Israelites did not have the option of sentencing a murderer to life imprisonment; there were no facilities to imprison someone for a long period of time. Remarkably, imprisonment was never used as a means of punishment for any crime. Obviously this restricted greatly their choice of punishment. Secondly, it is likely that the death penalty was rarely utilised. This probably ensured that its use did not have the effect of devaluing human life. To make frequent recourse to capital punishment might suggest that human life is of little esteem, thus negating the very reason for adopting it. Whatever form of punishment we endorse, as Christians we must always ensure that it does not undermine the sanctity of human life.

(d) The subject matter of this section is distinctive. It encourages both a caring attitude towards the weak and vulnerable members of society (i.e. aliens, widows, orphans, the needy, and the poor) and a concern that the legal system be totally impartial. Those involved in disputes are to favour neither the rich, by accepting a bribe (23:8), nor the poor (23:3). Everyone, irrespective of their class, is to be treated equally (23:6, 9). A witness must not be swayed by social pressure (23:2), and should ensure that his or her testimony is truthful (23:1, 7).

The commands found here seek to inculcate a standard of behaviour which goes beyond the letter of the law. A human court is unlikely to prosecute someone for failing to return his enemy's straying animal; nevertheless God demands that his people should overcome evil with good (23:4–5; cf. Mt. 5:43–48; Rom. 12:19–21). In the light of the special relationship being established between God and the people it is surely significant that at the middle of this section is the command, 'you are to be my holy people' (22:31). We see here how God's holy people should live.

14.9. Instructions Concerning the Sabbath and Religious Festivals

In the fourth section of the Book of the Covenant the Israelites are reminded of their obligation to worship the LORD alone: 'Do not invoke the names of other gods; do not let them be heard on your lips' (23:13).[7] Such worship lies at the heart of the three annual festivals, which celebrate the LORD's benevolence towards Israel, and the Sabbath. The observance of the Sabbath is exceptionally important because it is the sign of the covenant being established between God and Israel (31:12–17). Anyone desecrating the Sabbath is guilty of renouncing this special relationship with God; the consequence is death (31:14–15).

---

[7] The material in 23:10–19 is carefully structured, falling into two halves, centred around verse 13, with each half subdivided into two parts. The first half deals with the seventh year (23:10–11) and the seventh day (23:12). Verses 14–19 are concerned with the three main festivals that the Israelites celebrated annually: Unleavened Bread; Harvest; Ingathering. The instructions in 23:17–19 correspond with the three feasts outlined in verses 14–16; note in particular how verse 17 parallels verse 14.

14.10. The Reciprocal Nature of the Covenant

The final part of the Book of the Covenant (23:20–33) highlights the reciprocal nature of the covenant being established between God and Israel. If the Israelites obeyed the LORD their God, then they would take possession of the land of Canaan (23:22–23). Furthermore, God's blessing would ensure their future comfort (23:25–26) and security (23:27–28). As a consequence of their relationship with the LORD, the Israelites had to distance themselves from the worship of other gods by destroying all pagan images and places of worship (23:24). For similar reasons, they were not to enter into any treaty with the inhabitants of Canaan lest this caused them to compromise their exclusive allegiance to the LORD (23:32–33). Such a warning was necessary because although God promised to remove from the land the nations already living there, they would be expelled only gradually in order to avoid the land becoming desolate (23:29–30).

14.11. The Ratification of the Covenant

After descending from the mountain, Moses relayed to the people God's words. Once more they expressed their willingness to do all that God commanded (24:3; cf. 19:8). There follows a brief account of the ceremony by which the covenant between the LORD and Israel was ratified (24:4–11). Interestingly, the activities outlined here reflect the three main sections of the LORD's speech to Moses (20:24–24:2). The building of an altar and the offering of sacrifices parallel the instructions given in 20:24–26. Moses then reads to the people 'the Book of the Covenant' (24:7), the middle section of the divine speech (21:1–23:33). After the Israelites again acknowledge their willingness to obey God (24:7), the covenant is sealed through the sprinkling of blood on the people (24:8). Finally, God's invitation to Moses and the elders to come up the mountain (24:9–11) corresponds to the third section of the divine speech (24:1–2).

14.12. Rebellion in the Camp

Having successfully ratified the covenant, Moses ascended Mount Sinai in order to receive instructions for the building of the tabernacle (25:1–31:18). However, his long absence of 'forty days and forty nights' (24:18) created an atmosphere of uncertainty in the Israelite camp. Perhaps fearful of what God may have done to Moses (cf. 20:19), the Israelites sought reassurance through the construction of an image which would represent the LORD's presence in their midst. Turning to Aaron, the people asked him to make 'gods', or better 'a god' (so NIV mg.), who would go before them (32:1).[8] Although the Israelites did not consciously reject the LORD as their God, their attempt to portray him as a golden calf was a major breach of the covenant stipulations which they had earlier accepted (cf. 20:4–6; 20:23).[9] Such an obvious violation of the LORD's instructions invited fierce condemnation (cf. 32:7–10).

Abhorring what took place, the LORD ordered Moses to return to the camp (32:7). God's anger was roused by the fact that the Israelites had so quickly turned away from his commands, and this in spite of repeated affirmations that they would do everything that the LORD had said (19:8; 24:3, 7). Such disrespect for God merited the harshest of punishments, death. In contrast to the people, Moses was assured that he would become 'a great nation', echoing God's earlier promise to Abraham (Gen. 12:3). Surprisingly, perhaps, Moses intervened and pleaded on behalf of the people for mercy, recalling God's marvellous deliverance of them from Egypt and his much earlier covenant with Abraham, Isaac and Jacob (32:11–13). His petition was based throughout on the character and honour of God. Moreover, he made no attempt to excuse the people's sinful behaviour. So compelling was his intercession that God relented from the immediate destruction of the people (32:14). Nevertheless, as the narrative subsequently reveals, the people did not go unpunished (32:28, 35).

When Moses eventually saw what had been happening in the camp, he too became enraged. By deliberately breaking the divinely inscribed stone tablets, containing the terms of agreement, Moses indicated that the covenant relationship between God and the Israelites was now ended.

Whereas the account in Exodus 32 is dominated by the rebellion of the Israelites and God's punishment of the people, attention switches in Exodus 33 to Moses, the faithful servant, and his remarkable friendship with the LORD. Moses' unique relationship with God provided the opportunity for him to intercede on behalf of the people; as a result, the covenant was renewed. This is attributed, not to some dramatic change of heart on the part of the people, but to the LORD's compassion and mercy. Consequently, Moses was instructed to bring up the mountain two stone tablets to replace those previously broken

---

[8] Several factors indicate that the image of the golden calf was meant to represent the LORD. According to the latter part of verse 4, the calf represented the god who delivered the people from Egypt; it was no new deity. Secondly, the festival, enthusiastically celebrated by the people (32:6), was described by Aaron as 'to the LORD' (32:5). Moreover, the festal activities resemble those recorded in Exodus 24 regarding the ratification of the covenant between the LORD and the Israelites.

[9] The narrator hints at this indirectly through his use of the Hebrew term *'ĕlohîm* 'god/gods' in verses 1, 4 and 8; when used with plural verbs *'ĕlohîm* normally refers to pagan gods; when used with singular verbs it normally refers to the LORD.

(34:1). Once more Moses wrote down the detailed covenant obligations (34:27; cf. 24:4),[10] and God inscribed on the new stone tablets the 'ten words' or Decalogue (34:28; cf. 20:3–17).[11]

14.13. Conclusion

The covenant at Sinai marked an important stage in God's relationship with the Israelites. At the centre of God's plans for his people was the hope that they should reflect his holy nature by being perfect in all they do, say and think. Unfortunately, the people soon displayed, through building the golden calf, their inability to keep the obligations set before them. As a result, the covenant relationship with God, which promised to be a source of great blessing, became for them, due to their disobedience, a source of divine cursing.

14.14. New Testament Connections

For religious Jews of the NT period it was exceptionally important to keep the Mosaic law; it was considered the essence of God's requirements for holy living. Not surprisingly, much discussion and debate took place to determine the precise requirements of the law, and different schools of thought adopted differing views on how the Mosaic law should be interpreted and related to contemporary situations. Against this background it is no surprise that the law figured prominently both in the teaching of Jesus and in various issues addressed by the early church.

14.14.1. Jesus and the Law

The four Gospels all indicate that Jesus frequently came into conflict with the religious leaders of his day concerning his attitude to the law. This is most apparent regarding the keeping of the Sabbath; the Gospels convey the impression that the Pharisees and teachers of the law regularly condemned Jesus' actions on the Sabbath, especially his willingness to heal (Mt. 12:9–14;

---

[10] The terms of the covenant, outlined in 34:11–26, parallel closely those found in the last two sections of the 'Book of the Covenant' (23:14–33), except that their order is here reversed.

[11] Although the subject of the verb is not clearly stated, it may be deduced from 34:1 that the tablets were inscribed by the LORD (cf. 32:16). It is not unusual in Hebrew narrative for the subject of the verb to change without this being clearly indicated.

Mk. 3:1–6; Lk. 6:6–11; 13:10–17; 14:1–6; Jn. 5:1–15; 7:21–24). Tension also existed regarding Jesus' attitude towards the laws on ritual cleanliness (Mt. 15:10–20; Mk. 7:1–8) and the Pharisees were quick to condemn Jesus' willingness to eat with 'sinners' (Mt. 9:10–11; 11:19; Mk. 2:15–16; Lk. 5:29–30; 7:34; 15:2). How then did Jesus view the OT law?

Two observations may be made. First, Jesus held the law in high regard. Although he did not conform to all the ways in which his contemporaries kept the Mosaic law, he constantly affirmed the importance of the law.

> I tell you the truth, until heaven and earth disappear, not the smallest letter, not the least stroke of a pen, will by any means disappear from the Law until everything is accomplished. Anyone who breaks one of the least of these commandments and teaches others to do the same will be called least in the kingdom of heaven, but whoever practises and teaches these commands will be called great in the kingdom of heaven. For I tell you that unless your righteousness surpasses that of the Pharisees and the teachers of the law, you will certainly not enter the kingdom of heaven (Mt. 5:18–20).

Moreover, when asked, 'Which is the greatest commandment in the law?' Jesus answered by stressing the need to love God and love one's neighbour (Mt. 22:37–39; Mk. 12:29–31). His answer summarises the twofold division found in the Ten Commandments. Love for God must come first, but it can never be divorced from love for one's neighbour; the former leads automatically to the latter.

Secondly, Jesus emphasised the true intention of the law. Jesus parted company from the other religious leaders of his day on the fundamental issue of the law's nature and function. His contemporaries viewed it as a line separating right and wrong behaviour. In the light of this, they sought to determine which actions were within the law and which were outside the law; that is, an individual was righteous as long as he or she did not go beyond the boundary established by the law. This approach, however, encouraged individuals to focus on the minimum requirements of the law and fostered a very legalistic attitude towards human behaviour. Furthermore, as Jesus pointed out, it created all kinds of anomalies and resulted in the law being used for unrighteous ends.[12] In marked contrast, Jesus viewed the law as a sign pointing to the type of behaviour that God desired. Jesus maintained that to keep the law fully one had to be perfect as God is perfect (cf. Mt. 5:48). Hence he called on his disciples to display a righteousness which surpassed that of the Pharisees and the teachers of the law (cf. Mt. 5:20). He reminded his

---

[12] We see this in his comments about making oaths (Mt. 5:33–37) and the law of Corban (Mt. 15:3–9; Mk. 7:9–13).

followers that to interpret the commandments as requiring only outward obedience was to misunderstand their purpose (Mt. 5:17–48). His approach is clearly seen in his understanding of the commandments, 'Do not murder' and 'Do not commit adultery'. These he interpreted respectively to mean 'Do not do, say or think anything which might lead to murder or adultery'. Furthermore, he indicated that the OT law occasionally permitted certain actions (e.g. divorce) not because it reflected God's perfect will but because God sought to accommodate the hardness of human hearts (Mt. 19:3–9). While the Pharisees and the teachers of the law exploited such divine accommodations, Jesus emphasised that each individual should seek to fulfil in his or her life God's original design for human existence.

14.14.2. *Paul and the Law*

Much has been written about Paul's view of the OT law. It is possible here only to make a few brief observations. Like Jesus, Paul condemned a legalistic understanding of the law which undermined its true purpose. In Galatians 3:15–25 he argues that the divine covenant made with Abraham takes precedence over the law given several centuries later at Mount Sinai. Whereas his opponents were advocating that believers must keep the law in order to be righteous, Paul responded by noting that the law, given later to fulfil a temporary role until Christ came, could never make anyone righteous; it merely indicated the righteousness required by God, not the means of achieving such righteousness. As such, it underlined the necessity of becoming righteous through faith.

14.14.3. *The New Covenant*

An important conviction among the early Christians was the belief that God had established through Jesus Christ a new covenant which superseded the covenant inaugurated centuries earlier at Sinai. Not surprisingly, such a view provoked considerable hostility from Jews whose religious outlook was centred on the Sinai covenant. This new covenant was introduced by Jesus at the last supper (Mt. 26:28; Mk. 14:24; Lk. 22:20; 1 Cor. 11:25) and sealed by his sacrificial death (Heb. 9:11–28). As regards its superiority over the older Sinai covenant, the author of Hebrews, quoting Jeremiah 31:31–34, makes a number of important points. First, the new covenant is unlike the one made at Sinai (Heb. 8:9). Although the Sinai covenant was intended to secure a lasting relationship between God and the Israelites, it did not succeed due to the fact that the people failed to keep the divine obligations that were placed upon them; their faithlessness caused God to turn away from them (Heb. 8:9). The success of the new covenant is guaranteed by God's ability to do for the people what they themselves could not achieve. Whereas the laws of the old covenant were inscribed on stone tablets, under the new covenant God puts his laws in the hearts and minds of believers (cf. 2 Cor. 3:6). Through an inner transformation, accomplished by the indwelling of the Holy Spirit, God enables his people to live as he had originally intended. A further consequence of the new covenant is a better knowledge of God: 'No longer will a man teach his neighbour, or a man his brother, saying, "Know the Lord," because they will all know me, from the least of them to the greatest' (Heb. 8:11). Finally, the new covenant brings divine forgiveness for human sin and wickedness (Heb. 8:12). Under the old covenant God's forgiveness was linked to the atoning duties carried out by the high priest on the Day of Atonement. Because this was repeated annually it guaranteed only limited forgiveness for the people. Since Christ's mediatorial role as a high priest far exceeds that of the Aaronic high priest, the new covenant provides a greater assurance of forgiveness.[13] Those who are justified by faith in Christ are divinely pardoned for all their sins, past, present and future.

The inauguration of a new covenant by Christ influenced the early church in another way. Those bound by the old covenant were expected to demonstrate their allegiance by keeping holy the seventh day of the week; the Sabbath was the sign of the Sinai covenant (Ex. 31:13–17). With the arrival of a new covenant, the strict observance of the Sabbath, like circumcision, was no longer binding upon Christians. Rather, to commemorate Christ's resurrection the early church met for worship on the first day of the week (cf. Acts 20:7; 1 Cor. 16:2). The Sabbath was replaced by the Lord's Day.

At the heart of the Sinai covenant was God's desire that Israel should be 'a kingdom of priests and a holy nation' (Ex. 19:6). This thought is echoed in 1 Peter 2:9–10:

> But you are a chosen people, a royal priesthood, a holy nation, a people belonging to God, that you may declare the praises of him who called you out of darkness into his wonderful light. Once you were not a people, but now you are the people of God; once you had not received mercy, but now you have received mercy (cf. Rev. 1:6; 5:10; 20:6).

That which the Sinai covenant failed to achieve, as a result of human disobedience, is now fulfilled through the new covenant inaugurated by Jesus Christ's death, resurrection and ascension.

---

[13] This is discussed more fully in chapter 17.

15

The Tabernacle

15.1. Summary

The final third of the book of Exodus focuses almost exclusively on the construction and erection of the tabernacle. The extent of the material highlights the importance of the tabernacle as God's dwelling place. Although it takes the form of a rectangular tent, the extensive use of gold and blue fabrics indicates that the tabernacle was a royal residence. Its portable nature ensured that the divine king would be with his people wherever they went. A further aspect which plays an important part in the design of the tabernacle and its furnishings is the holy nature of God's being. The outer curtain fence separates sinful people from a holy God, and the bronze altar stands as a vivid reminder that only those who have made atonement for their sin and uncleanness may approach God. Finally, the tabernacle is designated 'the Tent of Meeting', indicating that it is the place where divinity and humanity commune together.

15.2. Introduction

The importance of the tabernacle is highlighted by the attention given to recording both God's description of how the tent and its furnishing should be manufactured (25:1–31:11), and the subsequent construction (35:1–40:33). Altogether, including the details relating to the consecration of the priests, approximately one-quarter of Exodus is given over to describing the making of the tabernacle. Chapters 25–31 consist of a very long divine speech outlining the preparations necessary for the construction of a special tent and the appointment of priests. Much of this material is repeated in 36:8–39:31, where we have an almost word for word record of the fulfilment of the instructions given by the LORD to Moses (see Table A). Such repetition is the author's way of underlining the importance of the tabernacle.[1]

---

[1] Remarkably, in spite of the space devoted to recording the making of the tabernacle, the present account does not provide all the information necessary to reconstruct fully the original tent.

Table A

Object	Instructions	Fulfilment
Tabernacle	26:1–11, 14–29, 31–32, 36–37	36:8–38
Ark	25:10–14, 17–20	37:1–9
Table	25:23–29	37:10–16
Lampstand	25:31–39	37:17–24
Incense altar	30:1–5	37:25–28
Anointing oil	30:25	37:29
Bronze altar	27:1–8	38:1–7
Bronze basin	30:18	38:8
Courtyard	27:9–19	38:9–20
Ephod	28:6–12	39:2–7
Breastpiece	28:15–28	39:8–21
Robe	28:31–34	39:22–26
Tunic, turban, sash	28:39	39:27–29
Gold plate	28:36–37	39:30–31

Whereas the initial divine instructions list the more important objects first, the account of their construction reflects the order in which the items were assembled when the tabernacle was erected (cf. 40:2–8, 12–14; 40:17–33) and conforms to the pattern found in other summaries of the tabernacle equipment (cf. 31:7–9; 35:11–18; 39:33–40; see Table B). Occasionally the divine instructions, but rarely the fulfilment, contain additional material relating to the use of a particular object (e.g. 30:6–10; 30:18–21). The similarity between the instructions and their fulfilment indicates that the people obeyed the LORD 'to the letter'. Everything was made just as Moses had been instructed. Exodus ends in dramatic fashion by describing how God's glory filled the tabernacle 'on the first day of the first month in the second year' (40:17) just in time for the people to celebrate the first anniversary of their deliverance from Egypt (cf. Num. 9:1–5).

Table B

Order of presentation in Exodus 25–30 and 36–39

Instructions		Fulfilment	
Ark	25:10–22	Tabernacle	36:8–38
Table	25:23–30	Ark	37:1–9
Lampstand	25:31–39	Table	37:10–16
Tabernacle	26:1–37	Lampstand	37:17–24
Bronze altar	27:1–8	Incense altar	37:25–28
Courtyard	27:9–19	Anointing oil	37:29
Ephod	28:6–14	Incense	37:29
Breastpiece	28:15–30	Bronze altar	38:1–7
Robe	28:31–35	Bronze basin	38:8
Gold plate	28:36–38	Courtyard	38:9–20
Tunic, turban, sash	28:39	Ephod	39:2–7
Incense altar	30:1–10	Breastpiece	39:8–21
Bronze basin	30:18–21	Robe	39:22–26
Anointing oil	30:23–25	Tunic, turban, sash	39:27–29
Incense	30:34–36	Gold plate	39:30–31

15.3. A Royal Tent

An important theme in the final part of Exodus is God's intention to dwell among the people (25:8; cf. 29:45–46). Having rescued them from the control of Pharaoh the king of Egypt and established a special covenant relationship with them, the LORD desires to accompany them into the promised land. Consequently, he commands Moses to construct a portable dwelling. Like his people, the sovereign LORD will dwell in a tent. However, his dwelling differs in the nature of the materials used in its construction. From the inventory of precious metals and bluish coloured fabrics (25:3–7;

cf. 35:5–9, 22–27) it is apparent that this is no common tent; it is for royal use. This is emphasised not only by the kinds of material used ('gold, silver, and bronze; blue, purple and scarlet yarn and fine linen') but also by their quantity. According to 38:21–31 approximately one ton of gold, four tons of silver and two-and-a-half tons of bronze were used to make the tabernacle and its furnishings.[2]

Initially Moses was instructed to make three items of furniture for inside the tent. The first of these was a rectangular wooden chest or box, covered 'with pure gold, both inside and out' (25:10–11). For ease of transportation the chest, or 'ark' as it is traditionally known, was to be constructed with gold rings and poles (25:12–15). Inside this container Moses would later place the stone tablets which were the 'Testimony', or 'terms of agreement', for the covenant between God and Israel (25:16, 21; Deut. 10:8 refers to the chest as the 'ark of the covenant'). The lid of the ark, made of pure gold, is designated an 'atonement cover' (25:17; cf. Heb. 9:5, 'place of atonement'). Leviticus 16:1–34 (esp. vv. 11–17) describes the annual ritual which took place when the high priest sprinkled blood on the ark's lid to make atonement for 'the uncleanness and rebellion of the Israelites, whatever their sins have been' (Lev. 16:16).[3] Two golden cherubim (or cherubs) were attached to the ends of the lid, facing each other with outspread wings.[4] Here, between the cherubim, God would later meet with Moses in order to communicate his instructions to the people (25:22; 30:36; cf. Lev. 16:2). Thus, apart from being a container, the ark also functioned as a seat, or, more specifically, as a throne protected by guardian cherubim (cf. 1 Sam. 4:4; 2 Sam. 6:2; 2 Kgs. 19:15; Ps. 80:2; 99:1; Isa. 37:16). Because of its importance as the LORD's throne, the manufacture of the ark is outlined first.

The second piece of furniture was a wooden table, overlaid with gold, and fitted with rings and poles (25:23–28). Plates, dishes and other utensils, all of gold, were to be provided, and the 'Bread of the Presence' was to be placed on the table at all times (25:29–30).

The third main fixture to be constructed was a gold lampstand with seven lamps (25:31–40). The lampstand was to be made in the pattern of a growing tree, decorated with 'flowerlike cups, buds and blossoms' (25:31). Three branches extended to either side of the central stem; the tops of the stem and branches were designed to hold lamps. No explanation is given to explain why

---

[2] Although the quantities involved appear large, they are by no means unusual when compared with contemporary practices in the ancient world.

[3] The Day of Atonement ritual is discussed more fully in chapter 17.

[4] Cherubim were the traditional guardians of holy places in the ancient Near East. Apart from the two described here, others were woven into the curtains which surround the tabernacle and which separate the Holy of Holies from the Holy Place (26:1, 31).

the lampstand should resemble a tree. Possibly it was meant to look like the tree of life in Genesis 3:22, symbolising the life-giving power of God.

The table and lampstand, together with the chest/seat, comprised the main items of furniture in an ancient home. As such they indicated that God lived within the tent. The abundant use of gold emphasised the importance of the occupant. The provision of bread (25:30) and light (27:21) were symbolic reminders that God was there at all times, both day and night.

Detailed instructions were provided next for the construction of the actual tent or tabernacle (26:1–37). Some uncertainty exists over how the various curtains and wooden frames fitted together. Since the entire structure was designed to be portable, its construction was probably similar to that used for other tents. The bluish fabrics and gold fittings were indicative of royalty. The rectangular structure was divided into two rooms by a curtain, one room probably being twice the size of the other (26:31–33). The ark of the Testimony was to be placed in the smaller of these rooms, in the western half of the tabernacle. Because the LORD was seated there, enthroned between the cherubim, this part was called the 'Most Holy Place' or 'Holy of Holies' (26:34). The larger room, to the east, was designated the 'Holy Place'; it was to be furnished with the golden table and lampstand (26:35). The curtain separating the two rooms contained woven figures of cherubim as a reminder that the way into the immediate presence of God was barred to sinful man (cf. Gen. 3:24).[5]

One further item of furniture was to be made for inside the royal tent, an incense altar (30:1–10). Made of acacia wood and plated with pure gold, it was to be placed in the Holy Place alongside the golden table and lampstand. Twice daily Aaron was to burn fragrant incense upon it (30:7–8), and once a year, probably on the Day of Atonement (cf. Lev. 16:15–19), he was to make atonement on its horns (30:10).[6]

15.4. A Holy Tent

Around the tabernacle or royal tent Moses was to construct a courtyard by erecting a curtain fence. The courtyard, a rectangular shape twice as long as it was broad, measured approximately fifty metres by twenty-five metres and was surrounded by a curtain about two-and-a-half metres high. The shorter sides were to the east and west. The only entrance was on the eastern side.[7] On

---

[5] For a fuller discussion of the problems involved in reconstructing the tabernacle, see 'Tabernacle', *IBD*, 1506–11.

[6] The altar had four horns, one at each of its top corners.

[7] For a plan of the tabernacle, see p. xxvii.

passing through this gateway a worshipper encountered first a large bronze altar before approaching the tabernacle which stood in the western part of the courtyard. The fence that surrounded the courtyard, along with the curtain that hung across the entrance, prevented those outside from looking into the courtyard. Separated from the rest of the Israelite encampment, the courtyard was set apart as a holy area; only the tabernacle, in which God dwelt, was considered to be more sacred.[8] This distinction between the holiness of the courtyard and the tabernacle is reflected in the value of the materials used in their construction. Whereas gold was regularly used within the tabernacle, the main metals utilised in the construction of the courtyard were silver and bronze. Just as Moses set a boundary around Mount Sinai to prevent the people from coming into the divine presence (19:12–13, 21–24), so the courtyard fence prevented them from approaching God inadvertently. As Exodus regularly emphasises only those who are holy can come into the divine presence; to approach God otherwise has fatal consequences. Without the courtyard functioning as a buffer zone, it would have been impossible for the Israelites to dwell in safety close to the LORD.

Since the area within the courtyard was holy ground, the priests, Aaron and his sons, assigned to serve there also had to be holy. To indicate this, they were provided with 'sacred garments'. The materials used in their production, 'gold, and blue, purple and scarlet yarn, and fine linen' (28:5), not only highlight the dignity and honour bestowed upon Aaron and his sons, but also clearly associated them with the tabernacle which was made of similar materials. As high priest Aaron was to wear a breastplate, an ephod, a robe, a woven tunic, a turban and a sash (28:4); his sons were to be given tunics, sashes and headbands (28:40).[9] Most attention is focused on the special items worn by the high priest, especially the 'ephod' (28:6–14) and 'breastpiece' (28:15–30).

The first item mentioned in the list of high priestly clothes is the ephod. Scholars refer to it by its Hebrew name *'epod* (*'ephod*) because the biblical text does not provide sufficient information to reconstruct it exactly.[10] Special reference is made to the two precious stones engraved with the names of the twelve tribes of Israel. Mounted 'in gold filigree settings' (28:11), they were fastened 'on the shoulder pieces of the ephod as memorial stones for the sons of

---

[8] The two rooms of the tabernacle also differed in their degree of holiness. The Holy of Holies which contained God's throne could only be entered by the high priest on the Day of Atonement. The Holy Place, however, was entered daily by some of the priests who ministered there.

[9] The lack of reference to footwear may indicate that the priests served barefooted; when God appeared in the burning bush Moses was commanded to remove his sandals because the ground was holy (cf. Ex. 3:5).

[10] On Christ's role as a high priest within the heavenly tabernacle, see chapter 17.

Israel' (28:12). They were a reminder that Aaron served God as high priest, not for his own benefit, but on behalf of all the Israelites.

The next item, designated a 'breastpiece', appears from its description to have been a square pouch that the high priest wore over his chest. The pouch was made of similar materials to the ephod and was attached to it. On the outside of the pouch were four rows of precious stones, with three stones in each row; each stone was to be inscribed with the name of an Israelite tribe. Although Aaron came from the tribe of Levi, as high priest, wearing the names of the tribes on his chest, he ministered on behalf of all the people. The use of precious stones symbolised the value that God placed upon his people Israel. Finally, instructions were given that 'the Urim and the Thummim' should be placed in the pouch (28:30). The precise form of the Urim and Thummim remains uncertain. However, they were probably used as a means of determining God's judgement (cf. 22:8, 9).[11]

Other items of clothing worn by the high priest are mentioned in 28:31–43. A blue robe, adorned with embroidered pomegranates and golden bells, was presumably worn under the ephod and breastpiece. The tinkling of the bells would serve to identify the one entering or leaving the Holy of Holies, enabling the high priest to come close to God in safety; anyone else venturing into the LORD's presence would die (cf. 19:12–13, 21–22, 24). As a further reminder of the sacred nature of priestly service, the front of Aaron's turban had a gold plate with the words, 'HOLY TO THE LORD' (28:36). Because he was set apart as holy, Aaron as high priest was able to mediate on behalf of the Israelites, ensuring that their sacrifices were acceptable to the LORD (28:38). Apart from the items already mentioned, Aaron was also to wear a tunic, turban and sash (28:39); the tunic appears to have been worn under the robe of the ephod (cf. 29:5). Because they do not relate directly to the 'dignity and honour' of the priests, the instructions concerning underwear were given separately. The priests were to wear 'linen undergarments' to prevent them from inadvertently exposing their genitalia in the Holy Place (cf. 20:26). Such nakedness was clearly inappropriate in the presence of the LORD (cf. Gen. 3:7, 10, 21). Moreover, since only the priests could enter the tabernacle, the command that they should wear undergarments would reassure those outside that nothing unseemly occurred within the tabernacle.

To minister in God's holy presence the priests had to be holy. The instructions in 29:1–46 reflect the various stages (mentioned briefly in 28:41) necessary for their consecration: clothe, anoint, 'fill the hands',[12] consecrate. After assembling the appropriate items (29:1–3), Moses was to wash[13] and

---

[11] For a brief description and picture of a modern reconstruction of the breastpiece, see 'Breastpiece of the High Priest,' *IBD*, 207.

[12] NIV 'ordain' does not translate accurately the Hebrew original.

[13] Purity and cleanliness are closely associated with being holy (cf. 19:10, 14).

clothe Aaron and his sons in their priestly garments (29:4–9). Then he was to anoint them with oil.[14] Next he had to offer up three different sacrifices, involving a bull and two rams. The first (29:10–14), best understood as a purification offering, involved the bull, and followed closely the instructions given later in Leviticus 4:3–12 relating to the unintentional sin of an anointed priest. In this instance, however, the blood was probably placed on the horns of the large bronze altar in the courtyard and not on the gold incense altar within the tabernacle (29:12; cf. Lev. 4:7). The blood purified the altar which had become defiled through contact with individuals who were considered unclean. The next sacrifice, a whole-burnt offering (29:15–18), follows exactly the instructions given later in Leviticus 1:10–13 for the offering of a ram. The whole-burnt offering atoned for the sins of Aaron and his sons. The total destruction of the animal was a vivid reminder that sinful man could not approach a holy God. The animal died as a substitute for those who were identified with it by the laying on of their hands on its head. The third sacrifice (29:19–34) resembles closely a fellowship or peace offering made as an expression of thankfulness (cf. Lev. 3:6–11; 7:12–15). However, the ritual described here has distinctive features, appropriate for this unique occasion. First, Aaron, his sons and their garments were to be consecrated by sacrificial blood (29:19–21); whatever the blood touched became holy.[15] Secondly, verses 22–35 focus on the remuneration which Aaron and his sons were to receive as priests. The NIV wrongly refers to this as 'the ram for the ordination' (29:22; cf. 29:26, 27, 31, 34); it is literally 'the ram of (the) filling'. This 'filling' refers to the portion which was to be given to the priests after they offered up different sacrifices (cf. Lev. 6:14–18, 25–29; 7:1–38). The ritual that Moses would later perform consecrated the right thigh and breast for priestly consumption. A distinction is drawn between the 'breast', which is 'waved', and the 'thigh', which is 'presented' (29:27). On this occasion the breast will be given to Moses as his reward for offering the sacrifice (29:26), and the thigh will be burnt on the altar, along with some bread (29:25). On future occasions, after the priests are consecrated, the breast of the fellowship sacrifice shall be presented to all the priests, and the thigh given to the priest who officiates (Lev. 7:28–36). Apart from the breast, thigh, and various fatty portions, the rest

---

[14] Special oil was to be manufactured for the anointing of the tabernacle, its furnishings, and the priests who served there (30:22–30). Since everything touched by this particular oil became holy, restrictions were placed upon its production and use (30:31–33). Similar instructions were given for the making and use of the incense which was to be burned within the tabernacle (30:34–38).

[15] 'The priest must have consecrated ears ever to listen to God's holy voice; consecrated hands at all times to do holy deeds; and consecrated feet to walk evermore in holy ways' (A. Dillmann, *Die Bücher Exodus und Leviticus* [2nd edn.; Leipzig: Hirzel, 1880], 465).

of the ram of (the) filling was to be cooked and eaten, together with the remaining bread, at the entrance to the tabernacle. Only the priests were to eat this holy food.

The ritual outlined in verses 1–34 was essential for the consecration of the priests. Most commentators believe on the basis of verse 35 that this ritual was repeated every day for seven days. Alternatively, the sacrifices outlined in verses 36–41 may have been offered during the next six days, with Aaron and his sons under strict instruction to remain within the courtyard of the tabernacle (cf. Lev. 8:33–35). In either case the process of consecration or sanctification required time. The fulfilment of the instructions regarding the consecration of Aaron and his sons is recorded in Leviticus 8:1–36.

Concerning the priests Moses was also told to make a bronze basin (30:17–21). This was to be placed between the tabernacle and the bronze altar so that Aaron and his sons could wash their hands and feet when serving within the tabernacle and courtyard (30:17–21). The requirement that the priests should wash symbolises their need to remain holy and pure (cf. 19:14; 29:4).

The Exodus narrative thus highlights in a special way the holy nature of the tabernacle and of those who ministered within it.

15.5. A Tent of Meeting

The tabernacle was not only a royal and holy tent but also a tent of meeting. This is highlighted in God's comments in 29:43: 'There … I will meet with the Israelites, and the place will be consecrated by my glory' (29:43). Like the Garden of Eden, the tabernacle was the place where divinity and humanity could commune together. However, to enable sinful people to meet a holy God, it was necessary for them to be sanctified from their sin and uncleanness. To this end God instructed Moses to construct a portable bronze-plated altar, which was to be situated in the courtyard near the entrance to the tabernacle (27:1–8). From its dimensions, this altar dominated the area in front of the tabernacle; it was 2.5 metres wide (half the width of the tabernacle) and 1.5 metres high. It consisted of a square hollow framework made of acacia wood overlaid with bronze. To create a draught for the incineration of the animal sacrifices the lower part of each side was comprised of a grating of bronze network. Its position between the courtyard entrance and the tabernacle indicated that a worshipper could only approach God after offering a sacrifice to atone for sin.[16]

---

[16] Instructions for the consecration of the altar are given in 29:36–37. Leviticus 1:1–7:38 details the various sacrifices that individuals were expected to offer.

Following the erection of the tabernacle, a cloud covered it, and the glory of the LORD filled it (40:34). God now dwelt in the midst of the people, and the tabernacle was designated 'the Tent of Meeting' (40:35; cf. 27:21), replacing the tent used earlier by Moses (cf. 33:7–11).[17] It differed from this other tent, however, in that God dwelt within the tabernacle and Moses stayed outside (40:35), whereas with the earlier tent Moses went inside and God remained outside (33:9). God's presence was visible to everyone through the cloud and fire that settled upon the tabernacle. From there he guided them on their journeys (40:36–38). Exodus concludes by noting the glorious presence of the sovereign God in the midst of his people Israel.[18]

15.6. The Provision of Materials and Skilled Craftsmen

The account of the making of the tabernacle also focuses on two practical matters regarding its construction. First, Moses was instructed to ask the people to make an offering to the LORD in order to provide the materials required for the construction of the tabernacle and related items (25:1–7). When Moses addressed the people (35:4–9) they responded generously (35:20–27). Indeed such was their generosity that later they had to be restrained from giving too much (36:3–7). Their freewill gifts reflect their deep gratitude to God for delivering them from Egypt.

---

[17] Exodus 33:7–11 records how Moses, prior to the erection of the tabernacle, was in the custom of pitching a tent at some distance from the main encampment in order to meet with God. Given its specific function, this tent was known as the 'tent of meeting' (33:7). Here Moses enjoyed a unique and personal relationship with God: 'The LORD would speak to Moses face to face, as a man speaks with his friend' (33:11). Although they were in close proximity to one another, even Moses the faithful servant was not permitted to look directly upon God; 33:9 implies that the tent curtain shielded Moses who was within from the LORD who was without. This 'tent of meeting' should not be confused with the tabernacle, also known as the Tent of Meeting (e.g. 40:2, 6), which was constructed only later (36:8–38) and which was pitched in the midst of the Israelite encampment (Num. 1:53; 2:2, 17), not 'outside the camp some distance away' (33:7).

[18] Although the Exodus narrative portrays the LORD as coming to dwell within the tabernacle, there are indications that the tabernacle was not viewed as his main residence. As Jacob Milgrom observes: 'From the fact that Moses is commanded to build the Tabernacle and its appurtenances according to the pattern that was shown to him on Mount Sinai (Ex. 26:30; cf. Ex. 25:9, 40; 27:8; Num 8:4), it is possible that he was shown the earthly sanctuary's heavenly counterpart.' See *Leviticus 1–16*, 141. In the light of this, it is interesting to note Moses' comment in Deuteronomy 26:15: 'Look down from heaven, your holy dwelling place, and bless your people Israel …'

Secondly, God informed Moses that he had chosen and equipped certain men with the skills necessary to produce the tabernacle and its furnishings (31:1–11). Singled out for particular mention are Bezalel and Oholiab whose special ability is attributed to the fact that they have been filled with the Spirit of God (31:3). Later, when placed in charge of the work (35:30–36:2), they also displayed their aptitude to teach others (35:34). Elsewhere, attention is drawn to the women who devote their natural abilities and skills to the LORD by spinning yarn (35:25–26).

15.7. Conclusion

Exodus 25–30 emphasises three aspects of the tabernacle: it was (a) a royal tent, (b) a holy tent, and (c) a 'Tent of Meeting'. The first two of these are clearly linked to God's nature; he is a sovereign and holy God. The third aspect focuses on the special relationship which God established with the people of Israel through the covenant at Sinai. The construction of the tabernacle enabled the people to commune more directly with their God and reassured them of his presence in their midst.

15.8. New Testament Connections

Although the tabernacle was replaced by a temple, modelled upon it and constructed first by Solomon and later rebuilt at the end of the sixth century BC, it is discussed in a number of NT passages. In general these reflect important developments in the way the tabernacle (and its successor, the temple) was perceived.

The early Christians emphasised the secondary nature of the tabernacle/temple. It was merely a 'copy and shadow of what is in heaven' (Heb. 8:5; cf. 9:11, 24). Consequently, the NT plays down the importance of the temple in Jerusalem, even to the extent of anticipating its destruction (Mk. 13:1–2), and, instead, focuses attention on the heavenly tabernacle. The demise of the Jerusalem temple is clearly linked to how the early church understood the death and resurrection of Jesus Christ. First, Matthew 27:51 records that when Jesus died the curtain in the temple, separating the Holy of Holies from the Holy Place, was torn from top to bottom. The tearing of this curtain revealed that, by his sacrificial death, Christ removed the barrier which existed between God and humankind (cf. Heb. 9:1–8). Secondly, Jesus was viewed as entering the heavenly sanctuary, rather than the earthly sanctuary, to serve as a high priest: 'For Christ did not enter a man-made sanctuary that was only a copy of the true one; he entered heaven itself, now to appear for us in God's presence'

(Heb. 9:24; cf. 9:11–28).[19] This emphasis upon the heavenly sanctuary, rather than the earthly temple in Jerusalem, is also reflected in Jesus' comments to a Samaritan woman concerning the right place to worship God:

> Believe me, woman, a time is coming when you will worship the Father neither on this mountain nor in Jerusalem. You Samaritans worship what you do not know; we worship what we do know, for salvation is from the Jews. Yet a time is coming and has now come when the true worshippers will worship the Father in spirit and truth, for they are the kind of worshippers the Father seeks. God is spirit, and his worshippers must worship in spirit and in truth (Jn. 4:21–24).

Here Jesus anticipates a time when worship will not be restricted to any particular earthly location.

From another perspective the NT draws a close parallel between Jesus and the tabernacle/temple. In Jesus, God is viewed as inhabiting human flesh just as he previously inhabited first the tabernacle and then the temple. John alludes to this when he writes, 'The Word became flesh and made his dwelling (lit. tabernacled) among us. We have seen his glory …' (Jn. 1:14). The same idea clearly underlies Jesus' own comment in John 2:19, 'Destroy this temple, and I will raise it again in three days.' John clarifies the meaning of this statement by observing, 'The temple he had spoken of was his body' (Jn. 2:21; cf. Mk. 14:58).

According to Paul every believer, due to the indwelling of the Holy Spirit, is a temple (1 Cor. 6:19; cf. 1 Cor. 3:16–17; 2 Cor. 6:16). Moreover, the Spirit's presence causes God's glory to be reflected in the lives of those who are Christ's followers: 'We, who with unveiled faces all reflect the Lord's glory, are being transformed into his likeness with ever-increasing glory, which comes from the Lord, who is the Spirit' (2 Cor. 3:18).

---

[19] On Christ's role as a high priest within the heavenly tabernacle, see chapter 17.

16

Be Holy

16.1. Summary

Leviticus is dominated by the topic of holiness. Its prominence derives from the fact that God is holy. Although Leviticus emphasises God's power to sanctify or make holy other people or objects, it also highlights the danger posed by the moral and ritual uncleanness associated with human behaviour. Holiness and uncleanness are presented as mutually exclusive. Consequently, for the Israelites to enjoy a meaningful and fruitful relationship with God, they must reflect his holiness in their daily lives. Since differing degrees of holiness and uncleanness exist, the Israelites are divinely exhorted, 'Be holy because I, the LORD your God, am holy' (19:2; cf. 11:44–45; 20:26).

16.2. Introduction

The book of Leviticus continues the story of Exodus by describing what took place in the thirteenth month after the Israelites' divine deliverance from Egypt (cf. Ex. 40:17; Num. 1:1). As a result, the books of Exodus and Leviticus, and, as we shall later observe, also Numbers, are closely connected. Leviticus both assumes the erection of the tabernacle which forms the climax of the book of Exodus (40:1–38), and records the consecration of Aaron and his sons as priests, fulfilling the instructions given to Moses by the LORD in Exodus 29:1–46. Leviticus must, therefore, be read in conjunction with Exodus, both books forming part of the continuous and carefully composed narrative which comprises the Pentateuch.

Although Leviticus continues the story of the Israelites' journey from Egypt to Canaan, almost ninety per cent of the book consists of divine speeches on a variety of topics. As a result, apart from numerous short introductions to these discourses (cf. 1:1; 4:1; 5:14; 6:1; 6:8; etc.), there are only two sections in which the narrator describes events rather than reports God's words. The first of these focuses on the consecration of the priests and the subsequent sin of Nadab and Abihu (8:1–10:20); the second passage is much briefer and deals with a man who blasphemes by cursing God (24:10–23). Even in this short episode more than half of the verses record what the LORD said to Moses (24:13–22). Leviticus is thus composed almost entirely of divine speeches. In this regard it closely resembles Exodus 20:22–24:2 and 25:1–31:17.

In Leviticus Moses continues his role of mediator between God and the Israelites. While the LORD nearly always speaks directly to Moses alone – on a few occasions Aaron is also included (11:1; 13:1; 14:33; 15:1) – his words are usually intended for either the Israelites (e.g. 1:2; 4:2; 7:23, 29; 11:2) or the priests (6:9, 20, 25; 21:2; 22:2). This distinction between the majority of Israelites and the selected few who were divinely appointed as priests is a significant feature in Leviticus. Not only is it reflected in many of the divine speeches, but also more importantly it lies at the very heart of the account of the consecration of Aaron and his sons as priests in Leviticus 8–9. Here the narrative highlights the three stages by which Aaron and his sons were set apart from the rest of the Israelites. First, they were brought out from the midst of the community (8:6) to be consecrated as priests. The special ritual, involving washing, clothing and anointing, endowed them with a degree of holiness that surpassed that of other Israelites (8:6–30).[1] Moreover, because Aaron was treated differently from his sons, he was recognised as being even holier. Secondly, the priests were to stay at the entrance to the tabernacle for seven days (8:31–36). Not only did this further emphasise their separation from the people, it also confirmed their holy status; unlike the rest of the population they remained in close proximity to God. Thirdly, on the eighth day there was a rite of incorporation by which the priests were once again brought into contact with the rest of the community (9:1–24). Although Moses provided instructions, the newly appointed priests offered up the sacrifices on behalf of the community, with Aaron, as high priest, performing the main tasks. By recording that 'fire came out from the presence of the LORD and consumed the burnt offering and the fat portions on the altar' (9:24), the account of the consecration of the priests concludes by highlighting God's acceptance of Aaron and his sons as the community's cultic representatives.[2] Leviticus thus emphasises the important distinction which God instituted between the priests and all other Israelites.

---

[1] For a fuller discussion of the different elements which comprised the ritual for the consecration of the priests, see chapter 15.

[2] The appearance of the glory of the LORD to all the people in 9:23 parallels what occurred immediately after the erection of the tabernacle (Ex. 40:34–35). On both occasions God expressed his approval and acceptance of what had just taken place by displaying his presence to the people.

As well as stressing the differing degrees of holiness which existed between the priests and other Israelites, the book of Leviticus, especially in chapters 11–15, also draws attention to the fact that ordinary Israelites belonged to one of two categories: clean or unclean. Various factors, including eating particular foods, suffering from certain types of skin disease[3] or experiencing particular bodily discharges, caused an individual, and sometimes even those who came into contact with them, to become unclean. Anyone designated as unclean had to undergo a process of purification before they could participate fully in the religious life of the community.

16.3. Holy, Clean and Unclean

The features noted briefly in the preceding paragraphs draw attention to three related categories that permeate almost all of the material in Leviticus; these are holy, clean/pure and unclean/impure. The importance of these three categories is underlined by the very frequent occurrence of these and associated words throughout Leviticus. Terms based on the Hebrew root *qādaš* (*qādash*) (e.g. 'holy', 'holiness', 'sanctify') come 152 times in Leviticus, representing about one-fifth of all occurrences in the OT. The adjective *tāhôr* 'clean' and associated words occur 74 times, representing more than one-third of all OT occurrences. The adjective *tāmē'* 'unclean' and cognate terms come 132 times, representing more than half of the total occurrences in the OT. These statistics highlight the importance of the categories holy, clean/pure and unclean/impure in Leviticus.

The existence of these three categories is reflected in the layout of the Israelite camp. At the heart of the camp stood the tabernacle courtyard, a holy area the rest of the camp had the status of a clean area, and everywhere outside the camp was unclean.[4] This same threefold division was also found among the people; the priests were considered to be holy, the Israelites clean, and non-Israelites unclean. Moreover, the places and people corresponded directly: the priests were associated with the tabernacle, the Israelites with the camp, and the non-Israelites with those outside the camp (see Diagram D).

Within these main categories, subdivisions also existed. As regards holiness, this is evident in a number of different spheres. First, differing degrees of holiness existed within the priesthood and laity. The high priest was

---

[3] Although these skin diseases have in the past been understood to be a form of leprosy, it is most unlikely that this was the case.

[4] While the entire area outside the camp was considered unclean, selected places were set apart as clean for the disposal of the ashes from the altar in the tabernacle courtyard (4:12, 21; 6:11; cf. the burning of the bull of the purification offering [Lev. 16:27]).

Diagram D

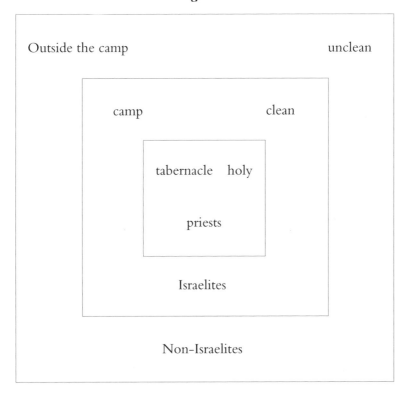

Outside the camp · unclean · camp · clean · tabernacle holy · priests · Israelites · Non-Israelites

distinguished from the other priests in a number of ways. Not only was the ritual for his consecration distinctive, as were his clothes, but he alone enjoyed the title of 'high' priest. At any time there could only be one high priest and each new appointee had to undergo a special consecration ritual. Of all the priests he alone was permitted to enter the Holy of Holies. The high priest was also required to adhere to much stricter rules regarding marriage, purity and mourning. A lesser category of priests consisted of those who suffered from some form of physical defect. Although they were prohibited from offering sacrifices, they were allowed to eat from the portions of sacrifices allocated to the priests. Next to the priests in holiness were the Levites. While they were not permitted to offer sacrifices, they assisted the priests with other duties concerning the tabernacle, especially its transportation and erection (Num. 4:1–49).[5] Whereas the priests and Levites enjoyed a special status of holiness arising from their ancestry and divine appointment, non-priestly Israelites

---

[5] While the Levites and the priests were all descended from Levi, the third oldest son of Jacob, only Aaron and his sons were designated priests. See chapter 19 for a fuller discussion of the relationship between the priests and Levites.

were given the opportunity to have a higher degree of holiness by becoming Nazirites. To attain this holier status an individual took 'a vow of separation to the LORD' which entailed (a) abstaining from the produce of the vine, and (b) not cutting one's hair (Num. 6:1–21). These subdivisions of people surface in different contexts within Leviticus. For example, whereas ordinary Israelites might touch any corpse, regular priests were only permitted to touch the corpse of a close relative (21:1–4), and the high priest was prohibited from having contact with any corpse (10:1–7).

Secondly, the tabernacle was divided into at least three distinct areas, each with differing degrees of holiness. The tent itself consisted of two rooms, the Holy of Holies and the Holy Place. The former of these, containing the ark of the covenant, was considered to be much holier than the adjacent room, the Holy Place, which contained the lampstand, the table for the 'Bread of the Presence' and the incense altar.[6] The tabernacle courtyard was less holy than the tent itself, although holier than the camp from which it was separated by a curtain fence. These different degrees of holiness within the tabernacle are also reflected in the access which people had. Only the most holy of the priests, the high priest, could enter the Holy of Holies, and even he was limited to one day in the year, the Day of Atonement. Although any priest could enter the Holy Place, ordinary Israelites were barred; they had access only to the courtyard.

Thirdly, the tabernacle furnishings also reflect the threefold pattern of holiness found within the different areas of the tabernacle. They do so in a number of ways depending upon (a) their location, (b) the materials used in their manufacture, (c) their accessibility to human beings, and (d) their use in religious rituals. Whereas the holiest furniture, made of pure gold, was placed within the tent, the altar and laver, made of bronze, were located in the courtyard. Although ordinary Israelites were permitted to view the bronze altar and laver, only priests could look upon the gold furnishings in the Holy Place with immunity (Num. 4:18–20). Within the tent, the ark of the covenant was set apart from the other items of furniture by being placed in the Holy of Holies. It was so holy that only the high priest could approach it, and even then he possibly used smoke from incense to conceal the top of the ark from view (16:12–13).[7]

Fourthly, particular days of the week and year exhibited differing degrees of holiness. The weekly Sabbath and the annual Day of Atonement were marked as especially holy by the prohibition of all work (23:3, 28). The pilgrimage

---

[6] For a detailed discussion of the layout of the tabernacle, see chapter 15.

[7] These distinctions between the items of furniture are also reflected in the instruction given in Numbers 4:5–33 regarding the activities of the Kohathites, Gershonites and Merarites in helping the priests transport the tabernacle.

festivals of Unleavened Bread, Weeks and Tabernacles and certain other days were considered less holy and therefore required only abstinence from regular work (23:7, 21, 25, 35). Finally, while the Israelites were expected to make special offerings on the first day of each month, they were permitted to work on these days, indicating that they were the least holy of all special days.

In the light of these four factors, it is apparent that the book of Leviticus envisages a world in which people, places, objects and even periods of time have differing degrees of holiness.

Just as there were varying degrees of holiness, so too with uncleanness.

1. The strength or weakness of an impurity was judged by its ability to communicate impurity to other objects or persons. Only more serious forms of impurity could pollute other people or objects. For example, if a man lay with a woman during her monthly period, she caused him to become unclean for seven days and, in turn, any bed upon which he lay also became unclean (15:24). Furthermore, anyone who touched this bed became unclean; however, this latter uncleanness lasted only for one day and could not be transferred to other people or objects.

2. Differing degrees of impurity were reflected by the way in which they polluted the sanctuary. The location of the pollution is indicated by where the blood of the purification offering was placed. Deliberate or intentional sins polluted the ark of the covenant in the Holy of Holies (cf. 16:16); unintentional or inadvertent sins by the high priest or the community polluted the incense altar in the Holy Place (4:2–21); lesser sins or impurities polluted the bronze altar in the courtyard (4:22–35).

3. Leviticus distinguishes between those impurities that could be rectified and those that could not. Regarding the former, considerable attention is given in chapters 12–15 to the rectification of uncleanness arising from skin diseases and various bodily discharges. In marked contrast, among those impurities that could not be rectified were sexual sins (18:20, 23–25, 27–30), idolatry (20:2–5), murder (Num. 35:16–21, 31) and profaning the sacred (e.g. 7:19–21; 22:3, 9). In these cases only the death of the guilty party could remove the pollution caused by his or her sin.

When rectification was possible, the process by which any uncleanness was purified varied depending upon its seriousness. Normally, a person or object was purified by (a) the passage of time, and (b) washing and/or laundering; those objects which could not be washed were disposed of by burial, burning or some other method. For minor impurities the length of time required for purification was one day (e.g. for touching the carcass of an animal, 11:39). More serious impurities required the passing of seven days (e.g. touching a human corpse, Num. 19:11). Longer periods of forty and eighty days respectively were necessary for a woman who gave birth to a son or daughter (12:2–5). As regards the washing of the body and the laundering of clothes, requirements again differed depending upon the degree of impurity. For example, whoever *touched* an animal carcass was unclean for a day; whoever *carried* an animal carcass sustained greater impurity and was required to wash his or her clothes (11:24–25, 27–28).[8]

From these observations concerning holiness and uncleanness/impurity, it is apparent that they formed a spectrum of closely associated categories. On the one side there was holiness, in the middle cleanness, and on the other side uncleanness/impurity (see Diagram E). The further one moved from the middle of this spectrum the greater the intensity of either holiness or uncleanness. For the ancient Israelites every person, object, place and period of time could be located somewhere on this spectrum.

Diagram E

Increasing   Increasing

◄——————————————— CLEANNESS ———————————————►

HOLINESS   UNCLEANNESS

So far we have discussed the concepts of holiness and uncleanness without attempting to define them. It is necessary, therefore, to clarify what was meant by these terms within the context of Leviticus. What was holiness? What was uncleanness?

16.4. Holiness

In Leviticus holiness is always associated with God. Four aspects of this are very significant:

(a) God is innately holy; he is the supreme manifestation of holiness. To be holy is to be God-like.
(b) Holiness emanates from God; he is the sole source of holiness. He alone endows other objects, places or people with holiness. Everything that is

---

[8] According to J. Milgrom, *Cult and Conscience: The ASHAM and the Priestly Doctrine of Repentance* (Leiden: Brill, 1976), 108–21, when an individual expressed remorse regarding a deliberate sin this had the effect of lessening the resulting pollution and thereby reduced the amount of rectification required.

given to God or belongs to him is holy. Since God radiates holiness to all that is close to him, the ark of the covenant, which functioned as his earthly throne, was the most holy item of furniture in the tabernacle. For the same reason the Holy of Holies was the holiest part of the tabernacle; indeed God's presence made it the holiest location upon the entire earth.

(c) Holiness describes the moral perfection and purity of God's nature. For this reason God's command to the Israelites, 'Be holy because I, the LORD your God, am holy' (19:2), comes in the context of imperatives governing the people's behaviour. Their actions and attitudes were to reflect God's perfect nature.

(d) Sanctification, the process by which someone or something becomes holy, is the result of divine activity. It is God who sanctified. This is reflected in the refrain 'I am the LORD, who makes you holy (who sanctifies you; NIV margin)' (20:8; 21:8, 15, 23; 22:9, 16, 32). Yet, while Leviticus notes the divine side of sanctification, it also emphasises the human side. Those made holy by God were expected to remain holy by doing nothing that would compromise their special status (cf. 11:44). The Israelites were also to keep holy anything sanctified by God. This applied, for example, to the Sabbath day. Because God had sanctified it, the Israelites were commanded to maintain its sanctity by refraining from all work (Ex. 20:8–11).

A natural extension of the belief that God is holy is the idea that holiness means wholeness or perfection. To be holy is to be unblemished or unmarred. It is to experience life in all its fullness as God had originally intended it to be. On one level this is reflected in the divine requirements regarding both priests and sacrifices. Priests with physical defects are not permitted to offer sacrifices (21:17–23). Similarly, it is regularly stated that the sacrificial offerings had to be without defect (1:3, 10; 3:1, 6; 4:3, 23, 28, 32; 5:15, 18; 6:6; 9:2–3, 14:10; 22:19–25; 23:12, 18; cf. Ex. 12:5); only in the case of a freewill offering was an exception made (22:23).[9] On another level holiness is associated with perfect moral behaviour (cf. 20:7; 22:32–33). This is revealed especially in chapter 19 (but compare also chapters 18 and 20) which contains a long list of commands governing personal behaviour. Interestingly, the material in this chapter echoes closely the Decalogue or Ten Commandments (Ex. 20:2–17) and the collection of moral instructions found within the Book of the Covenant (Ex. 22:21–23:9). To be holy is to live in a way that reflects the moral perfection of God; it is to live a life marked by love, purity and righteousness, these being the three most important hallmarks of perfect behaviour.

---

[9] Interestingly, the defects that disqualified both priests and sacrificial animals correspond very closely (21:18–20 and 22:22–24).

16.5. Uncleanness

In simple terms, uncleanness is the opposite of holiness. It represents all that is less than God-like. Although Leviticus never identifies the original source of uncleanness, we may surmise that it was believed to emanate from that which opposed God. Interestingly, uncleanness is associated with human beings in two ways. First, certain forms of uncleanness or impurity arise as a natural consequence of being human. These included suffering from specific skin diseases and experiencing bodily discharges. These and related forms of uncleanness all appear to be linked in one way or another to death. By associating some bodily diseases and conditions with death, the regulations of Leviticus indicate that death dominates human existence. Only by becoming holy can a human being escape the domain of death and experience the life-giving power of God.

Secondly, there are other forms of uncleanness that human beings have the power to control. These occur when individuals by their actions transgress any boundary established by God. People who wilfully ignore God's commands, decrees, or laws are a source of uncleanness and defile all that they touch. Their actions both distance them from God and bring them further under the domain of death.

16.6. The Relationship Between Holiness and Uncleanness

Leviticus highlights two important factors regarding the relationship between holiness and uncleanness. First, holiness and uncleanness are totally incompatible. Not only was it impossible for anyone or anything to be holy and unclean at the same time, but, more importantly, no holy object or person was normally permitted to come into contact with anything unclean.[10] This incompatibility between holiness and uncleanness accounts for the existence of many of the regulations found in Leviticus. For example, it explains the necessity of the complex sacrificial system, outlined in chapters 1–7, which enabled those who were by nature unclean to become pure and holy. Without the offering of sacrifices, it would have been impossible for the Israelites to live in close contact with the LORD their God.[11]

Secondly, both holiness and uncleanness were perceived by the ancient Israelites as being dynamic in nature; that is, they had the ability to transmit their

---

[10] When such contact occurred it either had a purifying or defiling effect, depending upon the specific circumstances.

[11] For a fuller treatment of sacrifice, see chapter 17.

nature to other people or objects. In this regard they differ significantly from the state of cleanness/purity; it was merely neutral, and was unable to make anything else clean or pure. Consequently, any clean person or thing was constantly in the middle of a struggle between the powers of holiness and uncleanness.[12] Since the status of an individual could change, Leviticus consistently underlines the danger posed by uncleanness to those who are holy or pure. This danger was greatest for the priests who worked within the tabernacle, a holy area, and handled the tabernacle furniture, holy objects. For a priest to serve in the tabernacle, it was essential that he remained holy. If he became unclean, he could no longer carry out his duties; to do so would have meant death.[13]

The dynamic nature of holiness and uncleanness also explains the antagonism which we find in Leviticus towards the inhabitants of Egypt and Canaan (cf. 19:1–37). Due to their uncleanness they were viewed as a major threat to the well-being of the Israelites. Because their uncleanness was dynamic and opposed to the holiness of the LORD, it had the potential to make the Israelites unclean, endangering their special relationship with the LORD. For this reason the inhabitants of Canaan had to be removed from the land. Any form of compromise would inevitably pollute the Israelites and subsequently God's sanctuary. To be a holy nation, Israel had to set itself apart from all that was unclean.

16.7. Conclusion

By dominating the book of Leviticus, the concept of holiness lies as the heart of the Pentateuch. Since the narrative in Genesis and Exodus moves towards the creation of Israel as a 'holy nation', it is hardly surprising that Leviticus should define in more detail what it means for the Israelites to be holy. This increased interest in holiness also follows on naturally from the creation of the tabernacle and God's occupation of it. Given that holiness emanates from God, the Holy One, his presence in the midst of the people brings into their daily lives an important new dynamic. Because their God is holy, the people themselves must be holy. This, however, will be a constant struggle for them due to those powers, both internal and external, which oppose God.

---

[12] Elsewhere in the OT this conflict is presented in terms of Yahweh's conflict with death.

[13] The danger posed by the holy furnishing of the tabernacle to an unclean person is also reflected in the regulations concerning an individual who unintentionally killed another person. They are instructed to cling to the horns of the altar. Only one who was morally clean might expect to touch the altar with immunity.

16.8. New Testament Connections

The concepts of holiness and uncleanness are frequently mentioned in the NT and reflect closely what we observe in Leviticus. As regards uncleanness, Jesus focused attention on those actions or attitudes that made a person unclean:

> What comes out of a man is what makes him 'unclean'. For from within, out of men's hearts, come evil thoughts, sexual immorality, theft, murder, adultery, greed, malice, deceit, lewdness, envy, slander, arrogance and folly. All these evils come from inside and make a man 'unclean' (Mk. 7:20–23; cf. Mt. 15:17–20).

In doing so he was highly critical of the Pharisees and teachers of the law who neglected these causes of uncleanness while concentrating on relatively minor aspects of ritual purity (cf. Mt. 23:23–28; Lk. 11:37–41). Paul, likewise, associated impurity with wickedness and immorality (e.g. Rom. 1:24; 6:19; 2 Cor. 12:21; Eph. 4:19; 5:3, 5). According to Paul, such sinful behaviour was to be shunned by believers 'for God did not call us to be impure, but to live a holy life' (1 Thes. 4:7; cf. 1 Cor. 1:2; 2 Tim. 2:8).

The NT references to purification highlight two complementary aspects. On the one hand, they underline that it is God who purifies those who are unclean (cf. Acts 15:9). More specifically, it is emphasised that purification is achieved through the sacrificial death of Jesus Christ: 'But if we walk in the light, as he is in the light, we have fellowship with one another, and the blood of Jesus, his Son, purifies us from all sin' (1 Jn. 1:7; cf. Jn. 15:3; Titus 2:14; Heb. 1:3; 1 Jn. 1:9). On the other hand, believers are exhorted to purify themselves: 'Since we have these promises, dear friends, let us purify ourselves from everything that contaminates body and spirit, perfecting holiness out of reverence for God' (2 Cor. 7:1; cf. Jas. 4:8).

The concept of holiness figures prominently in all of the NT Epistles. Holiness of life is to be the ambition of every believer. Peter expresses this most clearly, quoting in the process Leviticus: 'But just as he who called you is holy, so be holy in all you do; for it is written: "Be holy, because I am holy" ' (1 Pet. 1:15–16; cf. Rom. 6:19, 22; 2 Cor. 1:12; Eph. 4:24; Col. 3:12; 1 Thes. 2:10; 3:13; 1 Tim. 2:15; Titus 1:8; Heb. 12:14; 2 Pet. 3:11). The author of Hebrews underlines the importance of holiness: 'Make every effort to live in peace with all men and to be holy; without holiness no-one will see the Lord' (Heb. 12:14). Such holiness is clearly linked to behaviour that is morally exemplary. Jesus instructed his followers:

> For I tell you that unless your righteousness surpasses that of the Pharisees and the teachers of the law, you will certainly not enter the kingdom of heaven … Be perfect, therefore, as your heavenly Father is perfect (Mt. 5:20, 48).

Significantly, there are thirty-three occasions in the NT (excluding Revelation) when believers are designated as 'saints' or 'holy ones' (e.g. Acts 9:13, 32; 26:10; Rom. 1:7; 8:27; 15:25, 26, 31; 16:2, 15).

Although believers are constantly exhorted to be holy, God's role in the process of sanctification is also recognised (1 Thes. 5:23). In Hebrews he is pictured as a father disciplining his children in order to produce holiness of character: 'But God disciplines us for our good, that we may share in his holiness' (Heb. 12:10). Most attention, however, tends to be focused on the role played by Jesus Christ and the Holy Spirit. On three occasions both are mentioned together in connection with the sanctification of believers (1 Cor. 6:11; Heb. 10:29; 1 Pet. 1:2). 2 Thessalonians 2:13 refers specifically to 'the sanctifying work of the Spirit' (cf. Rom. 15:16). This is obviously linked to the belief that the Holy Spirit dwells within believers: 'Do you not know that your body is a temple of the Holy Spirit, who is in you, whom you have received from God?' (1 Cor. 6:19) As God's presence made the tabernacle holy, so too the presence of the Holy Spirit sanctifies believers. Elsewhere, the sanctifying work of Jesus Christ is highlighted; he is 'the one who makes men holy' (Heb. 2:11; cf. Acts 26:18; 1 Cor. 1:2). Significantly, this is linked to Christ's death: 'we have been made holy through the sacrifice of the body of Jesus Christ once for all' (Heb. 10:10; cf. Col. 1:22; Heb. 10:14; 13:12).

A number of incidents recorded in the Gospels focus on the relationship between the holy and the unclean. When Jesus touched those who were unclean with skin diseases, he displays his power both to heal and to purify (Mt. 8:1–4; Mark 1:40–44; Luke 5:12–14). The same was true when the woman who had been suffering from bleeding for twelve years touched Jesus (Mt. 9:20–22; Mk. 5:24–34; Lk. 8:42–48). Similarly, when Jesus restored the dead to life, he revealed his power over death, a primary source of uncleanness (Mt. 18:23–25; Mk. 5:35–43; Lk. 7:11–17; 8:49–56). Jesus' holy nature was also recognised by his disciples (Jn. 6:69; cf. Acts 3:14; 4:27, 30; Heb. 7:26) and by the unclean spirits or demons who refer to him as 'the Holy One of God' (Mk. 1:24; Lk. 4:34).

17

The Sacrificial System

17.1. Summary

When Moses and the Israelites completed the building of the tabernacle it became possible for God to dwell in their midst. However, to enable the people to live in close proximity to the Holy One of Israel, God instituted through Moses a sacrificial system by which the people could atone for their sins. At the heart of this system lay a number of different sacrifices which complemented each other by addressing differing facets of human wrongdoing. For example, the purification offering cleansed the tabernacle of pollution caused by sin. Of all the sacrifices offered throughout the year those presented on the Day of Atonement were the most important. Annually the high priest entered the Holy of Holies to atone for the sin of the whole nation and to purify the most sacred part of the tabernacle. Without this and other rituals it would have been impossible for the people to live in harmony with the LORD their God.

17.2. Introduction

The first seven chapters of Leviticus consist of regulations governing the offering of sacrifices. These come between the account of the erection of the tabernacle in Exodus 40 and the consecration of the priests in Leviticus 8–9. Since the instructions for the erection of the tabernacle and the consecration of the priests were given together in Exodus 25:1–31:17, we might have expected the description of their fulfilment to be placed side by side. They are separated, however, by the sacrifice regulations. Nevertheless, the present location of the sacrifice instructions is very apt. First, their location at the very beginning of Leviticus emphasises their importance; they are central to Israel's relationship with God. Secondly, overseeing the offering of sacrifices was the foremost duty of the priests. It is, therefore, quite appropriate that these instruction should be placed immediately prior to the account of the consecration of the priests in Leviticus 8–9.

Several features of the material in Leviticus 1–7 are noteworthy. First, the information provided about the sacrifices is in the form of instructions or regulations. These fall into two sections. Whereas the instructions in 1:2–6:7 and 7:22–34 are addressed to the Israelite laity, those in 6:8–7:21 are for the priests. Two sets of instructions are provided because the ordinary Israelites and the priests performed different functions when it came to offering sacrifices.

Secondly, the instructions cover five different types of sacrifices. In the NIV these sacrifices are termed burnt offering, grain offering, fellowship offering, sin offering and guilt offering. Some scholars, however, prefer the designations purification and reparation for the sin and guilt offerings respectively. As we shall see below, these alternative titles reflect more accurately the distinctive functions of these offerings. The differences between the various types of sacrifices will be discussed later.

Thirdly, the order in which these sacrifices are presented differs in the two sections. This is due to the location of the peace offering (see Table C). Whereas it comes in the middle of the list of regulations addressed to the laity, it comes at the end of the rules for the priests. In the first list the peace offering is grouped with the burnt and grain because all three are 'food offerings' which produce 'a soothing aroma for the LORD'. The purification and reparation offerings are discussed separately due to their distinctive functions. In the second section the order is determined by the holiness of the meat associated with each sacrifice. The peace offering was placed last in the list because ordinary Israelites could eat this meat. In both sections the burnt offering comes first because it was viewed as the most important of all the sacrifices.

Table C

Regulations for laity	Regulations for priests
Burnt offering 1:2–17	Burnt offering 6:8–13
Cereal offering 2:1–16	Cereal offering 6:14–23
Peace offering 3:1–17	Purification offering 6:24–30
Purification offering 4:1–5:13	Reparation offering 7:1–10
Reparation offering 5:14–6:7	Peace offering 7:11–21

Fourthly, for both sections the order of the sacrifices does not reflect the sequence in which they were normally offered. Although the burnt offering, as the most important sacrifice, is mentioned first, it was often only presented after a purification offering had been made. This is evident in the case of the sacrifices offered by a Nazirite at the end of his or her period of separation. Although the burnt offering is mentioned first in Numbers 6:14–15, in practice it was presented after a purification offering (Num. 6:16–17). A similar situation can be observed regarding the purification ritual for someone suffering from a skin disease. The purification offering is made first (Lev. 14:19–20), although in the list of offerings it comes after the burnt offering (14:10; the ewe lamb for the purification offering is mentioned after the male lamb for the burnt offering).[1] Interestingly, the presentation of a purification offering prior to other sacrifices appears to have been a common pattern in the sacrificial rituals of other ancient Near Eastern societies.

17.3. The General Pattern for Animal Sacrifices

Of the five main types of sacrifices listed in the early chapters of Leviticus all but one involve the offering up of an animal. Although there are important differences in detail regarding the procedure for these animal sacrifices, which will be considered below, a common pattern was adopted for each offering. This falls into two parts: the first involves the actions of the Israelite worshipper; the second concerns the duties of the priest. An individual wishing to make a sacrifice brought an animal to the tabernacle courtyard (1:3; 4:4, 14). There the worshipper laid a hand on the animal's head (e.g. 1:4; 3:2, 8, 13), before slaughtering it (e.g. 1:5, 11; 3:2, 8, 13). The blood from the animal was collected by the priest and usually sprinkled against the sides of the bronze altar (1:5, 11, 15; 3:2, 8, 13); in the case of the purification offering some of the blood was put to special use (4:7–8, 16–18, 25, 30, 34). Next the whole animal, or selected parts, was placed on the altar to be consumed by fire (e.g. 1:6–9, 12–13, 16–17; 3:3–5, 9–11, 14–16; 4:8–10, 19–20, 26, 31, 35). Finally, the priests or Israelites usually consumed any meat that was not burnt up upon the altar (e.g. 6:26–29; 7:6; 7:15–21).

Two aspects of this pattern require further consideration. (a) The laying of a hand upon the animal's head has been understood in a variety of ways. It probably indicated at the very least ownership of the animal. By leaning on the animal the worshipper signalled that this was his or her sacrifice to God. An extension of this idea is that of association. The worshipper associated himself or herself with what happened to the animal. Since the death of the animal was meant to atone for the sin of the worshipper, by touching the animal the worshipper acknowledged that in reality he or she should be put to death. This understanding may even have extended to the belief that the animal was a substitute for the worshipper.[2] Some scholars have argued that the laying of a hand on the animal symbolised the

---

[1] In this case a reparation offering (14:12–18) preceded both the purification offering and burnt offering.

[2] Against the idea of substitution, however, is the fact that the meat of some sacrifices was consumed by the priests or even by the worshipper.

transference of sin from the worshipper to the animal. However, a clear distinction may need to be drawn between the act of placing one hand on the animal's head and placing two hands. With two hands it is undoubtedly a case of transference. This is clearly illustrated in the ritual of the scapegoat that was sent off into the wilderness on the Day of Atonement (16:20–22). The high priest was instructed 'to lay both hands on the head of the live goat and confess over it all the wickedness and rebellion of the Israelites' (16:21). The text then specifically states, 'The goat will carry on itself all their sins to a solitary place' (16:22). In the case of a single hand being laid on the head of an animal no passage states clearly that the transference of sin took place.

(b) For all animal sacrifices special instructions are given regarding the use or disposal of the animal's blood. As we shall see in more detail below, with the purification offering the sacrificial blood was used to cleanse sacred objects within the sanctuary which were defiled or polluted due to human sin or impurity. With the other types of sacrifices the blood was collected and sprinkled against the sides of the bronze altar (1:5, 11, 15; 3:2, 8, 13; 7:2). These ritual actions reflect the importance with which the ancient Israelites viewed blood; it symbolised life. For this reason sacrificial blood was a powerful antidote to the deathly consequences of sin and impurity.[3]

17.4. The Five Types of Sacrifices

The early chapters of Leviticus provide instructions for five main types of sacrifices. Although they share common features, each type has its own distinctive elements. Naturally, the existence of five different types of sacrifices suggests that each type had its own function. For the purification and reparation offerings it is possible to be reasonably certain about their differing purposes. As regards the other sacrifices, we can only make tentative suggestions.

17.4.1 The burnt offering (Lev. 1:2–17; 6:8–13)

The burnt offering was easily distinguished from all the other sacrifices by the fact that the entire animal was burnt upon the altar. For all other sacrifices only selected portions of the offering were placed upon the altar, with the remainder of the offering being eaten by the priests and/or other worshippers.[4] Of the

---

[3] The special importance of blood is also highlighted in the food regulations; see chapter 18.

[4] For this reason the burnt offering is sometimes described as the whole-burnt offering or holocaust.

different sacrifices the burnt offering was viewed as the most important. It comes first in both sets of instructions and the worshipper is clearly expected to present his or her best animal; this is implied by the brief comment that the offering was to be 'a male without defect' (1:3, 10). Although the burnt offering was intended to be costly, allowance was made for those who were poor and were able only to bring 'a dove or a young pigeon' (1:14).

Few details are given regarding the specific function of the burnt offering. The repetition of the phrase 'an aroma pleasing to the LORD' (1:9, 13, 17) suggests that it was intended to gain divine favour (cf. Gen. 8:20–21). This understanding of the sacrifice is probably to be linked to the comment in 1:4, 'it will be accepted on his behalf to make atonement for him'. The concept of atonement in the OT has two distinctive meanings: it can mean either 'to cleanse' or 'to pay a ransom'. In the case of the burnt offering the latter of these meanings seems the more likely. Within the judicial systems of ancient Israel and her neighbours it was sometimes possible for a guilty party to substitute in place of the death penalty a ransom (cf. Ex. 21:30). Thus, the animal offered as a burnt offering was presented as an alternative to the death penalty imposed by God for human sin. By paying this 'ransom' the worshipper appeased God's righteous anger against his or her own sin and uncleanness. God's justice demanded the death of an animal as a substitute for the judicial death of the worshipper. Given that burnt offerings were used to restore broken relationships between God and human beings, it is hardly surprising that such offerings figure prominently in the ratification of divine/human covenants (e.g. Gen. 8:20–9:17; 22:1–19; Ex. 24:3–11).

17.4.2 The cereal offering (Lev. 2:1–16; 6:14–23)

The cereal offering is unique in that of the five main types of sacrifices it was the only one not involving animals. It consisted of an offering made of fine flour, which could be presented either cooked (2:4–7) or uncooked (2:1–2). After the worshipper presented the offering, part of it was burnt upon the bronze altar, the rest being allocated to the priests who were dependent upon it for their daily food.

Like the burnt offering, the cereal offering was clearly intended to evoke a pleasing response from God (cf. 2:2, 9). However, whereas the whole of the burnt offering was consumed by fire, only a portion of the cereal offering was burnt on the altar. Most of it was handed over as a gift to the priests in recognition of their unique service for the people (cf. 8:22–31). Interestingly, the Hebrew term for a 'cereal offering' (*minhâ*; *minkhâ*) is translated in other contexts as 'gift' or 'tribute'. Sometimes it has the idea of a gift intended to ingratiate the giver to someone else (e.g. Gen. 32:13–21; 2 Kgs. 8:7–8).

Elsewhere it can refer to the money given by a lesser king to a greater in order to guarantee a peaceful relationship (e.g. Judg. 3:15–18; 1 Kgs. 4:21; 10:23–25; 2 Kgs. 17:3–4). This suggests that the cereal offering was possibly viewed as a gift or tribute paid to God in recognition of his divine sovereignty. In this case the priests received it as God's representatives.

17.4.3 The peace offering (Lev. 3:1–17; 7:11–21)

The peace offering is distinguished from the other offerings by the fact that most of the meat from the sacrificial animal was retained by the worshipper for a festive meal. Certain portions, however, were set apart for God and the priests: the fat associated with the kidneys and liver was burnt on the altar to produce 'an aroma pleasing to the LORD' (3:5, 16); the right thigh was given to the officiating priest and the breast shared among the other priests (7:28–34). Whereas the burnt offering required that the larger sacrificial animals be male, for the peace offering females could also be offered. Since a meal was an important aspect of the sacrifice, doves and pigeons were excluded as suitable offerings. Under the general heading of peace offerings further divisions existed. According to Leviticus 7, the peace offering could be an expression of thankfulness (vv. 12–15), the result of a vow or a freewill offering (vv. 16–21). For the first of these the meat of the animals had to be consumed on the day it was offered. In the second and third cases the meat could also be eaten on the second day, but if any remained until the third day it had to be burnt up.

   Due to the festive nature of the peace offering it is sometimes referred to as the fellowship offering (cf. NIV). The Hebrew name for the sacrifice *šělāmîm* (*shělāmîm*) has traditionally been linked to the concept of peace (cf. Hebrew *šālôm* [*shālôm*]). Since 'peace' in Hebrew thought implied well-being in general it is likely that an important element of the peace offering was the acknowledgement of God as the source of true peace.

17.4.4 The purification offering (Lev. 4:1–5:13; 6:24–30)

The distinctive nature of the purification offering is highlighted by the special use made of the animal's blood to cleanse sacred items within the tabernacle. Although Leviticus 4 focuses on different types of purification offering, attention is drawn on each occasion to how the priest placed or sprinkled the sacrificial blood on particular items within the tabernacle. The examples in Leviticus 4 are given in descending order, with the most serious offences being listed first. If the anointed priest or whole community of Israel sinned, the blood was placed on the horns of the golden incense altar which stood within the Holy Place (4:7, 18). If a leader committed the sin, the blood was put on the horns of the bronze altar that was located in the tabernacle courtyard (4:30, 34).

Traditionally, the purification offering has been known as the 'sin offering'. This is due to the fact that the Hebrew word used to designate the sacrifice, *ḥaṭṭā't* (*khaṭṭā't*), frequently means 'sin'. However, the title 'purification offering' is preferable because it indicates more precisely the purpose or function of the sacrifice. As we have already noted in chapter 16, sin and uncleanness had the power to defile or pollute sacred objects; the more serious the sin, the greater the pollution. Consequently, if the anointed or high priest,[5] who was expected to be especially holy and blameless, sinned unintentionally this polluted the golden incense altar in the Holy Place. In contrast, a tribal leader's sin defiled the bronze altar. For the purification offerings outlined in Leviticus 4:1–5:13 the blood was placed on the sacred furnishings and not on the people responsible for the sin, indicating that it was the pollution caused by the sinner which was being cleansed rather than the actual sinner. On other occasions, however, the blood was applied to people in order to cleanse and sanctify them (e.g. making of the covenant at Sinai; the consecration of the priests).

17.4.5 The reparation offering (Lev. 5:14–6:7; 7:1–10)

Few details are given concerning the ritual of the reparation offering. Most attention is focused on the circumstances requiring such a sacrifice. Regarding the sacrifice itself, special emphasis is placed upon the bringing of a 'ram from the flock, one without defect and of the proper value in silver, according to the sanctuary shekel' (5:15 cf. 5:18; 6:6). The animal was slaughtered, its blood sprinkled against the altar, and the fatty portions associated with the kidneys and liver were burnt upon the altar (7:2–5). The rest of the animal was given to the priests who alone were permitted to eat the meat (7:6).

Some English translations refer to this sacrifice as the 'guilt offering'. The Hebrew name *'āšām* (*'āshām*) can mean 'guilt'. However, it can also mean 'reparation' or 'compensation'. This latter understanding seems to be more appropriate as regards the function of this sacrifice. The emphasis placed upon the value of the ram and the references to adding 'a fifth of the value' in order to make restitution suggest that the sacrifice was intended to compensate God for wrongs committed against him (cf. 5:16; 6:5). In this regard the reparation sacrifice resembles in part the practice of redemption outlined in Leviticus 27.

---

[5] The title 'anointed priest' is used only in Leviticus 4:3, 5, 16 and 6:22. Although all priests were anointed, most commentators accept that this designation must be a reference to the high priest who was viewed as having received a special anointing (cf. Num. 35:25).

From the preceding survey of the five main types of sacrifices mentioned in Leviticus 1–7, it is clear that each sacrifice had a distinctive function. These functions reflect the different ways in which the divine/human relationship is affected by human sin and uncleanness. Together these different sacrifices sought to restore human beings to a harmonious relationship with God.

17.5. The Day of Atonement (Lev. 16:1–34)

The ritual associated with the Day of Atonement was also important for maintaining a harmonious relationship between God and the people of Israel. This ritual falls into three main parts: (a) the purification of the sanctuary, (b) the sending away of the scapegoat, and (c) the presentation of two burnt offerings. The first part parallels closely the ritual noted above for the offering of a purification offering. The second part is unique to the Day of Atonement. The final part is mentioned only briefly, fuller details being unnecessary in the light of those already given in 1:2–17 and 6:8–13. An important aspect of the ritual on the Day of Atonement was that it centred on the high priest, named here as Aaron. He alone bore responsibility for what took place and the onus was on him to ensure that atonement was achieved for all the people.

17.5.1 *The purification of the sanctuary*

Annually on the Day of Atonement the high priest, wearing his special priestly clothing (16:4), passed through the curtain which separated the Holy of Holies from the Holy Place. Inside the Holy of Holies he sprinkled blood on and before the cover of the ark of the covenant, cleansing it and the Holy of Holies from pollution caused by sin. This process was repeated twice. On the first occasion a bull was sacrificed as a purification offering; its blood atoned for the sins of the high priest and his family. Afterwards one of two male goats was sacrificed and its blood brought into the Holy of Holies by the high priest to atone for the sins of the whole community of Israel (16:15–16). The high priest entered the Holy of Holies a second time and placed some of the goat's blood on the cover of the ark of the covenant before sprinkling more blood seven times before the ark of the covenant. He then performed a similar ritual in the Holy Place before the golden altar of incense.[6] The high priest next put some of the blood from the bull and the goat on the horns of the bronze altar in the courtyard (16:18). Finally, he sprinkled more of this blood seven times on the altar to cleanse it (16:19). Later, the remains of the bull and the goat were

---

[6] This is implied in 16:16–17.

taken outside the camp and burned (16:27). The man designated to perform this task had to wash himself before returning to the camp (16:28).

17.5.2 The scapegoat

At a preliminary stage in the Day of Atonement ritual two goats were brought before the high priest. Lots were cast to determine which of the two would be sacrificed as a purification offering. After the high priest had purified the tabernacle with the blood of the first goat, he took the second goat and, placing both hands upon it, confessed over it 'all the wickedness and rebellion of the Israelites – all their sins' (16:21). This goat was then led to an uninhabited place in the desert and released. Finally, the man responsible for taking the goat into the wilderness washed himself before coming back into the camp (16:26).

17.5.3 The burnt offerings

Apart from the animals listed as purification offerings, it is mentioned that two rams were sacrificed as burnt offerings. The first was provided by the high priest (16:3); the second by the Israelites (16:5). Following the purification of the sanctuary and the sending away of the scapegoat, the high priest took off his special garments and washed himself. He then offered up both rams in order to atone for himself and the people (16:23–24).

The Day of Atonement was probably the most important occasion in the cultic calendar of ancient Israel, designed to atone for those sins which were not covered by sacrifices offered throughout the rest of the year. The seriousness of the pollution caused by these sins is indicated by the fact that the high priest had to cleanse with the blood of the purification offering the most sacred part of the tabernacle, the Holy of Holies. The expulsion of the scapegoat that removed the people's sin from the camp was a visible sign of the special cleansing achieved on this important occasion.

17.6. Conclusion

The detailed attention given to the sacrificial system in the opening chapters of Leviticus underlines its importance. In the light of humanity's disposition to sin against God, the provision of means by which atonement may be made represents a gracious and unmerited response from God. By instituting the sacrifices and associated rituals outlined in Leviticus, the LORD places at the disposal of the Israelites a way of restoring and maintaining a harmonious relationship with their God.

17.7. New Testament Connections

The concepts associated with the OT sacrificial rituals influenced strongly the way in which NT writers viewed the death of Jesus Christ. In particular, they believed that through the offering of a unique sacrifice by a unique high priest it was possible for the divine/human relationship to be restored to complete harmony. While this was central to the faith of the early Christians, we should not overlook the brief observation by the author of Hebrews that it was never God's desire that sacrifices should be offered. Their existence was due to the failure of human beings to keep God's commands (Heb. 10:5–9).

17.7.1 Jesus Christ as a sacrifice

The New Testament writers frequently understand the death of Jesus Christ in sacrificial terms. This is highlighted, for example, by the description of Jesus as 'the Lamb of God, who takes away the sin of the world' (Jn. 1:29; cf. 1 Pet. 1:19) and various references to the 'blood' of Jesus Christ (e.g. Acts 20:28; Rom. 5:9; Eph. 2:13; Col. 1:20; 1 Pet. 1:2; Rev. 7:14; 12:11). Similarly, Paul refers to the death of Jesus as a 'sacrifice of atonement' (Rom. 3:25), and it is recorded in Hebrews 9:26 that Christ 'appeared once for all at the end of the ages to do away with sin by the sacrifice of himself'.

For the author of Hebrews Christ's death was the ultimate sacrifice, of which the OT sacrifices were merely an illustration (Heb. 9:9–10; 10:1). The inadequacy of the OT sacrifices is highlighted by the fact that they had to be repeated; they could never make perfect for all time those who offered them (Heb. 10:1). Christ, however, constituted the perfect offering. Consequently, his sacrificial death was all-sufficient, and further animal sacrifices became unnecessary. For this reason the early church dismissed as irrelevant and superfluous the temple sacrifices in Jerusalem. Nevertheless, the OT regulations about sacrifices had continuing significance because they shed light on the nature of the atonement achieved through Christ's death.

Special attention is drawn to the cleansing associated with Christ's sacrificial blood. Whereas the blood of animals was able to cleanse objects and people who outwardly were ceremonially unclean, the blood of Christ is viewed as superior in that it can cleanse or purify inner, human consciences (Heb. 9:14; cf. Titus 2:14). Since the forgiveness of sins comes through the shedding of blood (Heb. 9:22; cf. Mt. 26:28; Eph. 1:7), those cleansed by the blood of Christ need no longer feel guilty (Heb. 10:2; cf. 1 Jn. 1:7).

A further link with the OT sacrifices may be observed in the celebration of the Lord's Supper or Eucharist. Paul alludes to this in 1 Corinthians 10:14–22 when he emphasises how believers, by eating bread and wine which represents respectively the body and blood of Jesus Christ, participate in his sacrificial death (cf. Jn. 6:53–56). As a result of Christ's atoning death individuals are made holy and perfect (cf. Heb. 10:10, 14; cf. 10:1; 13:12).

17.7.2 Jesus Christ as high priest

Closely associated with the description of Christ's death in sacrificial terms is his portrayal as a high priest. To this end the author of Hebrews argues that although Jesus did not belong to the family of Aaron, he was divinely appointed to be a high priest in the 'order of Melchizedek' (5:10; 7:11–22).[7] Furthermore, he differs from all previous high priests by the fact that he alone is 'holy, blameless, pure, set apart from sinners, exalted above the heavens' (7:26). Also, whereas the Aaronic priests served in the earthly tabernacle, 'a copy and shadow of what is in heaven' (8:5; cf. 9:24), Christ serves in the heavenly tabernacle (8:1–5). While the Aaronic high priest of necessity had to purify the earthly tabernacle each year on the Day of Atonement, Christ, by the offering of himself, purified the heavenly temple once and for all (Heb. 9:23; 13:11–12). Moreover, because his priestly mediation was completely acceptable to God, having entered the heavenly temple, there was no need for him to leave. Consequently, he is able continually to represent others before God (Heb. 9:25), and, because God accepts Christ's high-priestly mediation, believers may have confidence that God also accepts them.[8]

By emphasising that Jesus Christ, as God's unique son, provided the sacrifice necessary to atone completely for human sin, the NT highlights two important aspects of God's character: his justice and his love. Motivated by love, God provides the sacrifice necessary to meet the demands of his own justice. It is God, in the person of his own son, who pays the price of forgiveness for human sin.

---

[7] By associating Jesus with Melchizedek the author of Hebrews presents Jesus as both a priest and a king. A further dimension to this may be noted. In Genesis 1–3 Adam is presented as a priest-king. Not surprisingly, therefore, Jesus was viewed as the Second Adam (Rom. 5:12–21; cf. Lk. 3:38 and 4:3).

[8] Another OT idea that may be linked to the death of Jesus Christ as a high priest is the belief that a high priest's death purged pollution.

The Clean and the Unclean Foods

18.1. Summary

The food regulations contained in the book of Leviticus highlight two important theological principles. The distinction between clean and unclean foods emphasises the divine calling of Israel to be a holy nation, different from the other nations of the earth; the clean and unclean animals symbolise Israelites and non-Israelites respectively. The law prohibiting the eating of blood derives from the idea that all life, both human and animal, is sacred. Although God sanctions the eating of meat, due respect must be shown for the life of any animal slaughtered for food; blood, as the symbol of life, must not be eaten.

18.2. Introduction

As we have already noted, most of Leviticus consists of divine speeches mediated through Moses to the Israelites. Although these speeches cover various topics, a major unifying theme is God's concern that the people should be a holy nation. To this end Leviticus contains regulations governing the offering of sacrifices (1–7) and the procedures for being purified from various forms of uncleanness (12–15). This latter block of material is preceded immediately by rules concerning those animals which the Israelites may and may not eat (11:1–47). These regulations divide all living creatures on the basis of specific criteria into two groups: clean and unclean. Only those animals that belong to the former category may be eaten by the Israelites. These regulations are repeated later in Deuteronomy 14:3–20.

At first sight it is difficult to see any connection between these food regulations and the divine desire that Israel should be a holy nation. In what way did the eating of particular animals fulfil Israel's calling to be a holy people?

18.3. The Food Regulations Summarised

The regulations defining clean and unclean animals are divided into three sections that correspond with the three main regions of habitation: land (11:1–8), sea (11:9–12) and air (11:13–23). All animals were categorised as clean or unclean on the basis of a single principle governing each location:

1. Only cloven-hoofed, cud-chewing land animals were clean; all other mammals were unclean.
2. Only fish with fins and scales were clean; all other fish were unclean.
3. Birds of prey and flying insects that walked, rather than hopped, were unclean; all other birds and insects were clean.

While the general principles are clearly stated in Leviticus 11 for land animals, fish and flying insects, in the case of birds it has to be deduced from the different types listed. However, even when the principle is given, further details are usually added to clarify particular cases. For example, regarding land animals special attention is given to the camel, the coney, the rabbit and the pig; they are all declared unclean even though they meet one of the two criteria for clean animals given in the general principle.[1]

18.4. The Function of the Food Regulations

Various explanations have been offered to account for the dietary rules in Leviticus 11 and Deuteronomy 14. Some commentators have suggested that the classification of the animals into two types symbolised people and their behaviour. An animal which chewed its cud resembled a human being who meditated on the divine law. The sheep was designated clean because the ancient Israelites viewed God as their heavenly shepherd. The pig was unclean because of its dirty habits which were reminiscent of a sinner's behaviour. Although the arbitrary nature of such explanations has led contemporary scholars to reject them, the basic idea that the two types of animal are symbolic of people is probably correct.

---

[1] There are three basic ideas which underlie Jewish dietary laws: (a) it is forbidden to consume blood (Deut. 12:23); (b) meat and dairy produce must not be eaten together (Ex. 23:19); (c) certain types of animals, birds and fish are classified as unclean and should not be consumed (Lev. 11:1–47; Deut. 14:3–21). Food which meets these requirements is described in Hebrew as *Kašer* (*kasher*; cf. Kosher) 'ritually fit', 'wholesome'.

Other writers have proposed that these ancient food regulations anticipate the findings of modern science regarding hygiene. Whereas the clean animals were safe for human consumption, the unclean animals were not. Several factors argue against this proposal. (a) While pork is often cited as an example of an unclean meat that is dangerous to human health, this is only true when the meat is not properly cooked. Thoroughly cooked, pork is as safe to consume as any of the meats which are classified as clean. Similarly, camel meat poses little danger to health; indeed Arabs view it as a delicacy. (b) If a danger to health was the reason behind the food regulations, it is strange that this motive is never mentioned in the Bible. Might we not have expected that the Israelites would have been warned of this danger in order to encourage them not to eat the unclean meats? In the light of these factors, the explanation of hygiene is unconvincing.[2]

Some commentators suggest that the Israelites were instructed to avoid the unclean animals because of their close association with non-Israelite religions. For example, archaeological evidence suggests that the pig was eaten in Canaanite rituals. Yet, while some unclean animals were clearly used in the cultic activities of ancient Israel's neighbours, it is not possible to demonstrate this for all the animals designated unclean. Furthermore, if this was the rationale behind the classification of the animals, it is surprising that the bull, which was prominent in both Egyptian and Canaanite religious rituals, was not included among the unclean animals. While the rationale of religious associations might account for certain cases, it fails to explain all of the distinctions made between clean and unclean animals.

The most satisfactory explanation of the food regulations rests on the observation that for the Israelites the animal world was structured in the same way as the human world. The clean and unclean animals parallel clean and unclean people (i.e. Israelites and non-Israelites). Within the category of clean animals two further classes may be observed, sacrificial and non-sacrificial; these correspond with the human classes of priestly and non-priestly.[3] By restricting their diet to clean animals the Israelites were reminded

---

[2] From a Christian perspective, a further reason can be added. How could Jesus Christ have abolished rules that were supposed to protect the health of those who abided by them?

[3] We have already noted the importance of the three categories of holy, clean, and unclean, in chapter 17. It is, therefore, not surprising that they should reappear in the context of the food regulations. Regarding the correspondence between priests and sacrificial animals, it is interesting to observe how Leviticus 21 and 22 parallel each other; Leviticus 21 deals with blemished priests and Leviticus 22 with blemished sacrificial animals.

of their obligation to be a clean people, distinct from others.[4] Consequently, each meal at which meat was served had religious implications for the Israelites; it spoke of their divine calling to be a holy nation. This link between the food regulations and Israel's divine election is clearly reflected in 20:24–26:

> I am the LORD your God, who has set you apart from the nations. You must therefore make a distinction between clean and unclean animals and between clean and unclean birds. Do not defile yourselves by any animal or bird or anything that moves along the ground – those which I have set apart as unclean for you. You are to be holy to me because I, the LORD am holy, and I have set you apart from the nations to be my own.

Moreover, the food regulations made it difficult for an Israelite to participate in meals provided by non-Israelites. They not only symbolised that Israel was to be a clean nation in contrast to other nations, but they also had the practical effect of limiting contact with other people which might compromise Israel's special status.

18.5. The Rationale Behind the Clean/Unclean Classification

While the distinction between clean and unclean peoples accounts for the purpose of the food regulations, it is still necessary to explain why some animals were considered clean and others unclean. Why, for example, was a sheep categorised as clean, but a pig unclean? Was this classification merely arbitrary, or were there particular reasons for designating some animals clean and others unclean? Although most scholars accept that some rationale must have governed the categorisation of the animals as clean and unclean, no explanation commands unanimous support. One factor, however, deserves special consideration.

A common factor among many of the unclean animals is that they depend upon the death of other creatures in order to survive.[5] A survey of those

---

[4] The dietary rules are placed immediately after material dealing with the separation of the priests from the rest of the Israelites. As the priests were set apart as holy from the rest of the Israelites, so was Israel set apart as holy from the rest of the nations.

[5] As if to highlight this association with death, much of Leviticus 11 focuses on the uncleanness which occurs through touching or carrying the carcasses of unclean animals (cf. vv. 24–38). Even the carcasses of clean animals – those which die by some means other than ritual slaughtering – communicate uncleanness to human beings (vv. 39–40).

animals which are declared unclean reveals one feature which is common to most of them: they eat meat. All of the birds listed as unclean in verses 13–19 are birds of prey; their diet consists of the meat of other animals. The same is true regarding the land animals; those designated unclean have paws (e.g. cats and dogs) and such animals are carnivorous. In marked contrast, cloven-hoofed animals do not eat meat. This distinction between carnivores and non-carnivores (or ruminants) is emphasised by the inclusion of the criterion of chewing the cud. The idea that animals associated with death should be viewed as unclean is in keeping with what we have observed in chapter 17; in Leviticus death and uncleanness are generally linked, being the opposites of life and holiness. By eating clean animals the Israelites distanced themselves from death which was perceived as the source of uncleanness.

18.6. The Blood Prohibition

Before concluding our discussion of the food regulations in Leviticus 11, it is important to say something about the prohibition against eating blood which is highlighted in 17:1–16 (cf. 3:17; 7:26–27; Deut. 12:16, 23–25). So serious was this prohibition that God commanded anyone who ate blood to 'be cut off' (17:14).

To understand the reason for this, it is necessary to refer back to the book of Genesis. Although God had initially created human beings to be vegetarian (Gen. 1:29), one result of Adam and Eve's rebellion in the Garden of Eden was that humanity thereafter desired to eat meat. As a result, human beings killed animals for food, apparently adding to the general violence of humankind that ultimately caused God to send the flood (6:11–13). After the flood, God appears to make a concession to Noah and his descendants regarding the eating of meat. They were permitted to do so, on the condition that they 'must not eat meat that has its lifeblood still in it' (Gen. 9:4). Although God allowed the taking of an animal's life, the prohibition against eating blood drew attention to the importance which he placed upon all life. The Israelites' attitude to the killing of animals, even for food, was to differ from that of their neighbours. They were to behave in a way that reflected their belief that God was the source of all life. Since God was the giver and sustainer of life, he alone had the right to sanction the taking of a life.[6]

In passing it should be observed that meat did not form part of the regular diet of the Israelites, especially during the wilderness wanderings. The absence of meat was a recurring reason for complaints against God. When meat was eaten it appears to have been within the context of religious celebrations.

---

[6] On the significance of blood within the sacrificial system, see chapter 17.

18.7. Conclusion

From the preceding discussion it is clear that the food regulations contained in Leviticus reflect important theological ideas. On the one hand, the distinction between clean and unclean animals emphasises the special calling of Israel to be a holy nation. On the other hand, the prohibition against eating blood underlines the value which God places upon all life, animal as well as human. In a remarkable way religious truths were reflected in the daily routine associated with eating.

18.8. New Testament Connections

The concept of clean and unclean foods appears in a number of NT passages. In the Gospels, the parallel passages in Matthew 15:1–20 and Mark 7:1–23 focus on Jesus' attitude towards eating something which is unclean. In these passages it is not specifically stated that the meat was unclean; rather, the issue centres on the fact that the disciples 'were eating food with hands that were "unclean", that is, unwashed' (Mk. 7:2). In response Jesus commented to the people: 'Nothing outside a man can make him "unclean" by going into him. Rather, it is what comes out of a man that makes him "unclean" ' (Mk. 7:15; cf. Mt. 15:11).

Later, Jesus explained the saying to his disciples.

> Don't you see that nothing that enters a man from the outside can make him 'unclean'? For it doesn't go into his heart but into his stomach, and then out of his body ... What comes out of a man is what makes him 'unclean'. For from within, out of men's hearts, come evil thoughts, sexual immorality, theft, murder, adultery, greed, malice, deceit, lewdness, envy, slander, arrogance, and folly. All these evils come from inside and make a man 'unclean' (Mk. 7:18–23; cf. Mt. 15:17–20).

Mark adds the brief, but significant, observation: 'In saying this, Jesus declared all foods "clean" ' (7:19).

The topic of clean and unclean foods also arises in the account of Peter's visit to Cornelius, a God-fearing Gentile (Acts 10:1–11:18). This is an important incident within the book of Acts because it marks the first occasion on which the gospel was proclaimed to Gentiles. Prior to being asked to visit Cornelius, Peter was commanded by God in a vision to kill and eat animals that were unclean. Although Peter objected strongly, God warned him not to 'call anything impure that God has made clean' (Acts 10:15). Later, when he visited Cornelius Peter commented on the significance of the vision: 'You are well aware that it is against our law for a Jew to associate with a Gentile or visit him. But God has shown me that I should not call any man impure or unclean' (Acts 10:28).

Whereas God had previously introduced the concept of clean and unclean foods in order to separate the Israelites from other nations, the distinction between clean and unclean foods was abandoned in the NT period in order to show that God no longer distinguished between 'clean' Jews and 'unclean' Gentiles. With the death, resurrection and ascension of Jesus Christ, the Gentiles were now recipients of God's grace and mercy. In the light of this, it was only natural that the divinely instituted regulations concerning clean and unclean foods should be abandoned; they no longer served any meaningful purpose. So significant was Peter's vision in shaping the outlook of the early church that it is recorded twice in Acts (10:9–16; 11:5–17). Later, at the Council of Jerusalem, Peter defended his action in taking the gospel to the Gentiles by commenting that God no longer made a distinction between Jews and Gentiles (Acts 15:7–9).

Although the early church abandoned the distinction between clean and unclean foods on theological grounds, it is interesting to observe that they still insisted that Gentiles should adhere to the principle of not eating blood. This is seen in the conclusion reached by the Council of Jerusalem, which was called to clarify the position of Gentiles regarding circumcision and the law of Moses. James summarised the Council of Jerusalem's findings by noting that Gentile believers should be instructed 'to abstain from food polluted by idols, from sexual immorality, from the meat of strangled animals and from blood' (Acts 15:20; cf. 15:29). Whereas the OT regulations concerning clean/unclean foods were no longer relevant under the new covenant established by Jesus Christ, the theological basis for the OT prohibition against the eating of blood remained unchanged as a result of the new covenant. Thus, there was good reason for insisting that both Jewish and Gentile believers should adhere to it.

Remarkably, although the early church insisted on maintaining the OT regulation concerning the eating of the blood of animals, several NT passages contain startling statements about eating the blood of Christ. The most striking of these is John 6:53–56:

> Jesus said to them, 'I tell you the truth, unless you can eat the flesh of the Son of Man and drink his blood, you have no life in you. Whoever eats my flesh and drinks my blood has eternal life, and I will raise him up at the last day. For my flesh is real food and my blood is real drink. Whoever eats my flesh and drinks my blood remains in me, and I in him.'

These comments, which highlight a special relationship between Jesus and those who eat his flesh and drink his blood, are clearly related to the celebration of the Lord's Supper or Eucharist. In commemorating the new covenant believers are to eat bread and wine, representing the body and blood of Jesus Christ (Mt. 26:27–28; Mk. 14:23–24). By doing so, they acknowledge their association with Jesus and participate in the benefits derived from his death (1 Cor. 10:16–21; 11:23–26). At the very heart of the meal instituted by Jesus Christ is communion with God.

19

Towards the Promised Land

19.1. Summary

Although the Israelites' encounter with the LORD at Sinai lies at the heart of the Pentateuch, Sinai is not their final destination. Consequently, the initial chapters of Numbers focus on the preparations carried out by the people prior to leaving Sinai for the land of Canaan. These preparations show that the Israelites will be required to defeat militarily the nations that already occupy the land. However, the middle chapters of Numbers reveal, as we shall examine in more detail in the next chapter, that the people's trust in God wavered in the face of opposition and as a result they failed to take possession of what God had promised them. Of all those who left Egypt as adults only Joshua and Caleb would enter the promised land. Nevertheless, in spite of this initial failure, the final chapters of Numbers reveal that the promise of land was renewed with the next generation of adults. God's promise to Abraham would not be thwarted by human disobedience.

19.2. Introduction

Whereas the book of Leviticus is dominated by divine speeches outlining regulations and laws for the people of Israel, with few descriptions of events, the reverse occurs in Numbers. Most of the book records events that took place in the forty-year period beginning shortly after the making of the covenant at Sinai and ending with the Israelites camped on the plains of Moab ready to enter the land of Canaan. Interspersed among these narrative passages are a number of sections which record further regulations and laws (e.g. Num. 5–6; 15; 18–19; 28–30).

Although the book of Numbers spans a forty-year period, the coverage is uneven: Numbers 1–10 record events which fall within a two month period; Numbers 11–24 focus on selected experiences scattered throughout the next forty years; Numbers 25–36 concentrate on developments which take place in the fortieth year. Whereas the opening and closing chapters are generally favourable in their portrayal of the Israelites, the middle section consists of a series of incidents which highlights the failure of the people to trust and obey the LORD. These observations suggest that the book falls into three major parts and several other features further support this.

1. The first and third sections begin with censuses of all those men who were twenty years old or more (1:1–54; 26:1–65). The account of the second census specifically mentions that of all those included in the first census only Caleb and Joshua remained alive (26:64–65). This second census marks a new stage in the narrative and highlights an important difference between the second and third sections of the book: whereas Numbers 11–25 record various events which describe the death of large numbers of Israelites, Numbers 26–36 mention no deaths; even during a battle with the Midianites no Israelite soldier was killed (31:49).

2. All of the material in Numbers 27–36 relates directly in one way or another to the occupation of the land of Canaan. This is highlighted by the fact that the final section of Numbers is framed by two episodes which focus on problems concerning the inheritance of land by the daughters of Zelophehad (27:1–11; 36:1–13).

In this chapter we shall concentrate on the first and last sections of Numbers. The middle section of the book shall be considered in the next chapter.

19.3. Preparations for the Journey

The events recorded in the initial chapters of Numbers all took place close to Mount Sinai. Although the material in these chapters appears somewhat diverse a common theme ties much of it together: Numbers 1–10 describe how the Israelites prepared to leave Sinai to occupy the land of Canaan.[1] The following features of these preparations are noteworthy.

First, the Israelites were to prepare for war against the inhabitants of Canaan. This is highlighted in the very first chapter of the book which records a census of the people that took place 'on the first day of the second month of the second year after the Israelites came out of Egypt' (1:1). The census was intended to number 'all the men of Israel twenty years old or more who are able to serve in the army' (1:3; cf. 1:45). This emphasises an idea,

---

[1] It should be noted in passing that the material in Numbers 1–10 is not in strict chronological order.

alluded to elsewhere (cf. Ex. 13:18), that the Israelites were expected to fight for the land which God had promised them. The Levites, however, were excluded from this census due to their special association with the tabernacle. Because of their responsibility for its care and transportation, the Levites were not to be involved directly in any killing that might occur during the taking of the land.[2]

Secondly, linked to the preparations for conflict was the requirement that those living in the camp should be pure. Anything that might defile the camp was a potential danger to the success of the Israelites' occupation of the land of Canaan. Thus, anyone, whether male or female, who was unclean, as a result of a skin disease, a bodily discharge or contact with the dead, was to be sent outside the camp (5:1–4). For the same reason, instructions regarding restitution for wrongs (5:5–10) and suspected adultery (5:11–31) are included here. Nothing was to be allowed to defile the camp.[3]

Thirdly, instructions are given regarding the layout of the camp (2:1–34). While these specify the location of the tribes around the tabernacle or Tent of Meeting in terms of north, south, east and west,[4] they also indicate the order in which the tribes were to set out when they journeyed from one location to another (cf. 2:9, 16, 24, 31). The travel aspect of these arrangements is especially emphasised in the comments regarding the tabernacle and the tribe of Levi (2:17).

Fourthly, apart from specifying the arrangement of the tribes when they journeyed, various other practical details are mentioned. In outlining the duties of the Levitical clans, special attention is drawn to the transportation of the tabernacle and its furnishings (4:5, 10, 12, 15, 19, 24, 25, 27, 31, 32). The account of the census of all the Levites ends by noting that 'At the LORD's command through Moses, each was assigned his work and told what to carry' (4:49). Subsequently, it is noted that the tribal leaders presented to the LORD 'six covered carts and twelve oxen' (7:3) which were handed over by Moses to the Levites in order to assist them with the transportation of some of the tabernacle furnishings. However, the holiest items of the tabernacle were to be carried on human shoulders rather than transported by animals (7:9). It is also noted that the LORD commanded Moses to make two silver trumpets that were to be used, among other things, 'for calling the community together and for having the camps set out' (10:2; cf. 10:5–6).

---

[2] A further reference to battle comes in 10:9 concerning the sounding of silver trumpets by the priests.

[3] Uncleanness also figures in Numbers 9 regarding the celebration of the Passover in the second month. For a fuller discussion of the topic of cleanness/uncleanness, see chapter 16.

[4] The east side of the tabernacle was viewed as the most important due to the fact that the entrance to the Tent of Meeting was located there.

Fifthly, the concept of travel is prominent in remarks about the cloud which covered the tabernacle in 9:15–23. This passage explains, even before the Israelites leave Sinai, how God will lead them during the journey from Sinai to Canaan. Attention is repeatedly drawn to the way in which the movement of the cloud determined whether the Israelite camp moved or remained where it was.

19.4. The Role of the Levites

Apart from highlighting the preparations necessary for the Israelites' journey to Canaan, the early chapters of Numbers also give prominence to the setting apart of the Levites. This is evident in a number of ways. At the outset the tribe of Levi is excluded from the census, the reason being that they were appointed to be in charge of the tabernacle and its furnishings (1:47–53; cf. 2:33). Moses is subsequently instructed by God to present the Levites to Aaron the high priest as special assistants (3:6–9). There follows immediately a lengthy passage which associates the setting apart of the Levites with the sparing of the Israelite first-born in Egypt (3:11–51; cf. Ex. 13:1–16). This passage also notes how God assigned different responsibilities regarding the tabernacle and its furnishings to the main Levite clans. More detailed instructions, which relate primarily to the transportation of the tabernacle by the three main branches of the Levites, are given to Moses in 4:1–49. Later, the LORD instructs Moses regarding the process by which the Levites were to be set apart (8:5–19). These instructions underline that the Levites were to purify themselves in order to 'do the work at the Tent of Meeting on behalf of the Israelites and to make atonement for them so that no plague will strike the Israelites when they go near the sanctuary' (8:19).[5] The actual setting apart of the Levites is recorded briefly in 8:20–22. This is followed by further instructions regarding the age of Levitical service at the tabernacle (8:23–26). In a variety of ways the opening chapters of Numbers highlight the special role of the Levites.

The setting apart of the Levites resembles in some respects the appointment of Aaron and his sons as priests (cf. Ex. 29:1–46; Lev. 8:1–36). However, it is clear that the Levites were not granted the same holy status as the priests. Although, like the priests, they served within the tabernacle, they were not permitted to touch directly the holiest of the tabernacle furnishings or to perform the duties assigned to the priests regarding the offering of sacrifices.

This distinction between the priests and the Levites is significant. Prior to the book of Numbers there are few references to the Levites. Their loyalty to

---

[5] In the light of this, the rebellious actions of Korah, a Levite, take on added significance.

God is noted in Exodus 32:26–28 and, apart from a brief mention in Exodus 38:21, there is only one other minor reference to them (Lev. 25:32–33). In the light of this, the detailed attention given to them in the early chapters of Numbers is striking. Their prominence at this stage is probably tied to later developments within the book. As we shall observe in more detail in the next chapter, the account of the rebellion of Korah in 16:1–50 centres on the relationship between the priests and the Levites. As a leading Levite, Korah is found guilty and punished for trying to usurp the position of the divinely appointed priests.

Closely associated with the appointment of the Levites are the instructions in 6:1–21 for the setting apart of ordinary Israelites as Nazirites. The inclusion of this material in the early chapters of Numbers reveals that the taking of a special holy status was freely available to all Israelites. Although non-Levites were prohibited from serving in the tabernacle, they were not excluded from adopting a special degree of holiness.

19.5. Further Preparations to Enter the Land of Canaan

The final part of the book of Numbers (26:1–36:13), like the first, begins with a census of 'all those twenty years old or more who are able to serve in the army of Israel' (26:2; cf. 1:3). The significance of this second census lies in the fact that of all those included in the previous census, forty years earlier, only Caleb and Joshua remained alive (26:64–65; cf. 32:11–12). This fact is clearly linked to the earlier account of the rebellion of the Israelite spies following their reconnaissance of the land (13:1–14:45) and the LORD's prediction that 'not one of you will enter the land I swore with uplifted hand to make your home, except Caleb son of Jephunneh and Joshua son of Nun' (14:30). Even Moses, as recorded later in Deuteronomy 34:1–8, died outside the promised land due to his failure to honour God in the sight of the Israelites at the waters of Meribah (Num. 20:9–12; cf. 27:13–14).

Whereas Numbers 11–25 catalogue a series of events that result in the death of the entire adult generation which was delivered from Egypt, Numbers 26–36 record no comparable events; no deaths are mentioned in the final section of the book. Even when the narrative recounts a major battle against the Midianites (31:1–24), it is specifically noted that not one soldier failed to return alive from the conflict (31:49). This contrast between the second and third sections of the book is particularly striking and highlights the fact that the death of the exodus generation was due to their failure to trust God. As we shall observe in the next chapter, the middle section of Numbers highlights various occasions on which large numbers of Israelites perished as a result of disobeying God.

All of the material coming after the census in Numbers 26 focuses in one way or another on the future occupation of the land of Canaan. With the death of all those who failed to enter the promised land on the first occasion, the narrative now focuses on the preparations for the second generation to possess Canaan. These preparations are framed by two accounts that involve the daughters of Zelophehad (27:1–11; 36:1–12). Significantly, both episodes address the topic of land inheritance. In the first instance, Zelophehad's daughters are guaranteed that they shall have 'property as an inheritance among their father's relatives' (27:7). On the second occasion they are required to marry within their own tribe in order that their inheritance should not pass to another tribe. In both episodes questions concerning inheritance are resolved before the Israelites enter the promised land.

Of the other episodes in the final section of Numbers, the land of Canaan figures prominently in Numbers 32 and 34–35. The first of these chapters focuses on the request of the tribes of Reuben and Gad to settle on the east side of the Jordan in the 'lands of Jazer and Gilead' (32:1). Their wish is only granted when it is made clear that they are prepared to assist the other tribes in obtaining their inheritance on the west side of the Jordan. Moses is deeply concerned that the desire of the tribes of Reuben and Gad to stay on the east side of the Jordan does not arise from wrong motives; they are not to follow the rebellious example of their fathers who refused to enter the promised land. Towards its conclusion Numbers 32 also notes that 'the descendants of Makir son of Manasseh went to Gilead, captured it and drove out the Amorites who were there' (32:39). As a result, half of the tribe of Manasseh was permitted to settle on the eastern side of the Jordan.

Numbers 34 falls into two parts, each focusing on the land of Canaan. The first half delineates the boundaries of the land to be possessed by the Israelites. The rest of the chapter lists the names of the leaders appointed from each tribe to assist Eleazar the priest and Joshua in assigning the land between the nine and a half tribes (34:17). Because of their separation from the other tribes to serve in the tabernacle, the Levites are not allocated a specific region of the land of Canaan. Rather, they are given forty-eight towns, each with some pastureland surrounding it, distributed throughout the twelve tribal regions. Six of these towns are designated 'cities of refuge, to which a person who has killed someone may flee' (35:6). Further details are added to explain how these cities should function as places of refuge for those who unintentionally kill another person (35:9–28). Interestingly, the chapter concludes by high-lighting yet again the theme of land: the Israelites must not defile the land because the LORD will be dwelling in their midst (35:34).

19.6. Conclusion

The opening and final sections of the book of Numbers are clearly linked to the overall development of the narrative plot in the Pentateuch. Whereas Numbers 1–10 describe the final preparations of the people before they leave Sinai to enter the promised land, Numbers 25–36 anticipate the next major development in the narrative, the possession of the land. However, as we shall observe in detail in the next chapter, Numbers 11–24 record a series of events which result in the death of the generation which left Egypt to go to the promised land. It is an entirely new generation of adults that prepares to occupy the land of Canaan.

19.7. New Testament Connections

Most of the main links with the New Testament will be considered at the end of the next chapter when we consider the central section of Numbers. As regards the theme of land, we have already discussed the relevant NT material in chapter 10.

20

Murmurings

20.1. Summary

Whereas the opening and concluding chapters of Numbers describe the preparations that the Israelites made before entering the promised land, the middle chapters provide a contrasting picture. Here various incidents portray the true nature of the exodus generation of adult Israelites. In spite of all that they had witnessed in Egypt and at Sinai, they display a remarkable lack of faith in the LORD's ability (a) to provide for their daily needs, and (b) to ensure their safety in the land of Canaan. Their complaints against the LORD form a recurring pattern in these chapters. Furthermore, there are frequent challenges to the hierarchical structures which God has introduced for the well-being of all the people. As a consequence of their rebellious actions the entire adult generation, with the exception of Caleb and Joshua, is consigned to remain in the wilderness for forty years until they all die.

20.2. Introduction

After highlighting certain preparations for the next stage of the journey from Egypt to Canaan, the early chapters of Numbers reach a climax in 10:11 with the departure of the Israelites from Sinai. The narrative now focuses on their future progress. At the outset a very positive picture is presented with the tribes setting out just as the LORD had commanded them (10:11–28). To underline this the narrator includes material which displays Moses' optimism as regards the future. When Hobab, his brother-in-law, talks of returning to his own land and people, Moses responds by commenting: 'If you come with us, we will share with you whatever good things the LORD gives us' (10:32). A similar confidence underlies Moses' words each time the ark sets out and comes to rest. 'Rise up, O LORD! May your enemies be scattered; may your foes flee before you' (10:35). 'Return, O LORD, to the countless thousands of Israel' (10:36). In these ways the second half of

Numbers 10 conveys a sense of confidence that the LORD will successfully bring the Israelites into the promised land of Canaan.

Against this brief, optimistic introduction the events of Numbers 11–25 contrast markedly. God's anger turns against the Israelites, eventually resulting in the death of the entire generation of those adults who left Egypt. As we shall explore in more detail below, a number of themes are prominent. We frequently encounter the people complaining about the conditions under which they must now live during their journey to the promised land. These complaints reflect a deep-seated failure to trust the LORD. A second related theme is that of rebellion against those exercising authority. Associated with both of these are two other motifs: the divine punishment of those at fault and the role of Moses and the Aaronic priests as mediators on behalf of the people. Also various episodes in Numbers parallel closely Exodus 15:22–17:17 where the theme of 'testing' is prominent.

20.3. Murmurings Against the LORD

As soon as the journey from Sinai to Canaan begins we encounter the first of a number of incidents in which the Israelites express their dissatisfaction with the LORD (11:1–3). While this brief account does not specify the reason for the people's unrest, it sets the tone for much that follows in Numbers 11–25. Various elements in this episode will reappear later:

(a) God's anger is roused against the people because of their complaints (11:1; cf. 11:10, 33; 12:9; 21:5).
(b) As a result they are divinely punished (11:1; cf. 11:33; 12:10; 21:6).
(c) Moses prays to the LORD on behalf of the people (11:2; cf. 12:13; 14:13–19; 21:7).
(d) The punishment is limited (11:2; cf. 12:13; 21:8–9).
(e) A particular name, reflecting some aspect of what has occurred, is given to the location of the event. On this occasion the place is called Taberah, which means 'burning', on account of the punishment by fire that comes upon the people (11:3; cf. 11:34; 20:13).

The incident at Taberah is immediately followed by another which is recorded in much more detail (11:4–34). As is often the case, the reason for the people's dissatisfaction with God is linked to their craving for food. In spite of the fact that the LORD has provided them with manna, the Israelites yearn to return to Egypt. The narrative conveys well this sense of longing: 'If only we had meat to eat! We remember the fish we ate in Egypt at no cost – also the cucumbers, melons, leeks, onions and garlic' (11:4–5). Their complaint is full of irony.

They forget, on the one hand, the terrible conditions under which they had laboured as slaves in Egypt, and, on the other hand, the fact that they are journeying towards a land 'flowing with milk and honey'. The former reflects their lack of gratitude for all that God has done for them in the past, and the latter displays their lack of faith regarding all that God will do for them in the future. Not surprisingly, the LORD interprets their complaint as a personal rejection of him (11:20). Although the LORD provides quails in abundance, he sends at the same time a severe plague, killing some of the people. Thereafter the place is called Kibroth Hattaavah (Graves of Craving; 11:34).[1]

The next occasion on which the people murmur against the LORD occurs following the return of the twelve spies from the land of Canaan. Sent to discover the nature of the promised land, the spies report back that the land 'does flow with milk and honey' (13:27). As evidence of this they display before the people a single cluster of grapes which two men are required to carry. However, they also describe the inhabitants of the land as powerful, living in large, fortified cities (13:28). While Caleb, and later Joshua, speaks up in favour of entering the land (13:30; cf. 14:6–9), the rest of the spies discourage the people from doing so. As a result, the Israelites grumble against Moses and Aaron, indicating their desire to return to Egypt (14:1–4). Joshua and Caleb outline the implications of this: not only will the people miss out on the opportunity to possess a land that is 'exceedingly good', but they are also rebelling against the LORD (14:7–9). This is confirmed by the LORD's comments to Moses: 'How long will these people treat me with contempt? How long will they refuse to believe in me, in spite of all the miraculous signs I have performed among them?' (14:11). In the light of this, the LORD states that he will destroy the Israelites with a plague and create a new nation through Moses. Moses, however, argues against the destruction of the people on the grounds that it will cause other nations to doubt the LORD's ability to bring his own people into the promised land.[2] While the LORD relents from wiping out the entire nation, he makes it abundantly clear that not one of the adults who witnessed his glory and miraculous power, both in Egypt and in the desert, will enter the promised land; the only exceptions will be Joshua and Caleb.

---

[1] The dissatisfaction of the people at Kibroth Hattaavah provides the setting and also frames the account of God appointing seventy of Israel's elders to assist Moses in the task of leading the people.

[2] One sees here various echoes of the golden calf incident at Sinai when God made a similar suggestion to make a new nation (Ex. 32:9–10). On this latter occasion Moses intercedes for the people by quoting the LORD's earlier comment about being 'slow to anger, abounding in love and forgiving sin and rebellion' (14:18). Interestingly, this statement was first made in the context of the people's rebellion at Sinai (Ex. 34:6–7).

Consequently, on account of the unfaithfulness of their parents, the children are subjected to forty years in the desert – one year for each of the forty days which the spies spent in the land.

As regards the story of the spies two further points are noteworthy. First, the spies who speak out against entering the land are punished immediately; a plague strikes them dead (14:36–38). Secondly, the people belatedly attempt to enter the land of Canaan. This, however, is viewed as a further act of disobedience, the LORD having just stated that they shall remain in the desert for forty years. Consequently, the Amalekites and Canaanites defeat them (14:39–45).

A further report of the people grumbling against Moses and Aaron comes in Numbers 16 in response to the divine execution of Korah and his followers. This time criticism is levelled at Moses and Aaron because they have 'killed the LORD's people' (16:41). This remark is a further indication of the distorted outlook of the people. Even in the dramatic and terrible death of Korah and his followers they fail to recognise the hand of God. Once more the LORD threatens to kill the whole assembly. Before Aaron, at Moses' command, can atone for them, 14,700 are struck dead by a plague.

Another incident involving grumbling is recorded in 20:1–13. On this occasion a lack of water prompts the people's complaint. Apart from wishing to return to Egypt, the Israelites state that it would have been better for them, like their brothers, to be struck dead by God (20:3). Once again the narrative highlights the rebellious nature of their comments (cf. 20:10). This time, however, the actions of Moses and Aaron come in for severest criticism by the LORD. By striking the rock twice and saying, 'Must we bring you water out of this rock?' Moses and Aaron dishonour God (20:10). As a result, the LORD announces that they shall not enter the promised land (20:12).[3]

Numbers records one further occasion when the people speak against God and Moses: 'Why have you brought us up out of Egypt to die in the desert! There is no bread! There is no water! And we detest this miserable food!' (21:5) Yet again their criticisms focus on food and water. When the LORD sends venomous snakes to attack the people, they soon acknowledge their sin and seek help from Moses. Remarkably, this is the first occasion when the people themselves acknowledge their sin. As a result, the LORD commands Moses to place a bronze snake on the top of a pole. When those bitten by the venomous snakes look to this bronze snake they do not die.

All of the episodes considered so far are linked by the common motif of the people's lack of trust in the LORD. Interestingly, their complaints about

---

[3] Although the narrative does not make it explicitly clear, it seems likely that this episode occurred in the fortieth year (compare 20:1 with 33:36–38). If so, this incident reveals that the next generation of adult Israelites is in danger of copying the rebellious behaviour of their parents.

food and water echo earlier incidents in Exodus 15:22–17:12. In the light of this, it is no surprise that Numbers 14:22 picks up the idea that through their disobedience the Israelites tested God. Although the concept of testing is only mentioned once in Numbers, it is clear from the material in Exodus that, whereas God intended the desert experience to test the faith and obedience of the Israelites (cf. Ex. 15:25–26; 16:4; cf. 19:20), it was they who tested God (Ex. 17:2, 7; Num. 14:22). Furthermore, Exodus 15:26 emphasises that if the people obey him, God will not bring upon them any of the diseases which came upon the Egyptians. In the light of this, it is interesting to observe the frequent references to plagues in Numbers 11–25.[4] Ironically, by longing to be back in Egypt, the Israelites bring upon themselves the same suffering that earlier afflicted the Egyptians.

20.4. Challenges Against Those in Authority

Interspersed between the episodes about the murmurings of the Israelites are others that focus on various challenges to those appointed by God to positions of authority. Remarkably, the first such challenge comes from the least likely source. Miriam and Aaron, Moses' own sister and brother, contest the uniqueness of his claim to speak on the LORD's behalf (12:1–2). No doubt their challenge was prompted by the authority which they already had, Aaron as the high priest and Miriam as a prophetess (Ex. 15:20). The LORD, however, soon responds and confirms Moses' special status: whereas the LORD speaks to prophets in visions and dreams, he speaks to Moses 'face to face, clearly and not in riddles' (12:8). Consequently, the LORD's anger burns against Aaron and Miriam with the result that Miriam is afflicted with a skin disease. Although her punishment is reduced due to the intercession of Moses, she is still required to remain outside the Israelite camp for seven days (12:15).

The sinful nature of the challenge by Miriam and Aaron is highlighted by the comment, 'Moses was a very humble man, more humble than anyone else on the face of the earth' (12:3). This clearly indicates that Moses himself did not emphasise unduly his own importance. In the light of Moses' attitude towards his own position, the challenge of Miriam and Aaron is all the more serious. Furthermore, because Moses did not relish the idea of having absolute authority over the nation, he involved seventy of the elders in the task of leading the people (11:24–30).

The next challenge to authority comes in Numbers 16 and centres on an attempt by Korah and certain Reubenites – Dathan and Abiram – to usurp

---

[4] Note how the different terms used for the plagues in Egypt are also used in Numbers.

the unique position of Moses and Aaron. Once again the challenge comes from those who already enjoy a special standing within the nation; Korah as a Levite has been previously set apart to assist in the work of the tabernacle; his supporters are described as 'well-known community leaders who had been appointed members of the council' (16:2). Their challenge is against the hierarchical structure introduced by God whereby Aaron and his sons, as priests, had a holier status than that of the Levites and other Israelites (cf. 8:5–26). In the light of the early chapters of Numbers there can be little doubt that Korah's actions run counter to God's instructions for the people.[5] Furthermore, Korah's sin is all the greater because he himself enjoyed a more privileged status than that of the majority of Israelites. While he should have been grateful for the opportunity to serve in the tabernacle, he uses this as a springboard to aspire to priestly status (see the comments of Moses in 16:8–11). As the basis for his challenge to Moses and Aaron, Korah claims that 'the whole community is holy, every one of them, and the LORD is with them' (16:3). Implicit in this is the idea that there is no reason for Moses and Aaron to restrict others from approaching the LORD.[6] The attitude of Dathan and Abiram to Moses is highlighted in 16:12–14. As far as they are concerned, Egypt, not Canaan, is the 'land flowing with milk and honey' (16:13). Not only has Moses led them away from all that is best materially, but he has failed to provide them with anything better; his motive throughout has been to lord it over the people and kill them in the desert. The response of God to both these challenges is dramatic. The families of Korah, Dathan and Abiram are swallowed up into the earth (16:31–34), and a further group of 250 supporters are consumed by fire (16:35). In passing it should also be noted that once again Moses is portrayed as interceding on behalf of the whole community (16:20–22).

In the light of Korah's challenge to the authority of Aaron, Numbers 17–19 take on a special significance. In the first of these Moses demonstrates the unique standing of the tribe of Levi by having twelve staffs, one for each ancestral tribe, placed in the Tent of Meeting.[7] When these are removed on the next day the staff of Aaron has 'budded, blossomed and produced almonds' (17:8), indicating the unique, and life-giving, status of the tribe of Aaron. Moses then commands that the staff be kept as a sign to 'the rebellious' that they should not 'grumble' against the LORD (17:10). To emphasise further the uniqueness of Aaron's position as high priest Numbers 18 records

---

[5] On the role of the Levites, see chapter 19.

[6] In believing that all of the Israelites are holy and can draw near to the LORD, Korah failed to appreciate one of the distinctive roles given to the Levites; they were to act as a barrier between the LORD and the other tribes (1:53; cf. 8:19).

[7] The Hebrew word for 'staff' can also mean 'branch' or 'tribe'.

divine instructions regarding the relationship between the priests and Levites. Here it is noted that the Levites are a 'gift' to Aaron 'to do the work of the Tent of Meeting' (18:6). Furthermore, the 'service of the priesthood' is also a divine gift (18:7). Since the priests and the Levites are divinely appointed to fulfil specific roles, it is wrong for others to usurp their positions. Numbers 19 also alludes back to the rebellion of Korah by focusing on the ritual involving the water of cleansing. First, it highlights the special mediatorial role of the divinely appointed priests. Second, it emphasises that anyone who sins becomes unclean and of necessity must undergo a process of purification. Korah's claim in 16:3 that the whole community is holy was clearly presumptuous.

Alongside these challenges to those in authority, we might also include the reaction of Moses and Aaron to the people's demand for water in 20:2–13. In their impatience with the people they claim responsibility for the miraculous appearance of the water, thus failing to acknowledge the LORD as the one who provided it from the rock.

20.5. Religious Apostasy

The long line of episodes in which the exodus generation of Israelites exhibit their lack of trust in the LORD comes to a conclusion in Numbers 25. On this occasion they are guilty of both religious apostasy, worshipping the Baal of Peor, and sexual immorality, having relationships with Moabite women. Once more the LORD's anger burns against the people with the result that 24,000 of them are killed by a plague. Three factors stand out in the story as significant:

(a) After the LORD's condemnation of their activity, the Israelites display a spirit of repentance, 'weeping at the entrance to the Tent of Meeting' (25:6).
(b) Phinehas, the grandson of Aaron, is commended for his willingness to kill a fellow Israelite who blatantly ignores the LORD's condemnation of idolatrous and immoral behaviour. The execution of the guilty party is presented as an act of atonement, with the result that the plague against the Israelites stops. Afterwards Phinehas is rewarded through being divinely granted 'a covenant of a lasting priesthood, because he was zealous for the honour of his God and made atonement for the Israelites' (25:13).
(c) As confirmed by the census of Numbers 26 (cf. 26:63–65), this incident marks the death of the last of the Israelites who left Egypt as adults. The forty-year period in the desert is almost complete.

20.6. Destination – the Promised Land

In spite of the people's rebellion and the death of the entire exodus generation of adult Israelites, the central chapters of Numbers contain clear indications that the occupation of the land of Canaan is still a priority in God's dealings with the Israelites. This is reflected in the following ways. First, instructions given by the LORD in Numbers 15 begin with the words, 'After you enter the land I am giving you as a home ...' (15:2). This introduction is significant in that it follows immediately the account of the people's failure to enter the land of Canaan. Furthermore, the instructions in Numbers 15 presuppose a situation in which the people are able to grow crops of grain and grapes. Secondly, Numbers 21 records the defeats of the Canaanite king of Arad (21:1–3), Sihon king of the Amorites (21:21–31) and Og king of Bashan (21:33–35). These victories contrast with the defeat recorded earlier in 14:44–45[8] and the backing away from battle with the Edomites in 20:14–21, and indicate a first step towards the possession of the promised land (cf. 31:1–24). Thirdly, the lengthy account of the activities of Balaam son of Beor in Numbers 22–24 reveals God's desire to bless rather than curse Israel. Although Balaam is hired by Balak king of Moab to curse the Israelites, he blesses them on four separate occasions (23:7–10; 23:18–24; 24:3–9; 24:15–19; cf. 22:12). In doing so he echoes briefly the promises made earlier to the patriarchs in Genesis: 'Who can count the dust of Jacob' (23:10; cf. Gen. 13:16; 15:5); 'The LORD their God is with them' (23:21; cf. Gen. 17:8); 'May those who bless you be blessed and those who curse you be cursed' (24:9; cf. 23:8, 20; Gen. 12:3); 'A star will come out of Jacob; a sceptre will rise out of Israel' (24:17; cf. Gen. 17:6, 16; 49:10).[9] In the light of these factors, it is apparent that, in spite of the death of the exodus generation, God still intends to bring his people into the promised land. This is further emphasised by the fact that almost all of the material in Numbers 26–36, as noted in the previous chapter, anticipates in various ways the possession of the land.

20.7. Conclusion

The central chapters of Numbers provide a very negative portrait of the Israelites. This is highlighted in a number of ways. In spite of their remarkable deliverance from slavery in Egypt, they are unwilling to enter the promised

---

[8] Note the mention of Hormah in 14:45 and 21:3.

[9] Although the Balaam story shows signs of being a once independent unit, it picks up a number of important themes found in Genesis. As it stands it has been carefully integrated into the Pentateuch as a whole.

land. Contemptuous of all that God has already done for them, they constantly complain and desire to return to Egypt. Furthermore, they challenge those whom God has placed in authority over them, and fail to see in the divine punishment of others, God's power at work, believing that those struck dead are the LORD's people. Finally, they commit idolatry, the ultimate rejection of and rebellion against the LORD. In the light of all these short-comings it is hardly surprising that the entire adult generation of those who came out of Egypt die in the desert, outside the promised land.

Whereas the exodus generation of Israelites shows no sign of learning from its experience in the desert, their children, while initially revealing similar characteristics of unbelief and rebellion, demonstrate a greater capacity to trust the LORD. They, at least, willingly acknowledge their own sin (21:7; 25:6). For this reason, the book of Numbers portrays them as making progress towards inheriting the land promised to the patriarchs.

20.8. New Testament Connections

The account of the Israelites' time in the wilderness is picked up in a number of ways in the NT. One of the most striking uses comes in the account of the temptation of Jesus (Mt. 4:1–11; Lk. 4:1–13). Indeed, it is impossible to understand fully the story of Jesus' temptation without appreciating how he is contrasted with the Israelites who came out of Egypt. Whereas the ancient Israelites were tested in the wilderness and failed, Jesus, as the new Israel, succeeds. This theme is reflected in all three temptations. In the first, Jesus, hungry after having fasted for forty days, is asked to turn stones into bread. Had he, however, like the ancient Israelites, given priority to his own physical appetite, he would have implied dissatisfaction with God's provision for him. The second temptation, following Matthew's order, focuses on God's ability to save. Here Jesus is challenged to follow the example of the earlier Israelites and test, rather than trust, God's might to protect him. The third temptation focuses on God's capacity to give to Jesus those kingdoms that are under the control of another. Whereas the Israelites had doubted God's strength to give them the land of Canaan, Jesus expresses complete confidence in God. Thus, in various ways Jesus' faith in God contrasts sharply with that of the Israelites who came out of Egypt.

Several passages in John's Gospel refer directly to the OT account of the Israelites' sojourn in the wilderness. In his conversation with Nicodemus, Jesus mentions briefly the incident of the bronze snake in Numbers 21:4–9: 'Just as Moses lifted up the snake in the desert, so the Son of Man must be lifted up, that everyone who believes in him may have eternal life' (Jn. 3:14–15).

Here Jesus draws an important parallel between himself and the bronze snake. While the ancient Israelites received life by trusting in the bronze snake, those who trust in Jesus will receive eternal life.

Later in John's Gospel, in a discussion that takes place shortly after the feeding of the five thousand, Jesus compares himself to the manna provided in the wilderness (Jn. 6:25–59). Like the manna, he has been sent from heaven to give life to those who feed upon him (6:33, 35–40, 50–51, 54–58). However, the life which Jesus offers, in contrast to that given by the manna, is eternal (6:47–51, 58). Interestingly, John observes that many of the Jews responded to Jesus' words by grumbling (6:41, 43). Like their unbelieving ancestors, they failed to appreciate what had happened in their midst. For them the miraculous feeding of the five thousand, which should have been a sign of Jesus' divine origin, conveyed nothing of significance.[10]

The experience of the Israelites in the wilderness is also used by Paul to warn the Corinthian Christians against pursuing various unrighteous practices. He writes,

> Now these things occurred as examples to keep us from setting our hearts on evil things as they did. Do not be idolaters, as some of them were; as it is written: 'The people sat down to eat and drink and got up to indulge in pagan revelry.' We should not commit sexual immorality, as some of them did – and in one day twenty-three thousand of them died. We should not test the Lord, as some of them did – and were killed by snakes. And do not grumble, as some of them did – and were killed by the destroying angel (1 Cor. 10:6–10).

Because Paul views the wilderness experience as a time of testing, he concludes by exhorting his readers to resist temptation.

> No temptation has seized you except what is common to man. And God is faithful; he will not let you be tempted beyond what you can bear. But when you are tempted, he will also provide a way out so that you can stand up under it (1 Cor. 10:13).

Here Paul shares an understanding of the Numbers material similar to that found in the Gospel account of Jesus' temptation.

Before leaving Paul's comments in 1 Corinthians 10, one other issue deserves mention. This concerns his comment that the ancient Israelites

---

[10] Apart from the very obvious parallels with Exodus already noted, it is interesting to observe that earlier in Numbers 6 brief reference is made to the 'Jewish Passover Feast' being near (v. 4) and the fact that Jesus tests Philip (v. 6). The latter is particularly noteworthy because it is absent from the Synoptic versions of the feeding of the five thousand.

'drank from the spiritual rock that accompanied them, and that rock was Christ' (1 Cor. 10:4). At first sight it seems remarkable that Paul should associate Jesus with an inanimate object. Two observations, however, are important. First, Paul seeks in 1 Corinthians 10 to draw a parallel between the wilderness experience of the Israelites and that of the Corinthian believers. He argues that because the ancient Israelites perished on account of eating food associated with idols, the Corinthian believers should not indulge in such activities. As part of this argument Paul compares the food and drink which the ancient Israelites received from God (1 Cor. 10:3–4) with the food and drink which the Corinthians eat at the Lord's supper (1 Cor. 10:16–17). To strengthen the parallels between the two situations Paul associates the food and drink of the wilderness with Christ; the source of the drink is a 'spiritual rock' and that rock is Christ. Secondly, in the OT God is sometimes entitled a Rock. In this regard, the Song of Moses in Deuteronomy 32 is significant, given that it is presented as having been composed at the end of the Israelites' period in the wilderness. On five separate occasions God is designated 'the Rock' (Deut. 32:4, 15, 18, 30, 31; cf. 32:37), making this one of the main divine titles in the entire song. Undoubtedly, Paul's reference to Christ is influenced by the designation of God as a Rock. Paul does not think of Christ as a physical rock; rather he is a 'spiritual rock'. By presenting Christ as the source of the drink which the ancient Israelites received, Paul, first, affirms Christ's divine status and oneness with the God of Israel, and, secondly, reinforces the parallel which he wishes to demonstrate between the situation of the Corinthians and the ancient Israelites.

The author of Hebrews also highlights the failure of the wilderness generation and uses this as a warning to his readers (Heb. 3:7–19). Quoting Psalm 95:7–11, which is one of a number of psalms to recount the Israelites' experience in the wilderness, he observes that they did not enter the promised land 'because of their unbelief' (Heb. 3:19; cf. 8:9).

21

Love and Loyalty

21.1. Summary

The book of Deuteronomy brings the Pentateuch to a significant climax. As the Israelites stand on the verge of entering the promised land, Moses outlines God's agenda for the future. This centres on the special covenant relationship which exists between the LORD and Israel. At the heart of this covenant is a commitment by both parties to love the other wholeheartedly and faithfully. For the Israelites this commitment will require them to be completely obedient to all of the obligations placed upon them by God. Obedience will ensure blessing in terms of material prosperity and national security; disobedience will have the opposite consequence, resulting in the expulsion of the Israelites from the promised land. As Moses invites the people to renew their covenant relationship with the LORD, he sets before them an important choice, a choice between 'life and death, blessings and curses' (30:19).

21.2. Introduction

The setting of the events described in Deuteronomy is introduced in the opening verses of the book. It is the end of the fortieth year since the Israelites left Egypt and the people are camped to the east of the river Jordan. At last they are on the brink of entering the land which God had promised to their ancestors, Abraham, Isaac and Jacob. Following the death of the first generation of adults who came out of Egypt, the next generation of Israelites is at a decisive point in its relationship with God. Will they, like their parents, fall at the hurdle before them, or will they through faith in the LORD cross the Jordan and possess the promised land?

Given the importance of the setting it is hardly surprising that Moses addressed the people at length. Having led their parents out of Egypt he reminds a new generation of adult Israelites of all that has happened in the preceding years and challenges them to affirm their personal commitment to the special covenant relationship with the LORD initiated at Mount Sinai. At the heart of Deuteronomy is the future of the relationship between Israel and her God.

Only in Deuteronomy does Moses address the people at length using his own words. Elsewhere he usually repeats what the LORD has told him. Here he speaks on his own behalf, persuading the Israelites to follow the LORD. As a result, Deuteronomy often reads like a sermon with frequent exhortations and much repetition. This gives the book a character not found elsewhere in the Pentateuch.

Moses' speeches take on added significance in that they were given shortly before his death, which is recounted in the final verses of the book (34:1–12). They are the final words of an elder statesman to his people, a father to his children, encouraging them to proceed in the right direction for the future.

Apart from brief comments by the book's narrator, the bulk of Deuteronomy consists of the words of Moses. Two main speeches dominate the book, the first coming in 1:6–4:40 and the second in 5:1–26:19. The former speech begins with a survey of Israel's relationship with the LORD since leaving Mount Sinai forty years earlier and concludes with exhortations to obey the LORD in the future. This provides a suitable introduction for the second speech which begins in 5:1 and continues unbroken until 26:19, constituting approximately two-thirds of the entire book of Deuteronomy. The narrator's introduction to this second speech (4:44–49) indicates that it forms the 'law' (Hebrew, *tôrâ*) that 'Moses set before the Israelites' (4:44). This understanding of the speech is confirmed by later comments which refer (a) to 'all the words of this law (*tôrâ*)' being inscribed on stones coated with plaster (27:2–8), and (b) to Moses 'writing in a book the words of this law (*tôrâ*) from beginning to end' (31:24). This 'Book of the Law' (*tôrâ*) was subsequently to be placed beside the ark of the covenant of the LORD (31:26). Instructions are also given by Moses to the priests and elders that they are to read this law (*tôrâ*) to the people every seventh year (31:9–13). We shall say more on the Book of the Law below.

The concluding chapters of Deuteronomy consist mainly of a number of shorter addresses, not all by Moses, introduced by brief narrative comments. The first of these speeches is comprised of instructions for the inscribing of the Book of the Law (*tôrâ*) on plaster-coated stones once the people have crossed the Jordan and entered the land of Canaan (27:1–8). The next speech, which also looks to the future occupation of the land, begins with instructions to the tribes of Israel for the pronouncement of blessings from Mount Gerizim and curses from Mount Ebal (27:11–13; cf. 11:26–32), followed by the recital of a list of curses by the Levites (27:14–26). To these instructions Moses adds a further exhortation encouraging the people to obey the LORD (28:1–68). Interestingly, Moses' exhortation mirrors the previous instructions by highlighting the blessings which will flow from obedience (28:2–14) and the curses which will come as a result of disobedience (28:15–68). While it might have been anticipated that equal weight would be given to both blessings and curses, this is not the case; in both parts of Moses' speech, greater prominence is given to the curses (27:15–26; 28:15–68). Following the blessings and curses, Moses once more exhorts the people to keep the terms of the covenant by highlighting that the choice before them is one of life or death (29:2–30:20). Next there is a brief passage which focuses on Joshua's appointment as Moses' successor (31:1–8). After this Moses commands the priests and elders regarding the reading of the law (*tôrâ*) every seven years (31:9–13). Significantly, the LORD then predicts that after entering the promised land Israel will soon forsake him and break the covenant (31:16–18). Consequently, Moses is instructed to teach them a song 'so that it may be a witness' for the LORD against them (31:19–22). Before reciting this song to the people (31:30–32:43), Moses tells the Levites to place the Book of the Law (*tôrâ*) beside the ark of the covenant so that it also may witness to the waywardness of the people (31:24–29). The remaining sections of Deuteronomy focus on the death of Moses. The LORD instructs Moses to go up Mount Nebo in order that he may see the promised land before dying (32:48–52). Next, Moses pronounces a series of blessing upon the Israelites (33:1–29). Finally, Moses' death is recorded, ending with a brief epithet concerning his greatness as a prophet (34:1–12).

21.3. Deuteronomy and Ancient Near Eastern Treaties

As we have already noted Deuteronomy is concerned with the renewing of the special covenant relationship between the LORD and the Israelites. Since the mid 1950s biblical scholars have discussed in some detail the similarities that exist between the covenant in Deuteronomy and other ancient documents, in particular political treaties and law-codes. While some scholars have argued that the book of Deuteronomy as a whole conforms to the pattern of certain second-millennium BC treaties, others have challenged this by observing that either the parallels are not particularly close or those parallels that do exist may be accounted for on the basis of mid first-millennium BC treaties. Without wishing to enter into this debate in detail some further comments are necessary.

The closest parallels to the covenant found in the book of Deuteronomy appear to come in ancient treaties made between kings of powerful nations and the rulers of weaker, vassal states. These treaties have a formal structure which may be outlined as follows:

1. A preamble; this introduces the treaty and those participating in it.
2. A historical prologue; this describes prior relationships between the parties.
3. Stipulations; these set out the obligations placed upon the weaker party to the covenant. They fall into two parts: (a) general, and (b) detailed.
4. Document clause.
5. Witnesses; this section lists the gods who witness the making of the treaty.
6. Curses and blessings; these list the consequences of either keeping or breaking the covenant stipulations.

According to some scholars this very treaty form is reflected in the text of Deuteronomy as it stands. Consequently, attempts are made to assign the material in Deuteronomy between the various elements of the treaty form. This can result in a proposal such as follows:

1.	Preamble:	1:1–5
2.	Historical prologue:	1:6–3:29
3a.	General stipulations:	4:1–40; 5:1–11:32
3b.	Detailed stipulations:	12:1–26:19
4.	Document clause:	27:1–26
5.	Witnesses:	not applicable due to the monotheistic outlook of Deuteronomy.
6.	Curses and blessings:	28:1–68

Other scholars, however, adopt a more cautious approach, suggesting that it is mistaken to find the treaty form replicated in the book of Deuteronomy as it stands. While the essential elements of the treaty form are reflected in the present narrative form of the text, the book itself is not an actual treaty document. There is much to commend this view, especially since Deuteronomy in its entirety does not claim to be a self-contained covenant document. At the very most only 5:1–26:19, including possibly 28:1–68, is presented as an independent document within the present text.[1]

Although formal correspondence between the whole of Deuteronomy and ancient near eastern vassal treaties is lacking, the process by which the covenant was ratified between the Israelites and the LORD does bear a striking resemblance to that found in vassal treaties. In each we have the formalising of a special relationship between two parties, one strong and one weak, with the listing of extensive obligations and the pronouncement of blessings and curses.

---

[1] Two references suggest that Deuteronomy 28 and perhaps other material should be included in the Book of the Law (see 28:58, 61).

While scholars will undoubtedly continue to debate the precise nature of this correspondence, there can be little doubt that an awareness of it enables us to appreciate better the main characteristics of the covenant in Deuteronomy.

21.4. Love the LORD

Although the book of Deuteronomy focuses on a formal renewal of the relationship between the LORD and the Israelites, considerable attention is given to the fact that the formal act of renewal by itself does not constitute the relationship. Rather, the relationship between the LORD and his people is to be based on the twin pillars of love and loyalty. To appreciate this better it may be helpful to consider a modern analogy. The relationship between God and Israel can in part be compared to that between husband and wife. In many societies the relationship between husband and wife is formally instituted by the taking of marriage vows. While the wedding ceremony formalises the relationship of husband and wife, it cannot of itself sustain the relationship. For the marriage relationship to exist and develop in a meaningful way, it is essential that there be mutual love and loyalty. If love and/or loyalty disappear from the relationship between a husband and wife, the fact that they have been formally united will mean little. Indeed, both partners may seek to have this formal bond removed by instituting another formal procedure, divorce. The making of the treaty between God and Israel resembles a marriage ceremony. While both parties promise allegiance to each other, the strength of the relationship between them depends not on the covenant ceremony itself, but on the love and loyalty which each has for the other. For this reason, Moses emphasises that the Israelites are to love the LORD with their whole being. He expresses it thus: 'Love the LORD your God with all your heart and with all your soul and with all your strength' (6:5; cf. 11:13; 13:3; 30:6). Without such love the covenant relationship will be meaningless.

Moses' frequent exhortations to love the LORD suggest that this was likely to prove difficult for the Israelites. Their ability to love stands in marked contrast to that of the LORD. Nowhere is there any suggestion that his love might cease towards Israel. On the contrary, Moses highlights God's lasting faithfulness towards his people. From the outset he was the one who initiated the relationship. Motivated by love he chose Israel and delivered her from slavery in Egypt (4:37; 7:8; cf. 10:15). For the same reason, he did not allow Balaam to curse his chosen people (23:5). Elsewhere Moses expresses confidence regarding God's love for the future; his love will continue for a thousand generations (5:10; 7:9).

Although Moses is absolutely certain that the LORD loves Israel and that he will be completely faithful to her, this is no open-ended guarantee of divine blessing and favour. On the contrary, the covenant relationship involves a commitment from each Israelite to love the LORD. Should they fail to love the LORD, the consequences are clearly set out; they will experience God's disfavour in the form of various curses which are listed at length in 27:15–26 and 28:15–68.

In the light of this, love in Deuteronomy is never presented as something emotional; it is not just a matter of feelings. Loving God had very practical implications for the people. They must fulfil the obligations placed upon them by the covenant. Thus Moses repeatedly draws attention to the link between loving the LORD and keeping 'his requirements, his decrees, his laws and his commands always' (11:1; cf. 5:10; 7:9; 10:12; 11:13, 22; 19:9; 30:16). True love will demonstrate itself in perfect obedience. On the other hand, disobedience indicates a failure to love God (cf. 13:3).

Given this link between love and obedience – if you love me, you will obey me – it is no surprise that the central core of Deuteronomy consists of a long list of obligations which the Israelites were expected to keep. These obligations constitute the Book of the Law (*tôrâ*), a designation used in 28:61, 29:21 and 31:26. Although the Hebrew word *tôrâ* has traditionally been translated as 'law', this is partially misleading. While it includes laws which might be enforced by a legal court, it also embraces commands or stipulations which by their nature are not 'laws'; for example, it would be wrong to categorise the divine commands in 6:6–9 – to teach *tôrâ* to one's children – as 'law'. For this reason, some scholars prefer to translate *tôrâ* as 'instruction'. While this avoids the legal connotations of the term 'law', it fails to convey adequately the judicial aspect of *tôrâ*. As 17:8–13 reveals, *tôrâ* includes legal decisions taught by Levitical priests. Since it is difficult to find in English a single word which reflects accurately the full meaning of the term *tôrâ*, it is perhaps best to retain the Hebrew term and understand it in terms of all the material found in 5:1–26:19.

The importance of *tôrâ* is underlined throughout Deuteronomy. Reference is made to it at the very beginning of the book in the brief comment, 'East of the Jordan in the territory of Moab, Moses began to expound this law (*tôrâ*)' (1:5). According to the narrator's remark in 4:44, the Book of the Law (*tôrâ*) begins in 5:1. Later, Moses instructs the people to have the Book of the Law (*tôrâ*) inscribed on plaster-coated stones on Mount Ebal (27:1–8), with a further copy being placed beside the ark of the covenant (31:24–26). Elsewhere, attention is drawn to the importance of the Book of the Law (*tôrâ*) in that future kings are to make a copy of it for their own use and are expected to read it all the days of their lives (17:18–20). It is also mentioned in the last of the curses recited by the Levites: 'Cursed is the man who does not uphold the words of this law (*tôrâ*) by carrying them out' (27:26).

Since Israel's obedience to the *tôrâ* demonstrates her love for the LORD, Moses underlines the importance of being familiar with all that it demands. Consequently, he instructs the Israelites not only to meditate on all that he commands them, but also to teach it to their children:[2]

> These commandments that I give you today are to be upon your hearts. Impress them on your children. Talk about them when you sit at home and when you walk along the road, when you lie down and when you get up. Tie them as symbols on your hands and bind them on your foreheads. Write them on the doorframes of your houses and on your gates (6:6–9; cf. 4:4; 11:18–21; 31:9–13).

For Moses the stipulations of the covenant were to be a vital part of everyday life for all God's people, both young and old. Familiarity with them was essential for the maintenance of a harmonious relationship with the LORD; to ignore them would bring disaster.

Conscious of the Israelites' strong tendency towards disobedience (see next chapter), Moses incorporates within his exhortations various comments to encourage obedience. These motivation statements are found throughout Deuteronomy. Interestingly, apart from the longer section of curses in Deuteronomy 28, Moses generally motivates the people by highlighting the positive aspects of obedience. Only rarely does he mention the consequences of disobedience (e.g. 8:19–20). The most common motive is the promise of divine blessing, mentioned on a number of occasions within the Book of the Law. When, for example, in 15:7–10 Moses encourages the Israelites to be generous towards the poor, he adds the comment: 'then because of this the LORD your God will bless you in all your work and in everything you put your hand to' (15:10). Similar remarks are found in 7:12–15; 14:29; 15:4, 18; 23:10. The promise of blessing, however, is developed most fully in Deuteronomy 28 where Moses lists not only the blessing that will flow from obedience (28:3–14), but also the curses which will result from disobedience (28:16–68). Here Moses spells out in detail the practical consequences of experiencing divine blessing or cursing. Since a detailed examination of this chapter lies beyond the scope of this work, some general observations must suffice.

First, there is an emphasis upon fruitfulness and prosperity. Blessed by God, the people will increase numerically, as will their livestock. Moreover, the land will produce abundant harvests enabling the people to prosper richly, so much so that other nations will come to borrow from them. Under God's curse, however, the reverse will occur. Diseases will strike down the

---

[2] It should be noted that the noun *tôrâ* is closely related to the Hebrew verb 'to teach' (cf. 17:11). *Tôrâ* is that which is taught (by God).

people, as well as their animals and crops.[3] Such will be the decline in their fortunes that the Israelites will be forced to borrow from the alien living in their midst.

Secondly, under God's blessing the Israelites will enjoy as a nation security from their enemies who will be easily defeated. Implicit in this promise, and in the references to the fruitfulness of the land, is the assurance that the Israelites will occupy the promised land. This picture of national security is reversed, however, should the people come under God's curse. Not only will they be defeated by their enemies, but significantly, they will be led out of the promised land into captivity elsewhere.[4] Interestingly, these two aspects of blessing and cursing – prosperity and security – occur frequently in the briefer motivation statements made by Moses. References to life and prosperity come in the following passages: 4:1, 40; 5:29, 33; 6:2–3, 18, 24; 7:13–15; 8:1; 11:9, 14–15; 12:25, 28; 16:20; 29:9; 30:16, 20; 32:47. The land is mentioned in 4:1, 40; 5:33; 6:3, 18; 7:13; 8:1, 6–9; 11:8–9, 14–15, 23; 16:20; 17:20; 23:20; 30:16, 20; 32:47.[5] Stated briefly, Moses constantly reminds the Israelites that obedience brings life; disobedience brings death. This choice between life and death, prosperity or destruction, comes at the climax of Moses' final speech to the Israelites:

> See, I set before you today life and prosperity, death and destruction. For I command you today to love the LORD your God, to walk in his ways, and to keep his commands, decrees and laws; then you will live and increase, and the LORD your God will bless you in the land you are entering to possess. But if your heart turns away and you are not obedient, and if you are drawn away to bow down to other gods and worship them, I declare to you this day that you will certainly be destroyed. You will not live long in the land you are crossing the Jordan to enter and possess (30:15–18).[6]

---

[3] The description of what will happen to the Israelites echoes the punishments that fell upon the Egyptians at the time of the exodus.

[4] We shall have more to say on this in the next chapter. Interestingly, the promise of blessing was both national and personal. This is reflected in comments concerning the future king who is promised a long reign for obeying the law (17:18–20).

[5] Deuteronomy 8:7–9 provides a very vivid picture of the 'good land':

> For the LORD your God is bringing you into a good land – a land with streams and pools of water, with springs flowing in the valleys and hills; a land with wheat and barley, vines and fig trees, pomegranates, olive oil and honey; a land where bread will not be scarce and you will lack nothing; a land where the rocks are iron and you can dig copper out of the hills.

[6] There are close links between Deuteronomy and Genesis as regards the concept of blessing and cursing.

21.5. Be Loyal to the LORD

While Moses stresses the importance of love for a secure relationship between the Israelites and God, he also emphasises equally the necessity of loyalty. The Israelites must be faithful in loving only the LORD. In religious terms this means that they are not to practise idolatry; they must worship the LORD alone. This aspect of the covenant relationship heads the list of obligations found in the Decalogue: 'You shall have no other gods before (besides) me' (5:7; cf. Ex. 20:3).

A number of important ideas are associated with idolatry in the book of Deuteronomy. While most of these are found in the Exodus account of the Sinai covenant, they are developed in greater detail at this stage. First, Moses commands the people not 'to follow other gods' (6:14; 8:19; 11:28; 28:14; cf. 13:2). They are to neither 'serve' or 'worship'[7] these gods (7:4, 16; 8:19; 11:16; 17:3; 28:14, 36, 64; 29:18; 30:17; cf. 13:2, 6, 13; 29:26), nor 'bow down' to them (8:19; 11:16; 17:3; 30:17; cf. 5:19; 29:26). Underlying this terminology is the idea that the relationship between the worshipper and deity resembles that between slave and master. Since for the Israelites true worship involved total obedience to all that the LORD demanded, it was not possible for them to give allegiance to any other deity. Ironically, by being restricted to worship only the LORD, the Israelites were freed from the difficulty of trying to meet the sometimes conflicting demands of different deities. Not only were the Israelites prohibited from worshipping other gods, but they were also prohibited from worshipping anything that God had made, in particular the sun, moon or stars (4:19; 17:3).

Secondly, Moses highlights the danger posed by the religious beliefs of the nations living in the land of Canaan; the Israelites will be enticed to worship their gods. In an attempt to prevent this occurring, they are commanded not to copy their religious practices (16:21–22; 18:14); such practices are described as 'detestable' to the LORD (12:31; 13:14; 17:4; 18:9, 12; 20:18).[8] The Israelites are also to destroy everything associated with the worship of other gods in the land of Canaan: 'Break down their altars, smash their sacred stones, cut down their Asherah poles and burn their idols in the fire' (7:5; cf. 7:25; 12:2–3). Most significantly, because they will encourage the Israelites to worship their gods, the nations of Canaan are to be destroyed completely (7:16; 20:17–18).

Thirdly, picking up another of the obligations found in the Decalogue (5:8–10; cf. Ex. 20:4–6), Moses warns the people against making idols (4:15–31). Since the LORD did not reveal his form at Sinai, the Israelites must not try to depict him using human or animal forms (4:15–18). Elsewhere

---

[7] The same Hebrew verb may be translated by the English words 'serve' or 'worship'.

[8] It is interesting to observe that in 25:16 dishonesty is included among the various things which are described in Deuteronomy as 'detestable' to the LORD.

in Deuteronomy it is made very clear that all idols are 'detestable' to the LORD (7:25–26; 23:16; 27:15; 29:17; 32:16; cf. 32:21).

Fourthly, those who engage in idolatrous activities are guilty of 'doing evil in the eyes of the LORD' (4:25; 9:18; 17:2; 31:29; cf. 13:5, 11; 17:5, 7). One consequence of this is that they provoke him to anger (4:25; 6:15; 7:4; 11:7; 29:24–29; cf. 9:7–8, 18–20; 13:5, 11; 17:5, 7). Consequently, those guilty of idolatry should be put to death (6:15; 7:4; 13:15; cf. 9:8, 14, 19–20, 25–26). Furthermore, the regulations within the Book of the Law (*tôrâ*) make it very clear that anyone who entices others to worship foreign gods must be put to death. The Israelites were to execute those who, possibly claiming to be prophets either of the LORD or some other deity, enticed others to worship gods they had not previously known (13:1–5; cf. 18:20). This rule applies even to the closest of relatives or friends (13:6–11). Moreover, entire Israelite communities were to be wiped out should they commit idolatry (13:12–16).[9] Should the nation as a whole be guilty of idolatry, the punishment would be destruction and exile (4:26–28; 29:24–28). Ironically, as part of this punishment the people 'will worship man-made gods of wood and stone, which cannot see or hear or eat or smell' (4:28; 28:36, 64).

These regulations against idolatry emphasise that the Israelites were expected to remain completely loyal to the LORD their God.

21.6. Conclusion

In the book of Deuteronomy the story of the LORD's relationship with Israel reaches an important landmark. As they stand poised to take possession of the land of Canaan, Moses sets before a new generation of adult Israelites the obligations which they must fulfil in order to enjoy God's blessing in the land of Canaan. At the heart of these obligations is the requirement to love the LORD wholeheartedly. Israel's future in the promised land is tied directly to their willingness and ability to fulfil their covenantal duties. While Deuteronomy holds out the prospect of divine blessing in the promised land, as we shall examine in more detail in the next chapter, it also envisages a future in which Israel, through failure to fulfil the covenant obligations, will come under God's curse.

---

[9] It is important to note that as regards idolatry the LORD intends to treat the Israelites in the same way as the nations already living in the land of Canaan; the same punishment would be applied to Israel as to these other nations.

21.7. New Testament Connections

The book of Deuteronomy is one of the most frequently quoted books in the NT.[10] Since, of all the OT books, it sets out most fully the essential requirements for a harmonious relationship with God, this is hardly surprising. It is often quoted as stating what the OT law requires (e.g. Mt. 5:31, 38; 15:4; 18:16; 19:18–19; Mk. 7:10; 10:19; Lk. 18:20; 1 Cor. 5:13; 9:9; 2 Cor. 13:1; Eph. 6:2–3; 1 Tim. 5:18).

Deuteronomy's influence pervades the teaching of Jesus. When asked by 'an expert in the law', 'Which is the greatest commandment?' (Mt. 22:36), Jesus responds by quoting first Deuteronomy 6:5: 'Love the Lord your God with all your heart and with all your soul and with all your mind.'[11] Elsewhere his commitment to the agenda set by Deuteronomy is clearly seen in the parallel accounts of his temptation (Mt. 4:1–11; Lk. 4:1–13). On each occasion that he is tested by the devil Jesus replies by quoting from Deuteronomy.[12] In doing so he highlights one of the principal tenets of the book: 'Worship the LORD your God, and serve him only' (Deut. 6:13, quoted in Mt. 4:10 and Lk. 4:8).

Even when the text of Deuteronomy is not quoted directly, its influence is still apparent. We see this in Jesus' insistence that his followers must be single-minded in their commitment to God: 'No one can serve two masters. Either he will hate the one and love the other, or he will be devoted to the one and despise the other. You cannot serve both God and Money' (Mt. 6:24).

Later, this principle is highlighted in the story of the rich young man (Mt. 19:16–30; Lk. 18:18–30). By insisting that he give his wealth to the poor, Jesus reveals that the man has divided allegiances. The idea of wholehearted commitment to God also appears in the parables of Jesus, especially those which involve a master/servant relationship (Mt. 18:23–35; 24:45–51; 25:14–30; Lk. 12:42–48; 19:12–27); these parables commonly emphasise the importance of loyalty and faithfulness.

---

[10] It is quoted some 83 times. The only other OT books to be referred to as often in the NT are Genesis, Psalms and Isaiah. Two factors, however, should be borne in mind in considering the number of times Deuteronomy is quoted in the NT. First, many of the quotations come in parallel accounts recorded in the Synoptic Gospels. Secondly, on a few occasions part of the Decalogue is quoted; in such instances it is possible to see the source of the quotations as either Exodus, Deuteronomy 20 or Deuteronomy 5 (e.g. Rom. 7:7; 13:9; Jas. 2:11).

[11] Parallel accounts come in Mark 12:28–34 and Luke 10:25–28. To emphasise an important consequence of loving God, Jesus also quotes Leviticus 19:18: 'Love your neighbour as yourself.'

[12] He quotes Deuteronomy 8:3; 6:16 and 6:13.

Another aspect of Deuteronomy that is developed briefly in the NT is that of cursing. Paul picks this up in his letter to the Galatians where he notes that 'All who rely on observing the law are under a curse for it is written: "Cursed is everyone who does not continue to do everything written in the Book of the Law"' (Gal. 3:10, quoting Deut. 27:26). Since, according to Paul, no one can keep the law fully, all are cursed. However, this for Paul is not the end of the matter. He then confidently affirms that Christ has 'redeemed us from the curse of the law by becoming a curse for us, for it is written: "Cursed is everyone who is hung on a tree"' (Gal. 3:13, quoting Deut. 21:23).

22

Why Israel?

22.1. Summary

By establishing a special covenant relationship with the Israelites, the LORD set them apart from all other nations as his people. God's choice of Israel is not linked to any special quality which they possess; it is not due to their righteousness or size. When the LORD promised them the land of Canaan, this was because the nations living there had forfeited, by their wickedness, their right to the land. Yet, whereas the Israelites were commanded to destroy completely the nations living in Canaan, it was God's intention that they should be a light to other nations, reflecting the righteousness which he expected of all people. Although the Israelites stood to benefit greatly from the privilege of being God's holy nation, their calling also carried with it important responsibilities. Failure to fulfil these would bring upon them God's disfavour.

22.2. Introduction

The book of Deuteronomy, as we have already noted in the previous chapter, revolves around the covenant which is renewed between the LORD and Israel. As a consequence of this Israel enjoyed a relationship with the LORD that differed markedly from that experienced by other nations. Various passages within Deuteronomy focus on the nature and purpose of this special relationship and indirectly a number of important theological issues are addressed. Why did the LORD choose Israel and deliver her from Egypt? Did the LORD display favouritism in wiping out the nations of Canaan in order to give their land to the Israelites? Did Israel, as a result of her special relationship with God, have an unfair advantage over all the other nations of the earth? The answers to these questions permeate the book of Deuteronomy.

22.3. The Election of Israel

Throughout Deuteronomy it is made clear that Israel as a nation had a unique relationship with the LORD. Moses summarised this as follows: 'For you are a people holy to the LORD your God. The LORD your God has chosen you out of all the peoples on the face of the earth to be his people, his treasured possession' (7:6; cf. 14:2).[1]

Here we encounter several distinctive ideas which occur elsewhere in Deuteronomy and which point to God setting Israel apart as his own special nation. First, on a number of occasions it is stated that God chose Israel 'out of all the nations on the earth' (14:2; cf. 4:37; 7:6–7; 10:15). The emphasis rests on the fact that it was the LORD who chose Israel, not Israel who chose the LORD. Secondly, the Israelites were to be *his* people (4:20; 7:6; 26:18; 27:9; 28:9–10; 29:13; cf. 9:26, 29; 21:8; 26:15). Israel alone was the LORD's people; no other nation could claim this. The uniqueness of this relationship is underlined by the comment that Israel was God's 'treasured possession' (7:6; 14:2; 26:18). The Hebrew term *sĕgullâ* 'treasured possession' is used elsewhere in the OT to describe the jewels and value objects in a king's treasury (1 Chr. 29:3; Ecc. 2:8); Israel was precious to the LORD. Elsewhere the closeness of this bond is presented in terms of a parent/child relationship (32:18–20). Thirdly, the distinctive relationship between Israel and the LORD is reflected in the designation 'holy nation' (7:6; 14:2, 21; 26:19; 28:9). Of all the nations on earth Israel alone was under a special obligation to exhibit the holiness of God's nature. This was necessary because God had committed himself to live in a unique way among the Israelites.

Further evidence pointing to the LORD's choice of Israel comes in the many references to what he had already done for them in the past. Some of these focus on the special promises, chiefly concerning the possession of the land of Canaan, which God made to the patriarchs (4:31; 6:18, 23; 7:8; 8:1; 9:5; 13:17; 19:8; 26:15; 31:20; 34:4). Others deal with their divine redemption from Egypt (5:6; 6:12; 7:8; 8:14; 9:26; 13:5; 15:15; 21:8; 24:18) and the defeat of their enemies (2:24–3:11). Deuteronomy frequently highlights how the LORD has acted uniquely and decisively on the people's behalf. One passage that is particularly vivid in this regard is the poetic description in 32:8–15:

> When the Most High gave the nations their inheritance, when he divided all mankind, he set up boundaries for the peoples according to the number of the sons of Israel. For the Lord's portion is his people, Jacob his allotted inheritance. In a desert land he found him, in a barren and howling waste. He shielded him and cared

---

[1] A similar description of Israel's unique status among the nations of the earth comes in Exodus 19:4–6.

for him; he guarded him as the apple of his eye, like an eagle that stirs up its nest and hovers over its young, that spreads its wings to catch them and carries them on its pinions. The LORD alone led him; no foreign god was with him. He made him ride on the heights of the land and fed him with the fruit of the fields. He nourished him with honey from the rock, and with oil from the flinty crag, with curds and milk from herd and flock and with fattened lambs and goats, with choice rams of Bashan and the finest kernels of wheat. You drank the foaming blood of the grape. Jeshurun grew fat and kicked; filled with food, he became heavy and sleek.

Deuteronomy, however, looks not only to the past to highlight Israel's relationship with the LORD, but also to the future. The concluding words of Moses' second speech emphasise in a special way one important aspect of the LORD's future for Israel:

He [the LORD] has declared that he will set you in praise, fame and honour high above all the nations he has made and that you will be a people holy to the LORD your God, as he promised (26:19).

Elsewhere the future benefits of Israel's election are highlighted indirectly through those sections of the legal material which presuppose the occupation of the land of Canaan. Although the Israelites have yet to cross the river Jordan and take possession of the promised land, many of the regulations outlined by Moses to the people anticipate their settlement in the land. Thus, to mention but some, rules are given regarding the eating of animals away from the tabernacle (12:15–25),[2] pilgrimage festivals (16:1–17), and the giving of tithes (14:22–27). All of these presuppose that the Israelites will occupy a large territory, with many of them living at a considerable distance from the tabernacle. Similarly, the giving of instructions to establish cities of refuge (19:1–9) also implies that the Israelites will be dispersed throughout the whole of Canaan.

Apart from providing evidence that Israel was set apart by God from all other nations, the book of Deuteronomy also sheds light on the reason for Israel's divine election. What caused the LORD to choose Israel rather than some other nation? Interestingly, in Deuteronomy this question is mainly answered by excluding certain possibilities. First, Israel's election is not due to her righteousness. This is clearly stated in 9:4–6:

---

[2] In Deuteronomy, the place where the tabernacle was to be located in the promised land is referred to using either the phrase 'the place the LORD will choose' (12:5, 11, 14, 18, 21, 26; 14:23–25; 15:20; 16:2, 6, 7, 11, 15, 16; 17:8, 10; 18:6; 26:2; 31:11) or the phrase 'to put his Name there for his dwelling' (12:5, 11; 14:23; 16:2, 6, 11; 26:2; cf. 12:21, 14:24).

> After the LORD your God has driven them out before you, do not say to yourself, 'The LORD has brought me here to take possession of this land because of my righteousness.' No, it is on account of the wickedness of these nations that the LORD is going to drive them out before you. It is not because of your righteousness or your integrity that you are going in to take possession of their land; but on account of the wickedness of these nations, the LORD your God will drive them out before you, to accomplish what he swore to your fathers, to Abraham, Isaac and Jacob. Understand, then, that it is not because of your righteousness that the LORD your God is giving you this good land to possess, for you are a stiff-necked people.

This passage is not alone in emphasising Israel's lack of righteousness for there are frequent references to the nation's waywardness. Moses reminds the people that when God tested their obedience through the wilderness experience (8:2–5), they rebelled and were punished (1:26–46; 9:7–24), and, but for the intercession of Moses, the LORD would have rejected them completely (9:18–20, 25–29; 10:10). Not only are they occasionally described as a stiff-necked people (9:4–6; 9:13; 10:16; 31:27), but Moses comments, 'You have been rebellious against the LORD ever since I have known you' (9:24; cf. 31:27). In these and other ways Israel is consistently portrayed as failing to achieve the high standard of righteousness demanded by the LORD. Even as regards the future, Deuteronomy highlights the Israelites' inability to fulfil the obligations placed upon them (e.g. 31:16–18; 32:15–35).[3] Clearly, God's election of Israel is not determined by the fact that they were morally superior to others.

Another factor that is briefly mentioned as regards the election of Israel is that of size. According to Moses, 'The LORD did not set his affection on you and choose you because you were more numerous than other peoples, for you were the fewest of all peoples' (7:7). It was not because of Israel's superiority in numbers and strength that God chose her; on the contrary, when God initiated his dealings with Israel, he started with one individual, Abraham.

If Deuteronomy dismisses Israel's righteousness and size as reasons for her divine election, is any other explanation provided? The only other factor mentioned is God's oath with her forefathers (7:8; 9:5; cf. 4:31; 6:18, 23; 8:1; 13:17; 19:8; 26:15; 31:20; 34:4). Yet, even here the emphasis rests on God's love and faithfulness to the oath which he swore (7:8–9). The part played by the patriarchs in the process of election is secondary to that of the LORD. Deuteronomy is consistent in emphasising that the LORD's election of Israel was not due to some inherent quality found in the people; rather, it resulted from his unmerited love for them.

---

[3] This is discussed more fully below.

Having observed how Deuteronomy emphasises the divine election of Israel, what does it say about the purpose underlying this? What did the LORD hope to achieve through choosing the Israelites to be his own people? The clearest answer to this question comes in 4:6–8:

> Observe them [God's decrees and laws] carefully, for this will show your wisdom and understanding to the nations, who will hear about all these decrees and say, 'Surely this great nation is a wise and understanding people.' What other nation is so great as to have their gods near them the way the LORD our God is near us whenever we pray to him? And what other nation is so great as to have such righteous decrees and laws as this body of laws I am setting before you today?

Underlying this passage is the idea that Israel is divinely chosen to be an example for others to emulate. Two aspects of this are highlighted here. First, the nearness of the LORD's presence is emphasised. Israel will enjoy an intimate relationship with God which will be seen in the LORD's willingness to hear the people's prayers. Secondly, others will praise the *tôrâ* ('body of laws', NIV), by which the nation shall regulate its affairs, because of the inherent righteousness of its decrees and laws. Naturally, this required that the Israelites should be consistent in keeping all the demands of the *tôrâ*. Israel's election is linked to her obligation to be a holy nation (cf. 7:7–11). Because the LORD has chosen Israel and promised to bless her abundantly, she has the responsibility of living up to her divine calling. Moses expresses this link between election, obedience to the LORD, and other nations, as follows:

> The LORD will establish you as his holy people, as he promised you on oath, if you keep the commands of the LORD your God and walk in his ways. Then all the peoples on earth will see that you are called by the name of the LORD, and they will fear you (28:9–10).

Given the importance that is placed upon Israel being a light to the nations, it is not surprising that much of Deuteronomy is devoted to outlining the regulations and laws which are intended to make Israel more righteous than other nations. While it is not possible to provide here a detailed survey of all the material in the Book of the Law (*tôrâ*), a number of general observations can be made. At the outset it should be noted that the regulations in Deuteronomy seek to promote a sense of brotherhood. An example of this comes in the regulations concerning kingship (17:14–20). Not only is it stated that the king 'must be from among your own brothers' (17:15), but later it is added that he 'must not consider himself better than his brothers' (17:20). The law (*tôrâ*) required that the king should not use his special status to promote his own interests above those of others. Linked to the concept of brotherhood is a concern for the weaker members of society. Throughout the Book of the

Law (*tôrâ*) special mention is made of the fatherless, the widow, the slave, the poor and the alien.[4] Because of their vulnerability, they must not be mistreated or exploited; all are to be shown dignity and respect. Furthermore, the law (*tôrâ*) is also concerned to promote a generous spirit (e.g. 10:18–19; 15:12–14). In their dealings with others the Israelites must reflect the LORD's generosity towards them.[5]

Deuteronomy also emphasises throughout the importance of Israel being a righteous nation. We see this highlighted, for example, in the refrain which occurs often in the Book of the Law (*tôrâ*): 'You must purge the evil from among you' (13:5; 17:7; 19:19; 21:21; 22:21; 22:24; 24:7; cf. 17:12; 19:13; 21:9; 22:22). It is also reflected in the LORD's description of Israel as Jeshurun 'the upright one' (32:15; 33:5, 26).[6] However, although Deuteronomy stresses the importance of Israel being righteous, it also allows for the possibility that should Israel fail in this regard, she would still be a witness to God's righteousness (cf. 29:24–28).[7]

Although Israel was the LORD's 'treasured possession', this did not give to the people a firm guarantee that they would always enjoy divine favour. As we have noted in the previous chapter, the covenant established between the LORD and Israel only guaranteed blessing when the people fulfilled the obligations placed upon them. Failure to meet these obligations would bring upon them the curses outlined at the end of the Book of the Law (*tôrâ*). While the Israelites enjoyed a unique and privileged position as regards their relationship with the LORD, they were expected to be especially righteous.

---

[4] The alien, the fatherless and the widow are mentioned together in the following verses: 10:18; 14:29; 16:11, 14; 24:17, 19–21; 26:12–13; 27:19. Elsewhere, positive attitudes towards aliens are commended in 1:16; 5:14; 10:19; 14:21; 23:7; 24:14; 26:11. On occasions, the Levites, who were dependent on the generosity of other Israelites for their daily needs, are mentioned alongside the alien, the fatherless and the widow (14:29; 16:11, 14; 26:12–13; cf. 26:11).

[5] Deuteronomy assumes that, because these laws are divinely given, they reflect God's righteous nature. It is therefore no surprise that Moses describes God's nature in terms which echo the regulations of the Book of the Law (*tôrâ*).

> For the LORD your God is God of gods and Lord of lords, the great God, mighty and awesome, who shows no partiality and accepts no bribes. He defends the cause of the fatherless and the widow, and loves the alien, giving him food and clothing (10:17–18).

[6] Apart from its occurrences in Deuteronomy, the term is used only once elsewhere in the Old Testament (Isa. 44:2).

[7] See below.

22.4. Israel and the Nations

Thus far we have focused our attention on the LORD's choice of Israel to be his people out of all the nations of the earth. What, however, does the book of Deuteronomy reveal about the LORD's attitude towards other nations? In addressing this question it needs to be noted that in Deuteronomy an important distinction is drawn between the nations living in the land of Canaan and those living elsewhere. To appreciate this it may be best to consider first what Deuteronomy has to say about the nations of Canaan.

Given that the whole movement in the book of Deuteronomy is towards the Israelite occupation of the land of Canaan, it is hardly surprising that considerable attention should be devoted to the issue of what should happen to those nations already living there. Since the land was in the possession of seven nations – the Hittites, Girgashites, Amorites, Canaanites, Perizzites, Hivites and Jebusites – how would Israel come to possess it? The response of Deuteronomy is unambiguous. The Israelites were to destroy totally all those inhabiting the land of Canaan. As Moses instructs the people, 'When the LORD your God has delivered them over to you and you have defeated them, then you must destroy them totally. Make no treaty with them, and show them no mercy' (7:2; cf. 20:16–17).

To justify such a policy towards these nations, Moses highlights two factors. First, the destruction of these nations is an act of divine punishment.[8] As Moses emphasises in 9:4–6 the Israelites were not being given the land as a reward for their own righteousness, 'but on account of the wickedness of these nations, the LORD your God will drive them out before you' (9:5; cf. v. 4). Although the nature of their wickedness is not explicitly mentioned, a major factor was their idolatrous worship and its associated practices.[9] Second, the complete annihilation of the nations living in the promised land is necessary in order to prevent the Israelites from worshipping their gods (20:16–18). For this reason, Moses commands the total destruction of everything associated with the worship of these gods (7:5, 25–26) and forbids the people from following their religious practices (16:21–22; 18:14). Although the treatment of the nations living in Canaan appears exceptionally severe, it should be noted that their punishment was not arbitrary. As Deuteronomy makes clear, the Israelites themselves would suffer similar punishment for idolatry.

---

[8] A similar view is expressed in Genesis 15:16 in connection with God's promise to Abraham that his descendants will possess the land of Canaan.

[9] Since Deuteronomy sees a link between religion and morality, it is more than likely that the ethical standards of the nations in Canaan were viewed as also meriting divine punishment.

In spite of the strength of the nations already in Canaan – 'seven nations larger and stronger than you' (7:1) – the Israelites are assured that the LORD will give them the victory (7:16–24; 9:1–3; 11:22–25; 31:3–8). Although the victory will be decisive, it will also be gradual (7:22). Furthermore, their victory is linked to their obedience to God's decrees and laws (11:22–23).

While the book of Deuteronomy adopts a very negative attitude towards the inhabitants of Canaan, the same is not true of all other nations. This is reflected in a number of ways. First, Moses draws attention to the fact that during their journey to the promised land the Israelites were not permitted by the LORD to attack certain nations in order to take possession of their land (2:1–23). This was so for the Edomites, Moabites and Ammonites. Concerning each of these nations Moses observes that the LORD was responsible for giving them their land (2:5, 9, 19). Since the LORD granted the land to them, the Israelites had no right to take any part of it. Interestingly, Moses observes a number of parallels between the Edomites, Moabites and Ammonites; all were given land by the LORD,[10] and all of them overcame powerful enemies in order to take possession of the land (2:10–12, 20–23). Implicit in Moses' comments about these nations is the suggestion that if the LORD has done this for these nations, then the Israelites should have confidence that he will achieve the same for them.

Secondly, when the Book of the Law (*tôrâ*) addresses the topic of war against other nations, a clear distinction is drawn between how the Israelites should deal with the nearby nations of Canaan and more distant peoples. While they were to spare none of the members of the nearby nations (20:16–17) – all were to be put to death, men and women, young and old – a different policy was to be adopted towards other nations. At the start of any conflict an offer of peace was to be made (20:10). If this was accepted, then no deaths resulted. If, however, this was refused, the Israelites were to 'put to the sword all the men' but spare 'the women, the children, the livestock and everything else in the city' (20:13–14).[11]

Thirdly, various minor remarks within Deuteronomy suggest that the Israelites were expected to adopt a positive attitude towards the well-being of the nations outside Canaan. Thus, they are commanded not to 'abhor an Edomite' or 'an Egyptian' (23:7). In spite of all that had happened in Egypt,

---

[10] Moses quotes the LORD as saying, 'I have given Esau the hill country of Seir as his own' (2:5). Similar statements are made concerning the Moabites (2:9) and Ammonites (2:19).

[11] In passing it is interesting to observe the ban against cutting down fruit trees during the siege of a city. Implicit in this seems to be a concern to enable life, for those who survive a siege, to return to normality as a soon as possible after the conflict has ended. Even in war, the Israelites were to have a humanitarian concern.

the Israelites were to allow 'the third generation of children' born to Egyptians to 'enter the assembly of the LORD' (23:8). A positive attitude towards foreigners is also reflected in the numerous references to aliens within the Book of the Law (*tôrâ*). As noted above, they, like widows and the fatherless, were to be cared for in a special way.

These differing approaches towards foreign nations are in keeping with what we observed earlier regarding the election of Israel. Since the nations of Canaan, through their wickedness, had forfeited their right to the land of Canaan, the land was to be given to the Israelites. It was in this territory that Israel was to establish herself as a holy nation. Furthermore, because Israel was to be a light to the nations, it was important that she reflected in her national life the lifestyle and values which were consistent with the single-minded service of the LORD. This required that the land be purged of everything that might undermine the divine purpose underlying Israel's election. Hence the Israelites were to destroy completely the nations already living in Canaan. However, as regards other nations, a different attitude was to prevail. At all times Israel was to follow a policy of non-aggression towards them. Only if they threatened the national security of Israel would they be in danger of attack.

22.5. Election and Responsibility

Although the LORD chose the Israelites to be his people, at no stage were they forced against their will to accept him as their God. At Sinai and on the Plains of Moab they are invited to enter freely into a covenant relationship with the LORD. However, once they entered into such an agreement, they were committed by the terms of the covenant to remain loyal to the LORD. While Moses emphasises in his speeches the benefits available to the Israelites as a result of their divine election, the book of Deuteronomy also highlights the serious consequences that would result from a failure to fulfil this calling. If the Israelites were to enjoy the benefits of being the LORD's people, they had to keep the obligations placed upon them by the covenant.

Although Moses strongly exhorts the people to obey the covenant obligations, Deuteronomy as a whole conveys the idea that the Israelites will fail to keep them. While the possibility of failure is introduced as early as 4:25–31, it is in the concluding chapters that it becomes most prominent. First, the likelihood that Israel will break the covenant obligations is suggested by the space devoted to the curses in Deuteronomy 27 and 28. Whereas twelve verses are given over to outlining the blessing which will reward obedience (28:3–14), the curses occupy sixty-five verses (27:15–26; 28:16–68). By devoting so much attention to the curses, the impression is conveyed that they are more likely to materialise than the blessings.

Secondly, although the list of curses does not specifically indicate that the Israelites will fail to keep the covenant obligations, this is stated emphatically shortly afterwards in three different speeches.

(a) In his final exhortation to the Israelites to keep the covenant with the LORD, Moses clearly envisages a future in which the land will be devastated (29:23) and the people exiled (30:1–4).

(b) In one of the few divine speeches recorded in Deuteronomy, the LORD tells Moses:

> These people will soon prostitute themselves to the foreign gods of the land they are entering. They will forsake me and break the covenant I made with them. On that day I will become angry with them and forsake them; I will hide my face from them, and they will be destroyed (31:16–17).

To remind future generations of Israelites of this prediction the LORD instructs Moses to teach the people a special song (32:1–43).

(c) When Moses orders the Levites to place the Book of the Law (*tôrâ*) beside the ark of the covenant, he comments:

> For I know how rebellious and stiff-necked you are. If you have been rebellious against the LORD while I am still alive and with you, how much more will you rebel after I die! Assemble before me all the elders of your tribes and all your officials, so that I can speak these words in their hearing and call heaven and earth to testify against them. For I know that after my death you are sure to become utterly corrupt and to turn from the way I have commanded you. In days to come, disaster will fall upon you because you will do evil in the sight of the LORD and provoke him to anger by what your hands have made (31:27–29).

Like the song in 32:1–43; the Book of the Law (*tôrâ*) will be a witness against the Israelites (31:26; cf. v. 19).

In the light of these developments towards the end of Deuteronomy, it is clear that the Israelites, due to their disobedience, will experience mixed consequences from their divine election. While they will initially enjoy God's favour in the promised land, this will be replaced in due course by divine cursing, resulting in their expulsion from the land. That Deuteronomy should envisage such a development is noteworthy. However, even in the process of being punished by the LORD, the Israelites will still be a witness to the nations regarding the righteousness of the LORD. When in the future foreigners ask why terrible disasters have come upon Israel (29:22–24), it will be stated,

> It is because this people abandoned the covenant of the LORD, the God of their fathers, the covenant he made with them when he brought them out of Egypt.

They went off and worshipped other gods and bowed down to them, gods they did not know, gods he had not given them. Therefore the LORD's anger burned against this land, so that he brought on it all the curses written in this book. In furious anger and in great wrath the LORD uprooted them from their land and thrust them into another land, as it is now (29:25–28).

Thus, even when divinely punished the Israelites would be a light to the nations.

Although Israel's election gave them advantages denied to other nations, in reality due to their rebellious nature, they would forfeit these. Nevertheless, in spite of their unfaithfulness, the LORD would not abandon them completely. If in exile they showed remorse for their actions, he would be compassionate towards them (30:1–10). Significantly, in anticipating the future restoration of exiled Israelites to the promised land, Moses alludes briefly to the fact that 'the LORD your God will circumcise your hearts and the hearts of your descendants, so that you may love him with all your heart and with all your soul, and live' (30:6). Here Moses envisages a time in the distant future when the LORD will intervene in order to overcome the inability of the Israelites to keep the covenant faithfully.

22.6. Conclusion

The book of Deuteronomy highlights why the LORD chose Israel to be his people and the consequences associated with this choice. They were to be a holy nation, keeping the covenant obligations found in the Book of the Law (*tôrâ*) in order that others might know and marvel at the righteousness of God. Yet, in spite of the special privileges bestowed upon them, Deuteronomy anticipates a future in which the Israelites will rebel against the LORD and break the covenant. As a result, after entering the promised land they themselves will be exiled and forced to live among other nations.

22.7. New Testament Connections

Within the NT the issue of Israel's divine election is perhaps most prominent in Paul's letter to the Romans. Here Paul addresses at length how the gospel has impacted the relationship between Jews and Gentiles. In his discussion Paul highlights the belief of his Jewish contemporaries that in the 'law' they have 'the embodiment of knowledge and truth' (Rom. 2:20). Such a belief is clearly derived from the way in which the law (*tôrâ*) is presented in the book of Deuteronomy. While Paul does not dispute this view of the law, he challenges the ability of his contemporaries to keep it. He even suggests that because of their inability to keep the law, 'God's name is blasphemed among the Gentiles' (Rom. 2:24; quoting Isa. 52:5; Ezek 36:22), an idea which may well have its roots in the book of Deuteronomy.

Next, Paul focuses on the topic of circumcision and argues that without a circumcision of the heart, implying complete obedience to God, outward circumcision is of no benefit. Although his Jewish opponents were stressing the importance of having the law and being circumcised, Paul argues that they are mistaken in thinking that this makes them more righteous than others: 'No-one will be declared righteous in his (God's) sight by observing the law; rather, through the law we become conscious of sin' (Rom. 3:20). Paul then proceeds to argue that there is a 'righteousness from God' which 'comes through faith in Christ to all who believe' (Rom. 3:22). This righteousness is available to both Jews and Gentiles, to everyone who, like Abraham, exercises faith. By focusing on this 'righteousness from God' Paul reflects the outlook of Deuteronomy that without a divinely given circumcision of the heart it would be impossible for the Israelites to keep the covenant.

Later, Paul picks up on the benefits which belong to the Israelites as God's chosen people.

> Theirs is the adoption as sons; theirs the divine glory, the covenants, the receiving of the law, the temple worship and the promises. Theirs are the patriarchs, and from them is traced the human ancestry of Christ, who is God over all, forever praised! Amen (Rom. 9:4–5).

Yet, in spite of these things, Paul willingly acknowledges that there are those Israelites who have failed to obtain the righteousness that comes by faith; rather they have sought to be righteous by keeping the law and have failed. On the other hand, Gentiles 'who did not pursue righteousness, have obtained it' (9:30). In the light of this Paul asks if the LORD has rejected his people, Israel. While he acknowledges the failure of many Jews to find salvation, he holds out the hope that 'all Israel will be saved' (11:26). Although the inclusion of the Gentiles within the people of God is a very significant development for Paul, he does not believe that this implies the complete exclusion of the Jews. Echoing Deuteronomy, Paul sees the divine election of Israel as leading to the salvation of the Gentiles.

Conclusion

From the preceding chapters it is apparent that the Pentateuch includes diverse material which has been brought together to form a narrative that is unified by a distinctive plot concerning God's special relationship with the descendants of Abraham, Isaac and Jacob. A central aspect of this plot is the creation of Israel as a nation. At the outset this is highlighted in terms of God's promise that Abraham shall have numerous descendants who will possess the land of Canaan. Later, the account of Israel's deliverance from Egypt and the making of the covenant at Sinai mark the formal establishment of Israel as God's chosen nation. The reality of this relationship is confirmed by the appearance of the divine presence at the tabernacle erected in the middle of the Israelite camp; God now dwells in the midst of his people.

Israel's privileged relationship with God, however, places special responsibilities upon the people. Most importantly of all they are to be holy, abiding by moral standards superior to those adopted by others. As well as being committed to a distinctive code of ethics, the people receive instructions regarding a wide variety of practices and rituals, all of which are designed to underline and maintain Israel's holy status. These range from instructions for offering sacrifices to prohibitions against eating certain foods. In a variety of ways the Israelites are to distinguish themselves from other peoples by being holy.

1. A Light to the Nations

Basic to God's choice of Abraham and his descendants is the intention that Israel will be a light to the nations. As a result of the disobedience of Adam and Eve the whole human race is alienated from God. Furthermore, every subsequent act of disobedience adds to this. Against this background the Israelites are to provide positive role models for others to follow. Through faithful obedience to God they will experience his blessing in a harmonious relationship. In addition, there will be harmony between the Israelites and their environment, evidenced by continuous human habitation in fertile and productive land.

Through her special relationship with God Israel is to reveal how creation may be restored to its original pristine condition. To this end Israel's life within Canaan reflects in part the situation that existed in the Garden of Eden prior to the disobedience and expulsion of Adam and Eve. Like Eden, the land of Canaan will be fruitful, a land 'flowing with milk and honey', and there the Israelites will commune with God in a personal and intimate way.

The Pentateuch, however, does not envisage the Israelite occupation of Canaan as heralding the full restoration of the idyllic situation that existed prior to the first act of human rebellion against God. While the Israelites are presented as having a unique relationship with God, it is not completely harmonious. From the outset, following their deliverance from Egypt, they repeatedly display their reluctance to trust God and obey him in everything. We see this prior to their arrival at Mount Sinai, during their stay there and afterwards when they journey towards the promised land. Throughout the books of Exodus to Deuteronomy there are many reminders of Israel's inability to live up to her divine calling to be a holy nation. Moreover, the concluding chapters of Deuteronomy emphasise that this failure will continue into the future, eventually resulting in the people being expelled from the land of Canaan itself.[1]

Although God intends that Israel should be a positive role model for other nations, even her disobedience serves God's purposes. As Deuteronomy 29:24–28 indicates, the later expulsion of the Israelites from the land, due to their waywardness, will be a lesson for all the nations. Both positively and negatively, Israel will be a witness to people everywhere regarding how each individual should live before God.

2. A Royal Descendant

While much of the Pentateuch focuses on the origin of the nation of Israel, the book of Genesis emphasises that the unique status of Israel must be understood against the background of God's desire to bless all the nations of the earth. From the perspective of the final narrator of the Pentateuch the destinies of Israel and all other nations are intertwined. Complementing the promise of nationhood is the divine promise that through Abraham's 'seed' God's blessing will be mediated to all the families of the earth.

Although Israel as a nation will play an important role in the outworking of God's purposes for the whole of humanity, particular attention is focused in Genesis on a unique lineage through whom God's blessing will be mediated to

---

[1] Apart from direct references to Israel's many shortcomings, the design of the tabernacle and the establishment of different rituals intended to deal with the consequences of human sinfulness indicate that a return to Eden is not envisaged in the immediate future.

people everywhere. Beginning with Adam, linear genealogies trace this line down to the patriarchs, Abraham, Isaac and Jacob. As the narrative develops Genesis associates this 'seed' with a future descendant of royal status. After Jacob the lineage is traced through Joseph and Ephraim, being tied to the one who receives the blessing of the first-born in each generation. However, Genesis also anticipates that the line of Joseph will eventually give way to a royal descendant from the tribe of Judah.

Although interest in this royal 'seed' fades into the background in the books of Exodus to Deuteronomy, it is not completely forgotten. As well as the special prominence given to the tribes of Ephraim and Judah, the appearance of a powerful, future king dominates the fourth of Balaam's oracles (Num. 24:15–19), and the establishment of an Israelite monarchy is anticipated in the book of Deuteronomy (Deut. 17:14–20). However, like the promise of nationhood, the promise of a future king through whom all the nations of the earth will be blessed remains unfulfilled by the end of the Pentateuch.

3. Beyond the Pentateuch

The promises associated with the patriarchs, Abraham, Isaac and Jacob, also set the agenda for the books of Joshua to Kings. The subject of nationhood is particularly prominent in Joshua, Judges and Samuel. Whereas Joshua gives a predominantly positive description of the Israelite settlement in the land of Canaan, this process is reversed in Judges due to the recurring apostasy of the Israelites. Only through the divine provision of the monarchy is Israel enabled to gain possession of all the land promised to Abraham. Consequently, during the reigns of David and Solomon the Israelites come to possess the land as far as the boundaries defined in Genesis 15:18–21 (cf. 2 Sam. 8:1–14; 1 Kgs. 4:21; 9:20–21).

The books of Samuel recount in detail the dramatic beginnings of the Davidic dynasty, fulfilling the expectation of Genesis that this royal line will be descended from Judah. Later, with the establishment of Solomon as David's successor, Israel enjoys a brief period when, under the control of a divinely empowered 'wise' king, the people experience the benefits of a government that brings justice, prosperity and security.

Although the narrative in Joshua to Samuel advances in significant ways the fulfilment of the divine promises to Abraham, one aspect of these promises is never fully realised, the blessing of the nations.[2] The fulfilment of this latter promise is delayed as Kings charts the gradual decline of both the nation of Israel and the Davidic dynasty. Initially, we witness the break-up of Solomon's

---

[2] A partial fulfilment of this promise is suggested by the events surrounding Solomon's dealings with non-Israelites.

kingdom, with ten tribes forming an independent state, Israel, under the control of Jeroboam, an Ephraimite.[3] Although Solomon's son, Rehoboam, continues to rule from Jerusalem, the southern kingdom of Judah is a mere shadow of the one established by David and Solomon.

After several centuries, the rebellious and sinful actions of the populations of both kingdoms bring upon them God's wrath. As a result they experience defeat at the hands of foreign nations and are carried off into exile. First to experience this is the northern kingdom of Israel; in 722/1 BC the Assyrians sack the capital city of Samaria and deport many of the people.[4] Although it is divinely protected from the Assyrians, the southern kingdom of Judah suffers a similar fate about a century later. Not only is the temple in Jerusalem, the symbol of God's presence in the midst of his people, plundered and destroyed by the Babylonians, but also the Davidic monarchy is forced to relinquish control of the nation.

The exiles experienced by both Israel and Judah stand in sharp contrast to the narrative plot that develops out of the promises in Genesis. Whereas the promises offer hope of divine blessing, the concluding events in Kings focus on God's judgement. Nevertheless, as the account in Genesis to Kings reveals on different occasions, although the consequences of human sin may delay their fulfilment, God's commitment to his promises never wavers. While Kings explains why God's judgement has descended with terrible severity upon the descendants of Abraham, Isaac and Jacob, there remains the hope that, in spite of this, God will yet bring to pass all that he has promised. Consequently, the books of Genesis to Kings convey the expectation that beyond the restoration of Israel from exile all the nations of the earth will be blessed through a Davidic king. Such hopes would have been especially relevant to those who were trying to come to terms with the Babylonian exile and may well explain why the books of Genesis to Kings were brought together to form one of the great literary works of the ancient world.

From the perspective of a Christian living in the twenty-first century AD these ancient writings continue to be highly relevant, especially given the NT proclamation that Jesus Christ is the son of Abraham and the son of David, who mediates God's blessing to all the nations of the earth.[5]

---

[3] In the light of the expectations found in the book of Genesis that a royal line would develop from the line of Ephraim, Jeroboam's appointment is likely to have been favourably received.

[4] In celebration of that event the Assyrian king Sargon II recorded the following words after his capture of Israel's capital city in 721 BC: 'At the beginning of my royal rule ... I besieged and conquered Samaria, led away as booty 27, 290 inhabitants of it' (*Ancient Near Eastern Texts*, edited by J.B. Pritchard, 284–5).

[5] See Alexander, *The Servant King*.

Recommended Further Reading

Commentaries

Items considered to be most suitable for beginners are marked with a ★★★.

Genesis

Aalders, G.C., *Genesis* (2 vols; BSC; Grand Rapids: Zondervan, 1981)

Alter, R., *Genesis* (New York: W.W. Norton, 1996)

Brueggemann, W., *Genesis* (Interpretation; Atlanta: John Knox, 1982)

Cassuto, U., *Commentary on Genesis* (2 vols; Jerusalem: Magnes, 1964)

Coats, G.W., *Genesis with an Introduction to Narrative Literature* (FOTL 1; Grand Rapids: Eerdmans, 1983)

Gibson, J.C.L., *Genesis* (2 vols; DSB; Edinburgh: St Andrew, 1981)

Gowan, D.E., *Genesis 1–11* (ITC; Grand Rapids: Eerdmans, 1988)

Gunkel, H., *Genesis* (trans. Mark E. Biddle; Mercer Library of Biblical Studies; Macon, GA: Mercer University Press, 1997)

Hamilton, V.P., *The Book of Genesis: Chapters 1–17* (NICOT; Grand Rapids: Eerdmans, 1990)

—, *The Book of Genesis: Chapters 18–50* (NICOT; Grand Rapids: Eerdmans, 1995)

Hartley, J.E., *Genesis* (NIBCOT 1; Peabody, MA/Carlisle: Hendrickson/Paternoster Press, 2000)

Jacob, B., *The First Book of the Bible: Genesis* (trans. by E.I. Jacob and W. Jacob; New York: Ktav, 1974)

Kidner, D., *Genesis* (TOTC; Leicester: IVP, 1967) ★★★

Maher, M., *Genesis* (OTM 2; Wilmington: Michael Glazier, 1982)

Mathews, K.A., *Genesis 1–11:26* (NAC 1A; Nashville: Broadman & Holman, 1995)

Rad, G. von, *Genesis* (OTL; London: SCM, 1961)

Ross, A.P., *Creation and Blessing. A Guide to the Study and Exposition of Genesis* (Grand Rapids: Baker Book House, 1988)

Sarna, N.M., *Genesis* (The JPS Torah Commentary; New York: Jewish Publication Society, 1989)

Skinner, J., *Genesis* (2nd edn.; ICC; Edinburgh: T. & T. Clark, 1930)

Speiser, E.A., *Genesis* (AB 1; Garden City: Doubleday, 1964)

Turner, L.A., *Genesis* (Readings, A New Biblical Commentary; Sheffield: Sheffield Academic Press, 2000)

Vawter, B., *On Genesis: A New Reading* (Garden City: Doubleday, 1977)

Wenham, G.J., *Genesis 1–15* (WBC 1; Waco: Word, 1987)

—, 'Genesis', in D.A. Carson, R.T. France, J.A. Motyer, G.J. Wenham (eds.), *New Bible Commentary (21st Century Edition)* (Leicester: IVP, 1994) ★★★

—, *Genesis 16–50* (WBC 2; Dallas: Word, 1994)

Westermann, C., *Genesis 1-11. A Commentary* (trans. John J. Scullion; London/ Minneapolis: SPCK/Augsburg, 1984)

—, *Genesis 12-36. A Commentary* (trans. John J. Scullion; London/Minneapolis: SPCK/Augsburg, 1985)

—, *Genesis 37-50. A Commentary* (trans. John J. Scullion; London/Minneapolis: SPCK/Augsburg, 1987, c1986)

—, *Genesis* (TI; Grand Rapids: Eerdmans, 1987)

Exodus

Alexander, T.D., 'Exodus', in D.A. Carson, R.T. France, J.A. Motyer, G.J. Wenham (eds.), *New Bible Commentary (21st Century Edition)* (Leicester: IVP, 1994) ★★★

Ashby, G.W., *Go out and Meet God: A Commentary on the Book of Exodus* (ITC; Grand Rapids/Edinburgh: Eerdmans/Handsel Press, 1997)

Cassuto, U., *Commentary on Exodus* (Jerusalem: Magnes Press, 1967)

Childs, B.S., *The Book of Exodus* (OTL; London: SCM, 1974)

Coats, G.W., *Exodus 1–18* (FOTL IIA; Grand Rapids: Eerdmans, 1999)

Coggins, R., *The Book of Exodus* (Epworth Commentaries; Peterborough: Epworth, 2000)

Cole, R.A., *Exodus* (TOTC; Leicester: IVP, 1973)

Durham, J.I., *Exodus* (WBC 3; Waco: Word, 1987)

Ellison, H.L., *Exodus* (DSB; Edinburgh: St. Andrew, 1982) ★★★

Gispen, W.H., *Exodus* (BSC; Grand Rapids: Zondervan, 1987)

Hyatt, J.P., *Exodus* (NCB; Grand Rapids: Eerdmans, 1971)

Janzen, W., *Exodus* (BCBC; Waterloo, Ontario: Herald Press, 2000)

Noth, M., *Exodus* (OTL; London: SCM, 1962)

Propp, W.H., *Exodus 1–18: A New Translation with Introduction and Commentary* (AB 2A; New York: Doubleday, 1999)

Leviticus

Bonar, A.A., *A Commentary on Leviticus* (Edinburgh: Banner of Truth, 1966)

Budd, P.J., *Leviticus: Based on the New Revised Standard Version* (NCB; London/ Grand Rapids: Marshall Pickering/Eerdmans, 1996)

Gerstenberger, E., *Leviticus: A Commentary* (OTL; Louisville, KY: Westminister John Knox Press, 1996)

Gorman, F.H., *Divine Presence and Community: A Commentary on the Book of Leviticus* (ITC; Grand Rapids/Edinburgh: Eerdmans/Handsel Press, 1997)

Harrison, R.K., *Leviticus* (TOTC; Leicester: IVP, 1980)

Hartley, J.E., *Leviticus* (WBC 4; Dallas: Word, 1992)

Knight, G.A., *Leviticus* (DSB; Edinburgh: St. Andrew, 1981) ★★★

Levine, B.A., *Leviticus* (The JPS Commentary; New York: Jewish Publication Society, 1989)

Milgrom, J., *Leviticus 1–16: A New Translation with Introduction and Commentary* (AB 3A; New York: Doubleday, 1991)

—, *Leviticus 17–22: A New Translation with Introduction and Commentary* (AB 3B; New York: Doubleday, 2000)

—, *Leviticus 23–27: A New Translation with Introduction and Commentary* (AB 3C; New York: Doubleday, 2001)

Noordtzij, A., *Leviticus* (BSC; Grand Rapids: Zondervan, 1982)

Snaith, N.H., *Leviticus and Numbers* (NCB; Grand Rapids: Eerdmans, 1967)

Wenham, G.J., *The Book of Leviticus* (NICOT; Grand Rapids: Eerdmans, 1979) ★★★

Wright, C.J.H., 'Leviticus', in D.A. Carson, R.T. France, J.A. Motyer, G.J. Wenham (eds.), *New Bible Commentary (21st Century Edition)* (Leicester: IVP, 1994) ★★★

Numbers

Ashley, T.R., *The Book of Numbers* (NICOT; Grand Rapids: Eerdmans, 1993)

Budd, P.J., *Numbers* (WBC 5; Waco: Word, 1984)

Davies, E.W., *Numbers: Based on the Revised Standard Version* (NCB; London/ Grand Rapids: Marshall Pickering/Eerdmans, 1995)

Gray, G.B., *Numbers* (ICC; Edinburgh: T. & T. Clark, 1903)

Harrison, R.K., *Numbers* (WEC; Chicago: Moody, 1990)

Levine, B.A., *Numbers 1–20: A New Translation with Introduction and Commentary* (AB 4A; New York: Doubleday, 1993)

Levine, B.A., *Numbers 21–36: A New Translation with Introduction and Commentary* (AB 4B; New York: Doubleday, 2000)

Maarsingh, B., *Numbers* (TI; Grand Rapids: Eerdmans, 1987)

Milgrom, J., *Numbers* (The JPS Torah Commentary; New York: Jewish Publication Society, 1990)

Naylor, P.J., 'Numbers', in D.A. Carson, R.T. France, J.A. Motyer, G.J. Wenham (eds.), *New Bible Commentary (21st Century Edition)* (Leicester: IVP, 1994) ★★★

Noordtzij, A., *Numbers* (BSC; Grand Rapids: Zondervan, 1983)

Olson, D.T., *Numbers* (Interpretation; Louisville, KY: John Knox Press, 1996)

Philip, P., *Numbers* (Waco: Word, 1987)

Riggans, W., *Numbers* (DSB; Edinburgh: St. Andrew, 1983)

Sakenfeld, K.D., *Journeying with God: A Commentary on the Book of Numbers* (ITC; Grand Rapids: Eerdmans, 1995)

Snaith, N.H., *Leviticus and Numbers* (NCB; Grand Rapids: Eerdmans, 1967)

Wenham, G.J., *Numbers* (TOTC; Leicester: IVP, 1981) ★★★

Deuteronomy

Christensen, D.L., *Deuteronomy 1–11* (WBC 6; Waco: Word, 1991)

Clifford, R., *Deuteronomy* (OTM 4; Wilmington: Michael Glazier, 1982)

Craigie, P.C., *The Book of Deuteronomy* (NICOT; Grand Rapids: Eerdmans, 1976)

Driver, S.R., *A Critical and Exegetical Commentary on Deuteronomy* (3rd edn; ICC; Edinburgh: T. & T. Clark, 1902)

Mann, T.W., *Deuteronomy* (Westminster Bible Companion; Louisville, KY: Westminster John Knox Press, 1995)

Mayes, A.D.H., *Deuteronomy* (NCB; Grand Rapids: Eerdmans, 1979)

McConville, J.G., 'Deuteronomy', in D.A. Carson, R.T. France, J.A. Motyer, G.J. Wenham (eds.), *New Bible Commentary (21st Century Edition)* (Leicester: IVP, 1994) ★★★

Miller, P.D., *Deuteronomy* (Interpretation; Louisville: John Knox, 1990)

Munchenberg, R.H., *Deuteronomy* (Adelaide: Lutheran Publishing House, 1987)

Payne, D.F., *Deuteronomy* (DSB; Edinburgh: St Andrew, 1985) ★★★

Ridderbos, J., *Deuteronomy* (BSC; Grand Rapids: Zondervan, 1984)

Thompson, J.A., *Deuteronomy* (TOTC; Leicester: IVP, 1974)

Tigay, J.H., *Deuteronomy: The Traditional Hebrew Text with the New JPS Translation* (The JPS Torah Commentary; Philadelphia: Jewish Publication Society, 1996)

Weinfeld, M., *Deuteronomy 1–11* (B 5; New York: Doubleday, 1991)

Wright, C.J.H., *Deuteronomy* (IBCOT 4; Peabody, MA/Carlisle: Hendrickson Publishers/Paternoster Press, 1996) ★★★

Wright, G.E., 'Deuteronomy', in *The Interpreter's Bible* (Nashville: Abingdon, 1953)

Special studies

The following works are recommended for those who wish to explore in more detail specific topics along the lines adopted in this book. It should be noted that the works listed here vary in the extent and depth of their treatment of these topics.

The genealogical structure of Genesis

Alexander, T.D., 'Genealogies, Seed and the Compositional Unity of Genesis', *TynBul* 44 (1993), 255–70
—, 'Royal Expectations in Genesis to Kings: Their Importance for Biblical Theology', *TynBul* 49.2 (1998), 191–212
Robinson, R.D., 'Literary Functions of the Genealogies of Genesis', *CBQ* 48 (1986), 595–608
Wilson, R.R., *Genealogy and History in the Biblical World* (New Haven: Yale University Press, 1977)
Woudstra, M.H., 'The Toledot of the Book of Genesis and Their Redemptive-Historical Significance', *CTJ* 5 (1970), 184–9

Blessing

Clines, D.J.A., *The Theme of the Pentateuch* (2nd edn.; JSOTSS 10; Sheffield: Sheffield Academic Press, 1996)
Muilenburg, J., 'Abraham and the Nations: Blessing and World History', *Int* 19 (1965), 387–98
Westermann, C., *Blessing in the Bible and in the Life of the Church* (Philadelphia: Fortress Press, 1978)

Land

Brueggemann, W., *The Land* (Philadelphia: Fortress Press, 1977)
Frymer-Kensky, T., 'The Atrahasis Epic and its Significance for Our Understanding of Genesis 1–9', *BA* 40 (1977), 147–55
Wenham, G.J., 'Sanctuary Symbolism in the Garden of Eden Story', *Proceedings of the World Congress of Jewish Studies* 9 (1986), 19–25

Abraham

Alexander, T.D., 'Abraham Re-Assessed Theologically: The Abraham Narrative and the New Testament Understanding of Justification by Faith', in R.S. Hess, G.J. Wenham and P.E. Satterthwaite (eds.), in *He Swore An Oath: Biblical Themes from Genesis* (2nd edn.; Grand Rapids/Carlisle: Baker Book House/Paternoster, 1994), 7–28
Gros Louis, K.R.R., 'Abraham: I', in K.R.R. Gros Louis and J.S. Ackerman (eds.), *Literary Interpretations of Biblical Narratives II* (Nashville: Abingdon, 1982), 53–70
—, 'Abraham: II', in K.R.R. Gros Louis and J.S. Ackerman (eds.), *Literary Interpretations of Biblical Narratives I* (Nashville: Abingdon, 1982), 71–84
Hansen, G.W., *Abraham in Galatians* (JSNTSS 29; Sheffield: JSOT Press, 1989)

Turner, L.A., *Announcement of Plot in Genesis* (JSOTSS 133; Sheffield: JSOT Press, 1990)

Passover

Alexander, T.D., 'The Passover Sacrifice', in R.T. Beckwith and M. Selman (eds.), *Sacrifice in the Bible* (Carlisle/Grand Rapids: Paternoster/Baker Book House, 1995), 1–24

Bokser, B.M., *The Origins of the Seder* (Berkeley: University of California, 1984)

Segal, J.B., *The Hebrew Passover From the Earliest Times to AD 70* (London Oriental Series 12; London: Oxford University Press, 1963)

Sinai Covenant

Alexander, T.D., 'The Composition of the Sinai Narrative in Exodus xix 1–xxiv 11', *VT* 49 (1999) 2–20

Chirichigno, C.G., 'The Narrative Structure of Exodus 19–24', *Bib* 68 (1987), 457–79

Moberly, R.W.L., *At the Mountain of God: Story and Theology in Exodus 32–34* (JSOTSS 22; Sheffield: JSOT Press, 1983)

Sprinkle, J.M., *'The Book of the Covenant': A Literary Approach* (JSOTSS 174; Sheffield: JSOT Press, 1994)

Tabernacle

Hart, I., 'Preaching on the Account of the Tabernacle', *EvQ* 54 (1982), 111–6

Koester, C.R., *The Dwelling of God: The Tabernacle in the Old Testament, Intertestamental Jewish Literature, and the New Testament* (CBQMS 22; Washington: Catholic Biblical Association of America, 1989)

Soltau, H.W., *The Holy Vessels and Furniture of the Tabernacle of Israel* (Grand Rapids: Kregel, 1969; first published 1865)

Holiness

Jenson, P.P., *Graded Holiness: A Key to the Priestly Conception of the World* (JSOTSS 106; Sheffield: JSOT Press, 1992)

Wright, D.P., 'Holiness (OT)', ABD 3:237–49

—, 'Unclean and Clean (OT)', ABD 6:729–41

Sacrifices

Anderson, G.A., 'Sacrifices and Sacrificial Offerings (OT)', ABD 5:870–86

Averbeck, R.E., זבח (zbḥ)', in *NIDOTTE* 1:1066–73

Kiuchi, N., *The Purification Offering in the Priestly Literature: Its Meaning and Function* (JSOTSS 56; Sheffield: Sheffield Academic Press, 1987)

Milgrom, J., *Cult and Conscience: The ASHAM and the Priestly Doctrine of Repentance* (Leiden: Brill, 1976)

Wenham, G.J., 'The Theology of Old Testament Sacrifice', in R.T. Beckwith and M. Selman (eds.), *Sacrifice in the Bible* (Carlisle: Paternoster, 1995), 75–87

Food Laws

Houston, W., *Purity and Monotheism: Clean and Unclean Animals in Biblical Law* (JSOTSS 140; Sheffield: JSOT Press, 1993)

Soler, J., 'The Semiotics of Food in the Bible', in R. Forster and O. Ranum (eds.), *Food and Drink in History* (Baltimore: Johns Hopkins University, 1979), 126–38

Wenham, G.J., 'The Theology of Unclean Food', *EvQ* 53 (1981), 6–15

Wright, D.P., 'Observations on the Ethical Foundations of the Biblical Dietary Laws', in E.D. Firmage, B.G. Weiss and J.W. Welch (eds.), *Religion and Law, Biblical-Judaic and Islamic Perspectives* (Winona Lake: Eisenbrauns, 1990), 193–8

Wilderness Wanderings

Olson, D.T., *The Death of the Old and the Birth of the New: The Framework of the Book of Numbers and the Pentateuch* (Chico: Scholars, 1985)

Deuteronomy

McConville, J.G., *Law and Theology in Deuteronomy* (JSOTSS 33; Sheffield: JSOT Press, 1984)

—, *Grace in the End* (Carlisle: Paternoster, 1994)

Millar, J.G, *Now Choose Life: Theology and Ethics in Deuteronomy* (New Studies in Biblical Theology; Grand Rapids: Eerdmans, 1999)

Selected Bibliography

In order to restrict the size of the bibliography, only books and articles in English have been included. Fuller bibliographies on each book of the Pentateuch may be found in the commentaries of Westermann, Wenham and Matthews on Genesis; Childs, Durham and Propp on Exodus; Hartley and Milgrom on Leviticus; Levine and Budd on Numbers; Christensen and Weinfeld on Deuteronomy.

Aalders, G.C., *A Short Introduction to the Pentateuch* (London: Tyndale Press, 1949)

—, *Genesis* (2 vols; BSC; Grand Rapids: Zondervan, 1981)

Abela, A., *The Themes of the Abraham Narrative: Thematic Coherence within the Abraham Literary Unit of Genesis 11, 27–25, 18* (Malta: Studia Editions, 1989)

Ackerman, J.S., 'The Literary Context of the Moses Birth Story', in K.R.R. Gros Louis and J.S. Ackerman (eds.), *Literary Interpretations of Biblical Narratives* (Nashville: Abingdon, 1974), 74–119

Aitken, K.T., 'The Wooing of Rebekah: A Study in the Development of the Tradition', *JSOT* 30 (1984), 3–23

Albright, W.F., *From the Stone Age to Christianity* (2nd edn.; Baltimore: Johns Hopkins, 1946)

—, 'From the Patriarchs to Moses: I. From Abraham to Joseph', *BA* 36 (1973), 5–33

Alexander, T.D., *A Literary Analysis of the Abraham Narrative in Genesis* (PhD, The Queen's University of Belfast, 1982)

—, 'Genesis 22 and the Covenant of Circumcision', *JSOT* 25 (1983), 17–22

—, 'Lot's Hospitality: A Clue to His Righteousness', *JBL* 104 (1985), 289–91

—, 'From Adam to Judah: The Significance of the Family Tree in Genesis', *EvQ* 61 (1989), 5–19

—, 'The Wife/Sister Incidents of Genesis: Oral Variants?' *IBS* 11 (1989), 2–22

—, 'The Hagar Traditions in Genesis xvi and xxi', in J.A. Emerton (ed.), *Studies in the Pentateuch* (SVT Vol. 41; Leiden: Brill, 1990), 131–48

—, 'Are the Wife/Sister Incidents of Genesis Literary Compositional Variants?' *VT* 42 (1992), 145–53

—, 'Genealogies, Seed and the Compositional Unity of Genesis', *TynBul* 44 (1993), 255–70

—, 'Abraham Re-Assessed Theologically: The Abraham Narrative and the New Testament Understanding of Justification by Faith', in R.S. Hess, G.J. Wenham and P.E. Satterthwaite (eds.), *In He Swore an Oath: Biblical Themes from Genesis* (2nd edn.; Grand Rapids/Carlisle: Baker Book House/Paternoster, 1994), 7–28

—, 'Exodus', in D.A. Carson, R.T. France, J.A. Motyer, G.J. Wenham (eds.), *New Bible Commentary (21st Century Edition)* (Leicester: IVP, 1994)

—, *From Paradise to the Promised Land: An Introduction to the Main Themes of the Pentateuch* (Carlisle: Paternoster, 1995)

—, 'Messianic Ideology in the Book of Genesis', in P.E. Satterthwaite, R.S. Hess and G.J. Wenham (eds.), *The Lord's Anointed: Interpretation of Old Testament Messianic Texts* (Grand Rapids/Carlisle: Baker Book House/Paternoster, 1995), 19–39

—, 'The Passover Sacrifice', in R.T. Beck and M. Selman (eds.), *Sacrifice in the Bible* (Carlisle/Grand Rapids: Paternoster/Baker Book House, 1995), 1–24

—, *Abraham in the Negev: A Source-critical investigation of Genesis 20:1–22:19* (Carlisle: Paternoster, 1997)

—, 'Further Observations on the Term "Seed" in Genesis', *TynBul* 48.2 (1997), 363–8

—, *Pentateuchal Criticism Today: A Guidebook for Beginners* (Leicester: Religious and Theological Students Fellowship, 1998)

—, 'Royal Expectations in Genesis to Kings: Their Importance for Biblical Theology', *TynBul* 49.2 (1998), 191–212

—, 'The Composition of the Sinai Narrative in Exodus xix 1–xxiv 11', *VT* 49 (1999), 2–20

—, 'Beyond Borders: The Wider Dimension of Land', in P. Johnston and P. Walker (eds.), *The Land of Promise: Biblical, Theological and Contemporary Perspectives* (Leicester: Apollos, 2000), 35–50

Alexander, T.D. and B.S. Rosner (eds.), *The New Dictionary of Biblical Theology* (Leicester: IVP, 2000)

Alter, R., *The Art of Biblical Narrative* (New York: Basic Books, 1981)

—, *Genesis* (New York: W.W. Norton, 1996)

Anbar, M., 'Genesis 15: A Conflation of Two Deuteronomic Narratives', *JBL* 101 (1982), 39–55

Andersen, F.I., *The Hebrew Verbless Clause in the Pentateuch* (JBL Monograph Series 14; Nashville/New York: Abingdon, 1970)

—, *The Sentence in Biblical Hebrew* (The Hague/Paris: Mouton, 1974)

Andersen, F.I. and A.D. Forbes, *The Computer Bible* (Wooster, Ohio: Biblical Research Associates, 1991)

Anderson, B.W., 'From Analysis to Synthesis: The Interpretation of Genesis 1–11', *JBL* 97 (1978), 23–39

—, 'Unity and Diversity in God's Creation', *CurTM* 5 (1978), 69–81

—, *Creation in the Old Testament* (Issues in Religion and Theology 6; Philadelphia/ London: Fortress Press/SPCK, 1984)

Anderson, G.A., *Sacrifices and Offerings in Ancient Israel: Studies in Their Social and Political Importances* (Harvard Semitic Monographs 41; Atlanta, GA: Scholars Press, 1987)

—, 'Sacrifices and Sacrificial Offerings (OT)', in *ABD* 5: 870–86

Andreasen, N.E., 'Genesis 14 in Its Near Eastern Context', in C.D. Evans (ed.), *Scripture in Context. Essays on the Comparative Method* (Pittsburg: Pickwick, 1980), 59–77

Armstrong, K., *In the Beginning: A New Interpretation of Genesis* (New York: Ballantine Books, 1997)

Ashby, G.W., *Go out and Meet God: A Commentary on the Book of Exodus* (ITC; Grand Rapids/Edinburgh: Eerdmans/Handsel Press, 1997)

Ashby, G.W.E.C., 'Reflections on the Language of Genesis 1 and 2', *Semitics* 6 (1978), 58–69

Ashley, T.R., *The Book of Numbers* (NICOT; Grand Rapids: Eerdmans, 1993)

Auffret, P., 'The Literary Structure of Exodus 6:2–8', *JSOT* 27 (1983), 46–54

—, 'Remarks on J. Magonet's Interpretation of Exodus 6:2–8', *JSOT* 27 (1983), 69–71

Averbeck, R.E., 'זבח (zbḥ)', in *NIDOTTE* 1:1066–73

Baker, D.W., 'Division Markers and the Structure of Lev 1–7', in E.A. Livingstone (ed.), *Studia Biblica. Papers on Old Testament and Related Themes* (JSOTSS Vol. 11; Sheffield: JSOT Press, 1979), 9–15

—, 'Diversity and Unity in the Literary Structure of Genesis', in A.R. Millard and D.J. Wiseman (eds.), *Essays on the Patriarchal Narratives* (Leicester: IVP, 1980), 189–205

Baker, J.A., 'Deuteronomy and World Problems', *JSOT* 29 (1984), 3–17

Baldwin, J.G., *The Message of Genesis 12–50: From Abraham to Joseph* (The Bible Speaks Today; Leicester/Downers Grove, IL: InterVarsity Press, 1986)

Balentine, S.E., *The Torah's Vision of Worship* (Overtures to Biblical Theology; Minneapolis: Fortress Press, 1999)

Bar-Efrat, S., 'Literary Modes and Methods in the Biblical Narrative', *Imm* 8 (1978), 19–31

—, 'Some Observations on the Analysis of Structure in Biblical Narrative', *VT* 30 (1980), 154–73

—, *Narrative Art in the Bible* (Sheffield: Almond, 1989)

Barker, P.A., 'Faithless Israel, Faithful Yahweh in Deuteronomy', *TynBul* 47.1 (1996), 173–6

—, 'The Theology of Deuteronomy', *TynBul* 49.2 (1998), 277–304

Barr, J., 'Reading the Bible as Literature', *BJRL* 56 (1974), 10–33

Bassett, F.W., 'Noah's Nakedness and the Curse of Canaan', *VT* 21 (1971), 232–7

Batto, B.F., 'The Institution of Marriage in Genesis 2 and in Atrahasis', *CBQ* 62.4 (2000), 621–31

Beattie, D.R.G., 'What Is Genesis 2–3 About?', *ExpTim* 92 (1980), 8–10

—, 'Peshat and Derash in the Garden of Eden', *IBS* 7 (1985), 62–75

Bechtel, L.M., 'What If Dinah Is Not Raped? (Genesis 34)', *JSOT* 62 (1994), 19–36

Bentzen, A., *Introduction to the Old Testament* (7th edn.; Copenhagen: G.E.C. Gad, 1967)

Berlin, A., *Poetics and Interpretation of Biblical Narrative* (Sheffield: Almond, 1983)

Bird, P.A., '"Male and Female He Created Them": Gen 1:27b in the Context of the Priestly Account of Creation', *HTR* 74 (1981), 129–60

Blenkinsopp, J., 'The Structure of P', *CBQ* 38 (1976), 275–92

—, 'Abraham and the Righteous of Sodom', *JSS* 33 (1982), 119–32

—, *The Pentateuch* (London: SCM, 1992)

—, 'An Assessment of the Alleged Pre-Exilic Date of the Priestly Material in the Pentateuch', *ZAW* 108 (1996), 495–518

Blocher, H., *In the Beginning: The Opening Chapters of Genesis* (Leicester: IVP, 1984)

Blythin, J., 'The Patriarchs and the Promise', *SJT* 21 (1968), 56–73

Bokser, B.M., *The Origins of the Seder* (Berkeley: University of California, 1984)

—, 'Unleavened Bread and Passover, Feast Of', in *ABD* 6:755–65

Bonar, A.A., *A Commentary on Leviticus* (Edinburgh: Banner of Truth, 1966)

Booif, T., 'Mountain and Theophany in the Sinai Narrative', *Bib* 65 (1984), 1–26

Boomershine, T.E., 'The Structure of Narrative Rhetoric in Genesis 2–3', *Semeia* 18 (1980), 113–29

Bratcher, R.G. and H. Hatton, *A Handbook on Deuteronomy* (UBS Handbook Series; New York: United Bible Societies, 2000)

Brenner, A., *Genesis: The Feminist Companion to the Bible* (Feminist Companion to the Bible; Second Series; 1; Sheffield: Sheffield Academic Press, 1998)

—, *Exodus to Deuteronomy: A Feminist Companion to the Bible* (Feminist Companion to the Bible; Second Series; 5; Sheffield: Sheffield Academic Press, 2000)

Brichto, H.C., *Toward a Grammar of Biblical Poetics* (Oxford: Oxford University Press, 1992)

—, *The Names of God: Poetic Readings in Biblical Beginnings* (New York: Oxford University Press, 1998)

Brock, S., 'Genesis 22: Where Was Sarah?', *ExpTim* 96 (1984), 14–7

Brodie, T.L., *Genesis as Dialogue: A Literary, Historical & Theological Commentary* (Oxford/New York: Oxford University Press, 2001)

Brueggemann, W., 'The Kerygma of the Priestly Writers', *ZAW* 84 (1972), 394–414

—, *The Land* (Philadelphia: Fortress Press, 1977)

—, *Genesis* (Interpretation; Atlanta: John Knox, 1982)

Brueggemann, W. and H.W. Wolff, *The Vitality of Old Testament Traditions* (Atlanta: John Knox, 1975)

Buck, D.W., 'Exodus 20:1–17', *LTJ* 16 (1982), 65–75

Budd, P.J., *Numbers* (WBC 5; Waco: Word, 1984)

—, *Leviticus: Based on the New Revised Standard Version* (NCB; London/Grand Rapids: Marshall Pickering/Eerdmans, 1996)

Butler, T.C., 'An Anti-Moses Tradition', *JSOT* 12 (1979), 9–15

Carmichael, C.M., *The Laws of Deuteronomy* (Ithaca, NY: Cornell University Press, 1974)

—, *Law, Legend, and Incest in the Bible: Leviticus 18–20* (Ithaca, NY: Cornell University Press, 1997)

Carr, D.M., *Reading the Fractures of Genesis: Historical and Literary Approaches* (Louisville, KY: Westminster John Knox Press, 1996)

Carroll R.M.D., *Rethinking Contexts, Rereading Texts: Contributions from the Social Sciences to Biblical Interpretation* (JSOTSS 299; Sheffield: Sheffield Academic Press, 2000)

Caspi, M. and S.B. Cohen, *The Binding (Aqedah) and Its Transformations in Judaism and Islam: The Lambs of God* (Mellen Biblical Press Series 32; Lewiston, NY: Mellen Biblical Press, 1995)

Cassuto, U., *The Documentary Hypothesis* (Jerusalem: Magnes Press, 1961)

—, *Commentary on Genesis* (2 vols; Jerusalem: Magnes Press, 1964)

—, *Commentary on Exodus* (Jerusalem: Magnes Press, 1967)

Cazelles, H., 'Theological Bulletin on the Pentateuch', *BTB* 2 (1972), 3–24

Cheon, S., *The Exodus Story in the Wisdom of Solomon: A Study in Biblical Interpretation* (Journal for the Study of the Pseudepigrapha; Supplement Series 23; Sheffield: Sheffield Academic Press, 1997)

Chew, H.C., *The Theme of 'Blessing for the Nations' in the Patriarchal Narratives of Genesis* (PhD, University of Sheffield, 1982)

Cheyne, T.K., *Founders of Old Testament Criticism* (London: Methuen, 1893)

Childs, B.S., *The Book of Exodus* (OTL; London: SCM, 1974)

—, *Introduction to the Old Testament as Scripture* (Philadelphia: Fortress Press, 1979)

Chirichigno, C.G., 'The Narrative Structure of Exodus 19–24', *Bib* 68 (1987), 457–79

Christensen, D.L., *Deuteronomy 1–11* (WBC 6; Waco: Word, 1991)

Clark, W.M., 'The Flood and the Structure of the Pre-Patriarchal History', *ZAW* 83 (1971), 184–211

—, 'The Righteousness of Noah', *VT* 21 (1971), 261–80

Clarke, E.G. and S. Magder, *Targum Pseudo-Jonathan: Deuteronomy* (Collegeville, MN: Liturgical Press, 1998)

Clements, R.E., *Abraham and David: Genesis XV and Its Meaning for Israelite Tradition* (Studies in Biblical Theology; 2nd Series 5; London: SCM, 1967)

—, 'gôy', in TDOT 2 (1977), 426–33

—, 'Pentateuchal Problems', in G.W. Anderson (ed.), *Tradition and Interpretation* (Oxford: Clarendon Press, 1979)

—, *Deuteronomy* (Old Testament Guides; Sheffield: JSOT Press, 1989)

—, *The Book of Deuteronomy: A Preacher's Commentary* (Epworth Commentaries; Peterborough: Epworth Press, 2001)

Clifford, R., *Deuteronomy*, (OTM 4; Wilmington: Michael Glazier, 1982)

Clifford, R.J., *The Cosmic Mountain in Canaan and the Old Testament* (Cambridge, MA: Harvard University Press, 1972)

Clines, D.J.A., 'Noah's Flood: 1: The Theology of the Flood', *Faith and Thought* 100 (1972), 128–42

—, 'Theme in Genesis 1–11', *CBQ* 38 (1976), 483–507

—, *The Theme of the Pentateuch* (JSOTSS 10; Sheffield: JSOT Press, 1978)

—, 'The Significance of the "Sons of God" Episode (Genesis 6:1–4) in the Context of the "Primeval History" (Genesis 1–11)', *JSOT* 13 (1979), 33–46

—, 'What Happens in Genesis', in *What Does Eve Do to Help? And Other Readerly Questions to the Old Testament* (JSOTSS Vol. 94; Sheffield: JSOT Press, 1990), 49–66

—, *The Theme of the Pentateuch* (2nd edn.; JSOTSS 10; Sheffield: Sheffield Academic Press, 1996)

Coats, G.W., *Rebellion in the Wilderness: The Murmuring Motif in the Wilderness Traditions of the Old Testament* (Nashville: Abingdon, 1968)

—, 'Abraham's Sacrifice of Faith: A Form-Critical Study of Genesis 22', *Int* 27 (1973), 389–400

—, 'The Joseph Story and Ancient Wisdom: A Reappraisal', *CBQ* 35 (1973), 285–97

—, 'Redactional Unity in Genesis 37–50', *JBL* 93 (1974), 15–21

—, *From Canaan to Egypt: Structural and Theological Context for the Joseph Story* (CBQMS 4; Washington, DC: Catholic Biblical Association of America, 1976)

—, 'Strife and Reconciliation: Themes of a Biblical Theology in the Book of Genesis', *HBT* 2 (1980), 15–37

—, 'Strife without Reconciliation: A Narrative Theme in the Jacob Tradition', in R. Albertz. (ed.), *Werden Und Wirken Des Alten Testament. Festschrift Für Claus Westermann*, Vandenhoeck und Ruprecht: Göttingen, 1980)

—, *Genesis with an Introduction to Narrative Literature* (FOTL 1; Grand Rapids: Eerdmans, 1983)

—, 'Lot: A Foil in the Abraham Saga', in J.T. Butler et al (eds.), *Understand the Word: Essays in Honor of Bernhard W. Anderson* (JSOTSS Vol. 37; Sheffield: JSOT Press, 1985), 113–32

—, *Exodus 1–18* (FOTL IIA; Grand Rapids: Eerdmans, 1999)

Cody, A., 'When Is a Chosen People Called a *goy*?', *VT* 14 (1964), 1–6

Coggins, R., *The Book of Exodus* (Epworth Commentaries; Peterborough: Epworth, 2000)

Cohn, R.L., 'Narrative Structure and Canonical Perspective in Genesis', *JSOT* 25 (1983), 3–16

Cole, R.A., *Exodus* (TOTC; Leicester: IVP, 1973)

Collins, J., 'A Syntactical Note (Genesis 3:15): Is the Woman's Seed Singular or Plural?' *TynBul* 48.1 (1997), 139–48

Coote, R. and D. Ord, *The Bible's First Historian: From Eden to the Court of David with the Yahwist* (Philadelphia: Fortress Press, 1989)

Craghan, J.F., 'The Elohist in Recent Literature', *BTB* 7 (1977), 23–35

Craigie, P.C., *The Book of Deuteronomy* (NICOT; Grand Rapids: Eerdmans, 1976)

Crenshaw, J.L., 'Method in Determining Wisdom Influence Upon "Historical" Literature', *JBL* 88 (1969), 129–42

—, 'Journey into Oblivion: A Structural Analysis of Gen 22:1–19', *Soundings* 58 (1975), 243–56

Cross, F.M., *Canaanite Myth and Hebrew Epic* (Cambridge, MA: Harvard University Press, 1973)

Cross, F.M. and D.N. Freedman, *Studies in Ancient Yahwistic Poetry* (The Biblical Resource Series; Grand Rapids/Livonia, MI: Eerdmans/Dove Booksellers, 1997)

Crusemann, F., *The Torah: Theology and Social History of Old Testament Law* (Minneapolis: Fortress Press, 1996)

Cryer, F.H., 'The Interrelationships of Gen 5,32; 11,10–11 and the Chronology of the Flood (Gen 6–9)', *Bib* 66 (1985), 241–61

Cryer, F.H. and T.L. Thompson, *Qumran between the Old and New Testaments* (JSOTSS 290; Sheffield: Sheffield Academic Press, 1998)

Culley, R.C., 'Structural Analysis: Is It Done with Mirrors?' *Int* 28 (1974), 165–81

—, 'Themes and Variations in Three Groups of OT Narratives', *Semeia* 3 (1975), 3–13

—, 'Oral Tradition and the OT: Some Recent Discussion', *Semeia* 5 (1976), 1–33

—, *Studies in the Structure of Hebrew Narrative* (Semeia Supplements; Philadelphia/Missoula, MT: Fortress Press/Scholars Press, 1976)

—, 'Action Sequences in Genesis 2–3', *Semeia* 18 (1980), 25–33

Dahlberg, B.T., 'On Recognizing the Unity of Genesis', *TD* 24 (1976), 360–7

Daly, R.J., 'The Soteriological Significance of the Sacrifice of Isaac', *CBQ* 39 (1977), 45–75

Damrosch, D., 'Leviticus', in R. Alter and F. Kermode (eds.), *The Literary Guide to the Bible* (Cambridge, MA: Harvard University Press, 1987)

Daube, D., *The Exodus Pattern in the Bible* (London: Faber and Faber, 1963)

Davidson, R., *Genesis 1–11* (The Cambridge Bible Commentary, New English Bible; Cambridge: Cambridge University Press, 1973)

—, *Genesis 12–50* (The Cambridge Bible Commentary, New English Bible; Cambridge/New York: Cambridge University Press, 1979)

Davies, D.J., 'An Interpretation of Sacrifice in Leviticus', *ZAW* 89 (1977), 387–99

Davies, E.W., *Numbers: Based on the Revised Standard Version* (NCB; London/ Grand Rapids: Marshall Pickering/Eerdmans, 1995)

Davies, G.F., *Israel in Egypt: Reading Exodus 1–2* (JSOTSS 135; Sheffield: JSOT Press, 1992)

Davies, G.I., *The Way of the Wilderness* (Cambridge: Cambridge University Press, 1979)

Davies, P.R. and D.J.A. Clines, *The World of Genesis: Persons, Places, Perspectives* (JSOTSS 257; Sheffield: Sheffield Academic Press, 1998)

Davies, R.P., 'The Sacrifice of Isaac and Passover', in E.A. Livingstone (ed.), *Studia Biblica. Papers on Old Testament and Related Themes* (JSOTSS Vol. 11; Sheffield: JSOT, 1979), 127–32

Davis, D.R., 'Rebellion, Presence, and Covenant: A Study in Exodus 32–34', *WTJ* 44 (1982), 71–87

Delaney, C.L., *Abraham on Trial: The Social Legacy of Biblical Myth* (Princeton, NJ: Princeton University Press, 1998)

DeWitt, D.S., 'The Generation of Genesis', *EvQ* 48 (1976), 196–221

Dillard, R.B. and T. Longman III, *An Introduction to the Old Testament* (Leicester: Apollos, 1995)

Dorsey, D.A., *The Literary Structure of the Old Testament: A Commentary on Genesis–Malachi* (Grand Rapids: Baker Book House, 1999)

Douglas, M., *Purity and Danger* (London: Routledge & K. Paul, 1969)

—, 'The Forbidden Animals in Leviticus', *JSOT* 59 (1993), 3–23

—, *Leviticus as Literature* (Oxford/New York: Oxford University Press, 1999)

Dozeman, T.B., *God on the Mountain: A Study of Redaction, Theology and Canon in Exodus 19–24* (SBLMS; Missoula: Scholars, 1989)

—, *God at War: Power in the Exodus Tradition* (New York: Oxford University Press, 1996)

—, 'The Yam-Sup in the Exodus and the Crossing of the Jordan River', *CBQ* 58.3 (1996), 407–16

Driver, S.R., *A Critical and Exegetical Commentary on Deuteronomy* (3rd edn.; ICC; Edinburgh: T. & T. Clark, 1902)

—, *An Introduction to the Literature of the Old Testament* (9th edn.; Edinburgh: T. & T. Clark, 1913)

Dumbrell, W.J., 'The Covenant with Abraham', *RefThR* 38 (1982), 42–50

—, *Covenant and Creation: An Old Testament Covenantal Theology* (Exeter: Paternoster, 1984)

—, *The End of the Beginning: Revelation 21–22 and the Old Testament* (Grand Rapids: Baker Book House, 1985)

Durham, J.I., *Exodus* (WBC 3; Waco: Word, 1987)

Eakin Jr, F.E., 'The Plagues and the Crossing of the Sea', *RevExp* 74 (1977), 473–82

Eakins, J.K., 'Moses', *RevExp* 74 (1977), 461–71

Eissfeldt, W., *The Old Testament. An Introduction* (Oxford: Basil Blackwell, 1965)

Elder, W.H., 'The Passover', *RevExp* 74 (1977), 511–22

Ellington, J., 'Miscarriage or Premature Birth?' *BT* 37 (1986), 334–7

Ellis, P.F., *The Yahwist. The Bible's First Theologian* (London: Chapman, 1969)

Ellison, H.L., *Exodus* (DSB; Edinburgh: St. Andrew, 1982)

Emerton, J.A., 'The Riddle of Genesis xiv', *VT* 21 (1971), 403–39

—, 'Judah and Tamar', *VT* 29 (1979), 403–15

—, 'The Origin of the Promises to the Patriarchs in the Older Sources of the Book of Genesis', *VT* 32 (1982), 14–32

—, 'An Examination of Some Attempts to Defend the Unity of the Flood Narrative in Genesis: I', *VT* 37 (1987), 401–20; and *VT* 38 (1988), 1–21

Endo, Y., *The Verbal System of Classical Hebrew in the Joseph Story: An Approach from Discourse Analysis* (Studia Semitica Neerlandica 32; Assen, the Netherlands: Van Gorcum, 1996)

Engnell, I., 'The Pentateuch', in J.T. Willis (ed.), *Critical Essays on the Old Testament* (London: SPCK, 1970)

Enns, P., *Exodus Retold: Ancient Exegesis of the Departure from Egypt in Wis 10:15–21 and 19:1–9* (Harvard Semitic Monographs 57; Atlanta, GA: Scholars Press, 1997)

Enz, J.J., 'The Book of Exodus as a Literary Type for the Gospel of John', *JBL* 76 (1957), 208–15

Eslinger, L., 'Freedom or Knowledge? Perspectives and Purpose in the Exodus Narrative (Exodus 1–15)', *JSOT* 52 (1991), 43–60

Exum, J.C., ' "You Shall Let Every Daughter Live": A Study of Exodus 1:8–2:10', *Semeia* 28 (1983), 63–82

Feyerick, A., C.H. Gordon and N.M. Sarna, *Genesis: World of Myths and Patriarchs* (New York: New York University Press, 1996)

Fields, W.W., *Sodom and Gomorrah: History and Motif in Biblical Narrative* (JSOTSS 231; Sheffield: Sheffield Academic Press, 1997)

Finkelstein, J.J., 'The Ox That Gored', *TAPS* 71 (1981), 5–47

Finn, A.H., *The Unity of the Pentateuch* (London: Marshall, n.d)

Fishbane, M.A., 'Composition and Structure in the Jacob Cycle (Gen 25:19–35:22)', *JJS* 26 (1975), 15–38

—, 'The Sacred Center The Symbolic Structure of the Bible', in M.A. Fishbane and P.R. Flohr (eds.), *Texts and Responses* (Leiden: Brill, 1975)

—, *Text and Texture. Close Readings of Selected Biblical Texts* (New York: Schocken Books, 1979)

—, *Biblical Interpretation in Ancient Israel* (Oxford: Clarendon Press, 1985)

Fisher, E., 'Gilgamesh and Genesis: The Flood Story in Context', *CBQ* 32 (1970), 392–403

Fisher, L.R., 'From Chaos to Cosmos', *Enc* 26:2 (1965), 183–97

—, 'The Patriarchal Cycles', *AOAT* 22 (1973), 59–65

Fokkelman, J.P., *Narrative Art in Genesis* (Studia Semitica Neerlandica 17; Assen: van Gorcum, 1975)

—, 'Exodus', in R. Alter and F. Kermode (eds.), *The Literary Guide to the Bible* (Cambridge, MA: Harvard University Press, 1987)

Forrest, R.W.E., 'Paradise Lost Again: Violence and Obedience in the Flood Narrative', *JSOT* 62 (1994), 3–18

Fox, E., *The Five Books of Moses: Genesis, Exodus, Leviticus, Numbers, Deuteronomy; a New Translation with Introductions, Commentary, and Notes* (The Schocken Bible 1; New York: Schocken Books, 1995)

Francisco, C.T., 'The Exodus in Its Historical Setting', *SwJT* 20 (1977), 7–20

—, 'Expository Themes in the Book of Exodus', *RevExp* 74 (1977), 549–61

Freedman, D.N., *The Anchor Bible Dictionary* (6 vols; New York: Doubleday, 1992)

Frerichs, E.S. and L.H. Lesko (eds.), *Exodus: The Egyptian Evidence* (Winona Lake, IN: Eisenbrauns, 1997)

Fretheim, T.E., 'The Jacob Traditions. Theology and Hermeneutic', *Int* 26 (1972), 419–36

—, 'The Reclamation of Creation: Redemption and Law in Exodus', *Int* 45 (1991), 354–65

Fretheim, T.E., *The Pentateuch* (Interpreting Biblical Texts; Nashville, TN: Abingdon Press, 1996)

Friedman, R.E., *Who Wrote the Bible?* (Englewood Cliffs, NJ: Prentice-Hall, 1987)

—, 'Tabernacle', in *ABD* 6:292–300

—, 'Torah (Pentateuch)', in *ABD* 6:605–22

—, *Commentary on the Torah: With a New English Translation* (San Francisco: Harper San Francisco, 2001)

Frishman, J. and L.V. Rompay, *The Book of Genesis in Jewish and Oriental Christian Interpretation: A Collection of Essays* (Traditio Exegetica Graeca 5; Louvanii: Peeters, 1997)

Frymer-Kensky, T., 'The Atrahasis Epic and Its Significance for Our Understanding of Genesis 1–9', *BA* 40 (1977), 147–55

Fung, Y.-W., *Victim and Victimizer: Joseph's Interpretation of His Destiny* (JSOTSS 308; Sheffield: Sheffield Academic Press, 2000)

Garcia Martinez, F. and G.P. Luttikhuizen, *Interpretations of the Flood* (Themes in Biblical Narrative 1; Leiden/Boston: Brill, 1998)

Garrett, D.A., *Rethinking Genesis* (Grand Rapids: Baker Book House, 1991)

Gaston, L., 'Abraham and the Righteousness of God', *HBT* 2 (1980), 39–68

Geller, S.A., 'The Struggle at the Jabbok: The Uses of Enigma in a Biblical Narrative', *JANES* 14 (1982), 37–60

Gerstenberger, E., *Leviticus: A Commentary* (OTL; Louisville, KY: Westminister John Knox Press, 1996)

Gevirtz, S., 'Simeon and Levi in "The Blessing of Jacob" (Gen. 49:5–7)', *HUCA* 52 (1981), 93–128

—, '*heret* in the Manufacture of the Golden Calf', *Bib* 65 (1984), 377–81

—, 'Naphtali in "The Blessing of Jacob" ', *JBL* 103 (1984), 513–21

Gianotti, C.R., 'The Meaning of the Divine Name Yhwh', *BS* 142 (1985), 38–51

Gibson, J.C.L., 'Light from Mari on the Patriarchs', *JSS* 7 (1962), 44–62

—, *Genesis* (2 vols; DSB; Edinburgh: St. Andrew, 1981)

Ginsberg, H.L., 'Abram's "Damascene Steward" ', *BASOR* 200 (1970), 31–2

Gispen, W.H., *Exodus* (BSC; Grand Rapids: Zondervan, 1987)

Glander, S., *The Good Creator: Literature and Theology in Genesis 1–11* (Atlanta, GA: Scholars Press, 1997)

Goldberg, M., 'Exodus 1:13–14', *Int* 37 (1983), 389–91

Goldingay, J., 'The Patriarchs in Scripture and Tradition', in A.R. Millard and D.J. Wiseman (eds.), *Essays on the Patriarchal Narratives* (Leicester: IVP, 1980), 11–42

Good, E.M., *Irony in the Old Testament* (London/Philadelphia: SPCK/Westminster, 1965)

Gooder, P., *The Pentateuch: A Story of Beginnings* (London: Continuum, 2000)

Gooding, D.W., *The Account of the Tabernacle: Translation and Textual Problems of the Greek Exodus* (Texts and Studies. Contributions to Biblical and Patristic Literature. New Series. 6; Cambridge: Cambridge University Press, 1959)

—, *An Unshakeable Kingdom: The Letter to the Hebrews for Today* (Grand Rapids: Eerdmans, 1989)

Gordis, D.H., 'Lies, Wives and Sisters: The Wife-Sister Motif Revisited', *Judaism* 34 (1985), 344–59

Gordon, C.H., 'The Patriarchal Narratives', *JNES* 13 (1954), 217–38

Gordon, R.P., 'Compositeness, Conflation and the Pentateuch', *JSOT* 51 (1991), 57–69

Gorman, F.H., *Divine Presence and Community: A Commentary on the Book of Leviticus* (ITC; Grand Rapids/Edinburgh: Eerdmans/Handsel Press, 1997)

Gossai, H., *Power and Marginality in the Abraham Narrative* (Lanham: University Press of America, 1995)

Gowan, D.E., *Eschatology in the Old Testament* (Philadelphia: Fortress Press, 1986)

—, *Genesis 1–11* (ITC; Grand Rapids: Eerdmans, 1988)

Grabbe, L.L., *Leviticus* (OT Guides; Sheffield: JSOT Press, 1993)

Gray, G.B., *Numbers* (ICC; Edinburgh: T. & T. Clark, 1903)

—, *Sacrifice in the Old Testament* (Oxford: Clarendon Press, 1925)

—, *Sacrifice in the Old Testament: Its Theory and Practice* (Oxford: Clarendon Press, 1925)

Grayson, A.K. and J. Van Seters, 'The Childless Wife in Assyria and the Stories of Genesis', *Or* 44 (1975), 485–6

Green, B., *What Profit for Us? Remembering the Story of Joseph* (Lanham, MD: University Press of America, 1996)

Green, W.H., 'Primeval Chronology', *BS* 47 (1890), 285–303

—, *The Unity of the Book of Genesis* (New York: Scribner's Sons, 1895)

Greenberg, M., 'The Thematic Unity of Exodus III–XI', *World Congress of Jewish Studies* 1 (1967), 151–4

—, 'The Redaction of the Plague Narrative in Exodus', in H. Goedick (ed.) *Near Eastern Studies* (Baltimore: Johns Hopkins, 1971)

Groningen, G.V., 'Interpretation of Genesis', *JETS* 13 (1970), 199–218

Gros Louis, K.R.R., 'Abraham: I', in K.R.R. Gros Louis and J.S. Ackerman (eds.), *Literary Interpretations of Biblical Narratives II* (Nashville: Abingdon, 1982), 53–70

—, 'Abraham: II', in K.R.R. Gros Louis and J.S. Ackerman (eds.), *Literary Interpretations of Biblical Narratives II* (Nashville: Abingdon, 1982), 71–84

Grossfeld, B. and L.H. Schiffman, *Targum Neofiti 1: An Exegetical Commentary to Genesis: Including Full Rabbinic Parallels* (New York: Sepher-Hermon Press, 2000)

Grossman, D., *The Second Book of Moses, Called Exodus* (Pocket Canon; Edinburgh: Canongate, 1998)

Gruber, M.I., 'Was Cain Angry or Depressed? Background of a Biblical Murder', *BARev* 6 (1980), 34–6

Guglielmo, A.D., 'The Fertility of the Land in the Messianic Promises', *CBQ* 19 (1957), 306–11

Gunkel, H., *The Legends of Genesis* (Chicago: Open Court Publishing, 1901)

—, *Genesis* (trans. by Mark E. Biddle; Mercer Library of Biblical Studies; Macon, GA: Mercer University Press, 1997)

Gunn, D.M., 'The Hardening of Pharaoh's Heart Plot: Character and Theology in Exodus 1–14', in D.J.A. Clines, D.M. Gunn and A.J. Hauser (eds.), *Art and Meaning: Rhetoric in Biblical Literature* (JSOTSS Vol. 19; Sheffield: JSOT Press, 1982), 72–96

—, 'New Directions in the Study of Biblical Hebrew Narrative', *JSOT* 39 (1987), 65–75

Gunn, D.M. and D.N. Rewell, *Narrative in the Hebrew Bible* (Oxford: Oxford University Press, 1993)

Habel, N.C., 'The Gospel Promise to Abraham', *CTM* 40 (1969), 346–55

—, *Literary Criticism of the Old Testament* (Philadelphia: Fortress Press, 1971)

Hamilton, V.P., *The Book of Genesis: Chapters 1–17* (NICOT; Grand Rapids: Eerdmans, 1990)

—, *The Book of Genesis: Chapters 18–50* (NICOT; Grand Rapids: Eerdmans, 1995)

—, *Handbook on the Historical Books: Joshua, Judges, Ruth, Samuel, Kings, Chronicles, Ezra–Nehemiah, Esther* (Grand Rapids: Baker Book House, 2001)

Hamlin, E.J., *A Guide to Deuteronomy* (SPCK International Study Guide 32; London: SPCK, 1995)

Hansen, G.W., *Abraham in Galatians* (JSNTSS 29; Sheffield: JSOT Press, 1989)

Haran, M., 'The Religion of the Patriarchs', *ASTI* 4 (1965), 30–55

—, 'The Passover Sacrifice', in *Studies in the Religion of Ancient Israel* (SVT Vol. 22; Leiden: Brill, 1972), 94–5

—, *Temples and Temple-Service in Ancient Israel* (Oxford: Clarendon Press, 1978)

—, 'Seething a Kid in Its Mother's Milk', *JJS* 30 (1979), 23–35

Hargreaves, J.H.M., *A Guide to Genesis* (2nd edn.; SPCK International Study Guide 3; London: SPCK, 1998)

Harland, P.J., *The Value of Human Life: A Study of the Story of the Flood (Genesis 6–9)* (SVT 64; Leiden/New York: Brill, 1996)

Harrison, R.K., *Introduction to the Old Testament* (Grand Rapids: Eerdmans, 1969)

—, *Leviticus* (TOTC; Leicester: IVP, 1980)

—, *Numbers* (WEC; Chicago: Moody, 1990)

Hart, I., 'Preaching on the Account of the Tabernacle', *EvQ* 54 (1982), 111–6

—, 'Genesis 1:1–2:3 as a Prologue to the Book of Genesis', *TynBul* 46.2 (1995), 315–36

Hartley, J.E., *Leviticus* (WBC 4; Dallas: Word, 1992)

—, *Genesis* (NIBCOT 1; Peabody, MA/Carlisle: Hendrickson/Paternoster Press, 2000)

Hasel, G.F., 'The Genealogies of Gen 5 and 11 and Their Alleged Babylonian Background', *AUSS* 16 (1978), 361–74

—, 'The Meaning of the Animal Rite in Gen. 15', *JSOT* 19 (1981) 61–78

Hauge, M.R., *The Descent from the Mountain: Narrative Patterns in Exodus 19–40* (JSOTSS 323; Sheffield: Sheffield Academic Press, 2001)

Haughton, R., *The Tower That Fell* (New York: Paulist Press, 1997)

Hauser, A.J., 'Linguistic and Thematic Links between Genesis 4:1–16 and Genesis 2–3', *JETS* 23 (1980), 297–305

—, 'The Theme of Intimacy and Alienation', in D.J.A. Clines, D.M. Gunn and A.J. Hauser (eds.), *Art and Meaning: Rhetoric in Biblical Literature* (JSOTSS Vol. 19; Sheffield: JSOT Press, 1982), 20–36

Heard, R.C., *The Dynamics of Diselection: Ambiguity in Genesis 12–36 and Ethnic Boundaries in Post-Exilic Judah* (Atlanta, GA: Society of Biblical Literature, 2001)

Helyer, L.R., 'The Separation of Abram and Lot: Its Significance in the Patriarchal Narratives', *JSOT* 26 (1983), 77–88

Hendel, R.S., 'Genesis, Book Of', in *ABD* 2:933–41

—, *The Text of Genesis 1–11: Textual Studies and Critical Edition* (New York/Oxford: Oxford University Press, 1998)

Hettema, T.L., *Reading for Good: Narrative Theology and Ethics in the Joseph Story from the Perspective of Ricoeur's Hermeneutics* (Studies in Philosophical Theology 18; Kampen: Kok Pharos, 1996)

Hillers, D.R., *Covenant: The History of a Biblical Idea* (Baltimore: Johns Hopkins, 1969)

Hoekveld-Meijer, G., *Esau: Salvation in Disguise: Genisis 36, a Hidden Polemic between Our Teacher and the Prophets About Edom's Role in Post-Exilic Israel through Leitwort Names* (Kampen, Netherlands: Pharos, 1996)

Hoffmeier, J.K., *Israel in Egypt: The Evidence for the Authenticity of the Exodus Tradition* (New York: Oxford University Press, 1997)

Honeycutt, R.L., Jr., 'Aaron, the Priesthood, and the Golden Calf', *RevExp* 74 (1977), 523–35

Hoop, R.D., *Genesis 49 in Its Literary and Historical Context* (Oudtestamentische Studien 39; Leiden/New York: Brill, 1999)

Hopkins, D.C., 'Between Promise and Fulfillment: Von Rad and the "Sacrifice of Abraham" ', *BZ* 24 (1980), 180–93

Houston, W., *Purity and Monotheism: Clean and Unclean Animals in Biblical Law* (JSOTSS 140; Sheffield: JSOT Press, 1993)

Houtman, C., 'Exodus 4:24–26 and Its Interpretation', *JNSL* 11 (1983), 81–105

—, 'The Pentateuch', in A.S. van der Woude (ed.), *The World of the Old Testament* (Vol. 2; Grand Rapids: Eerdmans, 1989)

Hunter, A.G., 'Father Abraham: A Structural and Theological Study of the Yahwist's Presentation of the Abraham Material', *JSOT* 35 (1986), 3–27

Hurowitz, V., 'The Priestly Account of Building the Tabernacle', *JAOS* 105 (1985), 21–30

Hurowitz, V.A., 'Who Lost an Earring? Genesis 35:4 Reconsidered', *CBQ* 62.1 (2000), 28–32

Hurvitz, A., 'The Evidence of Language in Dating the Priestly Code', *RB* 81 (1974), 24–56

—, *A Linguistic Study of the Relationship between the Priestly Source and the Book of Ezekiel* (CahRB 20; Paris: J. Gabalda, 1982)

—, 'Dating the Priestly Source in Light of the Historical Study of Biblical Hebrew a Century after Wellhausen', *BZAW* 100 (1988), 88–99

—, 'The Historical Quest for "Ancient Israel" and the Linguistic Evidence of the Hebrew Bible: Some Methodological Observations', *VT* 47 (1997), 310–5

Hyatt, J.P., *Exodus* (NCB; Grand Rapids: Eerdmans, 1971)

Irwin, W.H., 'The Course of the Dialogue between Moses and Yhwh in Exodus 33:12–17', *CBQ* 59.4 (1997), 629–36

Isbell, C., 'Exodus 1–2 in the Context of Exodus 1–14: Story Lines and Key Words', in D.J.A. Clines, D.M. Gunn and A.J. Hauser (eds.), *Art and Meaning: Rhetoric in Biblical Literature* (JSOTSS Vol. 19; Sheffield: JSOT Press, 1982), 37–61

Jacob, B., *The First Book of the Bible: Genesis* (trans. by E.I. Jacob and W. Jacob; New York: Ktav, 1974)

Jacob, B. et al, *Das Buch Exodus* (Stuttgart: Calwer, 1997)

Jacobsen, T., 'The Eridu Genesis', *JBL* 100 (1981), 513–29

Janzen, J.G., 'What's in a Name? "Yahweh" in Exodus 3 and the Wider Biblical Context', *Int* 33 (1979), 227–39

—, *Exodus* (Westminster Bible Companion; Louisville, KY: Westminster John Knox Press, 1997)

Janzen, W., *Exodus* (BCBC; Waterloo, Ontario: Herald Press, 2000)

Jenson, P.P., *Graded Holiness: A Key to the Priestly Conception of the World* (JSOTSS 106; Sheffield: JSOT Press, 1992)

Jobling, D., *The Sense of Biblical Narrative* (JSOTSS 7; Sheffield: JSOT Press, 1978)

Johnson, L.T., 'The Use of Leviticus 19 in the Letter of James', *JBL* 101 (1982), 391–401

Johnson, M.D., *The Purpose of the Biblical Genealogies with Special Reference to the Setting of the Genealogies of Jesus* (SNTSMS 8; London: Cambridge University Press, 1969)

Johnson, R. and T. Johnson, *Discovering Genesis* (Crossway Bible Guides; Leicester: Crossway Books, 2001)

Johnstone, W., 'Reactivating the Chronicles Analogy in Pentateuchal Studies, with Special Reference to the Sinai Pericope in Exodus', *ZAW* 99 (1987), 16–37

—, 'The Decalogue and the Redaction of the Sinai Pericope in Exodus', *ZAW* 100 (1988), 361–85

—, *Exodus* (OT Guides; Sheffield: JSOT Press, 1990)

—, *Chronicles and Exodus: An Analogy and Its Application* (JSOTSS 275; Sheffield: Sheffield Academic Press, 1998)

Joosten, J., *People and Land in the Holiness Code: An Exegetical Study of the Ideational Framework of the Law in Leviticus 17–26* (SVT 67; Leiden/New York: Brill, 1996)

Kaiser, O., *Introduction to the Old Testament* (Oxford: Blackwells, 1975)

Kaufman, S.A., 'The Structure of the Deuteronomic Law', *Maarav* 1/2 (1978), 105–58

Kearney, P.J., 'Creation and Liturgy: The P Redaction of Ex 25–40', *ZAW* 89 (1977), 375–87

Kessler, M., 'Rhetorical Criticism of Genesis 7', in J.J. Jackson and M. Kessler (eds.), *Rhetorical Criticism: Essays in Honor of J. Muilenburg* (Pittsburgh: Pickwick, 1974)

Kidner, D., 'Genesis 2:5,6: Wet or Dry?' *TynBul* 17 (1966), 109–14

—, *Genesis* (TOTC; Leicester: IVP, 1967)

Kiene, P., *The Tabernacle of God in the Wilderness of Sinai* (Grand Rapids: Zondervan, 1977)

Kikawada, I., 'The Shape of Genesis 11:1–9', in J.J. Jackson and M. Kessler (eds.), *Rhetorical Criticism: Essays in Honor of J. Muilenburg* (Pittsburgh: Pickwick, 1974)

—, 'Literary Convention of the Primeval History', *AJBI* 1 (1975), 3–22

—, 'The Unity of Genesis 12:1–9', *Proceedings of the Sixth World Congress of Jewish Studies* (1977), 229–35

—, 'Genesis on Three Levels', *AJBI* 7 (1981), 3–15

Kikawada, I. and A. Quinn, *Before Abraham Was: The Unity of Genesis 1–11* (Nashville: Abingdon, 1985)

Kilmer, A., 'The Mesopotamian Concept of Overpopulation and Its Solution as Reflected in the Mythology', *Or* 41 (1972), 160–77

Kirkland, J.R., 'The Incident at Salem: A Re-Examination of Genesis 14:18–20', *StudBT* 7 (1977), 3–23

Kitchen, K.A., *Ancient Orient and Old Testament* (Leicester: IVP, 1967)

—, *The Bible in Its World* (Exeter: Paternoster, 1978)

Kiuchi, N., *The Purification Offering in the Priestly Literature: Its Meaning and Function* (JSOTSS 56; Sheffield: Sheffield Academic Press, 1987)

Klein, R.W., 'The Yahwist Looks at Abraham', *CTM* 45 (1974), 43–9

Kleinig, J.W., 'On Eagle's Wing: An Exegetical Study of Exodus 19:2–8', *LTJ* 21 (1987), 18–27

Kline, M.G., *Images of the Spirit* (Grand Rapids: Baker Book House, 1980)

Knierim, R.P., *Text and Concept in Leviticus i, 1–9* (Tübingen: J.C.B. Mohr, 1992)

Knight, G.A., *Leviticus* (DSB; Edinburgh: St. Andrew, 1981)

Knight, G.A.F., *The Song of Moses: A Theological Quarry* (Grand Rapids: Eerdmans, 1995)

Knohl, I., *The Sanctuary of Silence: The Priestly Torah and the Holiness School* (Minneapolis: Fortress Press, 1995)

Kodell, J., 'Jacob Wrestles with Esau (Gen 32:23–32)', *BTB* 10 (1980), 65–70

Koester, C.R., *The Dwelling of God: The Tabernacle in the Old Testament, Intertestamental Jewish Literature, and the New Testament* (CBQMS 22; Washington: Catholic Biblical Association of America, 1989)

Kok, J.L.T., *The Sin of Moses and the Staff of God: A Narrative Approach* (Studia Semitica Neerlandica; Assen, Netherlands: Van Gorcum, 1997)

Kraus, H.-J., *Worship in Israel: A Cultic History of the Old Testament* (Oxford: Basil Blackwell, 1966)

Kselman, J.S., 'The Book of Genesis: A Decade of Scholarly Research', *Int* 45 (1991), 380–92

Kugel, J.L., *The Bible as It Was* (Cambridge, MA/London: Belknap Press of Harvard University Press, 1997)

—, *Traditions of the Bible: A Guide to the Bible as It Was at the Start of the Common Era* (Cambridge, MA: Harvard University Press, 1998)

Kunin, S.D., *The Logic of Incest: A Structuralist Analysis of Hebrew Mythology* (JSOTSS 185; Sheffield: Sheffield Academic Press, 1995)

Kuntz, J.K., *The Self-Revelation of God* (Philadelphia: Westminister, 1967)

Laffey, A.L., *The Pentateuch: A Liberation-Critical Reading* (Minneapolis: Fortress Press, 1998)

Lambert, W.G., 'A New Look at the Babylonian Background of Genesis', *JTS* 16 (1965), 287–300

Larsson, G., 'The Chronology of the Pentateuch: A Comparison of the MT and LXX', *JBL* 102 (1983), 401–9

—, *Bound for Freedom: The Book of Exodus in Jewish and Christian Traditions* (Peabody, MA: Hendrickson, 1999)

Latvus, K., *God, Anger and Ideology: The Anger of God in Joshua and Judges in*

Relation to Deuteronomy and the Priestly Writings (JSOTSS 279; Sheffield: Sheffield Academic Press, 1998)

Lawlor, J.I., 'The Test of Abraham: Genesis 22:1–19', *GTJ* 1 (1980), 19–35

Lawton, R., 'Irony in Early Exodus', *ZAW* 97 (1985), 414

Le Tellier, R.I., *Day in Mamre, Night in Sodom: Abraham and Lot in Genesis 18 and 19* (Biblical Interpretation Series 10; Leiden/New York: Brill, 1995)

Lehmann, M.R., 'Abraham's Purchase of Machpelah and Hittite Law', *BASOR* 129 (1953), 15–8

Lemche, N.P., 'The Chronology in the Story of the Flood', *JSOT* 18 (1980), 52–62

—, *Prelude to Israel's Past: Background and Beginnings of Israelite History and Identity* (Peabody, MA: Hendrickson, 1998)

Levine, B.A., *In the Presence of the Lord* (Leiden: Brill, 1974)

—, *Leviticus* (The JPS Commentary; New York: Jewish Publication Society, 1989)

—, 'Leviticus, Book Of', in *ABD*, 4:311–21

—, *Numbers 1–20: A New Translation with Introduction and Commentary* (AB 4A; New York: Doubleday, 1993)

—, *Numbers 21–36: A New Translation with Introduction and Commentary* (AB 4B; New York: Doubleday, 2000)

Levinson, B.M., *Deuteronomy and the Hermeneutics of Legal Innovation* (New York: Oxford University Press, 1997)

Lewis, J.O., 'The Ark and the Tent', *RevExp* 74 (1977), 537–48

Lewis, J.P., *A Study of the Interpretation of Noah and the Flood in Jewish and Christian Literature* (Leiden: Brill, 1968)

Lichtenstein, M., 'Dream-Theophany and the E Document', *JANESCU* 1/2 (1968), 45–54

Loewenstamm, S.E., 'The Divine Grants of Land to the Patriarchs', *JAOS* 91 (1971), 509–10

Long, V.P., *The Art of Biblical History* (Leicester: Apollos, 1994)

Longacre, R.E., 'The Discourse Structure of the Flood Narrative', *JAAR* 47 (1979), 89–133

Louth, A. and M. Conti, *Genesis 1–11* (Ancient Christian Commentary on Scripture 1; Downers Grove, IL: InterVarsity Press, 2001)

Luke, K., 'Two Birth Narratives in Genesis', *ITS* 17 (1980), 155–80

—, 'The Nations of the World (Gen 10)', *BibBh* 8 (1982), 61–80

Lundbom, J.R., 'God's Use of the Idem Per Idem to Terminate Debate', *HTR* 71 (1978), 193–201

—, 'Abraham and David in the Theology of the Yahwist', in C.L. Meyers and M. O'Connor (eds.), *The Word of the Lord Shall Go Forth: Essays in Honor of David Noel Freedman* (Winona Lake: Eisenbrauns, 1983), 203–09

Luttikhuizen, G.P., *The Creation of Man and Woman: Interpretations of the Biblical Narratives in Jewish and Christian Traditions* (Themes in Biblical Narrative 3; Leiden/Boston: Brill, 2000)

Maars, R., 'The Sons of God (Genesis 6:1–4)', *ResQ* 23 (1980), 218–24

Maarsingh, B., *Numbers* (TI; Grand Rapids: Eerdmans, 1987)

Mabee, C., 'Jacob and Laban: The Structure of Judicial Proceedings (Genesis xxxi 25–42)', *VT* 30 (1980), 192–207

Maccoby, H., *Ritual and Morality: The Ritual Purity System and Its Place in Judaism* (Cambridge/New York: Cambridge University Press, 1999)

Magonet, J., 'A Response to P. Auffret's "Literary Structure of Exodus 6:2–8", *JSOT* 27 (1983), 73–4

—, 'The Rhetoric of God: Exodus 6:2–8', *JSOT* 27 (1983), 56–67

Maher, M., *Genesis* (OTM 2; Wilmington: Michael Glazier, 1982)

—, 'The Transfer of a Birthright: Justifying the Ancestors', *PIBA* 8 (1984), 1–24

Malamat, A., 'Tribal Societies: Biblical Genealogies and African Lineage Systems', *Archives Europeénnes de Sociologie* 14 (1973), 126–36

Maly, E.H., 'Genesis 12,10–20; 20,1–18; 26:7–11 and the Pentateuchal Question', *CBQ* 18 (1956), 255–62

Mann, T.W., *Deuteronomy* (Westminster Bible Companion; Louisville, KY: Westminster John Knox Press, 1995)

Marshall, J.W., *Israel and the Book of the Covenant: An Anthropological Approach to Biblical Law* (Atlanta: Scholars Press, 1993)

Martens, E.A., *Plot and Purpose in the Old Testament* (Leicester: IVP, 1981)

Martin, W.J., '"Dischronologized" Narrative in the Old Testament', *SVT* 17 (1969), 179–86

Mathews, K.A., *Genesis 1–11:26* (NAC 1A; Nashville, TN: Broadman & Holman, 1995)

Maxwell-Mahon, W.D., ' "Jacob's Ladder": A Structural Analysis of Scripture', *Semitics* 7 (1980), 118–30

Mayes, A.D.H., *Deuteronomy* (NCB; Grand Rapids: Eerdmans, 1979)

—, *The Story of Israel between Settlement and Exile: A Redactional Study of the Deuteronomistic History* (London: SCM, 1983)

—, 'On Describing the Purpose of Deuteronomy', *JSOT* 58 (1993), 13–33

Mazar, B., 'The Historical Background of the Book of Genesis', *JNES* 28 (1969), 73–83

McCarthy, D.J., 'Moses's Dealings with Pharaoh', *CBQ* 27 (1955), 227–348

—, 'Three Covenants in Genesis', *CBQ* 26 (1964), 179–89

—, 'Plagues and Sea of Reeds: Exodus 5–11', *JBL* 85 (1966), 137–58

—, 'berît in Old Testament History and Theology', *Bib* 63 (1972), 110–21

—, 'Exodus 3:14: History, Philology and Theology', *CBQ* 40 (1978), 311–22

McComiskey, T.E., *The Covenants of Promise: A Theology of Old Testament Covenants* (Grand Rapids: Baker Book House, 1985)

McConville, J.G., *Law and Theology in Deuteronomy* (JSOTSS 33; Sheffield: JSOT Press, 1984)

—, 'Abraham and Melchizedek: Horizons in Genesis 14', in R.S. Hess, P.E. Satterthwaite and G.J. Wenham (eds.), *He Swore an Oath: Biblical Themes from Genesis 20–50* (2nd edn.; Grand Rapids/Carlisle: Baker Book House/ Paternoster, 1994), 93–118

—, 'Deuteronomy', in D.A. Carson, R.T. France, J.A. Motyer, G.J. Wenham (eds.), *New Bible Commentary (21st Century Edition)* (Leicester: IVP, 1994)

—, *Grace in the End* (Carlisle: Paternoster, 1994)

—, 'The Old Testament Historical Books in Modern Scholarship', *Them* 22 (1997), 3–13

McCullough, J.C., 'Melchizedek's Varied Role in Early Exegetical Tradition', *NETR* 1/2 (1978), 52–66

McEvenue, S., 'Word and Fulfilment: A Stylistic Feature of the Priestly Writer', *Semitics* 1 (1970), 104–10

—, *The Narrative Style of the Priestly Writer* (Analecta Biblica 50; Rome: Biblical Institute Press, 1971)

—, 'A Comparison of Narrative Styles in the Hagar Stories', *Semeia* 3 (1975), 64–80

—, 'The Elohist at Work', *ZAW* 96 (1984), 315–32

McGuire, E., 'The Joseph Story: A Tale of Son and Father', in B.O. Long (ed.), *Images of Man and God* (Sheffield: Almond Press, 1981), 9–25

McKane, W., *Studies in the Patriarchal Narratives* (Edinburgh: Handsel, 1979)

McKenzie, B.A., 'Jacob's Blessing on Pharaoh: An Interpretation of Gen 46:31–47:26', *WTJ* 45 (1983), 386–99

McKenzie, J.L., 'The Sacrifice of Isaac (Gen 22)', *Scripture* 9 (1957), 79–83

McKenzie, S., 'You Have Prevailed: The Function of Jacob's Encounter at Peniel in the Jacob Cycle', *ResQ* 23 (1980), 225–31

McKeown, J., *A Study of the Main Unifying Themes in the Hebrew Text of the Book of Genesis* (PhD, The Queen's University of Belfast, 1991)

McKnight, E.V., *The Bible and the Reader: An Introduction to Literary Criticism* (Philadelphia: Fortress Press, 1985)

McNamara, M., *Targum Neofiti 1, Deuteronomy* (Collegeville, MN: Liturgical Press, 1997)

McNamara, M., E.G. Clarke and S. Magder, *Targum Neofiti 1, Numbers* (Collegeville, MN: Liturgical Press, 1995)

Mendenhall, G., 'Covenant Forms in Israelite Tradition', *BA* 25 (1954), 66–87

Menn, E.M., *Judah and Tamar (Genesis 38) in Ancient Jewish Exegesis: Studies in Literary Form and Hermeneutics* (Supplements to the Journal for the Study of Judaism 51; Leiden/New York: Brill, 1997)

Milgrom, J., *Cult and Conscience: The ASHAM and the Priestly Doctrine of Repentance* (Leiden: Brill, 1976)

—, *Studies in Cultic Theology and Terminology* (SJLA 36; Leiden: Brill, 1983)

—, 'Ethics and Ritual: The Foundations of the Biblical Dietary Laws', in E.D. Firmage, B.G. Weiss and J.W. Welch (eds.), *Religion and Law: Biblical-Judaic and Islamic Perspectives* (Winona Lake: Eisenbrauns, 1990), 152–92

—, *Numbers* (The JPS Torah Commentary; New York: Jewish Publication Society, 1990)

—, *Leviticus 1–16: A New Translation with Introduction and Commentary* (AB 3A; New York: Doubleday, 1991)

—, 'Numbers, Book Of', in *ABD* 4:1146–55

—, 'Priestly ('P') Source', in *ABD* 5:454–61

—, *Leviticus 17–22: A New Translation with Introduction and Commentary* (AB 3B; New York: Doubleday, 2000)

—, *Leviticus 23–27: A New Translation with Introduction and Commentary* (AB 3C; New York: Doubleday, 2001)

Millar, J.G., 'The Ethics of Deuteronomy: An Exegetical and Theological Study', *TynBul* 46.2 (1995), 389–92

—, *Now Choose Life: Theology and Ethics in Deuteronomy* (New Studies in Biblical Theology; Grand Rapids: Eerdmans, 1999)

Millard, A.R., 'The Etymology of Eden', *VT* 34 (1984), 103–6

Miller, P.D., *Genesis 1–11. Studies in Structure and Theme* (JSOTSS 8; Sheffield: JSOT Press, 1978)

—, *Deuteronomy* (Interpretation; Louisville: John Knox, 1990)

—, *Israelite Religion and Biblical Theology: Collected Essays* (JSOTSS 267; Sheffield: Sheffield Academic Press, 2000)

Mirsky, A., 'Stylistic Device for Conclusion in Hebrew', *Semitics* 5 (1977), 9–23

Miscall, P.D., 'The Jacob and Joseph Stories as Analogies', *JSOT* 6 (1978), 28–40

—, 'Literary Unity in Old Testament Narrative', *Semeia* 15 (1979), 27–44

—, *The Workings of Old Testament Narrative* (Philadelphia: Fortress Press, 1983)

Mitchell, J.J., 'Abram's Understanding of the Lord's Covenant', *WTJ* 32 (1969), 24–48

Moberly, R.W.L., *At the Mountain of God: Story and Theology in Exodus 32–34* (JSOTSS 22; Sheffield: JSOT Press, 1983)

—, 'The Earliest Commentary on the Akedah', *VT* 38 (1988), 302–23

—, *Genesis 12–50* (OT Guides; Sheffield: JSOT Press, 1992)

—, *The Bible, Theology, and Faith: A Study of Abraham and Jesus* (Cambridge Studies in Christian Doctrine; Cambridge/New York: Cambridge University Press, 2000)

Morrow, W.S., *Scribing the Center: Organization and Redaction in Deuteronomy 14:1–17:13* (Atlanta, GA: Scholars Press, 1995)

Muilenburg, J., 'Abraham and the Nations: Blessing and World History', *Int* 19 (1965), 387–98

—, 'Form Criticism and Beyond', *JBL* 88 (1969), 1–18

Mullen, E.T., *Ethnic Myths and Pentateuchal Foundations: A New Approach to the Formation of the Pentateuch* (SBL Semeia Studies; Atlanta: Scholars Press, 1997)

Munchenberg, R.H., *Deuteronomy* (Adelaide: Lutheran, 1987)

Myers, J.M., 'The Way of the Fathers', *Int* 29 (1975), 121–40

Naylor, P.J., 'Numbers', in D.A. Carson, R.T. France, J.A. Motyer, G.J. Wenham (eds.), *New Bible Commentary (21st Century Edition)* (Leicester: IVP, 1994)

Neff, R.W., 'The Birth and Election of Isaac in the Priestly Tradition', *BR* 15 (1970), 5–18

—, 'The Annunciation of the Birth Narrative of Ishmael', *BR* 17 (1972), 51–62

Newman, M.L., *The People of the Covenant* (Nashville: Abingdon, 1962)

Newman, R.C., 'The Ancient Exegesis of Genesis 6:2,4', *GTJ* 5 (1984), 13–36

Nicol, G., 'Genesis xxix.32 and xxxv:22a. Reuben's Reversal', *JTS* 31 (1980), 536–9

Nicholson, E.W., *Deuteronomy and Tradition* (Oxford: Blackwell, 1967)

—, *Exodus and Sinai in History and Tradition* (Oxford: Oxford University Press, 1973)

—, 'The Interpretation of Exodus xxiv 9–11', *VT* 24 (1974), 77–97

—, 'The Decalogue as the Direct Address of God', *VT* 27 (1977), 422–33

—, 'The Covenant Ritual in Exodus xxiv 3–8', *VT* 32 (1982), 74–86

—, *The Pentateuch in the Twentieth Century: The Legacy of Julius Wellhausen* (Oxford: Clarendon Press, 1998)

Niehaus, J.J., *God at Sinai* (Grand Rapids: Zondervan, 1995)

Nielsen, E., *Deuteronomium* (Tübingen: J.C.B. Mohr, 1995)

Ninow, F., *Indicators of Typology within the Old Testament: The Exodus Motif* (Friedensauer Schriftenreihe. Reihe a, Theologie, Bd. 4; New York: P. Lang, 2001)

Nolland, J., 'Genealogical Annotation in Genesis as Background for the Matthean Genealogy of Jesus', *TynBul* 47.1 (1996), 115–22

Noordtzij, A., *Leviticus* (BSC; Grand Rapids: Zondervan, 1982)

—, *Numbers* (BSC; Grand Rapids: Zondervan, 1983)

North, R.G., *The Biblical Jubilee, after Fifty Years* (Analecta Biblica 145; Roma: Editrice Pontificio Biblico, 2000)

Noth, M., *Exodus* (OTL; London: SCM, 1962)

—, *A History of Pentateuchal Traditions* (Englewood Cliffs: Prentice-Hall, 1972)

O'Brien, M.A., 'The Contribution of Judah's Speech, Genesis 44:18–34, to the Characterization of Joseph', *CBQ* 59.3 (1997), 429–47

O'Callaghan, M., 'The Structure and Meaning of Genesis 38: Judah and Tamar', *PIBA* 5 (1981), 72–88

Oden, R.A., 'Divine Aspirations in Atrahasis and in Genesis 1–11', *ZAW* 93 (1981), 197–216

—, 'Transformations in Near Eastern Myths: Genesis 1–11 and the Old Babylonian Epic of Atrahasis', *Rel* 11 (1981), 21–37

Olbricht, T.H., 'The Theology of Genesis', *ResQ* 23 (1980), 201–17

Olson, D.T., *The Death of the Old and the Birth of the New: The Framework of the Book of Numbers and the Pentateuch* (Chico: Scholars, 1985)

—, *Numbers* (Interpretation; Louisville, KY: John Knox Press, 1996)

Onkelos et al, *Targum Onkelos to Numbers: An English Translation of the Text with Analysis and Commentary* (based on A. Sperber's edition; Hoboken, NJ: Ktav, 1998)

Orlinsky, H.M., 'Enigmatic Bible Passages: The Plain Meaning of Genesis 1:1–3', *BA* 46 (1983), 207–9

—, 'The Plain Meaning of Genesis 1:1–3', *BA* 46 (1983), 207–9

Osborn, N.D., 'This Is My Name Forever: "I Am" or "Yahweh" ', *BT* 39 (1989), 410–5

Osborn, N.D. and H. Hatton, *A Handbook on Exodus* (UBS Handbook Series; New York: United Bible Societies, 1999)

Pagolu, A., 'Patriarchal Religion as Portrayed in Genesis 12–50', *TynBul* 47.2 (1996), 375–8

Parke-Taylor, G.H., *Yahweh: The Divine Name in the Bible* (Waterloo, Ontario: Wilfrid Laurier University Press, 1975)

Parry, R., 'Source Criticism & Genesis 34', *TynBul* 51.1 (2000), 121–38

Patrick, D., 'The Covenant Code Source', *VT* 27 (1977), 145–57

—, *Old Testament Law* (London: SCM, 1986)

Patte, D. and J.F. Parker, 'A Structural Exegesis of Genesis 2 and 3', *Semeia* 18 (1980), 55–75

Paul, M.J., 'Genesis 4:17–24: A Case-Study in Eisegesis', *TynBul* 47.1 (1996), 143–62

Payne, D.F., *Deuteronomy* (DSB; Edinburgh: St Andrew, 1985)

Petersen, D.L., 'A Thrice-Told Tale: Genre, Theme and Motif', *BR* 18 (1973), 30–43

—, 'Genesis 6:1–4, Yahweh and the Organization of the Cosmos', *JSOT* 13 (1979), 47–64

Philip, P., *Numbers* (Waco: Word, 1987)

Phillips, A., 'A Fresh Look at the Sinai Pericope: Part I', *VT* 34 (1984), 39–52

—, 'A Fresh Look at the Sinai Pericope: Part II', *VT* 34 (1984), 282–94

—, 'The Laws of Slavery: Exodus 21:2–11', *JSOT* 30 (1984), 51–66

Plastaras, J., *The God of Exodus* (Milwaukee: Bruce Publishing, 1966)

Polzin, R., ' "The Ancestress of Israel in Danger" in Danger', *Semeia* 3 (1975), 81–97

—, *Moses and the Deuteronomist* (New York: Seabury, 1980)

—, 'Deuteronomy', in R. Alter and F. Kermode (eds.), *The Literary Guide to the Bible* (Cambridge, MA: Harvard University Press, 1987)

Power, W.J.A., 'The Book of Genesis', *PSTJ* 37 (1984), 1–56

Prewitt, T.J., 'Kinship Structures and the Genesis Genealogies', *JNES* 40 (1981), 87–98

Propp, W.H., 'The Skin of Moses' Face – Transfigured or Disfigured?' *CBQ* 49 (1987), 375–86

—, 'Did Moses Have Horns?' *BRev* 4 (1988), 30–7

—, *Exodus 1–18: A New Translation with Introduction and Commentary* (AB 2A; New York: Doubleday, 1999)

Rad, G. von, *Genesis* (OTL; London: SCM, 1961)

—, *Old Testament Theology* (2 vols; Edinburgh: Oliver & Boyd, 1962)

—, *The Problem of the Hexateuch and Other Essays* (Edinburgh: Oliver & Boyd, 1966)

—, *The Problem of the Hexateuch and Other Essays* (London: Oliver & Boyd, 1966)

Radday, Y.T., 'Chiasm in Tora', *LB* 19 (1972), 12–23

—, 'Chiasmus in Hebrew Biblical Narrative', in J.W. Welch (ed.), *Chiasmus in Antiquity* (Hildesheim: Gerstenberg, 1981), 50–117

—, 'The Four Rivers of Paradise', *HS* 23 (1982), 23–31

—, 'Genesis, Wellhausen and the Computer', *ZAW* 94 (1982), 467–81

Redford, D.B., *A Study of the Biblical Story of Joseph (Genesis 37–50)* (SVT 20; Leiden: Brill, 1970)

Rendsburg, G.A., *The Redaction of Genesis* (Winona Lake: Eisenbrauns, 1986)

—, 'The Inclusio in Leviticus xi: An Examination of a Distinctive Literary Device for Bracketing within Pentateuchal Law and Hebrew Poetry', *VT* 43 (1993), 418–21

Rendtorff, R., 'Traditio-Historical Method and the Documentary Hypothesis', *Proceedings of the World Congress of Jewish Studies* 5 (1969), 5–11

—, 'The "Yahwist" as Theologian? The Dilemma of Pentateuchal Criticism', *JSOT* 3 (1977), 2–10

—, *The Old Testament: An Introduction* (London: SCM, 1986)

—, *The Problem of the Process of Transmission in the Pentateuch* (JSOTSS 89; Sheffield: JSOT Press, 1990). Translated by John J. Scullion from *Das überlieferungsgeschichtliche Problem des Pentateuch* (BZAW 17; Berlin: W. de Gruyter, 1977)

Reyburn, W.D. and E.M. Fry, *A Handbook on Genesis* (UBS Handbook Series; New York: United Bible Societies, 1997)

Rice, G., 'The Curse That Never Was (Genesis 9:18–27)', *JRT* 29 (1972), 5–27

Ridderbos, J., *Deuteronomy* (BSC; Grand Rapids: Zondervan, 1984)

Riemann, P.A., 'Am I My Brother's Keeper?' *Int* 24 (1970), 482–99

Riggans, W., *Numbers* (DSB; Edinburgh: St. Andrew, 1983)

Robertson, O.P., *The Christ of the Covenants* (Phillipsburg, NJ: Presbyterian and Reformed, 1980)

Robinson, B.P., 'Israel and Amalek. The Context of Exodus 17.8–16', *JSOT* 32 (1985), 15–22

—, 'Zipporah to the Rescue: A Contextual Study of Exodus iv 24–6', *VT* (1985), 227–61

—, 'Symbolism in Exod. 15:22–27 (Marah and Elim)', *RB* 94 (1987), 376–88

—, 'Acknowledging One's Dependence: The Jethro Story of Exodus 18', *TNB* 69 (1988), 139–42

Robinson, R.D., 'Literary Functions of the Genealogies of Genesis', *CBQ* 48 (1986), 595–608

Rodd, C.S., 'Shall Not the Judge of All the Earth Do What Is Just?' *ExpTim* 83 (1971), 137–9

Rodriguez, A.M., 'Sanctuary Theology in the Book of Exodus', *AUSS* 24 (1986), 127–45

Rofe, A., *Introduction to the Composition of the Pentateuch* (Biblical Seminar 58; Sheffield: Sheffield Academic Press, 1999)

Rogers, C.L., 'The Covenant with Abraham and Its Historical Setting', *BS* 127 (1970), 241–56

Rogerson, J.W., *Old Testament Criticism in the Nineteenth Century* (London: SPCK, 1984)

—, *Genesis 1–11* (OT Guides; Sheffield: JSOT Press, 1991)

—, *W.M.L. De Wette Founder of Modern Biblical Criticism: An Intellectual Biography* (JSOTSS 120; Sheffield: JSOT Press, 1992)

—, *The Pentateuch* (The Biblical Seminar 39; Sheffield: Sheffield Academic Press, 1996)

Ross, A.P., 'The Table of Nations in Genesis 10 – Its Structure', *BS* 137 (1980), 340–53

—, *Creation and Blessing. A Guide to the Study and Exposition of Genesis* (Grand Rapids: Baker Book House, 1988)

Ryken, L., 'Literary Criticism of the Bible', in K.R.R. Gros Louis and J.S. Ackerman (eds.), *Literary Interpretations of Biblical Narratives* (Nashville: Abingdon, 1974), 24–40

Sailhamer, J., 'Exegetical Notes: Genesis 1:1–2:4a', *TJ* 5 (1984), 73–82

—, *The Pentateuch as Narrative: A Biblical-Theological Commentary* (Grand Rapids: Zondervan, 1992)

Sakenfeld, K.D., *Journeying with God: A Commentary on the Book of Numbers* (ITC; Grand Rapids: Eerdmans, 1995)

Samuel ben, M. and M.I. Lockshin, *Rashbam's Commentary on Exodus: An Annotated Translation* (Brown Judaic Studies 310; Atlanta, GA: Scholars Press, 1997)

Sanders, P., *The Provenance of Deuteronomy 32* (Oudtestamentische Studien 37; Leiden/New York: Brill, 1996)

Sarna, N.M., 'Abraham in History', *BARev* 3 (1977), 5–9

—, 'Genesis Chapter 23: The Cave of Machpelah', *HS* 23 (1982), 17–21

—, *Genesis* (The JPS Torah Commentary; Philadelphia: Jewish Publication Society, 1989)

Sasson, J.M., 'A Genealogical "Convention" in Biblical Chronography', *ZAW* 90 (1978), 171–85

—, 'The Tower of Babel as a Clue to the Redactional Structuring of the Primeval History (Gen. 1–11:9)', in G.A. Rendsburg et al (eds.), *The Bible World: Essays in Honor of Cyrus H. Gordon* (New York: Ktav, 1980), 211–9

Savage, M., 'Literary Criticism and Biblical Studies: A Rhetorical Analysis of the Joseph Narrative', in C.D. Evans (ed.), *Scripture in Context. Essays on the Comparative Method* (Pittsburg: Pickwick, 1980), 78–100

Sawyer, J.F.A. and M. Douglas, *Reading Leviticus: A Conversation with Mary Douglas* (JSOTSS 227; Sheffield: Sheffield Academic Press, 1996)

Schearing, L.S. and S.L. McKenzie, *Those Elusive Deuteronomists: The Phenomenon of Pan-Deuteronomism* (JSOTSS 268; Sheffield: Sheffield Academic Press, 1999)

Schierling, M.J., 'Primeval Woman: A Yahwistic View of Woman in Genesis 1–11:9', *JTSoA* 42 (1983), 5–9

Scholz, S., *Rape Plots: A Feminist Cultural Study of Genesis 34* (Studies in Biblical Literature 13; New York: P. Lang, 2000)

Scullion, J.J., 'New Thinking in Creation and Sin in Genesis 1–11', *ABR* 22 (1974), 1–10

—, 'Genesis, the Narrative Of', in *ABD* 2:941–62

Seebass, H., 'The Joseph Story, Genesis 48 and the Canonical Process', *JSOT* 35 (1986), 29–53

—, *Genesis* (Neukirchen-Vluyn: Neukirchener, 1996)

Seely, P.H., 'The Geographical Meaning of "Earth" and "Seas" in Genesis 1:10', *Westminster Theological Journal* 59.2 (1997), 231–56

Segal, J.B., *The Hebrew Passover From the Earliest Times to AD 70* (London Oriental Series 12; London: Oxford University Press, 1963)

Segal, M.H., 'El, Elohim, Yhwh in the Bible', *JQR* 46 (1955), 89–115

—, 'The Composition of the Pentateuch; a Fresh Examination', *Scripta Hierosolymitana*, 8 (1961), 68–114

—, *The Pentateuch* (Jerusalem: Magnes Press, 1967)

Seybold, D.A., 'Paradox and Symmetry in the Joseph Story', in K.R.R. Gros Louis and J.S. Ackerman (eds.), *Literary Interpretations of Biblical Narratives* (Nashville: Abingdon, 1974), 74–119

Siebert-Hommes, J., *Let the Daughters Live!: The Literary Architecture of Exodus 1–2 as a Key for Interpretation* (Biblical Interpretation Series 37 ; Leiden/Boston: Brill, 1998)

Skaist, A., 'The Authority of the Brother at Arrapha and Nuzi', *JAOS* 89 (1969), 10–7

Skinner, J., *Genesis* (2nd edn.; ICC; Edinburgh: T. & T. Clark, 1930)

—, *The Divine Names in Genesis* (London: Hodder & Stoughton, 1914)

Smith, F.G., 'Observations on the Use of the Names and Titles of God in Genesis and the Bearing of Exodus 6:3 on the Same', *EvQ* 40 (1968), 103–9

Smith, G.V., 'Structure and Purpose in Genesis 1–11', *JETS* 20 (1977), 307–19

Smith, M.S., 'The Literary Arrangement of the Priestly Redaction of Exodus: A Preliminary Investigation', *CBQ* 58.1 (1996), 25–50

Smith, M.S. and E.M. Bloch-Smith, *The Pilgrimage Pattern in Exodus* (JSOTSS 239; Sheffield: Sheffield Academic Press, 1997)

Snaith, N.H., *Leviticus and Numbers* (NCB; Grand Rapids: Eerdmans, 1967)

Snijders, L.A., 'Genesis XV: The Covenant with Abraham', *OTS* 12 (1958), 161–279

Soggin, J.A., *Introduction to the Old Testament* (Philadelphia: Westminster, 1976)

Soler, J., 'The Semiotics of Food in the Bible', in R. Forster and O. Ranum (eds.), *Food and Drink in History* (Baltimore: Johns Hopkins University, 1979), 126–38

Soltau, H.W., *The Holy Vessels and Furniture of the Tabernacle of Israel* (Grand Rapids: Kregel, 1969 [1865])

Sonnet, J.-P., *The Book within the Book: Writing in Deuteronomy* (Biblical Interpretation Series 14; Leiden/New York: Brill, 1997)

Speiser, E.A., ' "People" and "Nation" of Israel', *JBL* 79 (1960), 157–63

—, *Genesis* (AB 1; Garden City: Doubleday, 1964)

Spencer, M., 'Redemption in Exodus', *Emmanuel* 90 (1984), 496–503

Sprinkle, J.M., *'The Book of the Covenant': A Literary Approach* (JSOTSS 174; Sheffield: JSOT Press, 1994)

Sternberg, M., *The Poetics of Biblical Narrative: Ideological Literature and the Drama of Reading* (Indiana: Indiana University Press, 1985)

Stieglitz, R.R., 'Ancient Records and the Exodus Plagues', *BARev* 13 (1987), 46–9

Stitzinger, M.F., 'Genesis 1–3 and the Male/Female Role Relationship', *GTJ* 2 (1981), 23–44

Stock, A., *A Way in the Wilderness* (Collegeville: Liturgical Press, 1969)

Stordalen, T., 'Man, Soil, Garden: Basic Plot in Genesis 2–3 Reconsidered', *JSOT* 53 (1992), 3–26

—, *Echoes of Eden: Genesis 2–3 and Symbolism of the Eden Garden in Biblical Hebrew Literature* (Leuven, Belgium: Peeters, 2000)

Stratton, B.J., *Out of Eden: Reading, Rhetoric, and Ideology in Genesis 2–3* (JSOTSS 208; Sheffield: Sheffield Academic Press, 1995)

Surburg, R.F., 'Wellhausenism Evaluated after a Century of Influence', *CTQ* 43 (1979), 78–95

Sutherland, D., 'The Organization of the Abraham Promise Narratives', *ZAW* 95 (1983), 337–43

Talmon, S., 'The Presentation of Synchroneity and Simultaneity in Biblical Narrative', *SH* 27 (1978), 9–26

Tate, M.E., 'The Legal Traditions of the Book of Exodus', *RevExp* 74 (1977), 483–509

Terrien, S.L., *The Elusive Presence: Towards a New Biblical Theology* (San Francisco: Harper and Row, 1978)

Thompson, J.A., *Deuteronomy* (TOTC; Leicester: IVP, 1974)

Thompson, R.J., *Moses and the Law in a Century of Criticism since Graf* (SVT 19; Leiden: Brill, 1970)

Thompson, T.L., *The Historicity of the Patriarchal Narratives* (BZAW 133; Berlin: de Gruyter, 1974)

—, 'A New Attempt to Date the Patriarchal Narratives', *JAOS* 98 (1978), 76–84

—, 'Conflict Themes in the Jacob Narratives', *Semeia* 15 (1979), 5–26

—, *The Origin Tradition of Ancient Israel: I. The Literary Formation of Genesis and Exodus 1–23* (JSOTSS 55; Sheffield: JSOT Press, 1987)

Tidball, D., *Leviticus: Crossway Bible Guide* (Crossway Bible Guides; Leicester: Crossway Books, 1996)

Tigay, J.H., *Deuteronomy: The Traditional Hebrew Text with the New JPS Translation* (The JPS Torah Commentary; Philadelphia: Jewish Publication Society, 1996)

Turner, L.A., *Announcement of Plot in Genesis* (JSOTSS 133; Sheffield: JSOT Press, 1990)

—, *Genesis* (Readings, a New Biblical Commentary; Sheffield: Sheffield Academic Press, 2000)

Van Groningen, G., *Messianic Revelation in the Old Testament* (Grand Rapids: Baker Book House, 1990)

Van Seters, J., *Abraham in History and Tradition* (New Haven/London: Yale University Press, 1975)

—, *In Search of History: Historiography in the Ancient World and the Origins of Biblical Historical History* (New Haven: Yale University Press, 1983)

—, 'The Place of the Yahwist in the History of Passover and Massot', *ZAW* 95 (1983), 169–70

—, 'The Plagues of Egypt: Ancient Tradition or Literary Invention?' *ZAW* 98 (1986), 31–9

—, 'Comparing Scripture with Scripture: Some Observations on the Sinai Pericope in Exodus 19–24', in G.M. Tucker, D.L. Petersen and R.R. Wilson (eds.), *Canon, Theology, and Old Testament Interpretation* (Philadelphia: Fortress Press, 1988), 111–30

—, *Prologue to History: The Yahwist as Historian in Genesis* (Louisville: Westminster/John Knox, 1992)

—, *The Life of Moses: The Yahwist as Historian in Exodus-Numbers* (Louisville: Westminister John Knox Press, 1994)

—, *The Pentateuch: A Social-Science Commentary* (Trajectories 1; Sheffield: Sheffield Academic Press, 1999)

Vater, A.M., 'A Plague on Both Our Houses: Form and Rhetorical-Critical Observations on Exodus 7–11', in D.J.A. Clines, D.M. Gunn and A.J. Hauser (eds.), *Art and Meaning: Rhetoric in Biblical Literature* (JSOTSS Vol. 19; Sheffield: JSOT Press, 1982), 62–71

Vaux, R. de, *Ancient Israel: Its Life and Institutions* (2nd edn.; London: Darton, Longman & Todd, 1965)

—, *Studies in Old Testament Sacrifice* (Cardiff: University of Wales Press, 1964)

Vawter, B., *On Genesis: A New Reading* (Garden City: Doubleday, 1977)

Vervenne, M., 'The Protest Motif in the Sea Narrative (Ex. 14, 11–12): Form and Structure of a Pentateuchal Pattern', *ETL* 63 (1987), 257–71

—, *Studies in the Book of Exodus: Redaction, Reception, Interpretation* (Bibliotheca Ephemeridum Theologicarum Lovaniensium 126; Leuven: Leuven University Press: Uitgeverij Peeters, 1996)

Vervenne, M. and J. Lust, *Deuteronomy and Deuteronomic Literature: Festschrift C.H.W. Brekelmans* (Bibliotheca Ephemeridum Theologicarum Lovaniensium 133; Leuven: Leuven University Press/Peeters, 1997)

Vogels, W., 'Lot in His Honor Restored: A Structural Analysis of Gen 13: 2–18', *EgT* 10 (1979), 5–12

—, *Abraham Et Sa Legende: Genese 12, 1–25, 11* (Lire La Bible 110; Montreal/Paris: Mediaspaul/Cerf, 1996)

Wagner, N.E., *A Literary Analysis of Genesis 12–36* (PhD thesis; Toronto: University of Toronto Press, 1965)

—, 'Pentateuchal Criticism: No Clear Future', *Canadian Journal of Theology* 13 (1967), 225–32

—, 'Abraham and David?' in J.W. Wevers and D.B. Redford (eds.), *Studies on the Ancient Palestinian World* (Toronto: University of Toronto Press, 1972), 117–40

Wallace, H.M., *The Eden Narrative* (HSM 32; Atlanta: Scholars, 1985)

Wallace, R.S., *The Story of Joseph and the Family of Jacob* (Grand Rapids/Edinburgh: Eerdmans/Rutherford House, 2001)

Walsh, J.T., 'Genesis 2:4b–3:24: A Synchronic Approach', *JBL* 96 (1977), 161–77

Waltke, B.K., 'The Creation Account in Genesis 1,1–3', *BS* 132 (1975), 25–36, 136–44, 216–28, 327–42

Walton, J., 'The Antediluvian Section of the Sumerian King List and Genesis 5', *BA* 44 (1981), 207–8

Walton, J.H. and V.H. Matthews, *The IVP Bible Background Commentary: Genesis–Deuteronomy* (Downers Grove, IL: InterVarsity Press, 1997)

Warner, S.M., 'Primitive Saga Men', *VT* 29 (1979), 325–35

Warning, W., *Literary Artistry in Leviticus* (Biblical Interpretation Series 35; Leiden/Boston: Brill, 1999)

Warren, A., 'Did Moses Permit Divorce? Modal Weqatal as Key to New Testament Readings of Deuteronomy 24:1–4', *TynBul* 49.1 (1998), 39–56

Watts, J.W., *Reading Law: The Rhetorical Shaping to the Pentateuch* (The Biblical Seminar 59; Sheffield: Sheffield Academic Press, 1999)

Wcela, E.A., 'The Abraham Stories: History and Faith', *BTB* 10 (1980), 176–81

Weinfeld, M., 'The Covenant of Grant in the Old Testament and in the Ancient Near East', *JAOS* 90 (1970), 184–203

—, *Deuteronomy and the Deuteronomic School* (Oxford: Clarendon Press, 1972)

—, *Deuteronomy 1–11* (AB 5; New York: Doubleday, 1991)

—, 'Deuteronomy, Book Of', in *ABD* 2:168–83

Weisman, Z., 'National Consciousness in the Patriarchal Promise', *JSOT* 31 (1985), 55–73

Welker, M., *Creation and Reality* (Minneapolis: Fortress Press, 1999)

Wellhausen, J., *Prolegomena to the History of Israel* (Edinburgh: Adam & Charles Black, 1885)

Wenham, G.J., 'The Coherence of the Flood Narrative', *VT* 28 (1978), 336–48

—, *The Book of Leviticus* (NICOT; Grand Rapids: Eerdmans, 1979)

—, 'The Religion of the Patriarchs', in A.R. Millard and D.J. Wiseman (eds.), *Essays on the Patriarchal Narratives* (Leicester: IVP, 1980), 157–88

—, *Numbers* (TOTC; Leicester: IVP, 1981)

—, 'The Theology of Unclean Food', *EvQ* 53 (1981), 6–15

—, 'The Symbolism of the Animal Rite in Genesis 15: A Response to G.F. Hasel JSOT 19 (1981), 61–78; *JSOT* 22 (1982), 134–7

—, 'The Date of Deuteronomy: Linchpin of Old Testament Criticism', *Them* 10 (1985), 15–20; and *Them* 11 (1985), 15–8

—, 'Sanctuary Symbolism in the Garden of Eden Story', *Proceedings of the World Congress of Jewish Studies* 9 (1986), 19–25

—, *Genesis 1–15* (WBC 1; Waco: Word, 1987)

—, 'Genesis: An Authorship Study and Current Pentateuchal Criticism', *JSOT* 42 (1988), 3–18

—, 'Method in Pentateuchal Source Criticism', *VT* 41 (1991), 84–109

—, 'Genesis', in D.A. Carson, R.T. France, J.A. Motyer, G.J. Wenham (eds.), *New Bible Commentary (21st Century Edition)* (Leicester: IVP, 1994)

—, *Genesis 16–50* (WBC 2; Dallas: Word, 1994)

—, 'The Theology of Old Testament Sacrifice', in R.T. Beckwith and M. Selman (eds.), *Sacrifice in the Bible* (Carlisle: Paternoster, 1995), 75–87

—, *Numbers* (Old Testament Guides; Sheffield: Sheffield Academic Press, 1997)

—, 'The Priority of P', *VT* 49.2 (1999), 240–58

Wenin, A., *Studies in the Book of Genesis: Literature, Redaction and History* (Bibliotheca Ephemeridum Theologicarum Lovaniensium 155; Leuven University Press/Sterling, VA: Peeters, 2001)

Westbrook, R., 'Purchase of the Cave of Machpelah', *ILR* 6 (1971), 29–38

—, 'Lex Talionis and Exodus 21, 22–25', *RB* 93 (1986), 52–69

Westermann, C., *Blessing in the Bible and in the Life of the Church* (Philadelphia: Fortress Press, 1978)

—, *The Promises to the Fathers* (Philadelphia: Fortress Press, 1980)

—, *Genesis 1-11. A Commentary* (trans. John J. Scullion; London/Minneapolis: SPCK/Augsburg, 1984)

—, *Genesis 12-36. A Commentary* (trans. John J. Scullion; London/Minneapolis: SPCK/Augsburg, 1985)

—, *Genesis 37-50. A Commentary* (trans. John J. Scullion; London/Minneapolis: SPCK/Augsburg, 1987, c1986)

—, *Genesis* (TI; Grand Rapids: Eerdmans, 1987)

—, *Joseph: Eleven Bible Studies on Genesis* (Minneapolis: Fortress Press, 1996)

Wevers, J.W., *Notes on the Greek Text of Deuteronomy* (Septuagint and Cognate Studies Series 39; Atlanta, GA: Scholars Press, 1995)

—, *Notes on the Greek Text of Leviticus* (Septuagint and Cognate Studies Series 44; Atlanta, GA: Scholars Press, 1997)

—, *Notes on the Greek Text of Numbers* (Septuagint and Cognate Studies Series 46; Atlanta, GA: Scholars Press, 1998)

White, H.C., 'The Initiation Legend of Isaac', *ZAW* 91 (1979), 1–30

—, 'Direct and Third Person Discourse in the Narrative of the "Fall"', *Semeia* 18 (1980), 92–106

—, 'The Joseph Story: A Narrative Which "Consumes" Its Content', *Semeia* 31 (1985), 49–69

—, *Narration and Discourse in the Book of Genesis* (Cambridge: Cambridge University Press, 1991)

Whybray, R.N., 'The Joseph Story and Pentateuchal Criticism', *VT* 18 (1968), 522–8

—, *The Making of the Pentateuch: A Methodological Study* (JSOTSS 53; Sheffield: JSOT Press, 1987)

—, *An Introduction to the Pentateuch* (Grand Rapids: Eerdmans, 1995)

Wicke, D.W., 'The Literary Structure of Exodus 1:2–2:10', *JSOT* 24 (1982), 99–107

Wifall, W., 'Gen 3:15 – a Protevangelium?' *CBQ* 36 (1974), 361–65

Wildavsky, A., 'Survival Must Not Be Gained through Sin: The Moral of the Joseph Stories Prefigured through Judah and Tamar', *JSOT* 62 (1994) 37–48

Williams, J.G., 'The Comedy of Jacob: A Literary Study', *JAAR* 46 (1978), 208

—, 'The Beautiful and the Barren: Conventions in Biblical Type-Scenes', *JSOT* 17 (1980), 107–19

—, 'Genesis 3', *Int* 35 (1981), 274–9

—, *Women Recounted: Narrative Thinking and the God of Israel* (Bible and Literature Series 6; Sheffield: Almond, 1982)

Williams, M.J., *Deception in Genesis: An Investigation into the Morality of a Unique Biblical Phenomenon* (Studies in Biblical Literature 32; New York: P. Lang, 2001)

Williams, P.A., *Doing without Adam and Eve: Sociobiology and Original Sin* (Theology and the Sciences; Minneapolis, MN: Fortress Press, 2001)

Williams, P.J., 'The LXX of 1 Chronicles 5:1–2 as an Exposition of Genesis 48–49', *TynBul* 49.2 (1998), 369–72

Williamson, P.R., *Abraham, Israel and the Nations: The Patriarchal Promise and Its Covenantal Development in Genesis* (JSOTSS 315; Sheffield: Sheffield Academic Press, 2000)

Willis, J.T., 'Some Recent Studies on Genesis and the Literary-Historical Approach', *ResQ* 23 (1980), 193–200

Willis, T.M., *The Elders of the City: A Study of the Elders-Laws in Deuteronomy* (Atlanta, GA: Society of Biblical Literature, 2001)

Wilson, I., *Out of the Midst of the Fire: Divine Presence in Deuteronomy* (Atlanta, GA: Scholars Press, 1995)

Wilson, R.R., 'The Old Testament Genealogies in Recent Research', *JBL* 94 (1975), 169–89

—, *Genealogy and History in the Biblical World* (Yale Near Eastern Researches 7; New Haven: Yale University Press, 1977)

Winnett, R.V., *The Mosaic Tradition* (Toronto: Toronto University Press, 1949)

Wisdom, J.R., *Blessing for the Nations and the Curse of the Law: Paul's Citation of Genesis and Deuteronomy in Gal 3.8–10* (Wissenschaftliche Untersuchungen zum Neuen Testament. 2. Reihe. 133; Tubingen: Mohr Siebeck, 2001)

Wiseman, D.J., 'Abraham in History and Tradition. Part I. Abraham the Hebrew', *BS* 134 (1977), 123–30

Wittenberg, G., 'The Tenth Commandment in the Old Testament', *JTSoA* 21 (1978), 3–17

Wolff, H.W., 'The Kerygma of the Yahwist', *Int* 20 (1966), 131–58

Woudstra, M.H., 'The Toledot of the Book of Genesis and Their Redemptive-Historical Significance', *CTJ* 5 (1970), 184–9

—, 'The Story of the Garden of Eden in Recent Study', *VR* 34 (1980), 22–31

Wright, C.J.H., 'Leviticus', in D.A. Carson, R.T. France, J.A. Motyer, G.J. Wenham (eds.), *New Bible Commentary (21st Century Edition)* (Leicester: IVP, 1994)

—, *Deuteronomy* (NIBCOT 4; Peabody, MA/Carlisle: Hendrickson/Paternoster Press, 1996)

Wright, D.P., *The Disposal of Impurity: Elimination Rites in the Bible and in Hittite and Mesopotamian Literature* (SBLDS 101; Atlanta: Scholars, 1987)

—, 'Observations on the Ethical Foundations of the Biblical Dietary Laws', in E.D. Firmage, B.G. Weiss and J.W. Welch (eds.), *Religion and Law, Biblical-Judaic and Islamic Perspectives*, Winona Lake: Eisenbrauns, 1990), 193–8

—, 'Day of Atonement', in *ABD* 2:72–6

—, 'Holiness (OT)', in *ABD* 3:237–49

—, 'Unclean and Clean (OT)', in 6:729–41

Wright, G.E., 'Deuteronomy', in *The Interpreter's Bible* (Nashville: Abingdon, 1953)

—, 'Israel in the Promised Land: History Interpreted by a Covenant Faith', *Enc* 35 (1974), 318–34

Wyatt, N., 'Interpreting the Creation and Fall Story in Genesis 2–3', *ZAW* 93 (1981), 10–21

—, 'The Significance of the Burning Bush', *VT* 36 (1986), 361–5

Wynn-Williams, D.J., *The State of the Pentateuch: A Comparison of the Approaches of M. Noth and E. Blum* (Berlin/New York: W. de Gruyter, 1997)

Yarchin, W., 'Imperative and Promise in Genesis 12:1–3', *StudBT* 10 (1980), 164–78

Young, E.J., *An Introduction to the Old Testament* (Grand Rapids: Eerdmans, 1949)

Scripture Index

Names Index